#2

Written and Compiled by

Patrick Sebranek, *Union High School, Union Grove, Wisconsin*

Verne Meyer, *Dordt College, Sioux Center, Iowa*

Dave Kemper, *Parkview Middle School, Mukwonago, Wisconsin*

Illustrated by **Chris Krenzke**

About the Handbook

Write Source 2000 handbook is an invaluable school and home resource for writers and students of all ages. The handbook stresses the fundamental principles of writing—the writing process, the paragraph, poetry, usage and mixed pairs, punctuation, spelling, capitalization, and so on. The handbook also contains sections on reading, speaking, thinking and writing, learning, the book review, literary terms, the classroom report, vocabulary skills, and a complete glossary of prefixes, suffixes, and roots. (A complete program of coordinating writing and learning materials is available for classroom use.)

Write Source 2000 is truly an all-school handbook: It includes a very helpful math section, a glossary of computer terms, a study skills and test-taking unit, and an 8-page, full-color map section. The handbook has been designed with the student in mind and contains interesting examples, plenty of white space, and numerous full-color illustrations.

Acknowledgements

Write Source 2000 is a reality because of the help, advice, and understanding given by our families: Judy, Julie, and Janae; Yvonne, Tim, and Todd; Katie; and Erin. Also, three of our students allowed us to use their papers as samples in the handbook: Mike Evans (friendly letter), Shayne Hauser (biographical report), and Lisa Servais (short phase autobiography and character sketch). We are also grateful to *Shoe Tree (The Literary Magazine by and for Young Writers)* for sharing the work of student-authors Amy Nathan (free verse poem), Scott J. Moser (multi-paragraph book review), and Sarah Terzo (short story).

And we must thank those people whose help and advice was invaluable: Lois Krenzke, Sherry Gordon, Mary Ann Hoff, Randall VanderMey, and John Janty. Finally, a special thank-you to Ellen, Judy, John, and Myrna, whose dedicated service helped us through many rough spots.

WRITE SOURCE EDUCATIONAL PUBLISHING HOUSE

Box J, Burlington, Wisconsin 53105

1st Edition	2nd Printing
ISBN 0-939045-33-8 (softcover)	ISBN 0-939045-34-6 (hardcover)

Using the Handbook

We have packed an incredible amount of information into *Write Source 2000*—so much that we had to pay special attention to the book's design. We think you'll be able to find what you're looking for quickly and easily. Here's how it works.

All the information in the handbook is arranged by index numbers (from 001 to 877). You'll find the index numbers in five different areas:

- in the *Table of Contents*,
- in the *Index* near the back of the book,
- on the top of each page in a colored bar,
- on the side of each page in a colored box,
- and within the handbook itself in "See" references which refer you to more information on a topic. They look like this: (See 077.)

◆ Index numbers are located in the Table of Contents.

◆ Index numbers are located at the top of each page.

◆ Index numbers are located in the Index in the back of the handbook.

◆ Index numbers are located in "See References" for more information.

◆ Index numbers are located along the side of each page.

Helpful HINT You can work from the *Table of Contents* when you're interested in a general topic. You can work from the *Index* when you're looking for a specific piece of information. Or, you can work from the middle, so to speak, by slowly fanning through the pages. (Chapter titles are listed on the top of each right-hand page.) In other words, you can "have it your way" when you look for information in *Write Source 2000*.

Table of Contents

THE STUDENT ALMANAC   796-863

001 An Invitation to Learning

We're in this together. You and I. We're members of an important club—maybe the most important club ever. A club with no dues, no merit badges, no regularly scheduled meetings. And we have been members ever since we were born. I'll bet you didn't know that.

Your parents belong to this club, so do your grandparents, your second cousins, so do all students, everywhere. The president belongs, the queen of England belongs, Nelson Mandela belongs, so does Michael Jordan, Jackie Joyner-Kersee, Sue Hinton, Tom Cruise, even the citizens of Aukland, New Zealand, on the other side of the world belong.

So what is this club anyway? Well, I'll give you a hint. We can talk, sing (in some manner of speaking), even whistle because of this club. We can thank this club for our ability to read and write. It influences our thinking and gets us interested in various activities. It leads us down different career paths when we grow older. It makes all of our learning possible. We're talking about a club with clout. And do you know what? We all have a lifetime membership.

Learning Inside Out

Now if I would ask you where the club meets—where you do most of your learning—you would answer "in school," right? But there is more to learning than what goes on inside of classrooms—much more. You don't believe me? Well, just think for a minute. (By the way, the club loves it when you think.) Think of the one ability you possess that means more to you than all of the others combined. No, not your skill at Nintendo. I want you to be serious about this. The ability I have in mind was mentioned in a previous paragraph. It's your ability to talk, to communicate. You learned how to do this without ever stepping foot in school.

Lessons or drills seldom accompany this type of learning. Can you imagine a parent saying to his or her three-year-old, "Listen up, Oscar. Today we are going to practice saying: 'I will not talk back anymore.'" And what about results? Well, who do you know that hasn't learned to talk?

"There is more to learning than what goes on inside of classrooms —much more."

Or who hasn't learned how to ride a bike or fish or French braid when he or she has wanted to. That's the neat thing about "learning on the outside." It often just happens naturally or when you want it to in a relaxed atmosphere, free from the pressure and stress of performance. You simply listen, observe, experience, and learn.

The opportunities for this type of learning are endless. The club sees to it. You can learn from family members, friends, and neighbors; join community and church groups; or volunteer your services to worthy causes. You can visit museums, attend concerts, tour businesses, meet new people, enjoy the outdoors. You can read books and magazines on every subject imaginable. You can write your own books, produce your own movies, and who knows what else in the years to come. All of this is just waiting for you.

002

Tuning Into Learning

Now for a name. We call this club—Club Ed. And it shouldn't be too hard for you to understand why since learning is what it's all about. Remember that Club Ed makes no demands on its members. So it's up to you to make its business your business. How? Just take advantage of the many learning opportunities available to you, both inside and outside of school.

And why should you? First of all, you owe it to yourself. Tuning into learning helps you better understand yourself and your place in the world. It makes you more confident, more curious, and more excited about life. And take it from someone who has been a club member a lot longer than you: learning makes you a far more interesting person to be around.

You also owe it to the rest of us. You are our future. You are the person we'll turn to in the year 2000 and beyond. You will be one of our teachers, our problem solvers, our global citizens. And we're counting on you. We're in this club together, remember?

Writing to Learn

An Invitation to Writing

Someone once said that writing is too much fun to be left to "writers." And that is true, especially when you write for yourself, free from the gravitational pull of grades and expectations. I know from experience because I write regularly in a personal journal. (Actually I use a word processor.)

I make discoveries in my personal writing. I ask questions and answer some of them. I dream and laugh and remember. I express honest feelings. I lose track of time, and I have fun. Personal writing is also practice time for me. I feel more comfortable with writing in general and more confident about my writing ability because of it.

Anyone who writes regularly in a journal or otherwise knows how rewarding it can be. But what about you? Will writing become an important part of your life? There's only one way to find out—by giving it a chance, by writing regularly on your own. (See 130 in your handbook for guidelines for personal writing.)

Preparing for Liftoff

And there's no better time to begin writing than right now, as in this very minute. Here's what I want you to do: Open your notebook and get your favorite pen or pencil in hand. Think of an experience to get you started: something that you did last weekend, last night, or last hour; or think of someone you like or someone who really grinds your beans.

Write for 10 minutes, nonstop (I'll even settle for 5). When you finish, you will already feel better about writing because you will have produced a lot of it, and all of it will be your very own. And don't be surprised if you learn something about yourself in the process.

Now for your countdown:

10 . . . 9 . . .   (Remember, write for the entire time.)

8 . . . 7 . . .   (Go where your pen and your thinking take you. You don't have to stick to one topic.)

6 . . . 5 . . .   (If you get stuck, write "I'm stuck" until something comes to mind.)

4 . . . 3 . . .   (Your hand might get a little stiff near the end, but you can tough it out.)

2 . . . 1 . . . (Write!)

Writing to Learn

Don't be puzzled by the title. We don't have it backwards. Writing to learn is just what we mean. But I can understand why you might be confused. You are, after all, in school to learn to write with the help of your teachers, your classmates, and our handbook. So what gives? Why did we call this section "Writing to Learn"? Read on and find out.

006   If you've read the previous page, you already know why "Writing to Learn" is a good title for this chapter. It is by writing that you learn to write. You can read about writing and you can talk about it until you're blue in the face, but unless you practice writing, you really can't expect to make any major improvements. That doesn't mean that reading and talking about writing aren't important, because they are. But they only make a difference if you regularly put pen to paper.

Anybody who becomes good at something that requires a certain amount of skill does so through practice. How do you think Michael Jordan became such a good basketball player? Did he do it by watching basketball games, by playing HORSE, by talking a good game? Of course he didn't. He practiced for hours on end, and I'm sure he still does.

(By the way, unless you think otherwise, writers aren't born with a special writing gene or blessed by the writing fairy. Some seem to come by the ability to write more easily than others, but it is still a skill that we must all practice.)

007 Writing Leads to Active Learning

There's another reason for the title. Writing can help you learn more effectively in any field or area, be it language arts or industrial arts, social studies or science. I know. It might sound like we're venturing a bit out of our orbit here and making too much out of writing. But let me just share a few ideas with you.

We all agree that to become good at something, you have to roll up your sleeves and get actively involved, right? And this is exactly what you should do to become good at learning. Most of you are already involved, for the most part. You listen in class and take notes. You read what's required of you, complete homework assignments, and study for tests.

> "I hear and I forget; I see and I remember; I write and I understand."
> **Chinese Proverb**

Writing Leads to Better Understanding

> But we now know that there's more to effective learning than being attentive to daily requirements. Writing experts have found that if you explore your thoughts and feelings about new information in writing, it helps you make it part of your own thinking, which in turn helps you learn it.

I'm not talking here about writing in which you show what you have already learned. I'm talking about writing in which you try to figure out what you understand and what confuses you about new information—writing in which you make connections between "new knowledge" and old. This is exploratory writing, freely composed, written for your own benefit, much like the personal writing you should do for practice. This is writing to learn.

So what kinds of things can you learn through writing?

■ You can learn about yourself.

Explore your experiences and memories in personal writing, and you'll come to better understand them and yourself. Have a problem? See if you can work it out by writing about it. (See 130 for guidelines.)

■ You can learn about your world.

A few weeks ago I did some grocery shopping at a local supermarket, one that is more warehouse than store. I couldn't believe how cold and impersonal it made me feel, so I wrote about it. That initial writing turned into a poem about the ideal corner store.

Try it yourself. When something you see or hear or read moves you for some reason, write about it and see what you can discover.

■ You can learn about others.

Here's another personal experience: I have always been a fan of Bob Dylan. A Saturday morning wouldn't be . . . well . . . Saturday morning unless I've heard his scratchy voice and harmonica. About a year ago I read that he had changed his name from Robert Zimmerman to Bob Dylan when he was just starting out as a musician.

Now I already knew this, but for some reason, when I was reminded of this fact, it bothered me; so I decided to write about it—to explore my feelings, to see what I could learn.

I'm sure the same thing often happens to you: You are affected by the actions of a friend, a family member, a new acquaintance, someone you've read or heard about. The next time this happens, see what you can discover about this person (and about yourself) through writing.

010 ■ **You can learn about LIFE through writing.**

Get engaged to what's happening outside of your own small world through writing. When I, for example, read about the dramatic political changes in eastern Europe or witness homeless people begging for money or hear an ambulance scream down my street, I am often moved to write. I don't necessarily expect to make sense out of these experiences, but writing about them helps me sort out my thoughts and gets me thinking about more than myself—about important issues like freedom, opportunity, dignity, and well-being.

■ **You can learn across the curriculum.**

Writing in any form—even something as simple as a brief note to your teacher—puts you in charge of your own learning. It provides you with an effective and painless way to evaluate your progress in all of your school subjects. (See 410 in your handbook for more on writing to learn, including a list of writing-to-learn ideas.)

■ **You can learn about a writing subject.**

Let's say Mr. Wilke, your social studies teacher, makes the following writing assignment: You're now principal of your school, and as your first order of business, you plan on making _____ mandatory. (Mr. Wilke asks you to select something controversial and explain your reasons for this decision.)

Being the fashion leader that you are, you decide to make uniforms mandatory in your school. And what will your reasons be for this decision? That's where writing to learn comes into play. By writing freely about a subject, you can learn about it and establish a starting point for the shaping of your paper. There is no better way to get a writing assignment underway. (See 037 for ideas for searching and shaping a subject.)

The Writing Process

What we offer you in this section is a good description of what generally goes on during the process of writing. We also offer you plenty of suggestions, guidelines, and insights along the way to help you develop your own writing.

Writing in Action

Before we talk about your writing, let's look at the way a professional writes. A professional usually "lifts off" by writing for himself—with only a hint of an idea or plan in mind. His initial purpose is to explore and discover potential starting points for writing. Once a writer hits upon one that he likes, he's on his way to learn what he can through his writing. And he won't "touch down" until his writing is ready to share with his readers.

"Writing is mind traveling — destination unknown."

What happens to the writing while it's in orbit depends on the project. Usually a writer will write something, read it, change it so some of the ideas are clearer, read it again, ask someone else to read it, make some more changes, and so on. There is a lot of forward and backward motion as a writer tries to make sense out of his writing and shape it for his or her readers. Writing is called a process because it goes through such a series of changes.

The Steps in the Process

We identify four steps in our discussion of the writing process: *selecting, collecting, connecting,* and *correcting*. **Selecting** refers to the process of choosing a subject to explore in writing. **Collecting** refers to all of the searching, gathering, thinking, talking, and planning that goes on during a writing project. (Note that I said during a project. It is ongoing.) **Connecting** refers to all of the writing you do to connect and shape your thoughts into a meaningful composition. **Correcting** refers to those finishing touches which are made as the writing is put into its final form. It includes editing and proofreading.

Helpful HINT

This section is meant to be read and talked about with your classmates. Have your parents read it as well, so they can help you with your writing.

Selecting: *Choosing a Subject*

The writing process starts as soon as you start thinking about writing for yourself or for an assignment. What you do at this initial point in the process depends. If you already have a subject in mind, there's little else you need to know; you're ready to move on. If, however, you don't have a writing idea in mind—which will often be the case for assigned writing—your first step into the process is selecting a subject. We provide you with all kinds of activities for doing this. And one of these activities might be the perfect cure if and when you ever come down with a case of the "what do I write about" blues.

Setting Out

My favorite selecting activities are free writing and clustering. For most types of writing, all I need is a general idea related to an assignment to get me started, and I can free-write or cluster my way to a possible subject. (See 035 for an explanation of these and other selecting activities.)

Let's suppose my assignment is to select a new rule for my school and give the reasons for my decision. Here's how I would go about a subject search: I would start by writing freely about the rules I already know. If the first one that comes to mind deals with hall passes, that is where I would start.

Keeping It Going

While writing rapidly and freely (usually for 5-10 minutes), I'd expect that some new rules—one of which might be the subject of my writing—will come to mind. If not, I at least have some information in front of me to continue my subject search.

Or, I might try clustering with "school rules" as the nucleus word. When you cluster, you basically list ideas around the nucleus word as they freely come to mind. One of the ideas in the cluster may turn out to be a good writing subject; if not, one or more of the ideas should at least point me toward a possible subject. If I'm still stuck, I would talk about the assignment with a friend or classmate.

Helpful HINT

Select a subject that truly interests you. Doing otherwise makes about as much sense as making a batch of peanut butter cookies when you're really interested in chocolate chip.

Collecting: *Searching and Shaping a Subject*

With a possible subject in mind, you may decide to "pass Go," collect your $200, and begin writing—that is, if you're very familiar with your subject. If not, it might be wise to collect your thoughts about your writing idea first—and then "pass Go."

Setting Out

What kinds of thoughts should you collect? That depends. First, you may want to see what you know and what you need to find out about your subject. We've listed a number of activities in your handbook to help you do this. (See 037.) Some of these activities are the same ones you can use to find a subject. You may also read about a possible subject and talk about it with classmates, friends, and family members. Then you'll want to do whatever else it takes to get ready to write. (The next three pages provide you with a number of "writing readiness" ideas.)

For some writing projects, you will do very little collecting. This is especially true for personal writing. On the other hand, collecting becomes very important if you're working on a lengthy writing project that requires a lot of research and planning.

But Not So Fast

If you have a good writing idea in mind, leave it there for a little while before you jump headfirst into your shaping and planning. Bug your little brother, help your parents with the housework, take in a movie, or do some other homework. While you're doing all of these things, your writing idea will be percolating through your mind.

"Bring ideas in and entertain them royally, for one of them may be king."
—Mark Van Doren

When I come up with a good idea for writing, I let the idea hover just outside my conscious mind. As I go about my other business, it pops in and out of my thinking. When I do this, something very productive almost always happens. I might think of some interesting things to say about my subject, I might think of some questions I would like to explore, or I might discover a starting point for my first draft. (You can also actively think about your subject with the help of your handbook. See 331.)

015   A Closer Look at Collecting

> Let's say you've thought about a subject, collected some ideas that you might want to include in your writing, and you've talked about it with friends or classmates; but you still don't feel ready to write. What should you do? My advice is try to write anyway. Write right through your worries. I'll even get you going. Start with "What I want to talk about is...," "Here's what I know...," "Here's what I don't know...," or "And another thing...." Write for five minutes—nonstop.

When I do this, a general idea or line of thought often comes, and I keep right on going until I come to a natural stopping point in my writing. If that seems a bit too daring, consider looking at your subject more closely in one or more of the following ways: (There's nothing sacred about referring to these ideas *before* you start writing. They can help you at any point during the process.)

- Taking Inventory of Your Thoughts
- Focusing Your Efforts
- Planning Your Way
- Writing an Opening Paragraph

016   Taking Inventory of Your Thoughts

The questions which follow will help you see how well you and your subject match up. After you inventory your thoughts, it should be easier to move ahead with your writing or to reconsider your subject if necessary.

Situation: What are the requirements of the assignment?
     Does my subject match up with these requirements?
Self: How do I feel about the subject?
     Is it worth spending additional time on?
Subject: How much do I know about this subject?
     Is there additional information available?
     Is my subject too general or too specific?
Readers: Who am I writing this for?
     How much do they care or already know about this subject?
     How can I get them interested in my ideas?
Style: In what form could I present my ideas (story, essay, poem, personal narrative, etc.)? See 041 for a complete list of writing forms.
     Can I think of an interesting way to start my paper?

| **Focusing Your Efforts** | **017** |

Sooner or later you will think of an interesting way to write about your subject. This is called your *focus*. A focus gives you some direction, a handle on your subject, a way to develop it. And it provides a general framework or plan for your writing. A focus statement is similar to a topic sentence, which is the controlling idea of a paragraph.

How do you find a focus?

Let's think in terms of pictures or visual images. Suppose as staff photographer for the yearbook, it is your responsibility to take photographs of the spring play. And photographs you do take—from the first tryout through the final performance. It is also your responsibility to help the photo editor select 10 photographs for the yearbook. Which 10 should you choose? It would be difficult, in fact, next to impossible, unless you were able to think of a focus for the selection process. You could highlight

- all of the work that goes into producing the play,
- the night of the final performance,
- the director, especially if it is his or her final production,
- or photographs that capture the most dramatic moments of the play.

To choose a focus for your writing, look at what you have, decide what is important and interesting, and emphasize that in your writing. Actually put your focus in writing. Study it. Make sure it expresses a feeling and establishes a direction for your writing that you feel good about. (See 081 for a handy formula for writing focus statements. Also, read the paragraph below to see how one student chose a focus for her writing.)

In Focus

Last year one of my students wrote about the band camp she attended the past summer. She could have focused on a number of ordinary things, but she decided to focus on something much more entertaining and interesting. She wrote about her flub-ups, her embarrassing moments. And she did her share of flubbing up. Her first one was a beauty: Here she was at band camp—100 miles away from home, mind you—unloading her luggage from her family car, and she discovered that she had forgotten her instrument. She went on to tell about three or four other flub-ups, including the time she dropped her food tray and received a hearty round of applause from her fellow campers.

018   Planning Your Way

Once I have a focus in mind, I'm ready to write. I'm not sure what to expect as I set out. That's part of the fun of the first writing for me. I like surprises. You may still want to proceed a bit more carefully. That's okay.

Many writers like to organize their thoughts in a list, a brief outline, or a cluster before they begin their first draft. (See 059 for an explanation of outlining and 035 for clustering.) This is a good idea especially when you don't have a lot of time to deal with surprises, when you've got to get something on paper **now**. It is also a good idea for extended reports and research papers when you have to sort through large numbers of facts and details.

All good writers—even the most creative ones—focus on organization at some point during the process. Good writing has a design. It moves logically from one point to the next. It leads readers somewhere. (See 084 for help with organizing your thoughts.)

 Sometimes reviewing the information you have collected and listing it in some kind of order will help you find a focus for your writing.

019   Writing an Opening or Lead Paragraph

Sooner or later you'll need to write an opening or lead paragraph. For many writers, it is later, after they have written their first draft. But other writers like to focus their attention on their opening lines sooner, before they jump into their first draft. There are so many different types of writing and so many different ways to write openings that it is difficult to talk about all of them at one time. You might

- begin with a funny story to set a humorous tone,
- start with a simple fact that will be important later,
- draw your readers into your writing with a question or two,
- gain your reader's attention with a startling fact, a confession, quotation, or a hint of what's to come,
- start out with dialogue,
- or simply identify the main points you wish to cover.

 By all means try to make your opening entertaining and interesting, but, more importantly, make it sound like it comes from you and reflects your true feelings.

Connecting: *Writing the First Draft*

I would love to have you feel good about your writing, have it stick to your ribs like it does to mine. But that may be wishful thinking on my part. So my hope is that you at least begin to feel better about your ability to write by following our suggestions. I mention that now because it is at this step in the writing process— the connecting step—that you should really come to appreciate the power of writing.

The Appeal of Writing

I've told you before that the real attraction in writing, the element that draws the professional writers back to the process time and time again, is the element of surprise that accompanies freely written first drafts.

Keep that in mind when you are ready to write a first draft. Write freely about your subject. Let your pen or pencil do the talking and connecting. Don't hesitate. Just write.

If you have trouble staying with your writing, time yourself. Write in short, spontaneous bursts of three to five minutes (or longer) and see what you can discover. I'm not suggesting that you rush through your first draft. I just want you to loosen up as you write and make as many connections as you can.

Making Meaning

Write as much of your first draft as possible in your first sitting while all of your collecting is fresh in your mind. Refer to a plan (if you have one), but keep an open mind. Write until you come to a logical stopping point.

- Write naturally, as if you were surrounded by a group of friends and you are telling them your story.
- Know your subject. You don't have to know everything when you start out, but a good knowledge base makes your job easier.
- Be honest. Let the real you come through in your writing. This is your paper. Make it sound like you.

Helpful HINT   Many writers like to *rehearse* their writing in their minds before they actually put pen to paper. Other writers like to talk through their writing with a friend or classmate. Try one of these activities and see if it helps you write your first draft.

021

Connecting: *Revising Your Writing*

> If you followed my advice and let yourself go during your first draft, you will have produced a lot of writing, probably far more than you usually produce. Some of it is going to be pretty bad. This is only natural when you write freely and "up-tempo." But you can also expect that some of it will be very good—perhaps some of your best writing ever—and will become the foundation of your writing as you move on and revise it.

Revising isn't that easy, especially for young writers. You're going to have a lot of questions as you set out to improve your writing. We've organized this section according to three general questions you and most other student writers will likely ask about revising.

- How do you get started?
- What changes should you make?
- How many changes should you make?

022

How do you get started?

Do you look at all of those words you've produced, scream "I've created a monster," crumple it up, and start over? That might be your first reaction—the temptation to produce something safe is a strong one. But resist it and stick with me.

Here's what I want you to do: First, put your writing aside. Get it out of your mind for awhile and relax. You deserve it. Finding a subject, thinking about it, and exploring it in a first draft(s) can be a lot of work.

Reading and Reviewing

When you get back to your writing, see how you feel about it. Start by reading it. Read it a number of times. Read it out loud. Pay special attention to those ideas or parts that you like. Look specifically for surprising details, smooth-reading sentences, and interesting ideas in your writing. Have friends, classmates, or family members read it as well. Find out what they like or dislike, and see how their thinking compares to your own.

 Helpful HINT

Make some marks on your first draft as soon as you can. Underline words, phrases, or ideas that you like. Cross out ideas that you know you won't use. This will remind you that your writing is a "work in progress."

What changes should you make?

That depends on how you feel about your initial writing. You might find that you like most of what you've written. If this is the case, you're lucky (and hopefully being honest with yourself). You might only need to make some minor changes—maybe some reordering and refining of ideas. If, however, there are problems with parts of your draft (which will usually be the case), there are a variety of things you'll need to do to work it into shape.

A Word of Caution

Now before you start looking for spelling errors and missed capital letters and periods, we better talk for a minute about what it really means to work your writing into shape. When inexperienced writers are faced with making changes in their writing, they generally want to make them in this order: spelling, neatness, mechanics, and then . . . maybe . . . evaluating and improving upon the ideas in their writing.

So I know how great the temptation is for you to check the spelling, correct the punctuation, erase the Chee-tos stains, and feel that you've made the necessary changes. But you really must make changes in the reverse order. Attend to the meaning of your writing first, and then attend to its appearance. Otherwise, you may end up not really changing your writing at all. (See 123 for help.)

Making the Right Moves

The guidelines which follow will help you work your writing into shape once you read and review it:

■ First, **look at the big picture**. Take it all in, whole hog. Decide if there is a focus or main idea either stated or suggested in your writing. If you can't find it, write one. Or, if your original thinking on your subject has changed, write a new focus statement.

■ Then **look at the chunks of information** (sentences and/or paragraphs) in your writing, and *reorder* them, if you feel they could be arranged more effectively.

■ Also,
   ❑ **cut information** that doesn't support your main idea or focus;
   ❑ **add information**, if you feel additional points need to be made. Make sure that your writing answers all of the questions your readers may have;
   ❑ **rewrite parts** that aren't as clear as you would like them to be.

■ Finally, look very closely at your writing and
   ❑ **refine it** so the specific words and sentences are accurate, smooth reading, and effective. (See 111 and 118 for help.)

024   How many changes should you make?

In one sense, this is a silly question. You should change what doesn't sound right to you or what might be unclear to your readers. In another sense, it is a very serious question, especially if it's a lengthy piece of writing and you're not really confident in your ability to make changes. Here's my advice: Talk to your teacher. Tell him or her that you aren't sure you can overhaul everything that needs to be changed, at least not now, not for this piece. Maybe the two of you can agree on one or two things that you can work on for this writing. It's worth a try.

025   Making the Final Moves

After making the changes in the main part of your writing, review your opening again (or write one if you have not already done so). Make sure it draws your reader into the main part of your writing and gives us at least a taste of your focus or main point.

A closing paragraph or idea is not always necessary, especially if your writing ends naturally after the last important point is made. When one is needed, it is used to answer questions left unanswered in the main part of the writing and to help readers see the importance of your message.

Helpful HINT

Check your writing for one last thing. Readers don't like to be told everything when they read. They like to see some things for themselves. You can help them "see" if you have included a lot of good description and one or two brief personal stories in your writing.

Topping Off Your Writing

Here's how to top off your writing with a good title. Think of your title as fish bait: it should look juicy, it should dance slightly, and it should have a hook in it. To look juicy, a title must have strong, colorful words in it (The Black Stallion, Brave New World). To dance, it must have rhythm (The Old Man and the Sea, not The Sea and the Old Man). And to hook your reader, it must grab the imagination (My Understanding with a Grizzly, not What I Did on My Summer Vacation; Never Cry Wolf, not Life Among the Wolves). List a number of possible titles, and select the one that provides the best bait for your reader.

"Sometimes people give titles to me, and sometimes I see them on billboards."
—Robert Penn Warren

Correcting: *Preparing the Final Copy*   **026**

There will come a point in each writing assignment when you'll be satisfied that you've made all of the necessary changes (or your due date is fast approaching). This is the time to get your writing ready to share. During this final step you should first check for missing words. You should also check for spelling, mechanics, usage, and grammatical errors. Then it is time to prepare a neat final draft and proofread it.

Correcting and Proofreading Checklist   **027**

The following guidelines will help you put the finishing touches on your writing:

Spelling (See 563.)

- Have you spelled all of the words correctly? (Read your writing backwards one word at a time when you check for spelling. Then you can't help but focus on each word and check it for spelling.)

Punctuation (See 458.)

- Does each sentence end with an end punctuation mark?
- Have you placed commas before the conjunctions *and, but,* or *or* in compound sentences? Have you used commas to set off items listed in a series?
- Are apostrophes in place to show possession or to mark contractions?
- Have you properly punctuated any dialogue or written conversation with quotation marks?

Capitalization (See 533.)

- Have you started sentences and dialogue with a capital letter?
- Have you capitalized specific names of people, places, or things?

Usage (See 574.)

- Have you misused any of the commonly mixed pairs of words: *there, their, they're; to, too, two; its, it's; are, our; your, you're.*

Grammar (See 695 and 090-114.)

- Do your subjects and verbs agree?
- Do your pronouns agree with their antecedents?
- Have you unintentionally used any sentence fragments or rambling or run-on sentences?

Group Advising

All writers like a good audience, especially one which offers constructive comments during a writing project. And who could make a better audience than your fellow writers? Some of you might work in writing groups, so you already know the value of writers sharing their work. If you haven't, start by working in small groups or teams of two or three classmates.

028 Writing Group Guidelines

The Author/Writer

1. Come prepared with a meaningful piece of writing. (Make copies for each group member if this is part of normal group procedure.)
2. Introduce your writing. But don't say too much.
3. Read your copy out loud.
4. As the group reacts to your writing, listen carefully and take brief notes. Don't be defensive about your writing, since this will stop some members from commenting honestly about your work. Answer all of their questions.
5. If you have some special concerns or problems, share these with your fellow writers.

The Group Members

1. Listen carefully as the writer reads. Take notes if you need to. Some groups just listen and then do a free writing after the reading. Still other groups use a critique or review sheet as a guide when they react to a piece of writing. (See "Commenting on Writing" on the next page for a critiquing checklist.)
2. Don't be afraid to share your feelings about a piece of writing.
3. Try, however, to keep your comments positive and constructive.
4. Ask questions of the author: "Why? How? What do you mean when you say . . .?" And answer questions the author might have of you.
5. Listen to other comments and add to them.

Helpful HINT
Seek the help of your writing group throughout the writing process. But it is especially helpful to seek their advice early after a first or second draft.

Maintaining Good Relations   029

When you're helping someone with his or her writing, focus your comments on things that you actually see or hear in the writing. For example, a comment such as "You used so many 'there is' statements at the beginning of your paper" will mean much more to a writer than a general comment such as "Your opening is really boring" or "Put some life into your opening." A specific comment helps a writer see a problem without hurting his or her confidence.

At first you might only be able to comment on the repetition of a certain word, the length of the writing, a point you don't understand, or the nice sound the writing has. As long as these comments are honest and sincere, offer them. Your ability to make comments about the writing will increase with practice.

Helpful HINT

Give praise when praise is due, but base it on something you've observed in the writing. Advising sessions shouldn't be popularity contests. (See 432 for more help with group advising sessions.)

Commenting on Writing

Use the checklist which follows to help you discuss writing during advising sessions.

■ **Purpose** . . . Is it clear what the writer is trying to do? Is he or she trying to explain how something works, share a funny story, describe someone or something, etc.

■ **Voice** . . . Does the writing sound honest and sincere? Does the writer sound interested in his or her writing?

■ **Audience** . . . Will the readers enjoy or appreciate the subject of this writing? Are all of the readers' questions answered?

■ **Content** . . . Does the writer know his or her subject? Has the writer included enough chunks of information to interest readers?

■ **Form** . . . Are the ideas presented clearly and logically so a reader can easily move from one point to the next?

■ **Writing Devices** . . . Does the writing include any personal thoughts or stories, specific detail, dialogue, or creative comparisons (metaphors)?

■ **Purpose Again** . . . Does the writing make a person smile, pound his or her fist, or react in some other way? What is especially good about the writing?

Starting Points

"Starting Points" provides you with a variety pack of guidelines and ideas—all of which will help you develop your writing more effectively. We start with a summary of the steps in the writing process and follow with all kinds of high-powered ideas for selecting and shaping subjects for writing. This is one section that you will turn to again and again when you are developing writing assignments.

030 The Writing Process

Selecting, collecting, connecting, and **correcting** refer to different steps in the writing process. Selecting refers to finding a subject for writing. Collecting refers to all of the thinking, talking, reading, and planning that goes into a writing project. Connecting includes all of the writing from the first draft to the final revision. Correcting refers to the finishing touches made as the writing is put into final form. (See 011 for a complete discussion of the process.)

031 Selecting

1. Select a subject that genuinely interests you and meets the requirements of the assignment.
2. Refer to your personal "SourceBank" of writing ideas, or begin your subject search with one of the selecting activities in your handbook. (See 033-036.)
3. Free writing, clustering, and listing are popular starting points.
4. The list of writing topics may provide you with a ready-made subject or at least point you toward a writing idea. (See 040.)

> "Writing to me is a voyage, an odyssey, a discovery, because I'm never certain of precisely what I will find."
> —Gabriel Fielding

Helpful HINT

If you give one (or more) of the selecting activities a chance—if you allow your mind to travel freely—you will discover something new and unexpected, something worth writing about.

Collecting

1. Collecting initially involves doing whatever it takes to start writing.
2. You might learn about your subject using one of the searching and shaping activities. (See 037.)
3. You might gather facts and details by reading and talking about your subject.
4. If you're not ready to write your first draft at this point, consider working on one or more of the following activities:
   - ❖ Taking inventory of your work (See 016.)
   - ❖ Finding an interesting way (focus) to write about your subject
   - ❖ Organizing the information you have collected
   - ❖ Writing the opening section or paragraph

Connecting

1. Write the first draft while your initial collecting is still fresh in your mind.
2. Write freely and honestly. "Talk" to your readers.
3. Read your first draft to see how you feel about it.
4. Work your writing into shape by adding, cutting, reordering, rewriting, and refining information. (See 021-025 for help.)

Special Note: You're writing not only for yourself, but also for your readers. Make sure your writing answers any questions a reader might have.

Correcting

1. Put the finishing touches on your writing by reading carefully for missing words and awkward sections and by checking for errors in usage, grammar, and mechanics.
2. Prepare a neat final copy and proofread it before turning it in.
3. Enlist the help of a friend, classmate, teacher, or family member when you correct and proofread. (See 026 for help.)

Creating a Writing "SourceBank"

Don't think that professional writers spend all of their time in front of their word processors or hidden behind good books. They are often very active people who get out and get involved. Discovering what's going on in their world is very important to writers. It's what inspires them to write. And what pack rats they are. They save every little nugget of experience they can, in hopes that it might be of some use to them in their writing.

To think like a writer, you should act like one and develop your own "SourceBank" of possible writing subjects. The guidelines and activities which follow will help you do this.

"Found" Writing Ideas Be alert for writing ideas you find unexpectedly as you read, ride the school bus, goof around, etc. For example, while on a walk, you and a friend might come across a well-cared-for, healthy plant perched in front of a neglected, ramshackle home. A "flower-in-the-rough" scene such as this one could bring to mind a number of writing subjects.

Helpful HINT Just taking notice of what goes on around you might not be enough. You've got to remember things so that you can make use of them later in your writing. Recording experiences in writing will help you "record" these experiences in your mind. Writers often carry small pocket notebooks to capture images and ideas they happen upon, or they regularly write about their daily experiences in their journals.

Experience Experience as many different aspects of your community as you can. Visit museums, churches, farms, parks, libraries, businesses, factories. As you expand the scope of your world, you will naturally build a supply of potential writing ideas.

Reviewing Reference Guides and Periodicals Prowl around your library for writing ideas. Take special note of lists of articles on current issues kept in the vertical file or nonfiction titles recently added to the library. An issue of the *Readers' Guide to Periodical Literature* can also be useful as a checklist of current topics. And magazines and newspapers can also remind you of the topics being written about today.

Maintaining a Writing Folder As you work on your writing in school, especially if you work in writing groups, new ideas for writing will constantly present themselves. There's no more fertile ground for ideas than talking about writing with your classmates. Reserve part of your folder to write these ideas down.

■ **Reading Like a Writer**   Reserve part of your writing folder for
interesting ideas that you come across as you read. These ideas could
be interesting names, character traits, details, surprising turns in the
stories, well-put sentences, etc. They will serve as a valuable resource
(and a source of inspiration) when you develop your own writing.

■ **Personal Almanac (Inventory)**   Take a close look at your life up to
this point, and list ideas, people, places, and things that have mattered
to you. Keep adding to your almanac as more ideas come to mind.
Here's what you might include:

- ❏ Areas of expertise
- ❏ Memorable firsts
- ❏ Memorable lasts
- ❏ School memories
- ❏ Unforgettable people
- ❏ Unforgettable places
- ❏ Favorite books, movies, etc.
- ❏ Things to change

■ **Life Map**   Writing teachers Dan Kirby and Tom Liner in their book
Inside Out suggest that you inventory important experiences on a life
map. They're not talking about a typical map from an atlas or like the
ones in your handbook. They're talking about a map which has only
one road on it, the road representing your life. This is a map of time
as much as it is a map of space. At different points along your life map
you illustrate important events in your life from birth to the present.
Each point you illustrate represents a story or, an experience in your
life. Think in terms of the hills and valleys or the highs and lows of
your life. (See the start of a life map below.)

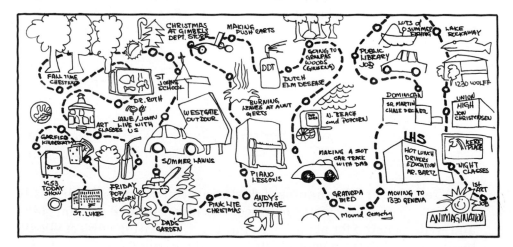

Selecting a Writing Subject

It will happen, as sure as waking up with a fever on the day of the first school dance. A paper will be due tomorrow, and you won't have done one bit of work on it. What should you do? Well, you can hope and pray that you *do* wake up tomorrow with a fever. You can think of some creative excuses why your paper isn't done. You can call Jill, the class brain, and see what she is writing about. Or should we say *has written* about. She's probably done. Or, you can use one of the following activities to help you get started. (We recommend the final course of action, but remember, a high temperature is nothing to fool around with.)

Special Note: See "Creating a Writing 'SourceBank'" (033) for creative ideas for developing a resource of writing subjects.

■ **Journal Writing**   Write on a regular basis in a personal journal. Explore your personal feelings, develop your thoughts, and record the happenings of each day. Underline ideas in your personal writing that you would like to explore in writing assignments. (See 129 for more on personal writing.)

■ **Free Writing**   Write nonstop for five or ten minutes to discover possible writing ideas. Begin writing with a particular idea in mind (one related to your writing assignment). Don't think—just write freely and rapidly. Underline ideas that might serve as starting points for your assignment.

■ **Clustering**   Begin a cluster with a *nucleus word*. Select a word that is related to your writing topic or assignment. Record words which come to mind when you think of this word. Don't pick and choose; record every word. Circle each word as you write it, and draw a line connecting it to the closest related word. (See the cluster example below.)

After three or four minutes of clustering, you will probably be ready to write. Scan your cluster for a word or idea that will get you going and write nonstop for about eight minutes. A writing subject should begin to develop from your clustering and writing.

■ **Listing**   Freely listing ideas as they come to mind is another **036** effective technique for searching for a writing subject. Begin with an idea or key word related to your assignment and simply start listing words. **Brainstorming**—the gathering and listing of ideas in groups—can also be an effective way to search for writing ideas.

■ **Imaginary Conversation**   Create an imaginary conversation between you and someone else or between two strangers. The subject should be an idea related to your writing assignment. Continue this conversation as long as you can.

■ **Sentence Completion**   Complete any open-ended sentence in as many ways as you can. Try to word your sentences so that they lead you to a subject you can use for a particular writing assignment. See the list below.

I wonder how...	I hope our school...	Our grading system...
Too many people...	I just learned...	Television is...
The good thing about...	One place I enjoy...	Cars can be...

 Try alternating responses with a friend or classmate and work from each other's ideas. Keep the ideas flowing as long as you can.

■ **Review the Essentials of Life Checklist**   Below you will find a checklist of the major categories into which most things we need to live a full life are divided. The checklist provides an endless variety of subject possibilities. Consider the first category, clothing. It could lead to writing about

❏ *the clothes you wish you were wearing;*
❏ *the wardrobe of a friend, classmate, or family member;*
❏ *your all-time favorite piece of clothing;*
❏ *clothing as a statement (the "we are what we wear" idea).*

clothing	machines	rules/laws
housing	intelligence	tools/utensils
food	history/records	heat/fuel
communication	agriculture	natural resources
exercise	land/property	personality/identity
education	work/occupation	recreation/hobby
family	community	trade/money
friends	science	literature/books
purpose/goals	plants/vegetation	health/medicine
love	freedom/rights	art/music
senses	energy	faith/religion

Searching and Shaping a Subject

The following activities will help you learn more about your subjects and develop them for writing. If you already have a good "feel" for a particular writing subject, you might attempt only one of the activities. If you need to explore your subject in some detail and time permits, you might attempt two or more of the activities. Read through the entire list before you choose.

■ **Free Writing** At this point, you can approach free writing in two different ways. You can do a *focused* writing to see how many ideas come to mind about your subject as you write. Or you can approach your writing as if it were an *instant version* of the finished product.

■ **Scrap Writing** Make a writing scrap by crumpling a piece of paper into a compact shape. Write the letters which correspond to the writing instructions (printed below) on six flat surfaces of your scrap. Then give your scrap a toss (at least four times). After each toss write freely about your subject, following the instructions of the letter which is most visible when you catch your scrap of paper.

    A. **Describe it.** *What do you see, hear, feel, smell, taste . . .?*

    B. **Compare it.** *What is it like? What is it different from?*

    C. **Associate it.** *What connections between this and something else come to mind?*

    D. **Analyze it.** *What parts does it have? How do they work (or not work) together?*

    E. **Apply it.** *What can you do with it? How can you use it?*

    F. **Argue for or against it.** *(seriously or humorously)*

Each time you toss your scrap and write freely, according to the writing instructions, you will learn something new about your subject.

■ **5 W's of Writing** Answer the 5 W's—*Who? What? Where? When?* and *Why?*—to identify basic information about your subject. (Add *How?* to the list for even better coverage.)

Keep asking the question *Why?* about your subject until you run completely out of answers. Sum up what you've learned.

■ **Precision Poetry** Write a poem about your subject (*cinquain, list, alphabet, name,* or *phrase* poetry, for starters). (See 233 in your handbook for guidelines.)

- **Clustering** This clustering will naturally be more focused than an **038** initial cluster since you now have a specific subject in mind.
- **Audience Appeal** Select a specific audience to address. Consider a group of preschoolers, a live television audience, readers of a popular teen magazine, a panel of experts, etc.
- **Offbeat (Unstructured) Questions** Creating and answering offbeat questions will help you see your writing idea in unexpected ways. The sample questions which follow suggest a number of offbeat ways to look at different types of writing subjects.

Writing About a Person
- ❏ What type of clothing is he (she) like?
- ❏ What does his menu look like?

Writing About a Place
- ❏ What is the place's best sense?
- ❏ Where does this place go for advice?

Writing About an Object
- ❏ What would make this object stand at attention?
- ❏ What does it look like upside down?

Writing About an Issue or Event
- ❏ What clubs or organizations would your argument or viewpoint join?
- ❏ Would your argument take the stairs or the elevator?

Writing to Explain a Process
- ❏ What restaurant is this process like?
- ❏ Where in a hardware store would this process feel most at home?

Writing a Narrative
- ❏ What fruit does this story resemble?
- ❏ What would your great-grandmother say about it?

"Your writing is trying to tell you something. Just lend an ear."

—Joanne Greenberg

- **Imaginary Dialogue** Create an imaginary dialogue between two people in which your specific subject is the focus of the conversation.
- **Twisted Version** Write a "twisted" version of your paper. You might write as if you were a different person or someone from a different time or place, or you might write an exaggerated or fairy-tale version of your paper.

Prompts, Topics, and Forms

What's that? . . . You can't think of anything to write about? . . . Nothing ever happens to you? . . . Your life's about as exciting as low tide? Well, I say baloney, balderdash, and bunkum to that. You have plenty to write about. Read on and I'll prove it to you.

039 Writing Prompts

Every day you do things that you feel good about. You hear things that make you mad. You become curious as to how something works. You're reminded of past experiences. These common, everyday thoughts and occurrences make excellent prompts or starting points for writing. And often that's all you really need. Once you start writing, the ideas should naturally start to flow, and you're on your way. Use the list of writing prompts which follow as starting points for all your writing.

▨ Best and Worst, First and Last

My worst day
My craziest experience at a restaurant
An unforgettable dream
The hardest thing I've ever done
My best hour
The worst thing to wait for
My best kitchen creation

▨ As My World Turns

My secret snacks
A day in the life of my pet
Last time I was at the mall, I . . .
When I played the rebel
Wheezing and sneezing
_____ caused a lump in my throat.
When I'm in charge

▨ Deep in Thought

List words that define you as a friend.
   (Write about the most important word.)
What car are you like and why?
List the duties of a good citizen.
   (Write about one [or more] of these.)

▨ Inside Education

My best class ever
Here's a look at the next episode of
   "As the School Swings."
Dear Blackboard,
Finally, a good assembly
I memorized every word.
A classmate I once worshipped

▨ It could only happen to me!

It sounds crazy but . . .
Putting my foot in my mouth
Guess what I just heard?
Creepy, crawly things
I looked everywhere for it.
Whatever happened to my . . .
I got so mad when . . .

▨ What If . . .and How About . . .?

Where do I draw the line?
What should everyone know?
Here is my wish list.
Why do people like to go fast?
What if I never forgot?

▨ Quotable Quotes

"Almost anything in life is easier to get into than out of."
"It's time for a change."
"My interest is in the future because I am going to spend the rest of my life there."
"Goofing off is a lost art."
"Everybody is ignorant, only on different subjects."

Writing Topics

Unless you spend most of your time in a closet, you come across any number of people, places, experiences, and things—all of which are potential topics for writing. We've listed a number of topics below (categorized according to different reasons for writing), so you'll get the idea.

■ **Describing**

People: teacher, relative, classmate, coach, neighbor, bus driver, someone you spend time with, someone you wish you were like, someone who bugs you

Places: a hangout, a garage, an attic, a rooftop, the alley, the bowling alley, the locker room, the zoo, the hallway, a corner, a barn, a bayou, a lake, a river, a cupboard, a yard

Things: a billboard, a poster, a video game, a monkey wrench, a key, a bus, a book, a boat, a drawing, a model, a doll, a junk drawer, a ladder, a locket, a locker

■ **Narrating** (Sharing)

stage fright, just last week, a big mistake, a reunion, getting lost, getting hurt, flirting, learning to _____, all wet, getting caught, cleaning up, being a friend

■ **Explaining**

How to . . . eat popcorn, make a taco, improve your memory, care for a pet, entertain a child, impress your teacher, earn extra money, get in shape, take a good picture

How to operate . . . control . . . run . . .	How to build . . . grow . . . create . . .
How to choose . . . select . . . pick . . .	How to fix . . . clean . . . wash . . .
How to store . . . stack . . . load . . .	How to protect . . . warn . . . wave . . .

The causes of . . . acid rain, acne, hiccups, tornadoes, shinsplints, dropouts, rust, cheating

Kinds of . . . music, crowds, friends, commercials, dreams, pain, neighbors, clouds, stereos, heroes, chores, homework, calendars, clocks

Definition of . . . "class," generation gap, a good time, hassle, a radical, a conservative, "soul," grandmother, school, loyalty, astrology, Kosher, algebra

■ **Persuading**

dieting, homework, the speed limit, smoking in public places, shoplifting, air bags, teen centers, something that needs improving, something that deserves support, something that's unfair, something that everyone should have or see or do, something . . .

Writing Forms

Have you ever written and designed a children's storybook? Have you ever written and designed your own bumper sticker, your own book of riddles, your own instructional manual? Just thinking about all of the forms of writing available to you might "prompt" you to write.

■ **Personal Writing** — journals, logs, diaries, free writing, clustering, listing, informal essays and narratives, brainstorming

■ **Creative Writing**—poems, myths, plays, stories, anecdotes, sketches, essays, letters, songs, jokes, parodies

■ **Subject Writing**—reports, reviews, letters, research papers, essays, news stories, interviews, instructions, manuals

■ **Persuasive Writing**—editorials, letters, cartoons, research papers, essays, advertisements, slogans, pamphlets, petitions, commercials

The Basic Elements of Writing

Developing Essays

When you explore, explain, or argue in your writing, you're developing an essay. At one extreme, an essay can be very informal and personal. At the other extreme, an essay can follow a specific pattern or design and result in a very orderly piece of writing, all spit and polish. Most of your essay assignments will fall somewhere in between these two extremes.

What follows are detailed guidelines for writing the personal essay and the traditional school essay, plus a number of additional insights into essay writing. Also included in this section are guidelines for building paragraphs and writing effective sentences.

An Essay by Any Other Name . . .

That Was Then

When I was in ninth grade, back in the Dark Ages, we wrote **themes**. (How long ago was that? I'll give you a hint: The Beatles made their television debut in America that year.)

We also wrote a lot of summary paragraphs and descriptive paragraphs and a library report or two. And who could forget book reports? But just about everything else we wrote that was longer than a paragraph and shorter than a report was a theme.

When we wrote about important events in our lives, we were developing themes. When we explained what "duty," "responsibility," or "progress" meant to us, we were writing themes. When we had to persuade our teacher (Mrs. Bransted was the only one who read our papers) that winter was the best season, that noon hour should be lengthened, that honesty may not always be the best policy, we were producing themes. Themes covered a lot of territory.

This Is Now

And themes still cover a lot of territory. Only I don't think they are called themes anymore, are they? Your teachers assign compositions or make writing assignments. Or maybe they have you write essays.

Essays seem to be gaining more and more popularity with teachers and students in all grades. And that's the term we will use in the discussion that follows. Just keep in mind that when we are talking about essays, we are also talking, for the most part, about themes, compositions, and longer writing assignments.

044 Writing the Personal Essay

Toddlers move at a different pace than most of us. If you've ever taken little ones for a walk, you know what I mean. They are forever stopping, picking things up, studying them, tasting them, dropping them, picking them up again, and so on.

That's how writers often develop personal essays. They kind of mosey along—freely picking up on whatever enters their minds as they write about a particular subject. They're in no hurry. If a certain idea interests them, they look at it very closely. They know that one good idea usually triggers another one if they stay with it long enough. In its most natural state, a personal essay simply follows the course of the writer's mind as he or she writes.

045 The Personal Essay vs. Autobiographical Writing

As its name suggests, a personal essay is largely based on personal experience. So much so, that it is sometimes hard to tell the difference between this form and autobiographical writing. The following writing situations should help you see the difference:

- Josie wants to recall a specific chapter in her life—the summers she spent living with her grandparents. (This is autobiographical writing because Josie is the subject.)
- Rachel wants to explore her feelings about the home video craze. (This is a personal essay because Rachel is dealing with a subject other than herself.)

Can you see the difference? The focus of autobiographical writing is the writer. It basically speaks about *one time in the life of one person*. The focus of the personal essay is *a subject other than the writer*. The personal essay opens up a discussion on a subject and, in this way, it speaks to us all.

Helpful HINT

The writer of autobiography says: I've written about an important time in my life. I hope you enjoy reading about this time. I also hope you learn something about me and maybe something about yourself in the process.

The writer of a personal essay says: I've written about a subject that I personally find fun (interesting, important). You might not agree with what I say about this subject, but that's okay. We all are entitled to our opinions. What matters to me is that you enjoy reading my essay and that it gets you thinking.

Selecting a Subject: *What do I write about?*

Personal essays are written on just about any subject imaginable. I've read great personal essays on everything from caring for pets to clothes, from cafeteria food to junk food, from baby-sitting to sitting in a doctor's waiting room.

So how do you find a good subject? My advice is not to look too far. You can find plenty to write about just by retracing a typical school day:

> "Let's see. I got up, showered, dressed, pulled my wallet and comb from my top drawer. (A top drawer is almost always a junk drawer, the contents of which contain any number of possible essay topics.) Then I went to the kitchen for breakfast. (Another possible topic. What is breakfast like at your house?) I sat in my usual seat on the bus. (Another topic. Who sits where on the school bus? and why? and what do you think about this?) I started worrying about the test I would have first hour. (What kinds of things do you worry about? and why?) Our bus was early, so I had to wait outside, which made me mad. (Why does this make you mad? What else gets your goat?)

I was able to find a number of subjects for this student before he even set foot in school. That's how easy it is. Just about anything in your life that interests you, amuses you, angers you, or gets you thinking is a possible topic for a personal essay. (*Note*: Review your personal journal. You'll find plenty of ideas for your essay.)

Here's another way to generate possible subjects for personal essays. On notebook paper, write the letters of the alphabet down the left-hand column. Skip at least one line between letters. Then list at least two possible subjects for each letter. For "a" you might list *attic* or *algebra* or *ATV* (all-terrain vehicle). For "b" you might list *brothers* or *band practice* or *blood pressure* (as in what gets yours to rise) and so on.

Collecting: *Gathering Your Thoughts*

Take some time to think about your subject. Consider why you picked it, how you might write about it, or, perhaps, what you hope to find out through your writing. The searching and shaping activities (037) will help you generate some initial ideas about the subject.

Share your thoughts with classmates. Let them know why you've picked this subject and how you generally hope to write about it. Take note of your classmate's ideas for writing. Read published essays in books and magazines. Ask your teacher if he or she has any model essays that might help you write about your particular subject.

048   **Connecting:** *Writing and Shaping Your Essay*

Write your first draft freely, but don't rush through it. Remember how a toddler walks along? That's how you want to write your first draft. Keep in mind that you are not trying to create the final word on your subject. A personal essay presents your viewpoint about something and nothing more. As you work on your writing, your goal should be to present this viewpoint in a way that will satisfy you and will interest your readers. (See 011 for additional guidelines for developing personal essays.)

Ask yourself Why? or How? or What if . . .? after you make important or interesting points. Push yourself to come up with some answers in your writing. This will help you see your subject in new and interesting ways.

049   # What Should a Personal Essay Look Like?

If you're not sure how to put your personal essay in finished form, read through the list of common forms which follows. One of them may match up perfectly with the subject of your writing.

■ **Free Form**   An essay in free form basically follows the course of the writer's mind as he or she writes. What's said is said. Any changes that are made are made for the sake of clarity. This form works well if your writing is mostly *reflective* (which means it consists of a lot of wondering and supposing).

■ **Traditional Form**   An essay that follows the traditional form begins with a planned opening, follows with developmental paragraphs (or sentences), and finishes with a few closing remarks. You're all familiar with this form. It's how you write your school-related paragraphs, essays, and reports. (See 053 for help with this form.) If you have a lot of information and ideas to sort through and organize, this might be the best form for your essay.

A possible approach: Let's say the contents of your junk drawer is the subject of your traditional essay, and you decide to classify this stuff according to those things that are gifts, souvenirs, and miscellaneous odds and ends. You should open your essay with an explanation of your approach to this subject, then work through the different "classifications," and conclude with a few closing remarks.

■ **Human Interest Story**   Many of the stories in your favorite maga- **050**
zines are human interest stories. They often look at familiar subjects
in entertaining ways and speak to a specific audience—teenagers,
senior citizens, mothers, etc.

A possible approach: Let's say you're writing about breakfast at your
house. It might be fun to think of yourself as being on assignment for
a popular teen magazine and write about this subject by contrasting
your "refined and proper" behavior with the "clumsy or coarse"
behavior of someone eating with you.

■ **Pet Peeve**   Pet peeves are those little everyday occurrences that bug
us, upset us, frustrate us:

> Doesn't it make you mad when the guy next to you starts sneezing
> and blowing his nose as soon as you're ready to dig into lunch . . .?

A possible approach: If you feel your subject could be classified as a pet
peeve, use this simple formula to develop your essay:
    1) Describe your pet peeve in a little story. 2) Then identify things
you have done (or things you would like to do) to remedy or counteract
this annoyance. 3) Indicate whether or not any of the remedies have
worked. 4) Then make some closing remarks—perhaps a final solution
to the problem.

■ **Editorial**   If the subject of your writing is something that's bother-
ing you, and it's something that should be treated more seriously than
a pet peeve, you can write about it in an editorial.

A possible approach: Perhaps there are some things about the home
video craze that bother you, and you want to share these feelings with
your classmates. You could do so in an editorial. (See "Writing an
Editorial" for additional guidelines.)

■ **Poem**   That's right. Some subjects might lend themselves well to
poetry. If "things that make you angry" is the subject of your writing,
you might develop a list poem by completing a series of "Anger is
when . . ." statements. (Review the poetry section in your handbook
and experiment with your subject.)

Correcting: *Setting It Straight*
051

   A personal essay is a record of your own thoughts on a particular
subject. Make sure that "record" is a clear and accurate one before you
share it with your readers. (See 026 for help.) Writing that is carelessly
thrown together at the last minute would make a good subject for a pet
peeve: *Don't you hate it when . . .*

052 Developing the School Essay

When you are asked to explain a process (*How to make a killer pizza*), to analyze something (*Progress reports do more harm than good and here's why*), to argue for or against something (*We need a video club in our school*), you are writing a traditional school essay. They've been around a long time—as long as story problems and spelling tests. (See 063 for a model.)

053 The Working Parts

The **opening** paragraph of a school essay usually states the subject (thesis statement), gains the reader's attention, and leads smoothly into the main part of the essay.

The **developmental** paragraphs make up the body (main part) of the essay. They should obviously be developed and organized as effectively as possible. In a how-to essay, for example, you will most likely use a step-by-step explanation. (See 084 for methods of organization.) A new paragraph is started whenever there is a shift or change to a new idea or topic.

The **closing** paragraph should tie all of the important points together. And it should leave the reader with a clear idea of the essay's importance.

 Use the guidelines which follow as well as the guidelines in the "The Writing Process" section to help you develop your essay.

Steps in the Process

054 Selecting

1. Select a general subject area that interests you and meets the requirements of your assignment.
2. Don't be satisfied with the first idea that comes to mind. Consider a number of possible ideas. The best idea yet may be just around the next turn in your thinking.

055 Collecting

3. List all of your initial thoughts or ideas about the subject.
4. Use your list to help you focus on a specific writing idea within the subject area.
5. Do any reading, researching, talking, and thinking necessary to learn about your subject.

Connecting

At this point you may continue planning, or you may write an early draft of your essay. The column on the left describes a traditional approach to the process. (If an outline is required follow these steps.) The column on the right is a much more informal approach.

<table>
<tr><td colspan="2">Traditional Essay</td><td colspan="2">Informal Essay</td></tr>
</table>

Traditional Essay	Informal Essay
6. Determine what it is you would like to say about this topic and write a starter statement which reflects this. (This is a working thesis statement.)	6. Write an early draft to discover the importance of your subject. Write freely and go where your writing takes you.
7. Work up a list of details which support your statement.	7. Review your early draft and decide on a controlling idea or focus for your essay.
8. Arrange this list of details into a well-ordered outline. (See 059.)	8. Add, delete, and rearrange ideas in your early draft so that the information in the main part of your essay supports your focus.
9. Do any additional reading and researching that you think is necessary.	9. Do any additional reading and researching that is necessary.
10. Write the first draft of your paper.	10. Develop a second draft which reflects the changes.

Correcting

11. Revise the first draft of your essay. Pay close attention to the style and the content of your writing. (See 021 for help.)

12. Correct any errors in spelling, mechanics, usage, and grammar in your revised version.

13. Prepare a final copy according to your teacher's guidelines. Proofread your essay at least once before turning it in. (See 027 for a checklist.)

MINI-lesson

Put some thought into the endings of your essays. The only rule that counts is this: stop when everything important has been said and nothing more is left out. (You'll have to decide for yourself what is important and what is not.) Avoid worn-out endings: 1) the simple moral, where you try to state the meaning of your writing in one last sentence, and 2) the dull restatement of something you said in the beginning. A good ending makes a reader think about everything that came before it. It seems natural, and it keeps the essay kicking.

---

058 Personalizing the School Essay

Peter Elbow, in *Writing with Power,* provides the following suggestions for adding some spark to your school essays (and having some fun in the process).

■ Pretend that you are the first person who has ever thought in a certain way about your subject and write excitedly and freely about your discoveries. Some fresh ideas are bound to develop.

■ Pretend that the subject of your writing is dangerous, scandalous, highly controversial, and argue against it.

■ Become the person whose ideas you are reading or writing about. Try to get inside of his or her mind and write as if you were that person.

■ At regular intervals ask yourself, "What am I trying to say?" And then answer the question in your mind or out loud. Pick up on anything that sounds better than the way you initially expressed yourself and work it into your essay.

> *"The essay is a literary device for saying almost everything about anything."*
>
> —**Aldous Huxley**

■ Look at your writing subject from a number of different angles. (See 037 for ideas.)

■ Get into your writing. Clench your fists when the words aren't coming the way you want them to. Clap your hands when you hit on the right way to say something. Fidget, squirm, move around when you really think you are on to something. (When I'm really on to a good idea, I can't sit still. I have to do something—get a cup of coffee, a cookie, some fresh air.)

■ Bend the rules (if your teacher allows it). If you don't feel like starting with a typical opening paragraph, open in a way that feels right to you—perhaps with a personal story that got you interested in your subject in the first place.

■ And if it just seems right to include a personal story in the body of your essay, do so—even though it may not have been part of your original planning. Wandering off the beaten path is not necessarily bad. It often is a sign that you are making your writing part of your own thinking, which is good.

■ Ask yourself some offbeat questions about your subject and formulate some creative answers. (See 038 for help.)

Organizing with an Outline

An **outline** is an organized list of what you plan to write about. It is a *sketch* of what your essay will look like. It is also a *guide* which will keep you on the right path when you are writing your first draft. In the early stages, your outline should be a changing, **working outline**; in its final form, your outline should be a "table of contents" of what you have "said" in your essay.

The details in an outline should be listed from *general to specific*, as they are in the following list: transportation, motor vehicle, car, Ford, Mustang (*Mustang* is a specific kind of transportation, a specific motor vehicle, a specific car, a specific Ford).

If, for instance, you were assigned to write a paper about "Trees" (*subject*), you might choose to write about "Trees used in landscaping" (*topic*). In the planning of your paper, you might decide to divide your topic into "Trees used for landscaping *in cold climates*" and "Trees used for landscaping *in warm climates*" (*subtopics*). You might then further divide your subtopics into the different kinds of trees suitable in each climate (*supporting details*). To complete your outline, you could list examples of each kind of tree (*specific examples*). It is important to remember that each additional division in an outline must contain information which is more specific than the division before it. (See the sample outline below.)

Outlining Details—General to Specific

Subject: Trees

Topic   Many trees can be used for landscaping.

I.   **Subtopic**   I.   Some trees are best suited for cold climates.

    A. **Supporting detail**   A.   Evergreens are hardy and provide year-round color.

        1. Specific example   1. Norway pine . . .
        2. Specific example   2. Scotch pine . . .

    B. **Supporting detail**   B.   Maples hold up well and provide brilliant seasonal color.

        1. Specific example   1. Red maple . . .
        2. Specific example   2. Silver maple . . .

II. **Subtopic**   II. Some trees are better suited for warm climates.

061   A **topic outline** is a listing of the *topics* or ideas to be covered in your writing; it contains no specific details. Topics (ideas) are usually stated in words and phrases rather than complete sentences. This makes the topic outline useful for short essays, especially those for which you have very little time (as on an essay test). Place your *thesis statement* or controlling idea at the top of your paper as a constant reminder of the specific topic. Use the form shown below for starting the lines of your outline. Do not outline your opening or closing unless your teacher tells you to do so.

Thesis statement: Africa will need all the help it can get to solve its hunger problem, yet it also can help itself.

OUTLINE FORMAT	I.
	  A.
	  B.
	    1.
	    2.
	      a.
	      b.
	        (1)
	        (2)
	          (a)
	          (b)
	II.
		TOPIC OUTLINE

		Opening

		I. Natural resources in Africa
		    A. Great area of unused resources
		    B. Capable of feeding Africa
		    C. Planning will take time

		II. India
		    A. A similar hunger problem
		    B. Planned for self-sufficiency
		    C. Solved a serious problem

Note: No new subdivision should be started unless there are at least two points to be listed in that new division. This means that each *1* must have a *2*; each *a* must be followed by a *b*.		III. "Harare Declaration"
		    A. A promise of self-sufficiency
		    B. United African countries
		    C. Already working in Somalia
		Closing

062   The **sentence outline** contains not only the major points to be covered in a paper, but it also lists many of the important supporting details as well. It is used for longer, more formal writing assignments; each point must be written in a complete sentence.

Opening
  I.   Africa is a land of many valuable resources.
    A. It contains great areas of unused land, water, and minerals.
    B. There are enough resources to feed all of Africa.
    C. Developing these resources will take time because many African countries are not very strong.
  II.   India should give African countries hope.
    A. They experienced a similar hunger problem.
    B. The government planned for self-sufficiency and began producing enough food for its people.
    C. India is in much better shape than it was 25 years ago.
  III. A group of agricultural officials produced the "Harare Declaration."
    A. This declaration promises self-sufficiency in Africa.
    B. This declaration also unified many African countries.
    C. Somalia is helping starving refugees from Ethiopia.
Closing

Sample Student Essay

Opening Paragraph

Thesis Statement

Transition

It is hard to ignore the hunger problem occurring in parts of Africa. For the past two or three years, television has shown us relief camps packed with homeless and hungry Africans. Headlines in our newspapers warn us of what could happen in the drought-stricken areas of Africa: "Millions in Africa Face Starvation" or "Starving Countries Must Be Helped." **The problem is so serious that Africa is going to need all the help it can get to save its hungry people. Yet Africa can also help itself.**

Africa is a land of many valuable and unused resources—farmable land, water, and minerals. Because of these resources, this continent has the ability to feed all of its people. According to one study, if the farmlands were used properly, not only could all of Africa be fed, all of western Europe could be fed as well. Unfortunately, many of the countries in Africa are new and having problems forming strong, healthy governments. As a result, **planning how to use the natural resources in the best possible way will take time.**

Transition

However, none of the countries in Africa should lose hope. Twenty-five years ago, India, a large country in Asia, was experiencing a hunger crisis. Many people predicted that this country would be in worse shape than Africa is in today. Yet India now produces enough food for its entire country because its government spent so much time on farm and economic planning. India still has problems—many poorly nourished people and a high infant death rate—but overall **India is in much better shape** than it was 25 years ago.

Transition

Encouraged by the progress made in India, 30 African officials produced an official document in 1984 called the "Harare Declaration." This document states that the responsibility to feed the hungry people rests on the African governments and the African people themselves. Its long-range goal is to make Africa a self-sufficient continent—a continent that produces all of its own food. Already in Somalia, a country in eastern Africa, the government has accepted thousands of hungry refugees from Ethiopia. The government is presently thinking of ways to give the refugees land in Somalia so that they can produce their own food.

Transition

In order to meet the goals of the "Harare Declaration," Africa will need the help of the United States and other countries. They especially need the emergency supplies for those people suffering the most from hunger. Organizations from many countries have been sending tons of food and medical supplies and have also been helping with the long-term needs of Africa. They are training Africans in new farming techniques and teaching mothers how to help their undernourished and sick children. If the relief continues until the most serious problems are solved, the African people can work at becoming self-sufficient. They have the resources to do it.

The closing leaves readers with an understanding of the essay's importance.

064 Writing the Comparison and Contrast Essay

The guidelines which follow will help you develop a comparison and contrast (C/C) essay.

- Start by doing some initial thinking and talking about the assignment. Select two suitable subjects to compare and contrast.
- Then write down all of the details which come to mind when you think of one of the subjects. (See "Venn Diagram" below for help.)
- Write down all of the details which come to mind when you think of the other subject.
- Review your work and share it with classmates. The give and take of ideas will help you see your subject in new ways.
- Write a first draft which focuses on all of the discoveries you have made up to this point. You should naturally pick up on the similarities and differences of the two subjects.
- Review your writing and share it with classmates.
- Make changes as necessary.
- Continue to work on your writing until it says what you want it to say.

What you discover as you read, write, and talk about your subjects is the focus of this kind of essay. The specific form your writing will take depends on you, the result of your first writing, and your teacher's guidelines.

065 The Venn Diagram

The Venn Diagram will help you develop ideas for comparison and contrast (C/C) essays. Here's how it works: Draw two overlapping circles as shown below. In the area marked **1**, list characteristics unique to one of the subjects. In the one marked number **2**, list characteristics unique to the second subject. In the area marked number **3**, list those characteristics the two subjects have in common.

To develop a C/C essay from your diagram, consider the following approach: Write about subject number one in paragraph number one. (Include an opening sentence or two which introduce the essay.) Write about subject number two in the next paragraph. Then write about the similarities between the two in a third paragraph.

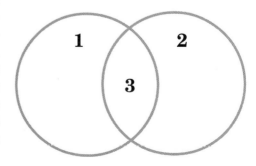

Additional Two-Part Essays

Many of the most challenging types of essays consist of two parts, much like the comparison/contrast essay. There's the *before* and *after* essay, the *cause* and *effect* essay, the *problem* and *solution* essay, and the opposing *points of view* essay. The guidelines which follow will help you develop each of these essay types.

■ **Begin** with a starter sentence about the subject of your essay once you have done some thinking, talking, and writing about it. Write a number of versions until you hit upon one you like. (We've made this easy for you by providing starter sentences for you to complete. See below.)

■ **Write freely** (shoot for 5 to 10 minutes) about the first part of your starter sentence.

■ **Review** your writing. (Share it with classmates.)

■ **Write freely** about the second part of your starter sentence.

■ **Review** your writing. (Share it with classmates.)

■ **Develop** an opening paragraph. Your opening paragraph should include your starter sentence plus a few additional sentences which add introductory detail.

■ **Make** any changes that are needed in the main part of your writing after you're opening paragraph is set.

■ **Continue** to work on your writing until it says what you want it to.

Starter Sentence

How to get started on an essay is often a problem, especially when you're working on a challenging two-part essay. That's why we've provided you with these starter sentences. Complete whichever one reflects your writing assignment; then use the guidelines above to continue your work.

Note: Change these sentences to meet the needs of your writing.

For *before and after* essays:
■ Once . . . but now . . .

For *cause and effect* essays:
■ Because of . . . we now . . .
■ When . . . happened , I (we, they) . . .

For *problem and solution* essays:
■ . . . has resulted in . . . .
■ . . . has caused us to . . . .

For writing about opposing *points of view*:
■ I (anyone) think . . . but he thinks or says . . . .
■ You can . . . but you can also . . .

Writing About a Person

Always try to write about someone you know well—or would like to know well. When you are familiar with your subject, you will be able to share a lot of good details with your readers. Use the suggested searching and shaping techniques (037) to gather as much information as you need. The following suggestions will also help. *Note:* Get permission from the person before you start writing. And don't say anything that will hurt your subject's feelings.

- **Observe** Begin gathering details by closely watching the person you are writing about. Take special note of any details which make this person different from others.

- **Investigate** What are your subject's goals, dreams, attitudes, concerns, pet peeves, hobbies, favorite things . . . ? Talk to your subject (in person, by phone, or by letter). Write down your questions ahead of time, but listen closely to the answers you get and ask new questions that occur to you. If possible, use a tape recorder so you can quote your subject accurately. (Read about your subject if he or she is well known and cannot talk to you personally.)

- **Define** Consider what type of person you are describing (child . . . adult; student . . . lawyer; amateur . . . stage performer; friend . . . stranger) and how he or she is like or not like other people of the same type.

- **Describe** List the important physical characteristics, mannerisms, and personality traits, especially those which help to make your subject different from other people. Notice the way your subject smiles, talks, sits, moves, dresses, and wears his or her hair.

- **Recall** Try to remember things your subject has said or done in the past. It would be interesting to include in your writing at least one story that reveals the kind of person your subject really is.

- **Compare** Compare your subject to other people. Who is he or she most like? a little bit like? not at all like? What object, thing, place, word, sport, plant . . . could he or she be compared to?

- **Analyze** Ask others about your subject. Often, they will be able to tell you things you would otherwise never have known. What are your subject's strengths and weaknesses?

- **Evaluate** Determine why this person is important to you and to others.

 Helpful HINT

After you have collected enough details, decide what overall impression your subject has made on you and use it as your starting point for your writing.

Writing About a Place

Whenever possible, write about a place you know well—perhaps a favorite place, or a least favorite place—one which left a big impression on you. Use the prewriting techniques (037) to help you gather the details that will capture your readers. The suggestions below are good starting points, too.

- **Observe**   Visit the place you are going to describe. (Use books, pictures, and audiovisual aids if you can't go there yourself.) Look closely at your subject and jot down what you see—especially those details that make this place different from others. (Remember to notice how other people are reacting to the place as well. Doing this well often spark new ideas and angles for your writing.)

- **Investigate**   Talk to people who know about the place (ticket agent in a train or bus station, hot-dog vendor at a ballpark, caretaker in a zoo, etc.). Ask questions about the past, present, and future of the place. You may even try talking to the place itself. Why not? Simply wonder to yourself, "If this place could talk, what would it tell me? What has it seen and heard? How does it think and feel?"

- **Define**   Consider what type of place you are describing (well-known landmark, landform, house or a room in it, amusement park, etc.) and how this place is like or not like other places of the same type.

- **Describe**   Tell about the age, size, shape, color, and other important physical features of your subject. What is the most outstanding feature of this place? And remember . . . looks aren't everything. Explain how your subject feels, smells, tastes, and sounds, as well as how it looks.

- **Recall**   Try to remember stories from the past about this place. Your readers will enjoy at least one anecdote.

- **Compare**   Compare your subject to other places. What other place is it most like? a little bit like? not at all like?

- **Analyze**   Ask others about your subject. What have they noticed about the place? How has it affected them? Does it remind them of other places? In what way? What are its strengths and weaknesses?

- **Evaluate**   Why is this place important to you and to others? Would you miss this place a little . . . a lot . . . somewhat if it were no longer there?

070 Writing About an Object

Pick an object you are familiar with or one in which you have a real interest. Begin gathering details—free writing, clustering, or listing may help. Also use the following suggestions.

- **Observe**   Look closely at this object to find out how it works. Notice how other people use this object and how they react to it. Do they take it for granted, for instance, or do they use the object with great care?
- **Investigate**   Read about this object. How was it discovered, built, first used? Ask others about their experiences with (or feelings about) this object.
- **Define**   What class or category does this object fall into? (See "Writing a Definition" below.) How is your subject different from or similar to other objects in the same category?
- **Describe**   Record the color, size, shape, and texture of this object. Describe the important parts and how they fit together. When writing, put your object in the middle of people and actions that will show rather than tell your readers the importance of your subject. A new ten-speed is interesting; but a new ten-speed, plus the beaming owner, plus a few gawking friends will say even more.
- **Recall**   Try to remember an interesting story about this object.
- **Compare**   What other objects is your subject most like? least like? Make a few "surprising" comparisons—what type of person does the object remind you of? what flavor of ice cream? what day of the week?
- **Analyze**   Consider this object's strengths and weaknesses. What changes would you make in it if you could?
- **Evaluate**   Why is this object important? Would you or anyone else miss this object if it suddenly disappeared?

071 Writing a Definition

Place the term you are defining into the *class* or category of similar objects. Then add the special *characteristics* which make this object different from the rest of the objects in that class.

Term - *A computer . . .*
Class - *is an electronic machine . . .*
Characteristic - *which stores and arranges information.*

Caution: Do not use the term or a form of it in your definition. *Example:* "A computer is a machine that *computes*."

Writing About an Event

Writing about an event should be more than giving out a few facts, although facts are important. It is, at its best, sharing how you feel about a certain happening... and about the people, places, and objects that make the event memorable. Be sure to write about something you have actually seen with your own eyes or participated in. (Watching the event on TV or interviewing someone who was part of the event can also work.) These suggestions will help.

■ **Observe**   Notice, if you are able, what is going on before an event. These details can be very interesting in your introduction, and will help set the mood for your readers. Watch the event closely, especially for anything which stands out in some way. (Low points can be just as important as high points—both deserve attention.) Use all of your senses. What does this event look like, smell like, feel like, taste like, and sound like?

■ **Investigate**   Read about the history of this kind of event. Talk to an "expert" on the subject. Ask other people about this particular event—get their impressions, disappointments, surprises, etc. Keep an ear open for their remarks while the event is going on.

■ **Describe**   List the *who, what, when, where, why,* and *how* of this happening— or at least as many of these six questions as you feel your reader needs to know. Write freely, as though you were telling your best friend about this event. Show your reader what makes this event special by including the background, people, actions, and overheard comments.

■ **Define**   What kind or type of event is this?

■ **Compare**   How is this event similar to or different from other events of this type that you have seen?

■ **Evaluate**   Why is this event important to you and to others? Do you or do you not want this event to happen again?

■ **Recommend**   What would you have changed to make this event more noteworthy?

■ **Decide**   After you have gathered all of your thoughts and details, decide how you feel about this event. What overall impression would you like to share with your readers?

Helpful HINT

Once you have gathered enough details, begin writing. Think of an unusual way to approach your subject. (How about a news report or fairy tale or ballad or . . . ?) If it doesn't work you can always go back to a more traditional form.

Writing an Explanation

Explanations are common in schools. Teachers often explain in several different ways: defining, reviewing, demonstrating, clarifying, etc. When you explain something in writing, you too are teaching—trying to make something easier to understand. Keep this in mind when you begin writing an explanation. The suggestions below should help.

- **Observe** Whenever possible, observe the person, place, thing, idea, event, or process you are going to explain in your writing. Notice the steps, parts, or details which will help you explain your subject to your reader.

- **Investigate** Talk to "experts" and others who have an understanding of your subject. Listen to their explanations and ask questions about anything you don't understand. Ask the *what, when, where, why, how* and *to what extent* questions.

- **Define** Write a simple, concise definition of your subject. (See model below.) Check reliable books on the topic and expand your definition to include the specific characteristics which make this person, place, thing, or idea different from others like it. (See 071.)

- **Describe** List each step, part, cause, etc. needed to understand your subject. List examples which clarify each point in your explanation. Describe the size, shape, color, sound, and smell to help your reader picture what it is you are trying to explain.

- **Compare** Compare your subject to others which are simpler or more familiar to your reader. Contrast: tell what your subject is "not" like.

- **Analyze** Break down your subject into its parts or steps. How do the parts work together to form the whole? What is the history or future or present condition of your subject?

- **Evaluate** Why is your subject important or worth knowing about? How might it help your reader?

Helpful
HINT

Explanations must be clear. Test what you have written by reading it out loud—and by reading it to someone else if at all possible. Revise as needed. Maybe you need more examples, illustrations, or comparisons. Maybe you have to explain each point (step) more carefully or more fully.

Writing to Persuade

When you write to persuade, you should choose a topic or issue which truly interests you, one which you have a definite opinion about. You should also *want* to convince your readers to feel the way you do. Persuading someone to agree with you requires careful thinking and planning. You must make the issue clear to your readers and include the facts and reasons that will give strong support to your opinion.

- **Reflect**   Begin by free writing, clustering, or listing your personal feelings about the issue and the reasons you feel that way.

- **Investigate**   Ask other people how they feel about this issue. Listen closely, especially to those who have a different opinion. Ask them why they feel the way they do; test your opinion and reasons on them. (Understanding how other people feel before you begin to write will help you form stronger arguments.)

- **Read**   Next, gather any facts and figures which you now realize must be included in your writing to be convincing. Use the *Readers' Guide to Periodical Literature* in your library to help you find current magazine articles on the issue. Take careful notes on what you read and use these notes to build a strong case.

- **Think**   Sound confident and sincere in your writing. Mention the reasonable arguments on the other side of the issue; then point out clearly why each argument is weak.

- **Show**   Use examples instead of statistics to illustrate your main points. ("Every day we bury in our dump sites enough garbage to completely cover the state of Rhode Island.") If you do use numbers, round them off. ("Each day we bury in our dump sites nearly 50 million tons of garbage.")

- **Organize**   Persuasive writing should be well organized:

  ❑ Write out a clear statement of your opinion in positive terms: ("Hall monitors should treat all students fairly," rather than "Hall monitors should not show . . . .")

  ❑ Place your topic (proposition) at the top of your paper. List your reasons underneath; under each reason, list the facts, figures, examples, or quotations which help support it.

  ❑ Prove to your readers that this really matters—they have something to gain by taking the same stand as you.

  ❑ Consider ending your writing with one of your strongest examples or reasons. Your readers may be waiting until the very end to decide.

Building Paragraphs

For many student writers, the key to writing well is being able to select a good topic and then sticking to it until they've supported it with plenty of details. This is especially true of writing that is done for assignments in school. One thing that can help you gain control of your writing is learning to write a good paragraph. The paragraph is a unit of writing which is easy to control and therefore works well for many writing assignments. The section which follows covers the paragraph and all that you need to know about writing and using it effectively.

075 What Is a Paragraph?

When you share information with your friends, you naturally include a beginning, a middle, and an end; and you do so without thinking much about it. You *begin* by identifying what it is you're going to talk about and getting your friends interested in it (*Guess what? . . .*). You continue in the *middle* part by filling in all of the important details (*And then . . .*). And you *end* by carefully putting the finishing touches on your story (*Finally, I . . .*).

It's a little different when you share something in writing. Much more thinking goes into how you will begin, how you will fill in the important details, and how you will end. Other sections in your handbook help you develop the three basic parts of stories and essays. The guidelines which follow here will help you develop the basic parts of the paragraph: the **topic sentence** at the beginning, the **body** or the middle of the paragraph, and the **closing** or **clincher sentence** at the end.

> "Every word must advance the focus of a paragraph."

One Topic, One Picture

A paragraph focuses on one specific topic, which can be "developed" in the form of a story, a description, an explanation, or an opinion. The form will depend upon your topic and the kinds of details you are able to gather and use in your paragraph. Whatever form it takes, your paragraph must contain enough information—enough supporting details—to give the reader a complete and interesting picture of the topic. Each sentence in the paragraph should add something to the overall picture. Then you'll have a good paragraph, one worth sharing with others.

The Basic Parts of a Paragraph

Beginning

The **topic sentence** tells the reader what the paragraph is going to be about. It also helps you keep your writing under control. (This is why a topic sentence is sometimes called the "controlling idea" of a paragraph.) Below you will find a sample topic sentence and a simple formula for writing good topic sentences:

> **Topic sentence**: Mr. Brown must have been a drill sergeant before he became our gym teacher.
>
> **Formula**: A specific subject (*Mr. Brown, our gym teacher*) + a specific feeling or attitude (*must have been a drill sergeant before*) = a good topic sentence.

Note: A sentence like "Mr. Brown is a teacher" would not make a good topic sentence because it does not follow the formula. This sentence contains a subject (Mr. Brown), but it does not express a specific feeling or attitude, so it does not add up to a good topic sentence.

Middle

The **body** is the main part of the paragraph. This is where you tell the reader about your topic by including specific details. All of the sentences in the body must relate to the specific topic of the paragraph and help it come alive for the reader. That is, all of the sentences in the body should contain details that make the topic more interesting or help explain it more clearly. These sentences should be organized in the best possible order. (See the sample paragraph on the next page.)

End

The **closing** or **clincher sentence** comes after all the details have been included in the body of the paragraph. The closing sentence reminds the reader what the topic of the paragraph is really all about, what it means. For example, let's say the topic sentence of a paragraph is "Mr. Brown must have been a drill sergeant before he became our gym teacher." A closing sentence for this paragraph could be something like the following:

> **Closing sentence:** I'm surprised that Mr. Brown doesn't make us march into the shower room after each class.

Note: This closing sentence reminds the reader that the specific subject of the paragraph is Mr. Brown, the gym teacher, and that he is like a drill sergeant (the specific feeling, attitude, or point of the paragraph).

Types of Paragraphs

Depending upon your topic and purpose for writing, you have several types of paragraphs to choose from: descriptive, narrative, expository, and persuasive.

A **descriptive** paragraph gives a single, clear picture of a person, place, thing, or idea. (See 068-070.)

Mr. Brown must have been a drill sergeant before he became our gym teacher. At the start of each class, we have to stand at attention in straight lines while he takes attendance. Then we have to suffer through his warm-up exercises. We begin by running in place until Mr. Brown can see that we are all "loosened up." Once we are good and loose, he instructs us to hit the floor for a "few" sit-ups. With no one to hold our ankles, the sit-ups are nearly impossible to do, especially when Mr. Brown barks out the pace we have to follow. But, Mr. Brown always saves the best till last—push-ups, and not just any old push-ups. We do them just as if we were in the army, and that means we have to keep our heads up, backs straight, and push up and down 25 times. I'm surprised that Mr. Brown doesn't make us march into the shower room after each class.

Topic Sentence: Mr. Brown must have been a drill sergeant before he became our gym teacher.

   I. At the start of each class, we have to stand at attention in straight lines while he takes attendance.
  II. Then we have to suffer through his warm-up exercises.
     A. We run in place until we are all "loosened up."
     B. Then we hit the floor for a "few" sit-ups.
        1. No one holds our ankles.
        2. Mr. Brown barks out the pace.
     C. His favorite is push-ups.
        1. We do them just as if we were in the army.
        2. That means we have to keep our heads up, backs straight, and push up and down 25 times.

Closing Sentence: I'm surprised that Mr. Brown doesn't make us march into the shower room after each class.

A **narrative** paragraph gives the details of an event or experience in story form or in the order they happened. (See 072.)   **078**

Mr. Brown does not allow any fooling around in his gym class. Unfortunately, two guys learned this the hard way. At the end of the first day of flag football, Mr. Brown blew his whistle. Most of us knew enough to stop and fall in line. He had made it very clear to us on the first day of class that when he blew his whistle, we had to stop our activity. Immediately! Kerry Schmidt and Jeremy Johnson ignored the whistle and continued throwing a football. With fire in his eyes, Mr. Brown quickly sent us in and went after them. We all watched from the locker room doorway while Mr. Brown made them duck-walk on the football field. By the time they reached the 50-yard line, they were really struggling. He sent them in after another 20 yards when their duck-walk had turned into more of a crawl. We couldn't help giving a few duck calls when Kerry and Jeremy limped into the locker room, but we didn't "quack" very loudly. We didn't want Mr. Brown to make us walk like a duck or any other type of animal for that matter.

An **expository** paragraph gives facts or directions, explains ideas, or defines terms. It is often used for writing assignments. (See 073.)   **079**

Complete one pull-up in Mr. Brown's gym class and you have really accomplished something. He makes us start by hanging from the bar with our arms straight. Our palms have to face forward on the bar. As we raise ourselves toward the bar, our bodies have to remain straight. Mr. Brown doesn't allow any kicking, wriggling, or squirming. He stands next to the bar and taps us on the stomach with a yardstick if we start to bend or wiggle. Our chins have to rest on the bar, if we are lucky enough to make it that far. We then have to lower ourselves until we are again hanging with our arms straight. This is one pull-up, unless Mr. Brown decides that something was done the wrong way.

A **persuasive** paragraph expresses an opinion and tries to convince the reader that this opinion is correct. (See 074.)   **080**

Mr. Brown might not be a popular teacher, but he has three qualities that make him a good teacher. First, he is well organized for every class period. He always starts us off with exercises. Then we either learn or practice some skill or divide up into teams and play some sport. We always know ahead of time what we will be doing because Mr. Brown posts the day's activities on a blackboard in the locker room. Second, he is always concerned that we do our best, no matter what the activity. He expects us to work as hard in a game of dodgeball as we do during physical fitness tests. Mr. Brown's third and most important quality is that he treats everyone fairly. It doesn't matter if you're a jock or not. You know exactly where you stand with him. If you don't work up to your ability, he lets you know about it. If you work hard, he's satisfied. Some guys think Mr. Brown expects too much, but they all work hard for him.

081 Writing the Paragraph

Selecting: *Choosing a Subject*

Selecting a specific subject for a paragraph should not be difficult. Your teacher will assign you the general subject for most of your paragraphs. You will then have to pick a specific topic from the general subject. Pick a topic that interests you and will interest your reader. *Remember:* It is important to have an interesting or exciting "story to tell." If you have trouble finding a specific topic, write freely or talk to friends and family members for ideas. (See 033 and 035 for help.)

Collecting: *Planning and Gathering*

The planning stage is very important in writing a paragraph. First, you must write a sentence which states clearly what your paragraph is going to be about. This topic sentence must identify the specific subject and state a feeling or attitude about the subject. Below is a sample.

> Uncle John is a real pest with his camera.
> A specific topic *(Uncle John)* + a specific feeling
> *(is a real pest with his camera)* = a good topic sentence.

After you have written a topic sentence, collect ideas and details to write about the topic. Again, you might want to write freely, talk to friends or family members, or do some reading on the topic to find details. Collect as many specific details as you can. Next, you should choose the best possible method of organization for your paragraph. (See 084.) Then, put the details into an outline, if you are required to do so.

Connecting: *Writing the First Draft*

As you write the first draft of your paragraph, start with the topic sentence, which is indented. Follow your topic sentence with the details that you have organized in your outline. Don't be afraid to add or take out details as you go along. End your paragraph with a closing sentence. This sentence will remind the reader of the topic and feeling stated in the topic sentence.

Improving the Writing

If you have planned your paragraph well, you won't need to do a lot of revising. As you do revise, make sure you have enough clear and creative details in your paragraph to make it understandable and entertaining. *Special note:* Level 3 sentences contain the specific details and examples needed for good paragraphs. (See "Levels of Sentence Detail," 085.)

Correcting: *Getting It Right*

Check the revised version of your paragraph for missing or misplaced words and other careless errors before turning it in.

The Details in a Paragraph   082

When you write a paragraph, the details should come naturally. They will usually come from your **personal experience**. When personal details aren't used, you will gather details from **other sources** you've read or heard about. Because details are so important in your writing, it might be helpful to know about the kinds of details you can use and how you can go about gathering them.

Personal Details

Personal details are those which you, the writer, gather by using your senses (*sensory details*), your memory (*memory details*), or your imagination (*reflective details*).

■ The first type of personal detail comes from the writer's own senses (*smell, touch, taste, hearing,* and *sight*) and is known as a **sensory detail**. These details are gathered through firsthand experience. By closely observing what is going on around you—in school, at home, on the bus—you will be able to gather plenty of sensory details about the person, place, or thing you are writing about. Sensory details are especially important when writing descriptive paragraphs.

> Mr. Brown not only looks like a drill sergeant, he talks like one.

■ The second type of detail comes from the writer's memory of past experiences and observations and is known as a **memory detail**. This might be a detail(s) you remember from yesterday or five years ago.

> When we shot free throws during basketball, Mr. Brown gave us five seconds before he gave the ball to the other team.

■ The third type of detail comes as a writer thinks creatively about the topic of the paragraph and tries to imagine what could have been or might yet be (*wonders, wishes, hopes*). This type of detail is known as a **reflective detail** and is often used in narrative and descriptive writing.

> I wonder how many pull-ups Mr. Brown can do.

Helpful
HINT
You can build a storehouse of personal details by writing in a personal journal and by developing a personal inventory of experience. (See 130.)

083 Details from Other Sources

When you are asked to write an expository or persuasive paragraph, start by gathering personal details of what you already know about the topic. Then, depending upon your topic, you may have to add details—facts, figures, reasons, examples—from other sources. You can find these "secondhand" details in a number of ways:

- **First**, you can simply ask another person—a parent, neighbor, teacher—anyone who has interesting information.
- **Second**, you can ask an "expert" or someone who has had a firsthand experience with your topic. (See "Interviewing," 405.)
- **Third**, you can write or call for information. (See "The Business Letter," 203.)
- **Finally**, you can gather details in your library—from magazines, newspapers, books, videotapes, filmstrips, or computer services.

084 Methods of Arranging Details

Wherever you get your information, you must make sure the details are accurate, up-to-date, and important to your topic. Don't use details just because they sound impressive or took a long time to get. Select carefully. Also, arrange your details in the most logical or effective order. The guidelines below should help you decide what the best method of arrangement is for your topic. (Also see 037 for suggestions on how to "think through" and further develop your details.)

❖ **Chronological** (time) **order**: You can arrange your details in the order in which they happened (*first, second, then, next, later, etc.*).

❖ **Order of location**: You can arrange your details in the order in which they are located (*above, below, alongside, beneath, etc.*).

❖ **Order of importance**: You can arrange your details from the most important to the least—or from the least important to the most.

❖ **Cause and effect**: You can begin with a general statement giving the *cause* of a problem and then add a number of specific *effects*.

❖ **Comparison**: You can explain a subject by showing how it is *similar* to another better-known subject.

❖ **Contrast**: You can use details which show how your subject is *different* from another better-known subject.

❖ **Illustration** (*general to specific*): You can arrange your details so that the general idea is stated first in the paragraph (*topic sentence*). Specific reasons, examples, facts, and other details are then added which *illustrate* or support the general statement.

Levels of Sentence Detail

What do we mean by "levels of sentence detail"? Well, first of all, you need to know that each sentence you write contains a certain "level" or depth of detail. A well-written paragraph, for instance, is made up of at least three levels of detail.

Sentences which contain general details are called *Level 1* or **controlling sentences**. These sentences (which include topic and closing sentences) name and control the topic of the paragraph. Sentences which contain details which make the topic clearer to the reader are called *Level 2* or **clarifying sentences**. *Level 3* sentences contain specific details and examples which complete the ideas started in Level 2 sentences. These sentences are called **completing sentences**.

Helpful HINT

Note below that all three levels of sentence detail are used in the paragraph about Mr. Brown. Each new level adds detail that is more specific, and each new level increases the reader's understanding. (The illustrations should help you understand what is meant by "levels" of sentence detail.)

Level One   Level Two   Level Three

- **Level 1**—*Controlling sentences* name and control the topic.

  Mr. Brown must have been a drill sergeant before he became our gym teacher.

- **Level 2**—*Clarifying sentences* help make the topic clearer.

  At the start of each class, we have to stand at attention in straight lines while he takes attendance. Then we have to suffer through his warm-up exercises.

- **Level 3**—*Completing sentences* add specific details.

  Mr. Brown always saves the best till last—push-ups, and not just any old push-ups. We do them just as if we were in the army, and that means we have to keep our heads up, backs straight, and push up and down 25 times.

Note: A good paragraph will usually have at least two or three Level 2 sentences and two or three Level 3 sentences.

086 The Sentences in a Paragraph

Write Smooth and Natural Sentences

Your sentences should sound natural and move smoothly from one point to the next. Short, simple sentences (or ideas) are often combined with special "linking words" to produce this smoothness. (See 089 and 102.) The simple sentences which follow have been combined into one longer sentence that reads more smoothly. (The linking words are underlined.)

> **Original sentences:** We shot free throws during basketball. Mr. Brown gave us five seconds. Then he gave the ball to the other team.
>
> **Combined:** <u>When</u> we shot free throws during basketball, Mr. Brown gave us five seconds <u>before</u> he gave the ball to the other team.

Use a Variety of Sentences

A good paragraph often contains a variety of sentence lengths and types. Having too many of the same type of sentence can make your paragraph sound immature. (See "Sentence Types," 711, for explanations and examples of the four types of sentences.) Notice the different types of sentences used in the following example:

> At the start of each class, we have to stand at attention in straight lines while he takes attendance. *(complex)* Then we have to suffer through his warm-up exercises. *(simple)* His favorite is push-ups. *(simple)* We do them just as if we were in the army, and that means we have to keep our heads up, backs straight, and push up and down 25 times. *(compound-complex)* We also run in place until Mr. Brown can see that we are all "warmed up." *(complex)*

Use a Variety of Sentence Beginnings

Sentences begin in different ways in a well-written paragraph. Sentences that all begin with the subject become monotonous and boring. Modifiers (individual words), phrases, and clauses can be used instead:

- We stand at attention in straight lines. *(sentence which begins with the subject)*
- Motionless, we stand at attention in straight lines. *(sentence which begins with a modifying word)*
- At the start of each class, we stand at attention in straight lines. *(sentence which begins with a phrase)*
- When each class starts, we stand at attention in straight lines. *(sentence which begins with a clause)*

Reviewing Paragraphs in Essays, Reports, and Longer Pieces of Writing

Look at each paragraph in your longer pieces in two ways: first, as an individual unit developing one idea and, second, as one part of the whole piece. (Use the paragraph symbol [¶] to indicate where each paragraph begins as you review your writing. This will remind you to indent each new paragraph in your final copy.)

■ Each paragraph should say enough to stand on its own. One common way to check the effectiveness of a paragraph is to form in your mind a title for it, as if it were the only thing you had written. Another common way to check the effectiveness of a paragraph is to form a simple question that the paragraph answers clearly. (If one of your paragraphs doesn't pass either of these tests, consider revising it or leaving it out.)

■ Change, rearrange, or delete any sentences which take away from the effectiveness of each paragraph. All of the sentences in a paragraph should be clear, meaningful, and smooth reading.

■ Think of an inverted pyramid when you review the opening paragraph. That is, an opening paragraph usually starts with *general* statements which get the reader's attention, and then states the *specific* subject or thesis in the last sentence or two.

Note: If you feel your opening paragraph is effectively structured in another way, leave it alone.

■ The concluding paragraph often begins with a general review of all of the important ideas discussed in the body. This paragraph ends with a statement(s) which reminds the reader of the importance of the paper.

■ All of the paragraphs in the body of your paper should help develop your thesis (main idea) in some way. A paragraph might *explain, define, compare,* or *classify* information to support your thesis statement. Another paragraph might relate a *personal experience* or recent incident. All these paragraphs should be organized so that they work together in the most effective way. Often the paragraph with the most important information comes right before the concluding paragraph.

■ Transitions should be used to connect one paragraph to the next. They unify the paragraphs, and they make your writing easier for the reader to follow and understand. (See 089 for a list of transitions.)

088 Summary: Writing the Paragraph

Collecting: *Selecting a Subject*

■ Select a specific topic that interests you and will interest your reader.

■ Make sure your topic is not too complicated and can be covered in one paragraph.

Preparing to Write

■ Write a specific topic sentence.

■ Gather details.

■ Select a method of organization.

■ Write an outline or plan, if required to do so.

Connecting: *Writing the First Draft*

■ Start with the topic sentence.

■ Follow with sentences that add interesting details.

■ Use your outline as a general guide.

■ Write a closing sentence.

Improving the Writing

■ Make sure the topic is made clear with plenty of good details.

■ Take out details that don't really add anything to the topic.

■ Make sure all your sentences are complete thoughts and that your sentences begin in different ways.

■ Make sure your sentences read smoothly; combine as necessary.

Correcting:

■ Check the word choice. Use strong, active words.

■ Check the mechanics—spelling, punctuation, and capitalization—and usage (*to* or *too*, *their* or *there*, etc.) of your writing. (See "The Yellow Pages.")

■ Write or type a neat final copy. Indent the first line. Proofread before turning in your final draft.

MINI-lesson

What will make readers "stand up" and listen to your writing—paragraphs or otherwise? Readers want *information;* they want to learn something. Readers want to be entertained; they appreciate good details and strong, vivid word pictures. Readers want writing that is original, that clearly moves from one point to the next. And readers want to hear the voice of the writer, the real you.

Transition or Linking Words

Words which can be used to show location:

above	behind	by	into	outside
across	below	down	near	over
against	beneath	in back of	off	throughout
along	beside	in front of	onto	to the right
among	between	inside	on top of	under
around	beyond			

Words which can be used to show time:

about	first	meanwhile	soon	then
after	second	today	later	next
at	third	tomorrow	afterward	as soon as
before	till	next week	immediately	when
during	until	yesterday	finally	

Words which can be used to compare two things:

in the same way	likewise	as
similarly	like	also

Words which can be used to contrast things (show differences):

but	otherwise	on the other hand	although
however	yet	still	even though

Words which can be used to emphasize a point:

again	truly	for this reason
to repeat	in fact	to emphasize

Words which can be used to conclude or summarize:

as a result	finally	in conclusion	to sum up
therefore	lastly	in summary	all in all

Words which can be used to add information:

again	another	for instance	finally
also	and	moreover	as well
additionally	besides	next	along with
in addition	for example		

Words which can be used to clarify:

in other words	for instance	that is

Composing Sentences

A common challenge for writers of all ages is being clear and concise. Sentences sometimes have a way of getting out of control. At times, they run on and on and on; other times, they are incomplete and unclear. Your goal as a writer is to compose sentences which express a complete thought and fit in clearly with the rest of the writing. The following guidelines should help.

Write Complete Sentences

Use only complete sentences in your writing. A complete sentence contains a subject and verb and expresses a complete thought. Sentence fragments, run-on sentences, and comma splices are errors which should be avoided. Also, avoid using rambling sentences.

090 Sentence Fragments

■ A *sentence fragment* may look and sound like a sentence, but it isn't. Instead, it is a group of words which is missing either a subject or a verb, or which doesn't express a complete thought.

◆ **Sentence fragment**: Thinks he's really funny.
   (The subject is missing.)
   Complete sentence: *My little brother* thinks he's really funny.
   (A subject has been added.)

◆ **Sentence fragment**: Not my definition of funny.
   (The subject and verb are missing.)
   Complete sentence: But *it is* not my definition of funny.
   (A subject and a verb have been added.)

◆ **Sentence fragment**: My brother and his bright ideas.
   (The thought is incomplete.)
   Complete sentence: My brother and his bright ideas *are going to drive me crazy*.
   (The sentence is now a complete thought.)

◆ **Sentence fragment**: Which is probably what he's trying to do.
   (The thought should be attached to the previous sentence.)
   Complete sentence: My brother and his bright ideas are going to drive me crazy, which is probably what he's trying to do.

Run-On Sentence

■ A *run-on sentence* occurs when two simple sentences are joined without punctuation or a connecting word.

Run-on sentence: I thought the ride would never end my eyes were crossed and my fingers were going numb.

(Punctuation needed.)

Corrected: I thought the ride would never end. My eyes were crossed and my fingers were going numb.

(Punctuation has been added.)

Comma Splice

■ A *comma splice* is an error made when you connect two simple sentences with a comma instead of a semicolon or end punctuation.

Comma splice: I never really enjoyed science, math is my favorite class.

(A comma is used incorrectly to connect or *splice* two sentences.)

Corrected sentences: I never really enjoyed science. Math is my favorite class.

(A period is used in place of the comma.)

Rambling Sentence

■ A *rambling sentence* can appear in your writing when you connect several simple ideas with the word *and*.

Rambling sentence: I went to the dentist yesterday and when I got there, I had to wait forever to see him and when he finally examined my teeth, he found four cavities and now I have to go back next week to get fillings and I don't want to go.

(Too many *and*'s are used.)

Corrected sentences: I went to the dentist yesterday. When I got there, I had to wait forever to see him. When he finally examined my teeth, he found four cavities. Now I have to go back next week to get fillings, and I don't want to go.

(The unnecessary *and*'s are omitted.)

Write "Agreeable" Sentences

Make sure the subject and verb agree in *number* in your sentences. That is, if you use a singular subject, make sure you use a singular verb. (John likes pizza.) If you use a plural subject, make sure you use a plural verb. (His friends like pizza, too.) Be especially careful that you don't make agreement mistakes in the following types of sentences.

094 Compound Subjects

■ Sentences with compound subjects connected by *and* need a plural verb.

Mike and Marty spend most of their spare time at the pizza parlor.

■ In sentences with compound subjects connected by *or* or *nor,* the verb must agree with the subject which is nearer the verb.

Neither *Mike nor Marty likes* anchovies on his pizza.
(Use a singular verb because the subject nearer the verb—*Marty*—is singular.)

Neither *Sarah nor her sisters like* olives on their pizza.
(Use a plural verb because the subject nearer the verb—*sisters*—is plural.)

095 Unusual Word Order

■ When the subject is separated from the verb by words or phrases, you must check carefully to see that the subject agrees with the verb.

John as well as his two friends works at the pizza parlor.
(*John*, not *friends*, is the subject, so the singular verb *works* is used to agree with the subject.)

■ When the subject comes after the verb in a sentence, you must check carefully to see that the "true" subject agrees with the verb.

There in the distance were the remains of the ghost town.
(The plural subject *remains* agrees with the plural verb *were*.)

Around the corner is my dad's store.
(The singular subject *store* agrees with the singular verb *is*.)

Has your sister read this book?
(The singular subject *sister* agrees with the auxiliary or helping verb *has*.)

Indefinite Pronouns

■ In sentences with a singular indefinite pronoun as the subject, use a singular verb. (Use a singular verb with these indefinite pronouns: *each, either, neither, one, everyone, everybody, everything, someone, somebody, anybody, anything, nobody,* and *another.*)

> ***Everyone* in John's family *likes* pizza.**

■ Some indefinite pronouns (*all, any, half, most, none, some*) can be either singular or plural.

> ***Some* of the pizzas *were* missing.**
>
> > (Use a plural verb when the noun in the prepositional phrase which follows the indefinite pronoun is plural. In the example sentence, the noun *pizzas* is plural.)
>
> ***Some* of the pizza *was* missing.**
>
> > (Use a singular verb if the noun in the prepositional phrase is singular. In the example sentence, the noun *pizza* is singular.)

There is additional information on indefinite pronouns, compound subjects, collective nouns, and agreement of subjects and verbs in "The Yellow Pages."

Collective Nouns

■ When a collective noun is the subject of a sentence, it can be either singular or plural. (A collective noun names a group or unit: *faculty, committee, team, congress, species, crowd, army, pair.*)

> **The crew of the sailboat is the best in the world.**
>
> > (The collective noun *crew* is singular because it refers to the crew as one group. As a result, the verb *is* must also be singular.)
>
> **The faculty are required to turn in their room keys before leaving for the summer.**
>
> > (The collective noun *faculty* is plural because it refers to the faculty as individuals within a group. As a result, the auxiliary verb *are* must also be plural.)

Note: Mumps, measles, news, mathematics, and *economics* require singular verbs.

Write Clear, Concise Sentences

Use sentences which are clear and to the point (concise). Any sentences which are confusing or wordy will make your writing assignments difficult to read. Use the guidelines which follow.

098 Problems with Pronouns

■ Avoid sentences in which a pronoun does not agree with its *antecedent*. (An antecedent is the word which the pronoun refers to. See 734.)

Agreement problem: Everyone going on the trip must bring their own lunch.

Corrected sentence: Everyone going on the trip must bring his or her own lunch.

(A pronoun must agree in number—singular or plural—with its antecedent. *Everyone* is singular so *his* or *her*, not *their*, is the correct pronoun to use to refer to *everyone*.)

■ Avoid sentences with a confusing pronoun reference.

Confusing pronoun reference: As he pulled his car up to the service window, it made a strange rattling sound.

Corrected sentence: His car made a strange rattling sound as he pulled up to the service window.

(It is unclear in the sample sentence which noun the pronoun *it* refers to—the window or the car. To clarify this, the sentence has been reworded.)

■ Avoid sentences which include a pronoun shift.

Pronoun shift: If *students* do not understand the assignment, *you* should ask for help.

Corrected sentence: If *students* do not understand the assignment, *they* should ask for help.

(Since *students* is a third-person subject, the pronoun which refers to it should also be in the third-person. That is why *you*—a second-person pronoun—has been changed to the third-person pronoun *they*. See 737-739 for an explanation of second- and third-person pronouns.)

■ Avoid sentences in which a pronoun is used immediately after the subject—the result is usually a double subject.

Double subject: Some *teachers they* don't offer many choices.

Corrected sentence: Some *teachers* don't offer many choices.

Misplaced Modifiers

099

■ Make sure that your modifiers, especially the descriptive phrases you use, are located as close as possible to the words they modify. Otherwise, the sentence can become very confusing.

Misplaced phrase: After seeing the movie, the space creatures seemed more believable than ever to all of us.
(*After seeing the movie* appears to modify *space creatures*.)

Corrected sentence: After seeing the movie, all of us felt the space creatures were more believable than ever.
(Now *After seeing the movie* correctly modifies *all of us*.)

Nonstandard Language

100

■ Avoid sentences which include a double negative.

Double negative: *Never* give *no* one the wrong time as a joke.

Corrected sentence: Never give anyone the wrong time as a joke.
(*No* was changed to *any* because the word *never* is a negative word. Do not include two negative words in the same sentence unless you understand how these words change the meaning of the sentence.)
Note: Do not use *hardly, barely,* or *scarcely* with a negative; the result is a double negative.

■ Avoid sentences which incorrectly use *of* for *have.*

Incorrect usage: It would *of* worked out better if it hadn't rained.

Corrected sentence: It would *have* worked out better if it hadn't rained.
(*Of* is incorrectly used in place of *have* because when *have* is said quickly, it sounds like *of.*)

Wordy Sentences

101

■ Make sure your sentences contain no unnecessary words *(in italics).*

Wordy sentence: The mountain climber was unable to descend *down* the mountain *by himself* and needed the help of another climber *to assist him.*

Corrected sentence: The mountain climber was unable to descend the mountain and needed the help of another climber.

Combining Sentences

What is sentence combining? Simply put, it is the act of making one smoother, more detailed sentence out of a bunch or short, choppy sentences. For instance, take a look at the following sentences:

A Trans Am screamed around the corner.
The Trans Am was fire red.
It screeched to a stop in front of the doors.
The doors led into the school.

Sound a little choppy? Here are two ways of combining these shorter sentences into one.

■ **The fire-red Trans Am screamed around the corner *and* screeched to a stop in front of the school doors.**

■ ***Screaming around the corner*, the fire-red Trans Am screeched to a stop in front of the school doors.**

102 Practice, Practice, Practice

Many researchers believe that practicing sentence combining will help you improve as a writer in the following ways:

■ You will gain a sense of ease and fluency in writing more detailed, smoother-reading sentences.

■ As writing these sentences becomes more automatic, you will be freed to concentrate on sharing your thoughts, ideas, and discoveries—the real purpose for writing anything.

■ You will begin to notice the variety of word combinations available to you in the English language. There are often many ways to combine the same set of shorter sentences, and you are free to choose whichever way best suits your writing.

■ Your ability to revise and edit your writing will be enhanced in two ways: (It may take you awhile to get used to the second skill.)

  ◆ When you spot choppy sections, you'll be able to combine the shorter sentences into longer, more effective ones.

  ◆ By "decombining" sentences into their separate parts, you will be able to spot unnecessary ideas, delete them, and then recombine the remaining thoughts into a clearer sentence.

A Word of Caution: Don't expect miracles. Sentence combining won't transform you into an accomplished writer. Only time and a lot of reading, writing, and practice will do that.

Guidelines for Sentence Combining

The guidelines which follow will help you transform short, choppy sentences into longer, smoother-reading sentences.

Use a Series of Words or Phrases   103

■ Ideas from shorter sentences can be combined into one sentence using *a series* of words or phrases.

◆ **Shorter sentences:** The cat is soft. The cat is cuddly. The cat is warm.

Combined sentence: The cat is soft, cuddly, and warm. (A series of three words was used to combine the three sentences into one.)

All of the words or phrases you use in a series should be parallel—stated in the same way. (All should be nouns or *ing* words or the same in some other way.) Otherwise, your sentences will sound awkward and unbalanced.

◆ **Awkward series:** The dog was friendly, reliable, and he showed exceptional intelligence.

Corrected sentence: The dog was friendly, reliable, and intelligent. (The three items in the series are now parallel. That is, all of the items are single-word adjectives.)

Use Compound Subjects and Compound Verbs   104

■ Ideas from shorter sentences can be combined using *compound subjects* and *compound verbs* (predicates). A compound subject includes two or more subjects in one sentence. A compound verb includes two or more verbs in one sentence.

◆ **Two shorter sentences:** John ran into the glass door. Sarah ran into the glass door.

Combined sentence with compound subject: *John and Sarah* ran into the glass door.

◆ **Two shorter sentences:** Mr. Fingers fumbled with the stack of papers. He dropped them down the stairs.

Combined sentence with compound verb: Mr. Fingers *fumbled* with the stack of papers and *dropped* them down the stairs.

As you continue working on your sentence skills, think about how different kinds of words and ideas best fit together. Soon you will be combining these ideas naturally as you write!

---

105   Use a Key Word

■ Ideas from shorter sentences can be combined by moving *a key word* from one sentence to the other sentence. This key word may be an adjective, a compound adjective, a participle, or an adverb.

◆ **Shorter sentences:** Julio's cat sat near the fishbowl. The cat is fat.
Combined sentence using an adjective: Julio's *fat* cat sat near the fishbowl.

◆ **Shorter sentences:** Those grasshoppers were delicious. They were covered with chocolate.
Combined sentence using a compound adjective: Those *chocolate-covered* grasshoppers were delicious.

◆ **Shorter sentences:** The lady told a joke. The lady giggled.
Combined sentence using a participle: The *giggling* lady told a joke.

◆ **Shorter sentences:** My brother is going to meet the president. He'll meet him tomorrow.
Combined sentence using an adverb: *Tomorrow* my brother is going to meet the president.

106   Use Phrases

■ Ideas from shorter sentences can be combined into one sentence using *prepositional, participial, infinitive,* and *appositive phrases.*

◆ **Shorter sentences:** The laser satellite guards the space fortress. The space fortress is on asteroid X-7.
Combined sentence using a prepositional phrase: The laser satellite guards the space fortress *on asteroid X-7.*

◆ **Shorter sentences:** Our best basketball player scored fifty points. The player is Biggy Small.
Combined sentence using an appositive phrase: Our best basketball player, *Biggy Small*, scored fifty points.

◆ **Shorter sentences:** The maid gave the detective a clue. She offered the clue to help him solve the mystery.
Combined sentence using an infinitive phrase: The maid gave the detective a clue *to help him solve the mystery.*

◆ **Shorter sentences:** Billy walked through the dark woods. He was whistling a nervous tune.
Combined sentence using a participial phrase: Billy, *whistling a nervous tune*, walked through the dark woods.

Use Compound Sentences

■ Ideas from shorter sentences can be combined into a *compound sentence*. A compound sentence is made up of two simple sentences which are *equal* in importance. The coordinating conjunctions *and, but, or, nor, for,* and *yet* are used to connect the two simple sentences. Place a comma before the conjunction in a compound sentence.

◆ **Two simple sentences:** A small brook trout looks like a minnow. It fights like a whale.

   One compound sentence: A small brook trout looks like a minnow, *but* it fights like a whale.

Use Complex Sentences

■ Ideas from shorter sentences can be combined into a *complex sentence*. A complex sentence is a type of sentence made up of two ideas which are *not equal* in importance. By combining two simple sentences into one complex sentence, you can make your ideas clearer and send a stronger message to the reader.

Helpful
HINT

The **more** important of the two ideas should be included in an *independent clause*, a clause which could stand alone as a simple sentence. The **less** important idea in a complex sentence cannot stand alone and is called a *dependent* or *subordinate clause*.

   The two clauses in a complex sentence can be connected with **subordinate conjunctions**. *After, although, as, because, before, if, since, when, where, while, until,* and *unless* are common subordinate conjunctions. The two clauses can also be connected with the relative pronouns *who, whose, which,* and *that*.

◆ **Two shorter sentences:** Janet returned to the team. We have won every game.

   One complex sentence: *Since* Janet returned to the team, we have won every game. (The complex sentence was formed by using the subordinate conjunction *since* in the dependent clause.)

◆ **Two shorter sentences:** Our coach works us very hard at practice. He is new this year.

   One complex sentence: Our coach, *who* is new this year, works us very hard at practice. (The complex sentence was formed using the relative pronoun *who* in the dependent clause.)

Styling Sentences

I know how important being in style is to you, and I know how much you think about it. You want to look right and wear the right clothes—no matter how many times your parents and teachers tell you it's not that important. Don't be fooled. They've been there themselves. They just don't want you to get carried away with your appearance. And they know that being in style is not cheap.

Your writing style says something about you, too, but not in the same way as your clothes and hairstyle do. This style reflects the you on the inside—your thoughts, your feelings, your enthusiasm. And you'll be glad to know that you don't have to give this style too much thought, at least not for now. Instead, let it (and you) develop naturally through your experiences as a writer.

109 Developing a Sense of Style

Here's how your style—your special way of saying something—can best develop:

- **Experiment with a variety of writing forms.** Write riddles and bumper stickers; write radio plays and essays. Write poems and short stories, notes and news stories. The "word" play you practice in writing riddles is just as important as the sense of order you practice in writing news stories.

- **Write about ideas and issues that are important to you.** Now this may not always be possible, especially when you are assigned specific topics to write about. But try to make something out of even the most uninteresting writing assignments. Become a different person in your writing. Address your writing to the president or a preschooler. Do something to make the writing your own; just make sure your teacher approves.

- **Be yourself in your writing.** How? Write in the first person (I) as much as possible, write freely and naturally, and don't be afraid to make mistakes or take risks.

> "I myself find that I trust my own writing most, and others seem to trust it most, too, when I sound like a person from Indianapolis, which is what I am."
> —Kurt Vonnegut

■ **Satisfy yourself.** You want your readers to appreciate your writing (and heck, who doesn't want a good grade), but you must first feel good about it yourself.

■ **Acquire an ear for good writing.** When you read, take note of sentences that you especially like for their sound, their detail, their surprises, their honesty. Write them down. Use these sentences as models for your own writing.

■ **Acquire a writer's eye.** Be on the lookout for those unique slices of life that can add so much to your writing. You'll enjoy this one recorded in Ken Macrorie's book *Uptaught*:

> A man returned to his parked car to find its hood and fenders gashed and crumpled. On the dashboard he found a piece of folded paper. Written in a neat feminine hand, the note said: "I just ran into your car. There are people watching me. They think I am writing down my name and address. They are wrong."

■ **Gain a general understanding of the rules of writing.** Don't worry. You don't have to become an expert grammarian. But you should become aware of some basic rules of grammar, mechanics, and usage. The list that follows is enough to get you started: (See "The Yellow Pages" for more information.)

   ❑ Write with a purpose or focus in mind or, at least, toward one.

   ❑ Have some sentence sense. Know what is and isn't a sentence.

   ❑ Know when capital letters are used and when periods are used. Know that commas are needed before *and*, *but*, or *or* in compound sentences and between words or ideas in a series.

   ❑ Stick to one tense and one person as much as possible. In a personal narrative, for example, you will write in the past tense and in the first person (I).

   ❑ Begin to build a writer's vocabulary. Learn, for example, what it means to write with details and examples. Learn the difference between abstract and concrete, between description and narration.

111 Sentence Style: A Closer Look

What follows are some more specific suggestions for improving your writing style.

- **Write clearly.** This is one of the most important principles of style. It is the foundation of good writing.

- **Strive for simplicity.** Essayist E. B. White advises young writers to "approach style by way of simplicity, plainness, orderliness, and sincerity." That's good advice from a writer steeped in style.

- **Know when to cut.** And as writer Kurt Vonnegut says, "Have the guts to do it." Give the axe to sentences that don't support your main idea and any words or phrases that don't strengthen your sentences.

- **Acquire a writer's sixth sense.** Know when your writing doesn't work. Watch for sentences that all sound the same and individual sentences that hang limp like wet wash.

Helpful HINT

"If all your sentences move at the same plodding gait, which even you recognize as deadly but don't know how to cure, read them aloud. You will begin to hear where the trouble lies. See if you can gain variety by reversing the order of a sentence, by substituting a word that has freshness or oddity, by altering the length of your sentences so they don't all sound as if they came out of the same computer."

—William Zinsser

- **Write with details (examples, figures of speech, anecdotes, etc.).** Writing without detail is like baking bread without yeast. One of the most important ingredients is missing. But don't wait too long for them. If nothing comes readily to mind, it probably wasn't meant to be. And be careful not to overdo the detail. Your writing may sound forced.

- **Write with specific nouns and verbs.** Writing with specific nouns (Gloria Estefan) and verbs (embraces) gives your writing energy. Writing with vague nouns (woman) and weak verbs (is, are, was, were, etc.) forces you to use a lot of qualifying modifiers. The end result? Tired, anemic sentences. (See 118-119 for more on word choice.)

- **Place nouns and verbs close to each other.** Don't make your readers work too hard by separating nouns and verbs by strings of modifiers.

- **And write active, forward-moving sentences.** Make it clear in your sentences that your subject is actually doing something.

Writers Writing Sentences

Professional writers don't write sentences that are easy for young writers to classify because they don't write with sentence types in mind. They don't say, "Gee, a compound sentence would sure look good here," or "It's high time that I use a simple sentence." They write to make meaning and to share this meaning in the most effective way they know how.

For the most part, writers work rather unscientifically. They go with what feels right in the heat of writing. Of course, when they revise, they pay special attention to sentences that don't work for them—often rewriting them many times until they have the right sound, balance, and substance. But even then, they don't necessarily think in terms of sentence types.

Sentence Variety

What you will find if you do study the writing of your favorite authors may surprise you. You may find sentences that seem to flow on forever, sentences that sort of sneak up on you, sentences that are so direct that they hit you right between the eyes, and "sentences" that aren't by definition complete thoughts. (Writers do break the rules occasionally.) And you may find that they write sentences of all shapes and sizes.

"Pause when you come across a well-put sentence or idea in your reading. Study it and learn from it."

Some of these sentences you'll want to try in your own writing because you like the way they sound or the way they make a point—not because they happened to be simple, compound, or complex sentences.

Note: Generally our favorite authors will write in a relaxed, somewhat informal style. This style of writing is characterized by sentences of many different sizes and shapes as well as by occasional sentence fragments or rambling ideas.

MINI-lesson

Search through your own writing for sentences you really like. Then see how many ways you can rewrite them. Also, exchange sentences with classmates for rewriting. This is an effective way to work on improving your sentence writing style.

A New Look at Sentences

For those of you who like to classify things, see if one of your favorite authors has used any of the four types of sentences which follow. They have to do with the way a writer adds detail and arranges words for rhythm and effect.

Sentences with Style

■ A **loose sentence** expresses the main idea near the beginning (in regular print below) and adds explanatory phrases and clauses as needed.

> We bashed the piñata for 15 minutes without denting it, **although we at least avoided denting one another's craniums and, with masks raised, finally pried the candy out with a screwdriver.**

■ A **balanced sentence** is constructed so that it emphasizes a similarity or contrast between two or more of its parts, including words, phrases, or clauses.

> Joe's unusual security system **invited burglars** and **scared off friends.** (*Invited* contrasts with *scared off* and *burglars* contrasts with *friends*.)

"It's not the structure professional writers vary so much as it is the way they add detail to the basic sentence."

■ A **periodic sentence** is one which postpones the crucial or most surprising idea until the end.

> **Following my mother's repeated threats of being grounded for life,** I decided it was time to propose a compromise.

■ A **cumulative sentence** places the general idea in the main clause (in regular print) and gives it greater precision with modifying words, phrases, or clauses placed before it, after it, or in the middle of it.

> **Eyes squinting, puffy, always on alert,** he showed the effects of a week in the forest, **a brutal week, a week of staggering in circles driven by the baying of wolves.**

MINI-lesson

See if you can build cumulative sentences (or one of the other sentence types described above). Start with simple sentences like *Joe is laughing* or *Julie is studying*. Now build on to these sentences with modifiers until you've created an interesting word picture.

Example: Joe is laughing, **half heartedly, with his head slightly tilted to one side, his eyes looking puzzled.**

Exercises in Style

If you're interested in expanding your writing repertoire, try some of the following activities:

- Change a piece of your writing from one form to another: a short story to a news story, an essay to a poem.
- Rework sections of a piece of writing that you are still not happy with, even after you have turned it in. (That takes a committed writer.)
- Rewrite a piece in a different tone or voice. Make something serious seem humorous, something light seem heavy.
- Make a longer piece shorter and a shorter piece longer.
- Experiment with beginnings.
- Predict the questions a specific audience might ask, perhaps a group of youngsters or a senior citizen's group, and then redo a piece.
- Rewrite the best parts of your writing. See how many variations you can come up with.

 Helpful HINT   If you're interested in improving your writing style, you've got to keep your fingers busy. That's the only way you'll make progress. If you get tired of writing in pencil, go to pen; when you tire of a pen, go to a typewriter or computer. When you get tired of that, put your writing tools away and try speaking into a tape recorder.

- Rework a piece by cutting the first half and starting right in the middle.
- Decide where it would be good or fun to digress in a piece and do so. Digressions are little stories that are interesting but not directly essential to the purpose of your writing.
- Identify the best sentence in a piece of writing, the second best sentence, the third best and so on. Explain the reasons for your choices.
- Draw a shape and limit your writing within the shape.
- Keep a file of favorite sentences from your writing, from the writing of your classmates, and from the writing of your favorite authors. Practice writing sentences like these. If you want a real challenge, try to explain why you like them.
- Write whole pieces like your favorite authors.
- Break some rules in your writing. Write with sentence fragments, with sentences that never end, with different spelling, with no connecting words, with no capital letters or periods.

The Art of Writing

Writing Naturally

Writing naturally might not sound like a difficult thing to do, but, for many of us, it is. For some reason, we switch to another personality when we write—the personality of someone who uses short, choppy sentences with strange, uninteresting words. And our writing sounds as if it were written by someone else. Before any of us can write well—tell a good story in words—we must be able to "speak" in an honest, sincere, and natural style.

If you're interested in working on your natural writing style, read the guidelines and models which follow. But don't stop there. Also included in this section are guidelines for improving your writing through revising and handy and helpful lists of writing techniques and terms.

Improving Your Style of Writing

116

A natural writing style will not only make writing enjoyable for you, but it will also make reading what you have written enjoyable for your classmates and teachers. Those students whose writing is most appreciated in your English class no doubt write in a natural style. Something in their writing moves you and makes you say, "Hey, I like that." That "something" is the ability of the writer to make his or her **voice** come through in the writing.

"Voice is the imprint of ourselves in our writing. Take the voice away . . . and there's no writing, just words following words."
—Donald Graves

Once the act of writing becomes easier for you, your style will "naturally" become more natural. You can practice writing naturally by keeping a personal journal or diary. (See 130 for guidelines.) Another way to practice is by "talking" to friends and close relatives in friendly letters. Write these letters as if your friend or relative were in the same room with you, and you were talking to this person.

Also, begin writing assignments by freely recording your thoughts about the subject of your writing. Keep writing nonstop until you can't think of anything else to say. Work some of these ideas into the actual writing assignment and your writing will start to sound more natural, more interesting, more like you.

117 Writing That's in Style

Read the parts of three stories which follow. The natural writing voice of the writer comes through in each selection.

> After that, I was underwater in a silent world, all alone. It was great. But my air was running out and I had to surface. I gave out a kick with my left leg; then two or three more and I surfaced. I dog-paddled to the side of the pool, paused, then lifted myself to the side. I was exhausted.

> While we were walking, I looked up and saw the moon was out. It made the fog seem to glow. Off in the distance, I heard a dog bark and then a chorus of barks. I felt a shiver crawl up my spine, probably just the cold.

> "I've thought it over. I'm not going on the Eagle."
> "But it'll be fun. C'mon!"
> "No! I just ate lunch. I'm not going on it."
> "Oh, gees! It's not that bad. You're not going to puke."
> "I know it, but I don't like going upside down."
> "Yes you do."
> "No I don't."
> "I'll give you a dollar."
> "Okay."
> We got into the last car of the roller coaster and locked ourselves in. We started to move and slowly submerged into the Eagle's tunnel. I felt like I was the camera on one of those <u>National Geographic</u> specials going into some creature's mouth and down its throat.

These selections make us pay attention to what is being said because each seems so real and so natural. And we can tell that each student writer is interested in telling a good story. In the first example, it is easy to visualize the writer kicking to the surface of the water. In the second example, we can share the writer's feeling of uneasiness while walking late at night. In the last humorous example, we can share the writer's fear and uncertainty of a roller coaster called the Eagle.

MINI-lesson

Writing voices are something like clothing styles. There is a different style for different occasions. You use a natural voice when you want to share information, a goofy mixture of voices when you're going for laughs, and somebody else's voice when you're trying to borrow a little bit of his or her attitude.

Improving Your Writing

Anytime you write a first draft, there will be parts of it which already sound interesting, creative, and natural. Leave those parts alone. However, there will also be parts of each writing assignment which simply don't sound right—something seems to be missing. Changes should be made in these sections so that the entire piece of writing will be enjoyable for your readers. The guidelines which follow will help you make these changes.

Use Strong, Colorful Words

A writer's style is greatly improved if he or she chooses the best words to use in any type of writing. The best words are the ones that effectively add to the meaning, feeling, and sound of the writing. Pay special attention to the nouns, verbs, and modifiers (adjectives and adverbs) that you use. These are the words that make your writing come alive. The guidelines given below will help you use attractive nouns, verbs, and modifiers.

■ **Choose specific nouns.** Some nouns are **general** *(car, house, animal)* and give the reader only a fuzzy picture. Other nouns are **specific** *(Corvette, igloo, llama)* and give the reader a much clearer, more detailed picture. In the chart which follows, the words on the top blanks are very general nouns. The words written in each of the second blanks are nouns which are more specific. Finally, each of the words in the bottom blanks is a very specific noun. These are the kind of specific nouns which can make your writing clear and colorful.

118

Choosing Specific Nouns

person	place	thing	idea
woman	city	drink	pain
actress	West Coast city	nutritious drink	headache
Jane Fonda	Los Angeles	fruit juice	migraine

MINI-lesson

Even the most successful writers make many changes before they are satisfied with their writing. Writer John Kenneth Galbraith makes this point very clearly: ". . . there are days when the result is so bad that no fewer than five revisions are required. In contrast, when I'm greatly inspired, only four revisions are needed."

119 ■ **Choose vivid verbs.** Use vivid, action-packed verbs to make your writing lively and interesting. For example, the vivid verbs *stared, glared, glanced, peeked,* and *inspected* all say more than an overused, ordinary verb like *looked.* The statement "Mr. Brown *glared* at the two tardy boys" is much more interesting than "Mr. Brown *looked* at the two tardy boys."

Helpful HINT

Avoid using the "to be" verbs *(is, are, was, were)* too often. Many times a better verb can be made from another word in the same sentence.

A "to be" verb: **Heapo is a powerful diver.**

A stronger verb: **Heapo dives powerfully.**

120 ■ **Choose words that "feel" right.** The words you include in your writing should not only be specific and colorful, but they should also have the right feeling or **connotation**. Let's say that you are writing about a friend who tried very hard to complete a 10-mile race, but couldn't quite make it. It wouldn't be right to say he tried "unsuccessfully" to finish the race because that word makes it sound like your friend is a failure, and that isn't true. A better word would be "bravely"—he tried "bravely" to finish the race.

Or, let's say you are writing about a particular dream. If this dream happens to scare the garbanzos out of you every time you think about it, 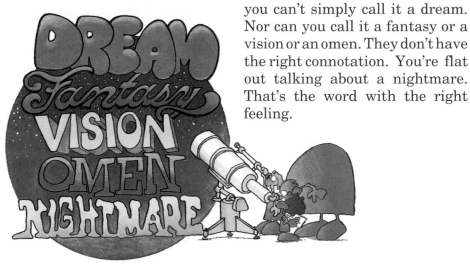 you can't simply call it a dream. Nor can you call it a fantasy or a vision or an omen. They don't have the right connotation. You're flat out talking about a nightmare. That's the word with the right feeling.

Note: You can use a thesaurus to help you find the best words for your writing. A thesaurus is, in a sense, the opposite of a dictionary: you use it when you already know the definition but need to find the right word. The thesaurus lists synonyms, words with the same meaning. You pick the word which best fits the meaning, feeling, and sound of your writing assignment. (See 302 for help.)

■ **Choose effective modifiers.** Use vivid, colorful **adjectives** to de-   **121**
scribe the nouns in your writing. Strong adjectives can help make the
nouns you choose even more interesting and clear to the reader. For
example, when you describe the Demon as "a wicked roller coaster," you
are making the ride much more interesting with the addition of the
adjective.

Avoid adjectives which are used so frequently that they carry
little meaning. Some of these adjectives are *neat, big, pretty,
small, cute, fun, bad, nice, good, dumb, great,* and *funny.*

Use **adverbs** when you think they can help describe the action (the
verb) in a sentence. For example, the statement "Rover ran *wildly* after
Rachel" is more action packed than "Rover ran after Rachel."

Note: Don't use two words—a verb and an adverb—when a single, vivid
verb would be better.

Verb and adverb: Joan sat quickly on the whoopee cushion.

A single vivid verb: Joan plopped on the whoopee cushion.

■ **Use figurative language.** You can also use figurative language from   **122**
time to time to make your writing interesting, clear, and creative. Three
common types of figurative language are the *simile, metaphor,* and *personification*—each compares two different things. (See 124 and 125 for
more examples.)

❑ A **simile** compares two different things using *like* or *as.*
Actually the pimple looks ferocious like a rhino horn.

❑ A **metaphor** compares two different things without using a
word of comparison such as *like* or *as.*
*The ferocious-looking pimple was a rhino horn that hurt half of
Hector's head.*

❑ **Personification** is a form of figurative language in which an
idea, object, or animal is given the characteristics of a person.
Hector's pimple curls up like it wants to ram into something.

If your writing is already clear, natural, and interesting,
remember to leave it alone. Add colorful words or figurative
language only when you feel they can improve your writing. If
you add too many colorful words and phrases, your writing will
sound flowery and artificial.

---

123 How do you really know what to change?

How do you really know what to change when you are ready to revise your writing? First, carefully review your rough draft. Make note of parts that you especially like or dislike. (See 022 for help.) Also, try writing about your work to sort out your thoughts and feelings about it. See what your classmates and teacher think of your writing. And make sure to consult your handbook for advice and writing models.

When you review your writing, look for the general problem areas described below. Any one of these areas could cause your writing to "malfunction." (See 023 for more on revising.)

1. **Your subject hangs lifeless, at half-mast.** It might be too general, too predictable, or too unimaginative ("What I Did on My Summer Vacation," for example). Don't necessarily give up on such an idea. See if a new twist will elevate it. Try something like "Invasion of the Killer Cousins."

2. **You're writing for the wrong reason.** Don't write only to please your teacher. Write to learn something. Write what you would like to read and what you think your classmates would like to read.

3. **Your writing doesn't sound like you.** If your writing sounds like you are trying to impress someone ("A good time was had by all"), try again. This time be honest. Express real feelings.

4. **Your first draft sounds boring.** Perhaps there is no focus to your writing, so it flows all over the place, like a glass of spilled milk. Find an interesting way to look at your subject, and put your writing in better focus.

   Or, maybe you've said too little or too much in your writing. If your first draft is all skin and bones, flesh it out with details, examples, dialogue, and personal feeling. And cut your writing back if it is bulging at the seams. Skim through less important ideas and develop important parts more thoroughly. Tell and show.

5. **Your sentences fall into a rut.** Do you begin many sentences with "He," "It," or "There"? Do you use many "be" verbs? Have you repeated words without knowing it? Replace any predictable or often used words with something more interesting and eye catching.

Helpful HINT

When you rework your writing, think of it as an opportunity, not a chore. Be unpredictable. Make your writing come to life. Try one or more of the searching or shaping activities if you need to refuel before you start out. (See 035 and 037.)

Writing Techniques

Even though you may not realize it, you use a number of "techniques" or special ways of treating words when you write, especially in your creative writing. See how many of the following techniques you are already familiar with. Also think about using those that are new to you. *Caution:* Don't use one of these techniques unless it fits well with your writing.

An **allusion** in literature is a reference to a well-known person, place, thing, or event.

Antithesis is a contrasting of ideas in the same or neighboring sentences. *Example:* "We decided to have the bear for supper before he decided to have us!"

Caricature is a description of a character in which his features or characteristics are exaggerated and distorted to the point of being funny or ridiculous.

A **dramatic monologue** is a speech in which a character tells a lot about himself by talking either to himself or to another character.

Exaggeration is stretching the truth. This can be used effectively in some instances in your writing. For example, a character frightened by a barking dog might say, "I thought that dog was going to bite my leg off!"

Figurative language is language used in a special way to create a special effect. It is made up of words and phrases which don't mean what they first appear to mean. *Example:* "You three *put your heads together* and plan the class party." (This does not mean *bump your heads together;* it means *share the ideas you have in your heads.*)

A **figure of speech** is a device used by authors to create a special meaning for their readers. (See *metaphor, personification,* and *simile.*)

In a **flashback**, the author goes back to an earlier time in the story and explains something that will help the reader understand the whole story better.

Foreshadowing is the writer's hints and clues about what is going to happen in the story.

Hyperbole is an exaggeration or overstatement used for emphasis: "My dad had a bird when he saw my grades."

Irony is using a word or phrase to mean the exact opposite of its normal meaning. *Example:* "My *favorite* pastime is cleaning my room."

Local color is the use of details which are common in a certain place (a *local* area). For example, a story taking place on the western seacoast would probably contain details about the ocean and the life and people near it.

A **metaphor** compares two different things without using a word of comparison such as *like* or *as*. *Example:* "That substitute teacher was a real ringmaster."

An **oxymoron** is a literary technique in which two contradictory words come together for a special effect. *Examples:* jumbo shrimp, inside out, tight slacks, original copy, old news, small fortune, random order.

A **paradox** is a statement that seems to go against common sense but is actually true. A construction worker or farmer may say, *"My muscles ache from working hard all day, but it's a good feeling."* (Because they are happy to have done a hard day's work, they are able to appreciate their sore muscles.)

Parallelism is the repeating of phrases or sentences that are written in the same way. *Example:* "We will *lie on the beach, swim in the ocean,* and *sleep under the stars."* Each verb *(lie, swim,* and *sleep)* is followed by a prepositional phrase.

Personification is a form of figurative language in which an idea, object, or animal is given the characteristics of a person. (See illustration.)

Poetic devices: (See 231-232.)

A **pun** is a word or phrase used in a way that gives it a funny twist. The words used in a pun sound the same, but they have different meanings. *Example:* "*I scream,* you scream, we all scream for *ice cream!"* (*I scream* sounds like *ice cream.)*

Sarcasm is the use of praise to ridicule or "put down" someone or something. The praise is not sincere and is actually intended to mean the opposite thing. Calling a turtlelike person *a real go-getter* would be sarcasm.

Satire is writing that ridicules or makes fun of people's mistakes and weaknesses. Satire is often used to raise questions about a current trend or political decision.

A **simile** compares two different things using either *like* or *as. Example:* "Everywhere giant-finned cars nosed forward like fish."

A **soliloquy** is a speech given in a play by a character who is alone on stage. Shakespeare was famous for his soliloquies.

Personification: The rock stubbornly refused to move.

A **submerged metaphor** is an implied comparison made in one or two words (usually verbs, nouns, adjectives). *Examples*: "Coach Smith *mended* the losing pitcher's hurt feelings." (Not literally; he just tried to make him feel better.)

A **symbol** is a concrete or real object used to represent an idea. *Examples:* A *bird,* because it can fly, has often been used as a *symbol for freedom.* Our *flag* is a *symbol of our nation,* the United States of America. Each star represents one of the fifty states and each stripe represents one of the thirteen original colonies.

Synecdoche is using part of something to represent the whole: "All *hands* on deck!" *(Hands* is being used to represent the whole person.)

Understatement is the opposite of exaggeration. The author restrains himself in his writing, thereby bringing special attention to an object or idea. The author Mark Twain once described Tom Sawyer's Aunt Polly as being "prejudiced against snakes." Since she hated snakes, this way of saying so is called *understatement.*

Writing Terms

Below you will find a glossary of words often used to describe some part of the writing process. These are simple, basic definitions. Check your index for the location of additional definitions, models, and explanations if necessary.

Analogy: A comparison of two or more similar objects; the analogy implies that since these objects are alike in some ways, they will probably be alike in other ways as well.

Anecdote: A brief story used to make a point. The story about Abraham Lincoln walking more than two miles to return several pennies he had accidentally overcharged a customer is an example of an anecdote which shows how honest Abe was.

Argumentation: Writing or speaking which uses reasons, arguments, and logic to make a point. (See 343.)

Arrangement: The order in which details are placed or organized in a piece of writing.

Audience: Those people who read or hear what you have written.

Balance: The arranging of words or phrases so that two ideas are given equal emphasis in a sentence or paragraph; a pleasing rhythm results.

Body: The writing (often paragraphs) between the introduction and conclusion which develops the main idea(s) of the writing.

Brainstorming: Collecting ideas by thinking freely and openly about all the possibilities; used most often with groups.

Central idea: The main point or purpose of a piece of writing, often stated in a thesis statement or topic sentence.

Cliche: A familiar word or phrase which has been used so much that it is no longer a good, effective way of saying something—as in "sharp as a tack" or "fresh as a daisy."

Clincher sentence: The sentence which summarizes the point being made in a paragraph, usually located last.

Coherence: Sticking together; putting your ideas together in such a way that the reader can easily follow from one point to the next.

Colloquialism: A common, everyday expression like *"What's happenin'?"* or *"How's it goin'?"* These expressions are used when talking to each other or when writing dialogue.

Composition: Writing in which ideas are combined into one, unified piece.

Description: Writing which paints a colorful picture of a person, place, thing, or idea using vivid details.

Details: The words used to describe a person, persuade an audience, explain a process, or in some way support the main idea; to be effective, details should be vivid, colorful, and appealing. (See 118-120.)

Diction: A writer's choice of words. There are many ways to describe the different kinds of words a writer can use: slang, colloquial, formal, etc.

Emphasis: Placing greater stress on the most important idea(s) in a piece of writing through special treatment; emphasis can be achieved by placing the important idea in a special position, by repeating a key word or phrase, or by simply writing more about one idea than the others.

Essay: A piece of factual writing in which ideas on a single topic are presented, explained, argued, or described in an interesting way.

Exposition: Writing which explains.

Extended definition: Writing which goes beyond a simple definition of a term in order to stress a point; it can cover several paragraphs and include personal definitions and experiences, similes, metaphors, quotations, etc.

Figurative language: Language which goes beyond the normal meaning of the words used; writing in which a figure of speech is used to improve the meaning. (See 122.)

Focus: Concentrating on a specific subject to give it emphasis or importance.

Form: The way in which the content of writing is organized: poem, essay, novel.

Free writing: Writing openly and freely on any topic; *focused* free writing is writing openly on a specific topic.

Generalization: An idea or statement which emphasizes the general characteristics rather than the specific details of a subject.

Grammar: The study of the structure of language; the rules and guidelines which are to be followed to produce acceptable writing and speaking. (See "The Yellow Pages.")

Idiom: A phrase or expression which means something different from what the words actually say. (See illustration.)

Issue: A point or question to be decided.

Jargon: The technical language of a particular group (musicians, journalists) which is inappropriate in most formal writing.

Journal: A daily record of thoughts, impressions, and autobiographical information; a journal can be a source of ideas for writing. (See 130.)

Juxtaposition: Placing two ideas (words or pictures) side by side so that their closeness creates a new, often ironic meaning.

Limiting the subject: Narrowing the subject to a specific topic which is suitable for a writing or speaking assignment.

Literal: The actual or dictionary meaning of a word; language which means exactly what it appears to mean.

Loaded words: Words which are slanted for or against the subject.

Logic: The science of reasoning; using reasons, facts, and examples to support your point. (See 343.)

Modifier: A word, phrase, or clause which limits or describes another word or group of words. (See *adjectives* and *adverbs*.)

Narration: Writing which tells a story or recounts an event.

Idiom: *"Now that's a horse of a different color"* for **"Now that's a completely different situation."**

Objective: Relating information without adding your feelings or opinions.

Personal narrative: Personal writing which covers an event in the writer's life; it often contains personal comments and ideas as well as a description of the event.

Persuasion: Writing which is meant to change the way the reader thinks or acts.

Plagiarism: Copying someone else's writing or ideas and then using them as if they were your own.

Point of view: The position or angle from which a story is told. (See 387.)

Process: A method of doing something which involves several steps or stages; the writing process involves prewriting, writing, and revising.

Prose: Writing or speaking in the usual or ordinary form; prose becomes poetry when it takes on rhyme and rhythm.

Purpose: The specific reason a person has for writing; the goal of writing.

Revision: Changing a piece of writing to improve it in style or content.

Sensory: Language or details which come to us through the senses and help the reader see, feel, smell, taste, and hear the subject.

Slang: Language used by a certain group of people when they are talking to each other. For example, "He's *totally awesome*" is a slang expression used by some people today. Many years ago, the slang expression "He's the *cat's pajamas*" would have meant the same thing.

Spontaneous: Doing, thinking, or writing off the top of your head with no planning.

Structure: The way writing is organized; much like *form*. When an author has something to say, he must fit his words into a form or pattern (poem, essay, editorial, etc.) in order to get his point across to the reader.

Style: *How* the author writes (his choice and arrangement of words) rather than *what* he writes (his message to the readers).

Subjective: Thinking or writing which includes personal feelings, attitudes, and opinions.

Supporting details: The details (examples, anecdotes, facts, etc.) used in writing to prove a point or bring a story to life.

Theme: The central idea in a piece of writing (lengthy writings may have several themes); a term used to describe a short essay.

Thesis statement: A statement of the purpose or main idea of an essay.

Tone: The writer's attitude toward the subject; a writer's tone can be serious, sarcastic, objective, etc.

Topic: The specific subject of a piece of writing.

Topic sentence: The sentence which contains the main idea of a paragraph.

Transitions: Words or phrases which help tie ideas together. (See 089.)

Trite: Expressions like cliches. They are used too much to be a very good way of saying something, especially in writing. *Examples:* true blue, red as a beet, hotter than blazes

Unity: A sense of oneness in writing in which each sentence helps to develop the main idea.

Universal: A topic or idea which applies to everyone, not just those around you.

Usage: The way in which people use language; language is generally considered to be standard (formal and informal) or nonstandard. You will use standard language for most of your writing assignments. (See 574-694.)

Vivid details: (See "Sensory.")

Personal Writing

Journal Writing

Let's say you want to make some sense out of a recent occurrence. You can write about this occurrence in a personal journal. Let's say you want to explore your thoughts and feelings about an important time in your life. You can write about this time in a phase autobiography. Or let's say you want to share a memorable experience with your classmates. You can do this in a personal experience paper.

You name a personal situation, and I'll give you both a reason to write and a writing form to help you shape your thoughts. And that's exactly what we do in this section. We begin with a look at journal writing and continue with guidelines for different types of autobiographical writing.

Keeping a Personal Journal

130

Hold on to your Walkmans if you think compact disc players, VCR's, video cameras, and Nintendo are where it's at. You ain't seen or heard nothin' yet. We're in the middle of a high-tech explosion. As one expert put it, "If a product works, it's already obsolete." That's how fast things are happening. Before too long, you'll see giant TV screens that hang like pictures on a wall, stereos that produce 3-D sound, and pocket-sized computers that you can talk to.

"For the majority of students, journals are yes places."
—Ken Macrorie

You and I have access to a lot of nice products now, and we have a lot to look forward to in the future. Part of me worries a little bit about all of this. I'm worried that some people are already becoming too plugged in to this high-tech equipment. And, as this equipment continues to improve, it will become more and more difficult to resist.

Don't get me wrong. I enjoy watching TV, love listening to music, and couldn't survive without my computer. But I also make plenty of time for myself—without the machines. One very important thing I do when I unplug is write in a personal journal. And I'd like you to make time to do the same.

All you need to do is set aside 15 to 20 minutes every day or every other day. (That's not much time—no matter how busy or plugged in you are.) You'll find journal writing to be an effective way to catch your breath and focus on yourself and your world. And while it might not be as exciting as 3-D sound, you will find it much more rewarding and meaningful.

Why Write in a Journal?

Journal writing will benefit you in a number of ways. It provides you with a valuable record of your thoughts, dreams, memories, and experiences. It offers you an easy and enjoyable way to practice writing. It helps you form new ideas, and serves as a useful resource for ideas for writing. Journal writing also supplies you with details of ready-made facts and details to use in writing assignments. All of this is located under one roof—your journal notebook.

Here's how to get started:

1. **Gather the tools of the trade.** All you really need is a spiral notebook and a supply of your favorite pens and pencils. I recommend a pen. Pencils need to be sharpened, and the temptation with a pencil is to erase, which stops you from writing. Some journal writers use different colored ink, depending on their mood when they write. And there's always a computer or typewriter—that is, if you know how to keyboard. Now might be a good time to learn.

2. **Find a comfortable time and place to write.** Set aside a regular time when you know you won't be distracted. And write where you feel comfortable. (You don't have to totally unplug either. There's nothing wrong with a little background music.)

3. **And write.** Try to write for sustained periods of time—at first, try bursts of three to five minutes. You're much more likely to make some interesting discoveries when you write nonstop. Time yourself if need be. (See 005 for help with your first writing.)

4. **Write about those things that are important to you.** Write about someone or something in school. Write about what you did last weekend or what you hope to do this coming weekend. Write about something silly that you saw. All you are looking for is a starting point. Once you start writing, new ideas will come. (See 039 for writing ideas.)

5. **Keep track of your writing.** Date your journal entries, and save them. Once you get into journal writing, you'll have fun reading some of your early entries. (Share your work with friends and family members as well.)

Helpful HINT If you regularly write for the same amount of time—let's say 10 minutes—count the number of words you produce. The number of words you are able to produce should increase over time—which means you are gaining fluency as a writer.

Journal Writing Sampler

If you have a reason to explore your personal thoughts and feelings, then you should be writing in a personal journal. If the "generic" personal journal doesn't fit your needs, one of the specific journal types described below might.

Dialogue Journal: In a dialogue journal, two individuals (two close friends, a father and a daughter, a dog and his master) carry on a written conversation. A dialogue journal helps the writers get to know each other better, helps them work through a problem together, or helps them share in some common interest. (A dialogue journal doesn't have to be limited to two individuals. It can be a group effort as well.)

Diary: A diary is a record of daily events, experiences, and observations with, perhaps, a little reflection or random thought thrown in for good measure:

> JULY 16: I helped Grandpa scrape and paint the garage today. Scraping is the pits, especially when it's hot and humid. He kept singing about goober peas. We finished at about 4:30, and he later took me out for supper at Eduardo's. The Cubs lost again. Why do they do this to me!

What's the difference between a journal and a diary? I make this distinction: A journal is freewheeling, a come-as-you-are record of thoughts and feelings. A diary is more exact and specific—a settling of the day's account.

Learning Log: A learning log gives students the opportunity to explore their thoughts and feelings about their course work. Writing about new concepts, facts, and ideas helps make them part of students' thinking. A learning log is an all-purpose personal learning tool. (See 409 for more information.)

Specialized Journal: When writers write about specific events or experiences, they are writing in a specialized journal. They might want to explore their thoughts and feelings while at summer camp, while participating in a team sport, while involved in a play production, or while working on an extended project in school.

Travel Log: In a travel log, writers simply explore their thoughts and feelings while vacationing or traveling. It's not only an effective way to preserve traveling memories, but it's also a productive way to kill time while in transit from one location to the next.

Writing Phase Autobiographies

This was the moment Rosie had been waiting for. Coach Anderson had just posted the final roster on the gym door, and her name was on it. The four months of conditioning and practicing with her older sister and her father had paid off. She was now a member of the McKinley Middle School basketball team.

Robb had known little about Mr. Cosford, other than he was old and suffered from emphysema. Then one day Robb's dad took him over to Mr. Cosford's for a visit. That visit led to others. And before Robb knew it, he had developed a special friendship with this neighbor.

133 And what about you?

Have you ever put all of your efforts into an activity like Rosie did? Have you ever, like Robb, come to know or appreciate someone more over time? Or, have you ever had to deal with a serious injury, with moving, with an addition to your family, or with a crisis among your friends?

At different points in our lives, we all live through "phases" such as these—extended periods of time that affect us, change us, make us better or make us different. They help make us who we are, yet how often do we really think about these times? Not very often, I'm afraid. We're too busy living life in the present, living through new phases.

134 Selecting: *Finding a Subject*

Let's see if we can forget about the present for a while. Take a deep breath. Relax. And don't worry about who you are going to sit with during lunch or what Mr. Guthrie is going to say when you tell him your report is not ready. Think back. Think about those times that were once very important to you, times that may seem unimportant or even silly to you now.

This really shouldn't be too difficult for you. Think of important or memorable periods of time in school, at home, or in your neighborhood. Think of friendships or relationships that have developed or ended. Think of hobbies or projects that have attracted your attention for a period of time. But don't panic if nothing readily comes to mind. You'll find helpful suggestions for selecting a subject on the next page.

Just freely list for ideas or . . .   135

The following activities will help you search for a subject for your phase autobiography.

■ Take out a piece of paper and freely list memories as they come to mind. Don't be choosy. Just keep listing. This is how many professionals get ideas for their writing. I'll even help you with your first memory. Complete one of the following ideas: "The first thing I remember about grade school is . . ." or "I'll never forget the time when . . . ."

■ If listing doesn't work, try something else: free writing, clustering, or just talking with a friend or classmate. Look at your life map or personal inventory of experiences if you have created one. All of these ways to unlock memories are described in your handbook. (See 033.)

Collecting: *Gathering Your Thoughts*   136

Review your work, looking for memories that are in some way related, and you have the makings of an important phase. It might help to think of a phase as a chapter in your life and the related memories as the detail that you will use to develop this chapter. For example, an important chapter in your life might develop out of memories related to a certain group of friends.

Let's see what you can remember about one of these phases by writing about it. Write freely and honestly. This writing is for you, so don't worry about how it sounds or looks. Simply write to see what you can remember about this time. And try to write as much as you can in one sitting. Then the ideas will begin to flow freely. And be prepared. If you honestly let yourself go in your writing, you're in for some real surprises because you're going to unlock some unexpected ideas and details.

"Free writing about your memories is like traveling in a time machine into your past."

Connecting: *Writing the First Draft*   137

I always look forward to the discoveries I make in my early drafts. It's one of the true joys of the process, and it's part of the magic that draws writers back to writing time and time again. That's why I want you to write your first draft freely and honestly—and for yourself. I want you to experience some of this magic, to feel good about your writing. Developing your finished piece will then become much more meaningful to you.

138 Reviewing Your Autobiography

Think of this initial draft (or drafts if you've already written more than one) as the ground breaking, the all-important first step in the development of your writing. You should now proceed with the actual building by planning and shaping your story for your readers. This gets at another aspect of the process that writers find so exciting and challenging—how to best share their discoveries with their readers.

You should first review your initial writing to see what you like about it, as well as to see what is missing or needs to be changed. Keep in mind that you are now thinking in terms of your readers. What will make your story interesting and entertaining for *them*? Make sure it's clear what you are writing about. Also, make sure that you have made all of the important points and that you have included enough detail, dialogue, and background information so that your readers can relive this phase with you.

139 Shaping Your Writing for Your Readers

An obvious way to shape a phase autobiography is in story form—telling what happens chronologically. This is how you probably shaped your initial writing. There's nothing wrong with this approach, especially if you have a good story to tell. Just remember to select only the best details; otherwise, your phase autobiography could go on forever.

If you want to be a bit more daring, consider one of the following forms for your writing:

> "As you continue writing and rewriting, you begin to see possibilities you hadn't seen before."
> —Robert Hayden

❑ Write about this phase in a letter (or a series of letters) to someone who was part of your life at this time. Create a conversation with someone linked to this time. Or, create a conversation with yourself—that is, between you then and you now.

❑ Report about this phase in a series of news articles.

❑ Fictionalize it in a short story or play.

❑ Write about this phase in a ballad; put your story to music.

140 Correcting: *Wrapping It Up*

After you have done all of your adding, cutting, rearranging, and fine-tuning, you're ready to put your writing into final form. Take special care at this stage to check for careless errors. Your story has to stand on its own two feet once you send it on its way to your readers. (See 026 for help.)

Model Short Phase Autobiography

In the sample phase autobiography which follows, the student author remembers a time in her life when she enjoyed dreaming up and pretending to be someone else. In fact, she did it so often that it became something she was "notorious for." This dress-up time in her life is considered a "phase," a period of time when a person does something day after day, week after week, sometimes month after month. Read the model and take note of the comments.

Fashionation

The writer begins with a clear, yet creative way of introducing her topic.

When I was younger, I was notorious for my strange dress-up games. One of these games was "Keeku." When I played Keeku, I would pin my hair up with plastic barrettes and hold a pair of red sunglass frames that only had one handle. With my costume complete, I would run around the house saying "Keeku! Keeku! Keeku!" It wasn't much of a game, but I guess I enjoyed it because I did it all the time.

The writer supplies plenty of details so the reader can get a clear picture of what she looked like.

I also spent a lot of time playing "Ginger." The main thing I needed to play this was my "Ginger dress" or squiggly skirt as it was sometimes called. It was a multi-colored tank top nobody wore anymore, and it was like a dress on me. I would put it on, tie a belt around it, and an amazing change would take place. I was no longer Lisa; instead, I was beautiful, glamorous Ginger from *Gilligan's Island*. I'd walk around the house calling my sisters and brothers Mary Ann, Gilligan, Skipper, or Mr. and Mrs. Howell. The title Professor was reserved for the St. Agnes statue in our living room which was just my size.

The student writer recalls a specific incident which adds to the overall picture we have of her.

Once when I was playing "Ginger," I added something new to the game; it was my Ginger hairstyle. This delicate design was created by sucking my hair up into the vacuum cleaner hose until it stood on end. I thought I was pretty beautiful until the neighbor boys began teasing me about it. I gave up my Ginger hairdo.

My days of make-believe sometimes included my sister Mary, who was my constant companion. We played long dresses or dressed up in our ballerina dresses. Hers was blue and mine was pink. They itched worse than poison ivy, but we'd wear them for hours. We wore them when we played house and store and restaurant . . . and even when we rode our Big Wheels down the driveway.

The writer concludes that everyone has a similar experience.

I guess all kids go through a pretending stage. Why dressing up was so important to me, though, I don't know. Today I wouldn't be caught dead looking like that.

142 Model Phase Autobiography

In *Me Me Me Me Me,* M.E. Kerr recounts her adventures as a young girl growing up in the state of New York. The particular phase reprinted here recalls a painful and revealing encounter with a new girl in school. Read the model carefully, and take special note of the comments which accompany it.

Mending a Wrong

One brief statement lets the reader know the extent of this phase, and it also adds suspense: before what *secret was out?*

Somehow you lasted for six months before your secret was out.

I first got wind of it overhearing a conversation my mother was having with one of her friends, on the telephone.

"Why, I never even thought of that!" was all my mother had to say to make my ears perk up. "She takes in the relatives? I'd be afraid to have them in my house."

I always counted on the fact my mother would be so caught up in new gossip that it would take her a while to perceive the danger of its being spread by what was huddled over in the chair behind her.

I would try not to even breathe so as not to remind her I was there.

Ms. Kerr continues to build suspense when she recreates one of her mother's phone conversations.

"I never knew that about Pam Burnside," she continued. "But when you think about it, they have to stay someplace. I never even thought about why we had so many of these tourist homes here. I just thought they were for vacationers, which we don't get that many of anyway. Of course—it all makes sense, and Pam would keep her mouth shut about it if anybody would. She's never been one to open her mouth much on any subject."

Anyone could hear a pin drop during the short intervals my mother listened. My foot was numb from staying under my bottom for so long, I was so afraid to change my position and remind her of me.

"So they're here because of him," she said. "Why that poor little girl, and I don't think she's popular with the other girls at all."

The dialogue and detailed description of the writer's position draw the reader into the phone conversation as if it were actually happening.

Pins and needles in my foot and leg became unbearable. I had to stand. The book I was reading clunked to the floor.

My mother said, "I can't talk now. Little pitchers have big ears, if you know what I mean."

When she hung up, I said, "Who's he?"

"I wasn't talking to a he."

"Who did you mean when you said they're here because of him?"

"No one," she said. "I didn't say anything like that."

"That's an untruth," I said, which was what my grandmother always called a lie—"an untruth."

The subject was dropped.

Somewhere in our small town the subject hadn't been

dropped, and the next day in school it was out in the open.

Even I drew a breath when Marilyn Monstarr confronted you. We called her Marilyn Monster, for she was hands down the bully's bully, the meanest mouth in town, and famous for saying if you squeezed acned Carrie Speck, pus would come out.

Ms. Kerr then recreates one more dramatic incident in which Millicent's secret is revealed in front of her classmates. She again speaks directly to Millicent.

She was saving her goodies for just before first class in the morning, while everyone was putting stuff in their lockers.

"Millicent?" she said to you in a big bully voice. "How do you like our pride and joy?"

You looked up at her while you were stooping down for books from your locker floor. You mumbled something, probably "What?"

"Our pride and joy," Marilyn Monster continued. Others were beginning to pay attention. "Our prison."

You seemed to flinch and go whiter in the face than you already were, but you managed to get out "I don't know" and shrug.

"Oh, don't you? I thought you'd know. Don't you visit your father there?"

I don't know what you did then. Finally, I was so ashamed I turned away.

The author ties everything together with a summary explanation and analysis.

Your secret was out. You and your mother had come to stay in our small town while your father served his sentence in the state prison. You and your little hat and gloves and shiny shoes, dressed so neatly and carefully, with your manicured nails, turning in the best compositions with the best penmanship and the straightest margins, were trying so hard to look and be like anything but a convict's daughter.

You made us think. I doubt that any one of us had ever thought about the relatives of the prisoners in our town before you came, though they had probably always been among us...staying in our many tourist homes.

Her final comments effectively bring this painful experience to a close.

You weren't with us very long. Even after your secret was out, you were never a part of us. We let up on you, but we never let you in.

After a while you went away—I don't know where or when.

But it was just as well, Millicent, because you never had a chance.

Final Thoughts: Ms. Kerr's "phase autobiography" covers a span of six months, but she doesn't tell the reader everything that happened. The main part of her writing focuses on only two incidents—a phone conversation and a dramatic encounter in school. That was all she needed to say. The two incidents bring this phase to dramatic life for the reader. And the final remarks let us know what the writer learned from the experience. (Consider reading all of *Me Me Me Me Me* by M.E. Kerr.)

Writing About Experiences

Have you ever met someone famous? Have you ever fallen flat on your face at the worst possible moment? Have you ever been lucky enough to win something or unlucky enough to lose something that was important to you? These are the kinds of experiences that come easily to mind and are fun to share with friends. They are also subject matter for a very satisfying and enjoyable type of autobiographical writing—the personal experience or incident paper. (See the model on the next page.)

144   Selecting: *Choosing an Experience*

Selecting a subject for your writing should be no problem. You're looking for a memorable experience—something unforgettable that happened to you over a relatively short period of time. This experience might have taken only a few minutes, or, perhaps, it extended over a couple of hours or over the better part of a day. You should have little trouble thinking of something to write about. But if you do, try any one of the searching and selecting activities—perhaps free writing or listing—described in your handbook. (See 035 for help.)

Note: "Unforgettable" and "memorable" mean different things to different people, so don't worry about the magnitude of the experience you write about. Not everyone has bumped into Warren Beatty on the street, won an all-expense-paid trip to Hawaii, or jumped from a burning building.

145   Collecting and Connecting: *Writing to Learn*

Many of the important details about the experience should already be clear in your mind. What you need to do is put pen to paper and uncover the hidden details.

Note: Write your initial draft as if it were an instant version of the finished product to get a good feel for your subject.

Carefully read and review your writing when you finish the first draft. You might find some gaps in the story that need to be filled in or discover that some ideas you included aren't necessary. Then again, you might find that your writing lacks detail or a clear focus. Whatever the case may be, you now must shape your writing so that your readers can experience what you experienced.

Correcting: *Getting It Right*

Edit and proofread your paper carefully. Clean, smooth-reading copy tells your reader that you take care and pride in your writing. This doesn't mean that your paper has to be perfect. We all miss a few mistakes. But you should always correct your writing to the best of your ability.

Model Personal Experience Paper

In this model, a student recalls an unforgettable experience—a time when he collected autographs from players on his favorite baseball team.

The student writer starts right in the middle of the action.

There I stood in the parking lot at the New York Met's training camp. I just hoped that I could get some autographs. I had my baseball cards in one hand and a pen in the other. Then suddenly a van pulled up and parked in the area reserved for the players. Everyone looked toward the van. All of a sudden Gary Carter got out. He was one of my favorite players. I thought I would drop my cards. I walked over to him with my heart beating as fast as it could.

I said, "Could you please sign this?" I held out his card.

He said, "Sure, I'd be glad to."

The writer shares with his reader the thrill of meeting a famous baseball player.

I couldn't believe it. I was hoping for any autograph, but I got Gary Carter's, one of the best players in the majors. I ran over to my mom and dad to show it to them. They were really happy for me.

A couple of minutes later Darryl Strawberry drove up in a black Corvette. I ran over to him with his card in my hand, and he signed it. After that I got Dwight Gooden's too. I was speechless. I couldn't even say thank you. When I caught my breath, I asked a few more players for autographs. Once most of the players were dressed and ready to practice, I asked many of them to autograph my baseball.

In the conclusion, the writer puts his experience in perspective.

Now that I look back on this experience, I think I was pretty lucky. I ended up with an autograph from about every player on the team—either on a baseball card or my baseball. I guess you could say on that day the ball really bounced my way.

Final Thoughts: This writer was clearly motivated to tell his story well because he was writing about an experience that was important to him. When we write about what we know and care about, we have a good chance of writing well.

Shaping Your Experience Paper

How can you tell what to leave in and what to take out, what to emphasize and what to downplay? That depends on what you want your experience paper to do.

If you want to make your readers laugh, you'll have to surprise them. Make them expect one outcome but show them another. Keep surprising your reader by either playing scenes up or playing them down. Writing for laughs isn't so hard. Some words and sentences are like balloons, and others are like pins. And you know what happens when those two come together!

Helpful HINT

When you've written something really funny, let it be! You will spoil the humor if you overexplain. Sometimes, follow a hilarious scene with a less funny one. The contrast will show off the humor of the first scene and help you prepare your readers for the next funny part.

If you want to keep your readers in suspense, leave out anything that blows the ending. Instead, feed them clues about what might happen, and hold back the key details until near the end. In fact, in your prewriting, you might want to make a list of the important things you purposely don't want to say. Good writers sometimes give out false clues so that the real outcome is a shock. Try it. Make a mystery out of your personal story.

If you want to inform your readers, feed them the main ideas clearly and in the best possible order. Writer Donald Murray suggests organizing ideas according to the 2-3-1 format. *Two* represents the second most important point. *One* represents the most important point. Why should you save this point for last? It keeps your writing kicking long after it's been read.

Remember: How you shape your story depends on what you want your story to do.

Helpful HINT

To make your beginnings click, put half of your story behind you and half of it ahead of you. Start there—in the middle of things. When you are ready to bring your writing to an end, look at the world around you. Take a hint from what you see. Cars screech to a halt. A jet trail flattens out and drifts away. A roller skater drags a rubber knob. Bathtubs swirl for a while, then gurgle. Your ending . . .

Personal Writing Sampler   **149**

You have a lot of memories stored up in that mind of yours, most of which focus on you and your experiences. But you also have collected countless thoughts and feelings about other people, animals, places, events, and objects. Give these subjects some "playing time" in your personal writing as well.

Memories of People: Think of someone you knew very well (and maybe still know) and share a memorable story about this person. Focus on a specific experience or period of time in this person's life and share with your readers his or her story. Remember, this is someone else's story, so stay in the background in your writing. (See 068 for help.)

A Variation: In your writing, highlight mannerisms, actions, or likes and dislikes of your subject, and give us a special look at this person.

"Unpeopled" Memories: Think of a time when you were out of doors and all alone and write about your experience. Focus on the natural scene itself. Or think of an experience with a pet or another animal, and make this the focus of your writing.

Memories of Places: Focus on a place that stands out in your mind. This could be a favorite place, a place you never want to see again, or a place that has changed over the years. (See 069 for help.)

Memories of Events: Write about an event that you witnessed when you were younger. Maybe you remember a fire in your neighborhood, an argument, a display of kindness, a hilarious situation, or a shocking development. (See 072 for help.)

Memories of Objects: We all have had favorite objects that deserve to be praised and preserved in writing. And we all can remember objects we'd like to bury in our writing (maybe a wooden spoon). Or, perhaps you can recall some odd or unusual object in your home or neighborhood. The sky's the limit here. (See 070 for help.)

Memories of Family Life: Write about memorable events and incidents dealing with your immediate family. Who knows? This might lead to something big—perhaps being designated as family historian.

MINI-
lesson

A memory piece comes out of your own experience; a story comes out of your imagination. Here's a challenge. Try writing in the grey area where memory writing turns into fiction or, stated in another way, where fiction is made out of real-life experience. (See 237 for help.)

Subject Writing

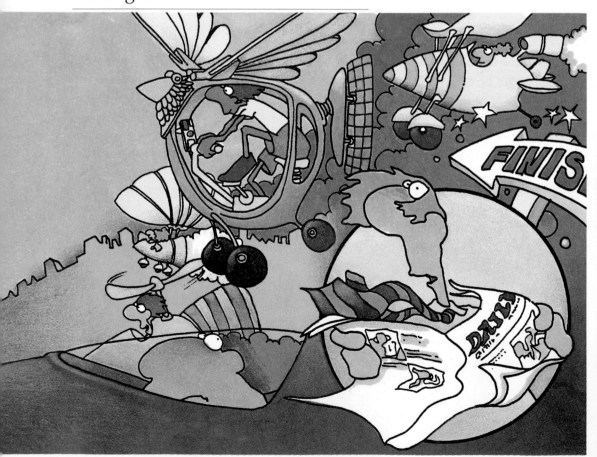

Writing Phase Biographies

I wish I had a hand-held 3-D Supersensory Biographical Single-Phase Translator. Then with a few twists of a knob I could tune in a picture of an interesting phase of someone else's life.

For example, I'd like to know

- when and why Abraham Lincoln decided to run for president,
- what life was like for your oldest living relative when he or she was your age, and
- all about an important period of change in the life of the most fascinating person you know.

Fortunately, I don't have to wait until 2001 A.D. for a 3-D SBSPT. You can invent one for me now by writing a "Phase Biography." But don't stop there. This section offers you encouragement and helpful guidelines to continue inventing.

What Is a Phase Biography?

151

A "phase bio" is a short, truthful story about an interesting or crucial period of somebody's life. It's something like the "phase autobiography," 133, except it's focused on somebody besides you. And memory won't be enough. You will need to do some poking around: maybe researching in books and magazines, maybe interviewing a person or others who knew that person, maybe tape-recording the interview. All that extra "legwork" will reward you with new insights and will make your biography one that you and your reader will appreciate.

Getting It Started

152

Look around. Your best subject might be very close at hand. Consider people in your life: friends at school, acquaintances of your parents, relatives. Some subjects may be more distant: ancestors, historical figures, famous people. You need to have a "nose" for interesting stories.

R.J. chose a friend of the family as the subject of his phase autobiography. His name is Armand and he's one of the best oil painters in the state of Michigan. More importantly, he is wise, powerful, and in love with nature in its unspoiled condition. He is more magnetic than anyone R.J. has ever met.

153 Investigating

First, R.J. **made note of his personal memories** of Armand. Next, he **asked** his parents what they knew about this man. As it turned out, they knew almost his whole life story. What fascinated R.J. most was a story about how, when Armand was only twelve years old, he used to hop trains and ride hundreds of miles away from home. That kindled R.J.'s curiosity and gave him specific **questions to ask:** Were you unhappy as a boy? What did you see on your travels? What was it like to hitchhike?

With so many questions to ask, R.J. could not wait to interview Armand himself. He called and got permission to come to the artist's studio, a converted chicken coop. Armand said he would be happy to let R.J. use a tape recorder. The boy and the older man spent quite a while talking pleasantly about whatever came to mind. At one point R.J. said, "Would it bother you if I turned on the tape recorder? What you're saying sounds important." "Not at all," said Armand. And they talked for nearly an hour and a half.

154 Putting It Together

R.J.'s interview left him excited about the biography he would write. Here's how it started:

> When Armand M., western Michigan's finest painter, was 12 years old, he was not sure then that he would become an artist. But he had a painful feeling that he was not fit to become anything else. The kids on the football field made him a blocker. That embarrassed him. Worse yet, he suffered from a childhood form of epilepsy, which doctors didn't understand. As he recalls, the family doctor told him he was just high-strung and needed some good hard work to straighten him out. But he remembers periods when he would black out. One time he woke up lying beside a railroad track, almost close enough to be run over. He had no idea how he got there. It wasn't long before he began to think of himself as a freak.
>
> His response to rejection and disapproval, he says, was to become a rebel. He began to look at the world around him with his own eyes and to draw what he saw. That habit, he says, never left him. It was at the heart of his growth as an artist . . .

Guidelines for Writing a Phase Biography

Here is a summary of useful ideas to consider and steps to take as you develop your own phase biography. The final form is up to you. It could be written as a basic story, but you could also try something more daring: a play, a TV news profile, or even a rap put to music.

Selecting: *Choosing a Subject*

▧ Take inventory of people you know or have heard about.

▧ Listen for stories people tell about others.

▧ Read biographical models such as you find in this book.

▧ List all of the potential subjects that come to your mind.

▧ Choose a subject that 1) you're truly interested in, 2) you think will interest others, 3) can be limited to a single "phase," and 4) you can find plenty of information about through reading, talking, and interviewing.

Collecting: *Gathering Your Thoughts*

▧ Jot down questions, facts, and bright ideas about your subject.

▧ Interview the subject if possible; otherwise, interview the person or persons who know the subject best. (See 405 for guidelines.)

▧ Read in books, newspapers, letters, old diaries, etc. to fill in background details.

▧ When you've collected more than enough information, reread it, and search through it for a "big idea" about a certain period of your subject's life. Make that idea the focus of your paper.

Connecting: *Writing and Revising*

▧ Figure out a way to begin that captures a little of the excitement you've found in your topic.

▧ Get a sense of what to show and what to tell to keep your subject interesting. Ordinarily, biographies are told chronologically, like stories. But you may wish to experiment and try a different approach.

▧ Write as many drafts as necessary to achieve your best ambition for the project. Add, cut, rearrange, and fine-tune your project for publication or performance.

Correcting: *Getting It Right*

▧ Use your *Write Source 2000* handbook to check all stylistic, grammatical, and mechanical details.

▧ Edit and proofread your work with extreme care. Do it with a partner if you can. You owe it to the subject of your biography to write his or her story effectively and accurately. (See 026 for help.)

Model Phase Biography

In *Extraordinary People: Understanding Savant Syndrome*, Dr. Darold A. Treffert describes what we know and don't know about the rare phenomenon called "savant syndrome," in which people who are mentally retarded can still perform miraculous feats of calculation, memory, or musical performance. Here is his introduction to an amazing musical genius called "Blind Tom." As you read, watch the comments along the left margin which explain some of the techniques the writer is using.

"Blind Tom"

Dr. Treffert frames the story with historical background facts.

The story of this memorable "idiotic musical genius" begins at a slave auction in Georgia in 1850 where his mother was sold as a slave by one Perry Oliver to a Colonel Bethune of a nearby county. Her fourteenth child was included in the sale "for nothing" because he was completely blind and was thought, therefore, to be useless and of no value. He was named Thomas Greene Bethune by his new master. On the colonel's Georgia plantation Blind Tom was allowed to roam the rooms of the mansion. Fascinated with sound of all types—rain on the roof, the grating of corn in the sheller, but most of all music—Tom would listen intensely to the colonel's daughters practicing their sonatas and minuets on the piano.

Dr. Treffert borrows information and quotes from different sources.

He would follow the music with his body movements. "Till 5 or 6 years old he could not speak, scarcely walk, and gave no other sign of intelligence than this everlasting thirst for music," notes his mother Sequin, "but at 4 years already, if taken out from the corner where he lay dejected, and seated at the piano, he would play beautiful tunes; his little hands having already taken possession of the keys, and his wonderful ear of any combination of notes they had once heard."

The author has begun by summarizing; now he highlights the moment of discovery with a brief story.

Late one night Colonel Bethune, who had no idea of the boy's talent, heard music coming from the drawing room in the darkened house. Thinking it must be one of his daughters playing, although that would be odd at such a late hour, he ventured downstairs and was startled to find the 4-year-old blind boy, so limited in other ways, playing a Mozart sonata—with flourish and without error. He had learned it by listening to one of the colonel's daughters, who had mastered it after weeks of practice. The colonel was astonished.

Model Biographical Report

This student writer decided to write about a distant ancestor. And it's no small wonder; the story she had to tell is a fascinating one.

Francis Ann Slocum

The opening questions draw readers into the report.

The writer provides introductory material.

I wonder if she knew what was going on or where they were taking her. She must have been scared. I wonder how they treated her and how she was able (at the age of five) to pick up their language so fast.

Francis Ann Slocum, my great-great-great-grandmother, was born in Rhode Island in the month of March in 1773. The next year her family moved to Pennsylvania. There, until she was five, she lived a happy childhood. But, on the second of November, in 1778, Delaware Indians raided her home during the absence of her father. The Indians didn't hurt anyone, but they seized Francis and carried her captive into the forest. She was lost to her relatives for 57 years.

The discovery of Francis Ann Slocum is recounted in great detail.

In January of 1835, a Colonel Ewing, who was a fur trader with Indians and understood their language, stopped at the house of a widow of the Chief of the Miami Indians. (The house was at the reservation in Miami City, Indiana.) Colonel Ewing became interested in the mistress of the house, whose features and whiteness of skin made him think she was not an Indian, though in all other ways she was a member of the tribe. Ewing later learned that she was born of white parents and that her father's name was Slocum. Colonel Ewing wrote a letter about her in 1835 saying that her husband was dead, that she was old, feeble, and did not have much longer to live. He sent the letter to a Lancaster, Pennsylvania, newspaper. Eventually the letter in the paper found its way to one of Francis' brothers, Joseph, who then went to see her. Talking through an interpreter he discovered that he had found his long-lost sister.

The book titles in the closing offer readers a way to learn more about this subject.

Francis spent so many happy years with the Indians that she refused to go back to her people. However, the family made several visits back to see her before she died at the age of seventy-four. Francis was buried in Wabash, Indiana, in a cemetery named after her, called the "Francis Ann Slocum Cemetery." There are two books written about her: *The Biography of Francis Ann Slocum* and also *The Lost Sister Among the Miamis.*

Biography Sampler

The feature editor is a gruff-looking veteran of the newspaper business. You enter his office for your first assignment. He looks up and says, "We need some stories about real people, interesting people, for our Sunday magazine. Get out there and see what you can come up with." That's it—no other guidelines or helpful hints. But don't worry. We've got you covered with the bio-writing forms described below. So go out there and see what you can find.

Oral History: Do you know an old woman with strong hands and a joyful, wise twinkle in her eye? Do you want to know how she got her twinkle? Ask her. Bring a tape recorder if she says that's okay. Have more questions to ask her, but let her tell you what she wants. Read about different periods in her life. Use your reading to help you give your interview shape when you write it up.

Bio-Poem: Here's a challenge: squeeze somebody's life into 11 fascinating lines. Make the first line the first name, the last line the last name. In between, make your character live and breathe. Here's one scheme: line 2, One key adjective; line 3, "Brother (or sister) of (fill in)"; line 4, "Lover of (name three things)"; line 5, "Who feels (three things)"; line 6, "Who needs (three things)"; line 7, "Who gives (three things)"; line 8, "Who fears (three things)"; line 9, "Who would like to see (three things)"; line 10, "Resident of (what city?)." But why use my idea? Whip up your own.

Chronicle: Write a story for your local newspaper about what some notable person did, either recently or far back in history. For example, maybe a local musician has recently joined a well-known rock band. Interview someone who knows him or her. Read about the person. Then choose an interesting angle and write a story which is both informative and entertaining.

Character Sketch

My Uncle John is normally a likeable and friendly man, but when there is a group of people and one of those instant cameras around, he becomes a real pest. No matter what the occasion, even something as uneventful as a few of our relatives getting together for a visit after work, Uncle John appoints himself photographer. He spends the whole time with one eye looking through the lens and the other scoping out the potential subjects . . .

Selecting: *Finding a Real Character*   **159**

A character sketch is a brief, colorful description based on a real person. It can exist by itself or as part of a longer piece of writing. As with all writing, the key to creating a good character sketch is selecting a good subject and bringing that subject to life. In this case, that means selecting an interesting character and giving life to both the outside (physical) and inside (personal) of the character. An "interesting" character can be anyone—a neighbor, teacher, friend, grandparent—anyone with a strong, strange, or appealing personality.

If you begin with the physical characteristics, you should include the appearance, the surroundings (including other people), and the background. By putting the person in a setting and establishing a personal history, you will create a more complete and interesting picture.

Collecting: *Gathering Details*   **160**

Don't overemphasize the physical characteristics of the person. Although it is important for your reader to "see" your subject, usually that means seeing the character inside as well as out. Consider the following:

Physical Characteristics
- What does he/she look like? Does she have any unusual characteristics? What does her face tell us about her personality?
- How does she walk? stand? sit? Does this person lean forward or backward when she sits? What does this tell us? Does she have any nervous habits?
- What is her speech like? Does she speak quickly? loudly? softly? only when spoken to? all the time?
- What kind of clothes, jewelry, makeup does she wear? What does this tell us about her? What about the way she wears her hair?

161 Personal Characteristics

■ Where is this character now? How can her surroundings add to the overall sketch?

■ What does she do for a living? How does she spend her spare time? How old is she? Does she have a nickname?

■ What about her background? Her family? What has she done in the past? What kind of education does she have? What does she plan to do in the future?

■ What kind of a person is she? What does she value most in life? Is she busy? relaxed? pleasant? thoughtful? intelligent? loyal? courageous? respected?

■ What kinds of thoughts are going on inside her head? Is she an emotional person? What does she believe in? What are her opinions on the important issues? How does she feel about life?

162 Connecting: *Bringing It All Together*

Once you have gathered all your details, you need to decide what they all add up to. You need to see your subject as a whole and then select those particular details which will help you re-create this single impression. Very often the impression you choose will be based on a strong characteristic, an incident, or a belief—one which will help your reader see "who this person really is." Here are some questions to get you started:

■ What do other people say about her? How do others react to her when she's around? Is she at all contradictory or changeable?

■ What seems to be a common thread or theme about this person that would tie her most important characteristics together? Who can you compare her to? Who is she not at all like? What is your overall impression of her?

163 *Getting It Down*

There is no right way or wrong way to go about writing a character sketch. Whatever works for you is the right way. What you must keep in mind, however, is the goal of this sketch: To present the reader with a single, sharp impression of your subject—and to support that impression with vivid details.

You might, for example, support your impression with a brief description which includes details about appearance, personality, lifestyle, values. You might then include an incident or two, showing your impression to be accurate. You could also describe "a typical day" in the life of your subject in which characters and dialogue are used to bring your subject to life. Or you might include your sketch in a short story.

Correcting: *Getting It Right*   164

As with all your writing, you will want to end up with a character sketch you can be proud to share with others. Proofread carefully. Listen as well as look. (*Remember:* For writing to be "right," it has to sound right as well as be technically correct.) Write or type neatly.

Sample Character Sketch   165

The sample below is a good example of a character sketch which brings the character to life. It is a good mixture of physical and personal details which let the reader see the subject inside and out.

> The old man grumbled a bit as he wiped his eye with the back of his gnarled hand. From his perch above the crowd, he watched. He glanced at his wife standing a short distance away. She too was old, but still he saw in her wrinkled face the pretty girl he had asked to share his life. As he watched her, his thoughts began to wander. He thought about the white and blue dishes on which she had so proudly served him his first "home cooked" meal. He seldom thought about such things, but at this moment they seemed very important to him. The chairs, the tables, the curtains, the things that had made the house seem more like a home, all somehow seemed very important to him.
>
> He watched as his wife turned and looked at the seemingly ancient saddles and bridles hanging on the back of one of the wagons. He followed her eyes and found himself thinking about their first team of horses and how hard they had worked together. He remembered the time he had taken the team to the County Fair horse pull, only to discover he didn't have the three-dollar fee needed to enter.
>
> The auctioneer's voice droned on. He shifted in the seat of his old John Deere. He patted the sweat-worn leather seat. John Deere had been a fine friend; now it would plow someone else's field. The things he had worked for all his life were being auctioned away, piece by piece. He could do nothing but watch. A half century of life and feelings went with each piece. The machinery, the furniture, the land were no longer his—but the farm and the home and the memories were his forever.

Observation Report

Do you want to make a spectator sport out of one of your writing assignments? You can if you write an observation report. In an observation report, you visit a location of interest, sit back, and take in all of the action. There's no need to ask questions of anybody and no need to get involved in any of the activity. You are there to observe and enjoy.

166 Selecting: *Choosing a Location*

What location should you choose for your observations? Why don't you try a local restaurant, a certain section of a park, a favorite spot in the woods, a convenience store, the school cafeteria, an airplane, etc. You get the picture. You're looking for an interesting place to put your mind, your eyes, and the rest of your senses to work.

167 Collecting: *Making Observations*

Take in as much of the setting as you can when you make your visit. Make note of the physical environment, the people, and animals (if there are any), and the nature of their activity. Keep track of what you observe by taking quick, but careful notes. Record as much as you can of the sights, the sounds, the smells, and the actions. And don't forget to record snippets of overheard conversations. (Some of you might want to use a "camcorder" for your collecting. It's fine by me, but check with your teacher first.)

> *"Somehow, if you really attend to the real, it tells you everything."*
> —**Robert Pollock**

168 Connecting: *Reporting on Your Observations*

The next step is to report on your observations. Two possible ways to develop your report are described below.

1. You can develop your report as a continuous flow of sights, sounds, and smells as they happened. This is sometimes called a sensory report. It is basically your field notes edited and developed just enough so your readers can appreciate your observations. It's pure descriptive writing. (See model on the next page.)

2. Or you can review your notes, decide on a main idea or focus for your writing, and develop your report accordingly. (Give your report some sight and sound by adding sensory details—perhaps the details you collected with a camcorder.)

Correcting: *Wrapping It Up*

Put the finishing touches on your report by checking for misplaced and misused words. Also, make sure that you "observe" the rules for spelling, punctuation, and grammar, and write or type a neat final copy of your report.

Model Observation Report

The model which follows records a writer's observations as they actually came to him, one after another. This type of report is sometimes called a sensory or saturation report. Take special note of all of the sensory detail the writer includes in his paper.

"Good Afternoon, Ladies and Gentlemen"

The writer first describes two passengers.

Safety belts are clicking all around with a sound like castanets. Up ahead all the middle seats are empty. One old man with a wide sunburned neck and grey curly hair wears a blue baseball cap with a red button at the peak. The blue visor has a red rim, green underneath. A woman comes on board, walks sideways down the center aisle studying the overhead compartments. She has black hair, china-white skin, and bright red lips.

Suddenly a warm soft voice comes from overhead: "Good afternoon, ladies and gentlemen. I'd like to welcome you aboard United flight 596, nonstop to Kansas City. We'll be underway in a few minutes. We hope you enjoy your flight."

Here, the writer picks up on some sounds and smells.

In the background, behind his voice, I hear the sounds of the cockpit. I smell jet fuel and feel rumbles under the floor. The whole plane quivers. A woman's voice comes on, not talking to the passengers: "Prepare doors."

A stewardess up front is fanning herself with one of the safety cards we have in the seat pockets before us. A bell quietly goes "boing." Now there are about six kinds of whines going on all at once, some steady like motors, some that would probably make a dog look around puzzled.

I feel hot, sweat trickles under my shirt; the nozzle overhead blows hot gasoliney air on my head. The stewardess reads over the intercom about slides that will self-inflate and aisle lights that will go automatically on. She acts out her words.

The writer makes a variety of sensory observations just prior to takeoff.

Some people reach up and try to turn the little nozzle to get cool air but get only more hot wind, judging from their gestures. The plane begins to rock and rumble and roll backwards. The flight attendant tells us to sit back, relax, and enjoy our flight to Kansas City, so I try.

Writing the News Story

For the second time this year, Waller Middle School and its students have been the victims of an overnight burglary. The school has lost another $2,000 worth of computer equipment—the students have lost the use of their Apple IIGS computer , a color monitor, a printer, two disk drives . . .

171 Off with a Bang

Like the short sample above, the news story should begin with a bang—or at least a pop. It must first have an attention-getting **headline** and a strong opening or **lead** which attract the reader and send a story on its way. The news story picks up momentum in the **body** with supporting and background details which answer questions readers will have after reading the lead. These details, however, lose their power and importance as the story continues. By the time a news story ends, the details have little impact. Only when a story is of great news value or very complicated will details near the end be important to a reader.

172 Selecting: *What to Look For*

As a news writer, you must always keep your eyes and ears open. You must look and listen for important news. A writer spots a potential story mainly by judging its **news value**. News has value when it exhibits at least one of the following traits:

- **Impact:** News has impact when it makes a difference in the lives of the readers. For example, new rules about talking during lunch or an increase in the price of admission at the local theater would have impact because each would make a difference to middle school readers.

- **Timeliness:** News is timely when it is current and new. A news story lives a short life, however.

- **Closeness:** News which is local has news value. Readers are usually interested in people and events connected to their own schools, neighborhoods, cities, and states.

- **Human Interest:** News which is touching, stirring, or otherwise interesting has "news value." For example, a janitor retiring after 30 years in a school would have news value because it would touch most readers.

Collecting: *Who, What, When, Where, Why, How?*

Like most news writers, once you have a story of news value, you should concentrate on the **lead** or opening to set the story in motion. The lead usually summarizes the main points of a news story in one or two sentences. News writers often develop the lead by asking themselves the five W's and H—*who, what, when, where, why,* and *how*—of a story. They then put the answers to these questions—at least the questions which are important—in the opening sentence(s) of the story.

Once a lead has been formed, a news writer must decide what additional facts and details must be collected to answer any important questions a reader might have after reading the headline and the lead paragraph. You probably won't know everything you need to know when you start writing your story so be prepared to do some background research and interviewing. (See "Interviewing," 405-407.)

Connecting: *Bring It Together*

If you have gathered plenty of good details, connecting them in a first draft should be easy. Begin with the lead and follow with the facts and details you feel are necessary to the story. Write freely at this point, and don't be afraid to move, add, or take out detail. News sentences and paragraphs are typically short and direct; paragraphs seldom contain more than three sentences. Each new paragraph should *not* depend on the following paragraph for explanation. A story can then end after any paragraph.

✏ NEWSWRITING TIP

The facts in a news story must be clearly stated. Make sure it is clear *who did what to whom, when things happened, and in what sequence they happened*. The facts in a news story must be accurately stated as well. Readers will not appreciate mistakes in times and dates, and people will not appreciate being misquoted. Always double-check facts before you turn in a story.

Since news is information, a news story must contain a lot of detail. Include descriptions of people and places and exact figures (final scores, total amounts, estimates, etc.). Remember to get complete names, addresses, and grade level or age of the people involved in a news story.

A news story must be presented without any favoritism. Let the facts speak for themselves. Finally, most news stories rely on good quotes. Alternate direct quotes (a source's exact words) with indirect quotes. Use direct quotes for colorful or memorable words.

175 Collecting and Correcting: *Shaping the Writing*

Begin your editing with a general reading. Make sure that the story flows smoothly and that the sentences are clear and direct. Then check for any missing information and information that might be misleading or misplaced. Also, double-check names, facts, dates, and spellings. A news writer must present clear and accurate information.

Carefully reread the lead as well. Will it grab the reader's attention? You should also write a headline for your story at this point, mainly as a test of your story's substance. If you have difficulty forming a headline, your story might lack a clear main idea.

Finally, check for errors in word choice, mechanics, and spelling. A news story that is clean or free of careless errors reflects favorably on you and on your newspaper.

176 Sample News Story

Statement Headline

Apple IIGS computer stolen

Byline *by Jamie Siegrist*

Lead Paragraph An Apple IIGS computer and its color monitor, two disk drives, and a printer were stolen from the Learning Resource Center early Tuesday morning, according to Rob Robinson, director of the center.

Robinson said the equipment was worth $2,000. He added that the center received it only a month ago.

Explanation and Amplification Software and manuals for the equipment were also taken from the LRC circulation desk, leading investigators to believe that the person who stole it knew the computer center fairly well. Robinson said police are investigating, but to his knowledge there are no suspects yet.

"Students would be the last people I would suspect because they are more trustable than the average person, and they have the most to lose if caught," said Robinson.

Background Information There are no signs of entry, but it is suspected that someone may have hidden in the center until after it was locked up. It is also possible that someone made a key, according to Robinson. He said a better security system is being discussed.

Earlier this year, six VCRs were stolen from the A-V room adjacent to the computer center, but the VCRs in the center were untouched, so it was thought that the center was safe. After that theft, locks in the A-V room were changed.

Feature Writing Sampler

A feature story is meant to entertain and inform. If often covers an interesting angle of a straight news story. For example, a feature might describe a particular scene, present a memorable character, or communicate a particular mood. Let's say a straight news story during a basketball tournament summarizes a particular game. A feature story might highlight the reactions of a certain spectator or describe the "action" around the concession stand during the game.

News Feature: A *news feature* is based on a current news story. It often provides related background information. For example, suppose a news story announces the schedule of events for the Annual Fun Night. A news feature might highlight the difficulties the committee had in deciding which games and activities to offer.

Informative Feature: An *informative feature* presents an interesting and appealing story not necessarily related to a timely news story. It is based on a news writer's interviews, observations, and reading. For example, suppose you were interested in architecture. You might research school architecture and develop an informative feature which proposes the ideal layout for a middle school or high school.

Historical Feature: A *historical feature* is often the result of a timely news story. For example, suppose a news story reports on the track team's first conference championship in 25 years. A historical feature might review that championship track team of 25 years ago.

Personality Story: A *personality story* presents a story about an individual who would be interesting or appealing to readers. For example, a day-in-the-life story of a local high school freshman would be interesting to middle school readers.

Firsthand Account: A *firsthand account* develops from the writer's personal experiences. For example, a writer might re-create his or her experience in an accident or special event.

Helpful HINT

The next time you are assigned a report, write it as a feature article designed for a popular magazine or newspaper. (Now make sure you get your teacher's approval before you go ahead with this.) Here are some things to remember before you get started: 1) Readers expect to learn something. 2) They expect an interesting angle or approach to the story. 3) They also like to hear about your firsthand experiences and conversations so that they know you are truly interested in the topic yourself.

Writing an Editorial

When Mrs. Martin asked each of us to present a short editorial, my first thought was, "I don't really have a strong opinion about anything the rest of the class wants to hear about." I mean, how many of you enjoy listening to other people—like me—give their opinions? Wouldn't you rather be watching MTV or listening to your favorite radio station? I know I would. And I guess that's my point. Today's students are not . . .

178 Why Write an Editorial?

An editorial is a short persuasive essay which usually contains the writer's opinion or reaction to a timely news story or event. Its primary purpose is to influence readers to think or act the same way the writer does. But, not all editorials take sides. There are four other purposes:

- **Inform:** Some editorials inform like straight news stories. Usually informative editorials deal with complicated issues which require careful explanation. (The effects of budget cuts on certain school programs might be the subject of an informative editorial.)
- **Promote:** Some editorials promote worthy activities. (The formation of a school soccer team might be promoted in an editorial.)
- **Praise:** Some editorials commend or praise worthy individuals or events. (The individuals who helped set up a teen center might be praised in an editorial.)
- **Entertain:** And some simply encourage or entertain their readers. (A serious or satiric what-to-do-in-our-town idea might be developed in an editorial.)

179 Selecting: *Choosing an Issue*

Choose a timely subject for your editorial, and make sure it is a subject that is of real interest to you and to most of your audience. Do whatever free writing is necessary to get your thoughts and feelings down. Then come up with a plan for putting your editorial together.

One way to start your editorial is with a clear statement of what you are trying to prove in your writing. Put your statement in positive terms. ("The student council should represent the entire student body" rather than "The student council does *not* represent the entire student body.") Or you might begin with a surprising statement, a quotation, a brief story, or any other interesting opening.

Collecting: *Gathering Support*

To convince others to believe as you do, you will need good supporting details. Gather as many details as possible using the questions which follow as a guide:

- What facts or evidence will support the case you're making? If you don't have this evidence now, where can you find it?
- Can you get statements from written sources or from authorities that will support your main point?
- Can you use comparisons to similar situations to support your argument?
- Is there a particular image or picture that you can use to strengthen your argument?
- Can you effectively answer the arguments on the other side (opposing viewpoints)?

Connecting: *Writing the First Draft*

The body of an editorial should develop logically with clear and accurate details and examples. Present your strongest arguments *first* and *last*. Give credit to any opposing viewpoints early, and point out the weaknesses in each. Offer a solution or suggest an action in your conclusion. Maintain a positive tone of voice throughout: too much emotion, sermonizing, or name calling will weaken your argument.

Correcting: *Getting It Right*

An editorial should be as appealing, clear, and forceful as you can make it. Use the checklist which follows to help you revise and edit:

- Write about issues. Your editorial should not be a character attack. Also, whenever possible, *praise* rather than criticize.
- Let the facts speak for themselves. Avoid preaching.
- Keep paragraphs brief and direct. A few effective examples or illustrations in an editorial are far more effective than a ton of details and statistics.
- Consider the timing and importance of the story. Don't write about old news or news that is not important to a large number of readers.
- Evaluate the clarity and directness of your ideas. Honesty and accuracy are absolute necessities.
- Keep the language in your editorial simple and direct. Don't try to "impress" your reader with your extensive vocabulary.
- Don't become too dramatic. Readers appreciate tasteful humor or wit on the editorial page.

183 Sample Student Editorial

The following editorial was written in response to a letter someone had written to a local newspaper. It takes a rather dry topic—the metric system—and turns it into an interesting, well-supported editorial.

A personal experience is used to begin the editorial.

Last week I read a letter to the editor in the <u>Casper Sentinel</u>. What I read was not surprising, but it was upsetting just the same. The man who wrote the letter had just returned from a fishing trip to Canada and was complaining to the whole world about how difficult it was to figure out the metric system.

The "other side" of the issue is covered.

He complained that he didn't know how much soda he got each time he bought a can. He also couldn't figure out the speed signs and how fast he was supposed to be going as he traveled from place to place. He couldn't even figure out how big his fish had to be before he could keep them. I'm surprised he found his way back home. His point, as summarized in his last two sentences, was this: "Leave things lay. We do not need the metric system in the U.S."

Examples are given of where the metric system is used.

I couldn't help but wonder whether this whole letter might have been a joke, someone pulling our leg. But then I realized this man's attitude was real and not much different from many other Americans', especially older Americans. Many of them simply do not understand the importance of having a universal system of measurement. Scientists and doctors adopted the metric system long ago, realizing how difficult and dangerous it would be to try to work with two systems of measurement in their professions. Pilots who fly from one nation to another also know its importance in keeping distance and speed measurements from causing a disaster.

Reasons for a change are offered.

But most Americans don't seem to catch on. While the rest of the world is learning English as a second language to help world communications, we remain one of only two nations not committed to the metric system. Instead, we cling stubbornly to a ridiculous, jumbled system based on the distance from some king's nose to his outstretched thumb and the average shoe size of the first 12 people to walk out of church one Sunday morning. We cling to a system that gives us fractions, remainders, mixed numbers, and a second set of wrenches for our bikes. Talk about confusing!

The editorial ends on a positive note.

The metric system is important to improved relations and clear communication throughout the world. It's time the United States does its part and joins the rest of the world. Then maybe we can once again lead, by good example, in other important areas as well.

Writing a Summary

The best test of how well you understand something you've read is whether you can tell or write an accurate summary of the important ideas in your own words. Being able to write summaries can greatly increase your ability to understand and remember what you have read.

To write a good summary, you must select only the most important ideas and combine them into clear, concise sentences. In most cases your summary should be no more than one-third as long as the original. Follow the guidelines below the next time you need to write a summary of something you have read.

Guidelines for Writing a Summary

184

- **Skim** the selection first to get the overall meaning.
- **Read** the selection carefully, paying particular attention to key words and phrases. (Check the meaning of any words with which you are unfamiliar.)
- **List** the main ideas on your paper—without looking at the selection!
- **Review** the selection a final time so that you have the overall meaning clearly in mind as you begin to write.
- **Write** a summary of the major ideas, using your own words except for those "few" words in the original which cannot be changed. Keep the following points in mind as you write:
    - ❏ Your opening (topic) sentence should be a clear statement of the main idea of the original selection.
    - ❏ Stick to the essential information—*names, dates, times, places,* and similar facts are usually essential; examples, descriptive details, and adjectives are usually not.
    - ❏ Try to state each important idea in one clear sentence.
    - ❏ Arrange your ideas into the most logical order.
    - ❏ Use a concluding sentence which ties all of your points together and brings your summary to an effective end.
- **Check** your summary for accuracy and conciseness by asking yourself the following questions:
    - ❏ Have I included all the main ideas?
    - ❏ Have I cut or combined the supporting details?
    - ❏ Could another person get the main idea of the selection by simply reading my summary?

185

Original

"Acid rain" is precipitation with a high concentration of acids. The acids are produced by sulfur dioxide, nitrogen oxide, and other chemicals which are created by the burning of fossil fuels. Acid rain is known to have a gradual, destructive effect on plant and aquatic life.

The greatest harm from acid rain is caused by sulfur dioxide, a gas produced by the burning of coal. As coal is burned in large industrial and power plant boilers, the sulfur it contains is turned into sulfur dioxide. This invisible gas is funneled up tall smokestacks and released into the atmosphere some 350-600 feet above the ground. As a result, the effects of the gas are seldom felt immediately. Instead, the gas is carried by the wind for hundreds and sometimes thousands of miles before it floats back down to earth. For example, sulfur dioxide produced in Pennsylvania at noon on Monday may not show up again until early Tuesday when it settles into the lakes and soil of rural Wisconsin.

Adding to the problem is the good possibility that the sulfur dioxide has undergone a chemical change while in flight. By simply taking on another molecule of oxygen, the sulfur dioxide could be changed to sulfur trioxide. Sulfur trioxide, when mixed with water, creates sulfuric acid—a highly toxic acid. If the sulfur trioxide enters a lake or stream, the resulting acid can kill fish, algae, and plankton. This, in turn, can interrupt the reproductive cycle of other life-forms, causing a serious imbalance in nature. If the sulfuric acid enters the soil, it can work on metals such as aluminum and mercury and set them free to poison both the soil and water.

Damage from acid rain has been recorded throughout the world, from the Black Forest in Germany to the lakes in Sweden to the sugar maple groves in Ontario, Canada. The result is a growing concern among scientists and the general public about the increasing damage being done to the environment by acid rain.

186

Summary

"Acid rain," the term for precipitation which contains a high concentration of harmful chemicals, is gradually damaging our environment. The greatest harm from acid rain is caused by sulfur dioxide, a gas produced from the burning of coal. This gas, which is released into the atmosphere by industries using coal-fired boilers, is carried by the wind for hundreds of miles. By the time this gas has floated back to earth, it has often changed from sulfur dioxide to sulfur trioxide. Sulfur trioxide, when mixed with water, forms sulfuric acid—a highly toxic acid. This acid can kill both plant and aquatic life and upset the natural balance so important to the cycle of life.

The Book Review

A book review is a special type of writing. In a book review, you state your reaction or your opinion about a book (or part of a book) you have read. You then support that opinion with specific facts and details taken from the book. The subject for a book review usually comes from one or more of the four main parts of a book—the *plot*, the *characters*, the *setting*, or the *theme*.

Reading and Understanding Your Book

187

To write a good book review, you need to read a book very carefully. And, you will need to reread those parts of the book you plan to use in your review. Also, you will need to know what kind of book you are reading—modern romance novel, historical novel, science fiction, biography, and so on. It would be wrong to criticize a biography because it lacks action and suspense. A biographer attempts to write about the life of an important person in a special way, a way that helps the reader understand that person better. A biographer isn't trying to write an action-packed story.

Selecting: *Choosing a Topic*

188

Also keep in mind that a review is a type of persuasive writing, writing which includes an opinion supported by facts and details; therefore, you must select an idea which is a statement of opinion for your review.

Helpful HINT   Use the list of ideas on the next page to help you choose a specific subject for your review. If you are asked to write a one-paragraph review, begin by choosing one of the basic parts of a story (*plot, characters, theme,* or *setting*) to write about. If you are assigned a longer book review, choose related ideas (*theme* and *character*, for example, or two strong characters).

189 Finding an Idea for Your Review

Plot (The action of the story)

- The story includes *a number (2, 3, 4 . . .)* of suspenseful and surprising events.
- The story includes *some/many* predictable events.
- Certain parts of the story are *confusing/hard to believe*.
- The climax (the most important event) changes the story *in an interesting way . . . in a believable way . . . in an unbelievable way*.
- There are *a number (2, 3, 4 . . .)* of important events which lead to the outcome or ending of the story.
- The ending is *surprising . . . predictable . . . unbelievable*.

Characters (The people—and sometimes animals—in the story)

- The main character changes from _____ to _____ by the end of the story.
- Certain forces or circumstances—people, setting, events, or ideas—make the main character or characters act as they do.
- A certain character acts *believably/unbelievably* when . . . .
- _____ is the main character's outstanding personality trait. (You may choose to point out more than one outstanding trait.)
- The main character does the right thing when . . . .
- I can identify with the main character when . . . .

Setting (The time and place of the story)

- The setting helps make the story exciting.
- The setting has an important effect on the main character.
- The setting (in a historical novel) increased my knowledge of a certain time in history.
- The setting (in a science fiction novel) creates a new and exciting world.
- The setting in this book offers nothing new and exciting.
- The setting could have played a more important role in this story.

Theme (The author's statement or lesson about life)

- *Ambition . . . courage . . . greed . . . happiness . . . jealousy . . .* is clearly a theme in (title of book).
- The moral, "Don't judge a book by its cover" . . . "Haste makes waste" . . . "Hard work pays off," is developed in (title of book).
- This book showed me what it is like to be . . . .

Model Book Review

The following is a model plan and book review paragraph about *Tom Sawyer*, a novel by Mark Twain. The writer decided that the novel's main character, Tom Sawyer, has a very adventurous spirit, and he used this important personality trait as the subject of his review. Four specific events from the book were used to support the writer's opinion or belief.

Plan

Topic Sentence: *Tom Sawyer's adventurous spirit makes his boyhood exciting and, at times, very dangerous.*

The following events show (display) this trait:

- Tom sneaks out of his house at midnight to join Huck Finn in a graveyard.
- Tom, along with Huck and another friend, runs away to be a pirate.
- Tom looks for hidden treasure.
- Tom reenters the same cave where he and Becky Thatcher almost lost their lives.

One-Paragraph Book Review

Tom Sawyer's adventurous spirit makes his boyhood exciting and, at times, very dangerous. One thing Tom likes to do is prowl around the town at all hours of the night. One night Tom sneaks out of his house at midnight and joins his friend Huckleberry Finn in the town's graveyard. Here, the boys witness Injun Joe killing the town doctor and are very nearly caught by the killer. Tom also likes to read adventure stories and imagine himself as a daring adventurer. At one point in the story, he decides to run away and become an adventurous pirate. He convinces Huckleberry and another friend to join him, and the newly formed band of pirates is off to Jackson Island. Another one of Tom's favorite pastimes is looking for hidden treasure. Once, while searching an old, abandoned shack, Tom and Huck find a hidden treasure belonging to Injun Joe, a dangerous criminal. At the end of the story, Tom reenters the cave where he and Becky Thatcher almost lost their lives once. Tom knows that Injun Joe has moved his treasure from the shack to the cave, and he can't resist going after it. His need for adventure and excitement gets Tom Sawyer into plenty of tight spots.

Opening episode grabs reader's attention

Imagine you've just been assigned the task of finding a treasure chest filled with pearls, precious gems, gold, and diamonds. But along the way, you have to dodge poisonous darts, worry about being shot at, and have a knife point stuck at your throat till you feel the sweat trickle down your spine. These are not once in a lifetime situations. Your life is constantly in danger—yet, all the while you have to keep your cool and make rational deductions.

Title and author are worked in naturally

Well, that's what Sherlock Holmes and his good buddy, Dr. Watson, have to do in The Sign of Four by Sir Arthur Conan Doyle.

Overall idea and plot are discussed

In this story, Holmes and Watson are hired by Miss Morstan to recover a treasure chest that used to belong to her father. Seven years ago, her father mysteriously disappeared overnight. Equally mysterious is Miss Morstan's receiving an extremely valuable pearl each year since her father's disappearance—and on the very date of her father's disappearance.

Comparison is made to a modern hero

All Sherlock Holmes books contain several adventures and The Sign of Four is no exception. One incident in the story was an action-packed boat chase. What happened was this: Sherlock Holmes knew that Jonathan Small, a vicious, money-hungry, peg-legged thief, had the treasure on board the steamboat "Auroa." As Holmes, Watson, and a police officer were chasing the "Auroa" in a police boat, Jonathan Small's partner, Tonga, a small, primitive savage, fired his blow gun at Dr. Watson and Sherlock Holmes. At the same time, Watson and Holmes fired their pistols at Tonga. Tonga's poison-tipped dart whizzed past Holmes' right ear, missing its target by a mere millimeter. Tonga missed, but Holmes and Watson didn't.

An opinion is given of the book and the author's style

As Tonga's body began to sink slowly into the Thames River, Jonathan Small threw over the treasure, one piece at a time, making it virtually impossible to retrieve.

An "inviting" ending is used

If you enjoy a mystery with a dash of high-risk adventure; if you'd enjoy an intellectual Indiana Jones who really gets you involved in trying to solve the mystery; if you enjoy your mysteries with a touch of humor sprinkled in by a fat, bumbling sidekick; then you'll love The Sign of Four.

Writing Letters

How would you like to receive 900,000 letters? Hank Aaron, the famous baseball player, received that many letters in 1974, the year he surpassed Babe Ruth's home run record. What did most of them say? Did he answer them? Why don't you write and ask him? There's a pretty good chance that he or someone on his staff will actually answer your letter.

Or what about writing to your favorite rock star or author, or your senator or congressman, or the president! The fact is, letter writing allows you to tear down the walls of your classroom and communicate with almost anyone in the world.

Why Bother?

If you are one of those who thinks letter writing is old-fashioned, time-consuming, dull work with little or no reward, you're not alone! Many students your age share this opinion, but those who have tried it will tell you that writing letters can truly be an adventure—you never know for sure what you'll get back. Here are some journal entries from students, like you, who decided to explore letter writing.

"I'm still waiting for my letter from U2. Why is it taking so long? Other kids have already heard back from the people they wrote to."

"I got a letter from my favorite author, Judy Blume. I show it to everyone. Lots of my friends think it's pretty neat. She thanked me for the letter and said she's glad I like her books. She also told me to keep writing, and someday . . . who knows, maybe I'll be getting letters from kids in school. She also sent me a list of student magazines where I could send my stories. So that's what I'm going to do. I'll probably never get one published, but . . . who knows?"

"When I did my report on whales, you [the teacher] suggested I write some letters to get information. I didn't like the idea at first, but I wrote anyhow, and now I may actually get a chance to see whales. You see, when I wrote to one of those places, they sent back a list of places that had special camps for kids interested in marine life, and I may get to go there this summer. Even if I don't go, I still have lots of information about whales."

193 Writing Letters to People You Do Not Know

Now, before you go wandering off looking for the president's address, there are a couple things you should know about writing to "people you do not know." First of all, many of these people get a great deal of mail each day. If you want them to read and respond to yours, it will have to be both clear and creative. Secondly, finding the president's address is easy; finding the address of your favorite rock star may not be. Without an address, your letter will get nowhere fast. (Ask your teacher or librarian for help.)

Many students start by writing to their favorite rock groups, actors, or athletes. The body of these first letters often goes something like this:

> *"You are my favorite drummer. I love your songs. Are you married? Where do you buy your clothes? Will you be performing in my area soon? How much will tickets cost and where can I get them? All of us think you're the greatest! Love . . . ."*

Although there is nothing "wrong" with this letter—it is, after all, honest and sincere—you could make it even better. How? First of all, try going beyond the typical "I really like your . . ." message. You should have a specific reason or purpose in writing, one which will set your letter apart from the others and give that person a reason to write back.

Helpful
HINT

If you can't think of a specific purpose or focus, do some research. Find out what "causes" this person may be involved in . . . something about his or her family or hometown . . . favorite pastimes and entertainers. Ask about your celebrity's background or training, views on world problems, anything that would help set your letter apart from all the others.

194 Guidelines for Writing "Fan" Letters

- Keep letters short and to the point.
- Use short, everyday words, but avoid overusing slang.
- Address the people you write to by their correct, official titles.
- Be specific when you offer compliments; show that you are a true "fan."
- Ask for a return letter and be sure to include your name and address (or a self-addressed stamped envelope if you request something specific).
- Answer these four questions when revising: Why did I write this letter? What is my purpose or focus? What facts, questions, or information have I included to support my reason for writing? Have I made it clear what I would like the reader to do?

Model "Fan" Letter

The letter which follows is a good example of a letter with a purpose— a letter which is clear, creative, and quite likely to get a response.

It is usually best to follow the form for a business letter when writing to someone you don't know. Notice the arrangement below and also see 203 for more information.

Heading

38391 Forest Drive
Madison, WI 53165
March 15, 1990

Inside Address

Mr. Paul Newman
711 Fifth Avenue
New York, NY 10022

Salutation

Dear Mr. Newman:

Body

I am writing to let you know how much I appreciate what you are doing for children. I read the article in <u>Life</u> magazine about the camp you have set up for them. I hope someday to work at a camp like yours during my summer vacations, but I'm only 13 at this time.

I know you also donate all the money from the sales of your salad dressing and spaghetti sauce to help feed hungry people. My mother always buys your products because of this and because she likes the humor: "Industrial Strength" and "Fine Foods Since February."

Why do you have such a big interest in hungry people? I am also concerned about children who do not have enough to eat. I am gathering information about the hungry people in our country for a classroom report, so I would appreciate receiving a letter from you that answers my questions. I know that this would get my classmates interested, too.

Thank you for helping take care of people. I wish more rich people would follow your example. If I am ever rich, I will remember there are needy people just as you have.

Closing

Sincerely,

Signature

Salli Laztellini
Salli Laztellini

The Friendly Letter

We all enjoy receiving cards and letters from friends and relatives, especially from those special people who have moved or live far away. Letters from friends may make a friendship stronger or renew an old friendship. Letters from relatives draw you closer to the many people who are related to you. So go ahead and give the people in your life a reason to write—a letter from you.

196 Form of a Friendly Letter

There are five basic parts in a standard friendly letter: the **heading**, the **salutation**, the **body**, the **closing**, and the **signature**. Your letter does not have to include all of these parts, especially in a friendly letter to a very close friend or relative.

However, in a friendly letter to someone you don't know very well, it is best to follow the standard form for a friendly letter. Given below is an explanation of the five parts of a standard friendly letter.

- The **heading** includes your address and the date. The heading is located in the upper right-hand corner of the letter.

- The **salutation** or greeting begins with the word *Dear* and is followed by the name of the person who will receive the letter. A comma is placed after the name. Write the salutation at the left-hand margin, two lines below the heading.

  > ***Dear Janet, Dear Grandma, Dear Uncle Eric,***
  > ***Dear Mr. Smith, Dear Miss Jones, Dear Dr. Long,***

- The **body** is the main part of the friendly letter in which you present (write) your information and ideas. Usually, the paragraphs in the body are fairly short for easy reading. Skip one line after the salutation before you begin the body. Also, you should skip one line between paragraphs.

- The **closing** is written two lines below the body of your letter. It begins just to the right of the middle of the letter. Only the first word is capitalized. The closing is followed by a comma.

  > ***Your friend, Sincerely, With love,***

- The **signature** is the final part of a friendly letter. It is written beneath the closing. Usually, you will just write your first name. Include your last name if you think there will be a question as to which Bob, Sue, John, or Julie you are.

Model Friendly Letter   197

2525 First Street   **Heading**
Muskego, WI 53150
November 12, 2000

Salutation   Dear Scott,

How have you been doing in the warm tropics? I know you are probably swimming in your pool and in the ocean. We're not so lucky back here. The last remaining leaves have just blown off the trees. On Monday we had the first trace of snow on the ground. It was so cold we nearly froze to death at the bus stop.

This month in school we're going to have a parent/kid exchange day. That means the parents are going to go to school instead of us. My mom said she would go while I stay home and watch all of the soaps. Are you doing something **Body**   like that in your school?

School has been going pretty well since my violin was hit by the bus. It was "totalled." I've been kind of lucky in school, though, because I haven't had a whole lot of home-work. My favorite class is math because I have a really nice teacher. Her name is Miss Johnson. Did Ray ever have her for math?

I haven't been doing too much since we've talked. In December I will be playing at the Domes with my school orchestra. We will be playing a whole mess of Christmas songs.

The reason I'm writing is because we have to write a friendly letter in my English class. My teacher says that we have been writing our letters the wrong way, and this is the right way. I hope. That is the reason why my letter is so different from the last one. I hope I get a good grade. Please write back soon!

Your best friend,

Closing

Mike

Signature

Writing a Friendly Letter

198 **Selecting:** *Choosing a Subject*

Write to someone who deserves a letter: a person you haven't written to in a long time, a person who has already written to you, or a special person you want to "talk to" personally in a letter.

199 **Collecting:** *Gathering Details*

Make a list of all of the main ideas you want to include in your letter. Gather all the details you will need to make each of these ideas clear and entertaining. Then decide the order in which these ideas will appear.

If this is a return letter, reread the letter you received. Make sure to answer any questions and think of one or two creative or "surprise" sections to make your letter more than just answers to the questions.

- Share a good joke or story.
- Re-create a conversation or write a poem.
- Describe a memorable day (hour by hour, etc.).
- Include a sketch, cartoon, photograph, or newspaper article.
- Start a story which your friend will continue or complete.

200 **Connecting:** *Writing the First Draft*

Write your first draft freely and naturally. Write as if you were face-to-face with your friend or relative, sharing stories and information. Be sure you cover all the main ideas you listed as you planned your letter.

 Helpful HINT If you haven't done much letter writing, or if you're writing to someone you don't know that well, the guidelines which follow will help:

- Start your letter in a way which gets your reader interested in your letter. Don't start by saying you don't really have much to say.
- Write in a style which will interest your reader. Don't say something like "School is okay this year," unless you add something to it such as "School is okay this year, but . . . ."
- Your reader will want to know what is going on in your life, so don't ask too many questions of him or her.
- If this is a return letter, answer any questions clearly. Repeat part of a question so that your reader will know what you are writing about: "You asked how Carol is doing in school this year."
- What you say in your letter has a lot to say about you, so avoid gossiping or saying something you'll later regret.
- End your letter in a positive way and ask for a return letter.

Revising Your Letter

Make sure that your letter is easy to read. This means your sentences should read smoothly; your paragraphs should be fairly short and each should develop one main idea. Include enough facts and details so your ideas are clear and entertaining.

Correcting: *Getting It Right*

Check your letter for spelling, capitalization, punctuation, and usage errors. (Your handbook can help.) Check the form of your friendly letter. It is especially important that your letter follow the standard form when you are writing to someone who is not a close friend or relative. A letter correctly written will make a good first impression.

Neatly write or type the final copy. Center your letter on the page, and keep your margins as equal as possible. Use at least one-inch margins on all sides. Address the envelope neatly and correctly, and make sure you fold your letter so that it fits into the envelope. (See 216.)

The Social Note

A special type of friendly letter is the social note. In a social note you don't share stories and information. Instead, you share a very short social message. This message may be an invitation or a reply to an invitation. A social note may also be a thank-you note for a gift or for someone's kindness. You can use the same paper or stationery you use for regular friendly letters or the special cards made for social notes.

Social notes usually begin with a salutation. (A heading is important if you expect an answer to an invitation.) The body of a social note is usually one or two paragraphs in length. These paragraphs are short and to the point. If you are sending an invitation and need to know how many people will be coming, ask for an answer in your letter. (Or you can add RSVP and your telephone number in the lower left corner.) "Sincerely" or "Love" are common closings.

Dear Grandma,

The book and the game you sent me are terrific. I'm on page 234 in the book and wondering what Elsie is going to do next. We have been playing the game every night after dinner—except Tuesday when I had to study for a spelling test. Aren't you glad to hear I'm studying! What a surprise, huh?

I always like your presents. I wonder how you always pick something that I want. But I also liked the letter you put in. It's nice to know that you think I'm a special person. I'll write a full letter next week. I just wanted you to know right away that I really like your presents.

Love,

Erin

The Business Letter

Sharing information with a friend or relative is not the only reason to write a letter. Writing a letter can also help you find information. In fact, writing a letter may be the best or the only way to get information about certain things. Often, the books, magazines, and newspapers which you read will contain addresses you can write to for free material on a variety of topics.

203   A business letter asking for information or answers should be written differently than the friendly letters you write to friends and relatives. It should be more "business-like" and follow the accepted form or style for a business letter. The business letter below requesting information on an endangered species is written very formally and follows the full-block style. (See 204.)

Heading
413 Chicago Street
Racine, WI 53405
March 1, 2000

Inside
Address
Director—Wildlife Notes
National Wildlife Federation
1412 16th Street NW
Washington, DC 20036

Salutation   Dear Director:

I am an eighth-grade student writing a science report on the American peregrine falcon.

I would appreciate any up-to-date information you have on this endangered bird. I am especially interested in the following types of information:

Body

1. The history of the peregrine falcon.
2. The falcon's nesting areas in the United States.
3. Present efforts to save the falcon.
4. A bibliography of current information.

Thank you for your help.

Closing   Sincerely,

Jim Bird

Signature   Jim Bird

Form of a Business Letter   **204**

The business letter is made up of six basic parts: the **heading**, **inside address**, **salutation**, **body**, **closing**, and **signature**. The placement of these parts is somewhat different in the two basic styles of business letters: the full-block style and the semiblock style. Note in the illustrations below the placement of the letter parts in the two basic styles of business letters:

Styles of the Business Letter

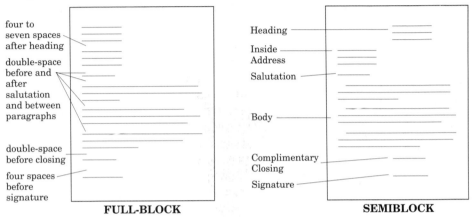

four to seven spaces after heading

double-space before and after salutation and between paragraphs

double-space before closing

four spaces before signature

FULL-BLOCK

Heading

Inside Address

Salutation

Body

Complimentary Closing

Signature

SEMIBLOCK

Heading: The heading for a business letter includes the sender's   **205** complete address and the full date. The heading is placed about an inch from the top of the page. In a business letter following the full-block style, the heading is placed at the left-hand margin. In a letter following the semiblock style, the heading is placed in the right-hand corner of the letter.

Inside Address: The inside address is placed at the left-hand mar-   **206** gin, four to seven spaces below the heading. It should include the name and complete address of the person and/or company you are writing. (Place a person's title after his or her name. Separate the title from the name with a comma. If the title is two or more words, place the title separately on the next line.)

Salutation: The salutation is placed two spaces below the inside   **207** address. For a specific person, use a salutation like *Dear Ms. . . . , Dear Mr. . . .* For a letter addressed to a person by title, use *Dear Sir, Dear Madam,* or *Dear* (Title). For a company, group, or organization, use *Gentlemen, Dear Sirs,* or *Dear* (Company name). Place a colon at the end of the salutation. (Check the first line of the inside address to determine the right salutation to use.)

208   **Body:** The body of the business letter is placed two lines below the salutation. The information in the body should be clearly and briefly written. Double-space between each paragraph. In a letter following the full-block style, do not indent the first line of each paragraph. In a letter following the semiblock style, indent the first line of each paragraph. (Indent five spaces if typed.)

209   **Closing:** The closing is placed two spaces below the body. Use *Very truly*, *Yours truly*, or *Sincerely* for a business letter closing. Place a comma at the end of the closing. In a full-block letter, the closing is placed at the left-hand margin; in a semiblock letter, the closing should line up with the heading.

210   **Signature:** End your letter by signing your name beneath the closing. If you are typing your letter, skip four lines and type your full name. Then, write your signature between the closing and your typed name.

211   Types of Business Letters

You're not in business, and business letters, by their very nature, are written for business reasons. So why should a junior high or middle school student know how to write a business letter?

You may need special information for a school report, as in the model business letter. As a member of your school and community, you may feel the need to "sound off" or express an opinion. As a consumer, you may need to order a product or complain about a product you've already bought. And as a teenager in need of money, you may want to apply for a part-time job. For these and other reasons it's important for you to know how to write a good business letter, especially *letters of inquiry*, *letters to an editor or official*, and *letters of complaint*.

212   Letter of Inquiry

One of the most common types of business letters is the **letter of inquiry.** A letter of inquiry is one in which you ask for information or answers to your questions. It should be short and to the point. Word your letter so that there can be no question as to what it is you need to know. (See 203 for model.)

Helpful HINT

There are many organizations which offer up-to-date information at no cost. (Others may charge a small fee.) When you are doing research for a school report, one of these organizations will very likely offer valuable facts about your report topic. Send your letter as soon as possible since it may take two to three weeks for your material to arrive.

Letter to an Editor or Official

A **letter to an editor or official** is written to complain, compliment, or clarify. Use the following guidelines:

■ Clearly explain the problem or situation.

■ Offer your opinion of the cause and possible solutions.

■ Support your opinions with facts and examples.

■ Suggest ways to change or improve the situation.

511 State Street
San Antonio, TX 78212
January 21, 2000

Editor
Goode Times
Goode Junior High
San Antonio, TX 78217

Dear Editor:

As we all know, the lunch hours here at Goode are a real mess! We are rushed through our lunches and then herded outside to stand around or goof off. What a waste of time!

What we need in our school is a more organized, meaningful noon hour for those students who don't like to waste their time. I have four suggestions as to how this could be done:

1. Those students who don't like to gulp down their lunches should be given more time in the cafeteria to enjoy their meals.
2. The gym should be opened for organized activities like volleyball and basketball.
3. The computer lab should be opened for students interested in computer activities.
4. A silent reading and study area should be created for those students who want to read or do homework.

I don't think my suggestions are out of line. We already have teachers and aides assigned to noon-hour supervision. I'm sure a teacher or aide would rather supervise or participate in more meaningful activities. And the students, at least all of my friends, would gladly participate.

If you feel the same way I do about the noon-hour situation, contact your student council representative. Talk to your teachers and Mr. Jones about the situation. Also, talk to your parents. Ask them to discuss this topic at the next Parent-Teacher Council meeting.

If we all work together, I'm sure we can make some much-needed improvements.

Thank you,

Dawn Smith

Dawn Smith

214 Letter of Complaint

When you have a problem with something you buy, your first step naturally will be to contact the store where you bought the product. Sometimes the local store can take care of the problem. Other times, however, the store will not be able to help you. Or, maybe you purchased the product by mail. In both cases, you will need to write a letter of complaint.

In a **letter of complaint**, be sure to include all the necessary information:

- Carefully and clearly describe the product.
- Describe the problem and what may have caused it. (Don't waste a lot of time explaining how unhappy you are.)
- Explain any action you have already taken to solve the problem.
- End your letter with the action you would like the reader (company) to take to solve the problem.

625 Oak Avenue
Fort Atkinson, WI 53538
October 5, 2000

Customer Service Manager
Rightway Fund Raisers
2525 Capital Drive
Springfield, IL 62701

Dear Sir:

At the beginning of the semester, I ordered a hooded sweatshirt from your company through a fund-raiser sponsored by our school's music department. When I received my sweatshirt, I experienced quite a shock. The hood was sewn on the wrong way.

The hood is on the front of the sweatshirt—the same side with our school name printed on it. I showed the sweatshirt to our music director who was as surprised as I was. He suggested that I return the sweatshirt along with a letter explaining my problem and a copy of my receipt.

I'm sure once you read this letter and inspect the sweatshirt, you'll want to send me a new sweatshirt with the hood sewn on the right way. I would appreciate receiving my new sweatshirt as soon as possible since I'm very anxious to wear it.

Sincerely,

Martin Miller
Martin Miller

Sending Your Letter

Addressing the Envelope

■ Place the full name and complete address of the person to whom the letter is being sent slightly to the left of the middle of the envelope.

■ Place your return address in the upper left-hand corner of the envelope.

■ Place the correct postage in the upper right-hand corner of the envelope.

MR JIM BIRD
413 CHICAGO ST
RACINE WI 53405

DIRECTOR WILDLIFE NOTES
NATIONAL WILDLIFE FEDERATION
1412 16TH ST NW
WASHINGTON DC 20036

There are two acceptable forms for writing the addresses on the envelope. In the traditional form, you use upper- and lowercase letters as well as punctuation and abbreviation. In the newer form preferred by the postal service, four important steps must be followed:

■ Capitalize everything in the addresses.

■ Use the list of common address abbreviations found in the ZIP Code Directory. (See 218.)

■ Don't use any punctuation.

■ Use the special two-letter state abbreviations found in the ZIP Code Directory. (See 217.)

Old vs. New: Note below the difference between the traditional form and the new form for addressing an envelope.

Old System	**New System**
Mr. James Evans	MR JAMES EVANS
512 North Adams Ave.	512 N ADAMS AVE
Winona, MN 55987	WINONA MN 55987

Also note the various combinations which are possible for addresses.

MISS TRISH DATON	ACCOUNTING DEPARTMENT	MR TEDDY BARE
BOX 77	STEVENSON LTD BLDG 18	PRESIDENT
HOUSTON TX 77008	2632 FOURTH ST	ACME TOY COMPANY
	DULUTH MN 55803	4421 RANDOLPH ST
		CHEYENNE WY 82001

216 Folding the Letter

The *preferred* method for folding a letter is used with a standard-sized (4-1/4" x 9-1/2") business envelope.

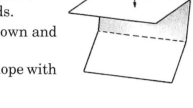

- Begin by folding the bottom edge of the letter so that the paper is divided into thirds.
- Next, fold the top third of the letter down and crease the edges firmly.
- Finally, insert the letter into the envelope with the open end at the top.

A second method of folding is used when your envelope is smaller than the traditional business envelope.

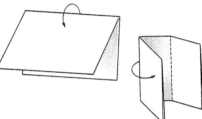

- Begin by folding the letter in half.
- Next, fold the letter into thirds.
- Insert the letter into the envelope.

217 State Abbreviations

	Standard	Postal		Standard	Postal		Standard	Postal
Alabama	Ala.	AL	Kentucky	Ky.	KY	Ohio	Ohio	OH
Alaska	Alaska	AK	Louisiana	La.	LA	Oklahoma	Okla.	OK
Arizona	Ariz.	AZ	Maine	Maine	ME	Oregon	Ore.	OR
Arkansas	Ark.	AR	Maryland	Md.	MD	Pennsylvania	Pa.	PA
California	Calif.	CA	Massachusetts	Mass.	MA	Puerto Rico	P.R.	PR
Colorado	Colo.	CO	Michigan	Mich.	MI	Rhode Island	R.I.	RI
Connecticut	Conn.	CT	Minnesota	Minn.	MN	South		
Delaware	Del.	DE	Mississippi	Miss.	MS	Carolina	S.C.	SC
District			Missouri	Mo.	MO	South Dakota	S.D.	SD
of Columbia	D.C.	DC	Montana	Mont.	MT	Tennessee	Tenn.	TN
Florida	Fla.	FL	Nebraska	Neb.	NE	Texas	Texas	TX
Georgia	Ga.	GA	Nevada	Nev.	NV	Utah	Utah	UT
Guam	Guam	GU	New			Vermont	Vt.	VT
Hawaii	Hawaii	HI	Hampshire	N.H.	NH	Virginia	Va.	VA
Idaho	Idaho	ID	New Jersey	N.J.	NJ	Virgin Islands	V.I.	VI
Illinois	Ill.	IL	New York	N.Y.	NY	Washington	Wash.	WA
Indiana	Ind.	IN	North			West Virginia	W.Va.	WV
Iowa	Iowa	IA	Carolina	N.C.	NC	Wisconsin	Wis.	WI
Kansas	Kan.	KS	North Dakota	N.D.	ND	Wyoming	Wyo.	WY

218 Address Abbreviations

	Standard	Postal		Standard	Postal		Standard	Postal
Avenue	Ave.	AVE	Lake	L.	LK	Road	Rd.	RD
Boulevard	Blvd.	BLVD	Lane	LN.	LN	Rural	R.	R
Court	Ct.	CT	North	N.	N	South	S.	S
Drive	Dr.	DR	Park	Pk.	PK	Square	Sq.	SQ
East	E.	E	Parkway	Pky.	PKY	Station	Sta.	STA
Expressway	Expy.	EXPY	Place	Pl.	PL	Terrace	Ter.	TER
Heights	Hts.	HTS	Plaza	Plaza	PLZ	Turnpike	Tpke.	TPKE
Highway	Hwy.	HWY	Ridge	Rdg.	RDG	Village	Vil.	VLG
Hospital	Hosp.	HOSP	River	R.	RV	West	W.	W

A Checklist for Writing the Business Letter 219

Use the following checklist to help you write, revise, and prepare a good business letter:

Selecting: *Choosing a Subject*

- Write a business letter
  . . . if you need to send for information.
  . . . if you want to express an opinion.
  . . . if you want to complain, compliment, or clarify.

Collecting: *Preparing to Write*

- Check your handbook for the requirements for the different types of business letters: *Letter of Inquiry, Letter to an Editor or Official, Letter of Complaint.*
- Gather all of the details and facts you need.
- Organize your ideas and facts into a general topic outline.

Connecting: *Writing the First Draft*

- Write honestly and naturally, but keep the style somewhat formal.
- Follow your topic outline.
- Write short paragraphs. (This does not mean that a paragraph should be only one or two sentences.)

Revising the First Draft

- Make sure you have included the necessary facts and details.
- Make sure you have written honestly and sincerely.
- Make sure your letter is easy to read.
- Make sure you have followed one of the business letter styles.

Correcting: *The Finishing Touches*

- Make sure you proofread for punctuation, capitalization, and usage. (Pay special attention to the capitalization and punctuation of the heading, inside address, and salutation.)
- Make sure your letter is neatly written or typed.
  - ❏ Center the letter and keep the margins even.
  - ❏ Use consistent and even spacing.
  - ❏ Use only one side of the paper.

Note: If the body of your letter carries over to a second page, the name of the person you're writing to should be placed at the top left-hand margin.

Creative Writing

Writing Poetry

Of all the forms of creative writing, none is more loved/hated than poetry. Many of those who love it have found that poetry allows them to share their thoughts and feelings in a unique way. Others enjoy reading and listening to the rhymes, rhythms, and images of poetry. As to those who "hate" it? Well, they probably haven't tried poetry lately—at least not in the way it is described on the following pages.

What Is Poetry?

The poet Marianne Moore defines poetry as "imaginary gardens with real toads in them." This definition may seem unusual to you. When you think of a definition, you probably think of something like "a verb is a word which expresses action or a state of being." Poetry, however, is too

"A poem is an imaginary garden with real toads in it."

creative and exciting to be effectively defined in such a factual way. That is why Ms. Moore chose such a different way to define poetry. She has given life to her definition and invites us to use our imaginations and share in her creation. A poem is an exciting and imaginative creation, an "imaginary garden." Poems come from our real world experiences—the "toads" which hop in and out of our lives every day.

"Imaginary gardens" might be new to you, but poetry is not. Your idea of poetry might be an old jump-roping jingle like "I like coffee/ I like tea/ I like the boys/ Do they like me?" Or, it might be the lyrics or words of your favorite song. More than anything, good poetry must present ideas in a new and different way, a way that makes poetry fun to listen to and interesting to read.

Poetry Is Not the Same as Prose

As you will see from the samples on the following pages, poetry comes in all shapes and sizes. For many years, it was written in lines and stanzas (groups of lines) and followed a certain pattern of rhyme and rhythm. Today, poetry doesn't have to rhyme. And it is often written with just words and phrases—not lines or sentences. Prose, on the other hand, is the writing you do every day in school, writing in which you use sentences and paragraphs to turn out reports, essays, and stories.

223 Poetry Can Add Life to an Idea

Suppose you are interested in writing about your family cat. How might you do this? You might describe this pet in a paragraph, develop a personal research report about house cats, or, perhaps, share some special thoughts and feelings about your cat in a poem. The writer of the following model decided that a poem was the best way to go. Even though poetry is usually briefer or shorter than prose, it can often give more life to an idea than "regular writing" can. And there is plenty of life in this poem as the writer makes a breakfast ritual come alive for the reader.

Breakfast for Two

Trudging down the stairs, 7:10 A.M.
And the cat whips by my ankles.
    I don't talk in the morning. Never
    Make me talk in the morning.
    Pull the cereal out
    Grab the milk,
    Get a spoon and a bowl.
And the cat skids and stops in his tracks as I pour my milk.
    All set, I raise
    The first spoonful
    To my mouth.
And the cat jumps up on the table and stretches out beside
My bowl, the perfect actor: the Prince.
    I start to crunch.
And the cat slowly, hesitantly, lifts his paw and slowly,
Hesitantly, tries putting it in my bowl for his first taste.
    I slap away his paw and
    Continue eating.
And the cat tries diving his head
    Right down into the bowl.
    I push away his head
    And then see that I am done,
    Just the sweetened milk
    Is left. I fill a spoon
    Full with it
    And lift it towards the cat.
And the cat sticks out his tiny
    Pink tongue and laps it up,
Squeezing his eyes
    Shut with pleasure.

Writing Your Own Poem

Selecting: *Finding a Subject*   224

Before you begin writing your own poem, you must first select a good subject or idea. Poems have been written on just about any topic you can imagine. Choose as a subject something that you know about or often think about. This will naturally be something specific like your favorite food, a special person, an unforgettable experience, or an unusual dream.

- Think of an important time or event in your life and try to write a poem about it—or about the moments just before or after it.
- Think of a subject that means a great deal to you. Pay special attention to it in a poem.
- Write a poem "commemorating" a time, place, or thing seldom noticed (a tattered old book used to prop open a window, the moment just after you crawl into bed, the space under the stairs).
- Write a poem as if you were someone else, someone older, younger, from another time and place.

Collecting: *Preparing to Write*   225

Once you have selected a subject, think of an interesting way to write about it. You might begin with a free writing. (A free writing will help you unlock the interesting or creative ideas hidden in your mind and help you gather details for your poem.) You might try clustering. (See 035.) The short, quick thought-groups required in clustering may lead naturally to poetry. Or you might try an open-ended question and repeat it several times—"What if . . . ? What if . . . ? What if . . . ?"

Connecting: *Writing the First Draft*   226

Once you have a specific subject and many interesting ideas or details about that subject, you are ready to write your poem. Don't worry about writing "the perfect poem" or a poem that looks or sounds like somebody else's. Write freely and naturally until you've said all that you need to say about the subject. Don't overlook the sounds, tastes, or smells of your subject—or how it looks or how you *feel* about it.

One of the nice things about writing poetry is that the form—the way it looks—is really up to you. You can arrange your details into any form you choose, as long as it looks good and makes sense to you. Very often the form of your poem will develop naturally as you write. Your poem might, for example, be a simple list of words and phrases, or it might be made up of complete sentences. As long as it makes sense to you and your reader, the poem can be anything you want it to be.

227 *Improving Your Poem*

You will revise your poem many times before you are satisfied that it captures your subject. Your poem should contain strong, active words that *show* rather than tell something. Note below the difference in the words used to describe the actions of the cat in the student poem.

Tell: The cat tries to taste the milk.

Show: And the cat slowly, hesitantly, lifts his paw and slowly,
Hesitantly, tries putting it in my bowl for his first taste.

The first example simply tells a reader what the cat is trying to do. The second example creates an effective image (word picture) that speaks for itself.

Does poetry have to rhyme? No. In fact, most modern poetry is called **free verse**, which means it is not written in any special form and doesn't require rhyme or rhythm. The model poem "Breakfast for Two" used earlier in this section is a free verse poem since it follows no special form. Only the traditional or older forms of poetry require rhyme and rhythm. This doesn't mean that you can't use rhyme—you certainly can—it merely means you can decide whether your poem will rhyme or not.

---

228 Additional Things to Check in Your Poem

- Check the title of your poem. Make sure it adds something to your poem and catches the attention of the reader.
- Check your poem to make sure it is clear and complete.
- Check the form of your poem. The way your poem looks and sounds should help the reader enjoy it.
- Check the way your poem ends. A poem that fizzles and dies at the end won't leave a reader with much of an impression.
- Check the capitalization of your poem. The first word in each line of a traditional poem is capitalized. In free verse poetry, this is not the case. You may decide to capitalize the first word of each line, but you don't have to. You might decide to capitalize only a few words for emphasis.
- Check the spelling, punctuation, and usage in your poem.
- Finally, write your final copy neatly and clearly.

Reading and Appreciating a Poem

To fully understand and appreciate poetry, you must not only write it, but also read it, talk about it, and listen to it. Below is a popular poem by one of America's most famous poets, Robert Frost. Read the poem using the suggestions at the bottom of the page.

Stopping by Woods on a Snowy Evening

Whose woods these are I think I know.   *(a)*
His house is in the village though;   *(a)*
He will not see me stopping here   *(b)*
To watch his woods fill up with snow.   *(a)*

My little horse must think it queer   *(b)*
To stop without a farmhouse near   *(b)*
Between the woods and frozen lake   *(c)*
The darkest evening of the year.   *(b)*

He gives his harness bells a shake   *(c)*
To ask if there is some mistake.   *(c)*
The only other sound's the sweep   *(d)*
Of easy wind and downy flake.   *(c)*

The woods are lovely, dark and deep   *(d)*
But I have promises to keep,   *(d)*
And miles to go before I sleep,   *(d)*
And miles to go before I sleep.   *(d)*

■ Read the poem very carefully.

■ Read the poem aloud. (If this isn't possible, "listen" to the poem as you read it silently.)

■ Read the poem over several times. Each reading will help you enjoy the poem more.

■ Try to catch the general meaning of the poem during your first reading. Knowing the general meaning will help you understand the more difficult parts of the poem.

■ Share the poems you enjoy with your friends.

230 | An Introduction to Traditional Poetry

> Most traditional forms of poetry follow exact patterns of rhyme and rhythm. To help you understand these forms better, the following pages cover the characteristics and forms of traditional poetry. With this introduction, you should be able to better understand and appreciate why poets write the way they do.

Most traditional forms of poetry require **rhyme**. The rhyme is organized in patterns called *rhyme scheme*s. Note the rhyme scheme of the model poem, "Stopping by Woods . . . ," (229). The lines that rhyme are labeled with the same letter: *aaba / bbcb / ccdc / dddd.*

Traditional forms of poetry are also written in **meter**. Meter is the rhythm or "pattern of accented (´) and unaccented (˘) syllables" in the lines of a poem. The regular beat or rhythm in a traditional poem comes from the meter. If you read a traditional poem carefully, you should be able to hear and identify its meter.

MINI-lesson

The "Stopping by Woods . . ." poem is written so that every other syllable is accented. This pattern of an unaccented syllable followed by an accented syllable is the poem's meter. (See the first two lines of this poem below; also see "Foot.")

> Whŏse woóds thĕse áre Ĭ thínk Ĭ knów.
>
> Hĭs hoúse ĭs ín thĕ víllăge thoúgh;

231 **Alliteration** is the repeating of beginning consonant sounds as in "**cr**eamy and **cr**unchy."

Assonance is the repetition of vowel sounds, as with the "i" sound in the following lines from "The Hayloft" by R.L. Stevenson.

> Till the sh**i**ning scythes went far and w**i**de
> And cut it down to dr**y**.

Consonance is the repetition of consonant sounds. This is a lot like alliteration except it includes consonant sounds anywhere within the words, not just at the beginning. Listen to the "s" sounds from "Singing."

> The **s**ailor **s**ing**s** of rope**s** and thing**s**
> In ship**s** upon the sea**s**.

End rhyme is the rhyming of words at the ends of two or more lines of poetry, as in the following lines from "The Night Light" by Robert Frost.

> She always had to turn a **light**
> Beside her attic bed at **night**.

Foot: A foot is one unit of meter. (*Meter* is the pattern of accented and unaccented syllables in the lines of a traditional poem.) There are five basic feet:

> *Iambic* —an unaccented syllable followed by an accented one (re peat´)
>
> *Anapestic*—two unaccented syllables followed by an accented one (in ter rupt´)
>
> *Trochaic*—an accented syllable followed by an unaccented one (old´er)
>
> *Dactylic*—an accented syllable followed by two unaccented ones (o´pen ly)
>
> *Spondaic*—two accented syllables (heart´break´)

Internal rhyme is the rhyming of words within one line of poetry, as in **Jack sprat** could eat no **fat** or **Peter Peter** pumpkin **eater**.

Onomatopoeia is the use of a word whose sound makes you think of its meaning, as in *buzz, gunk, gushy, swish, zigzag, zing,* or *zip*.

Quatrain: A quatrain is a four-line stanza. Common rhyme schemes in quatrains are *aabb, abab,* and *abcd*.

> I wish I had no teachers.
> That's what I'd like to see.
> I'd do whatever I wanted to,
> And nobody'd yell at me.

Repetition is the repeating of a word or phrase to add rhythm or to emphasize an idea, as in the following lines from "The Raven."

> While I nodded, nearly napping, suddenly there came a tapping,
> as of someone gently **rapping, rapping** at my chamber door—

Stanza: A stanza is a division in a poem named for the number of lines it contains. Below are the most common stanzas.

Couplet	...............two-line stanza	*Sestet*	...........six-line stanza
Triplet	.............three-line stanza	*Septet*	......seven-line stanza
Quatrain	...........four-line stanza	*Octave*	......eight-line stanza

Verse: Verse is a name for a line of traditional poetry written in meter. Verse is named according to the pattern of accented and unaccented syllables in the line (See "Foot.") and the number of patterns repeated. The names for the number of patterns or feet per line are given below.

Monometer	.....................one foot	*Pentameter*	.............five feet
Dimeter	..........................two feet	*Hexameter*	...............six feet
Trimeter	......................three feet	*Heptameter*	.........seven feet
Tetrameter	.....................four feet	*Octometer*	.............eight feet

The Forms of Traditional Poetry

Poetry has been around for centuries, beginning with bards and messengers who used poetry to pass along news, songs, and stories as they traveled from town to town. Today, we find poetry in songs, greeting cards, posters, gift books, and a variety of other places.

Ballad: A ballad is a poem which tells a story. Ballads are usually written in four-line stanzas called *quatrains*. Often, the first and third lines have four accented syllables; the second and fourth have three. (See "Quatrain" for possible rhyme schemes.)

> **Ballad of Birmingham** (first stanza)
>
> Mother dear, may I go downtown
> Instead of out to play,
> And march the streets of Birmingham
> In a Freedom March today?

Blank Verse: Blank verse is unrhymed poetry with meter. The lines in blank verse are 10 syllables in length. Every other syllable, beginning with the second syllable, is accented. (*Note:* Not every line will have exactly 10 syllables.)

> **Birches** (first three lines)
>
> When I see birches bend to left and right
> Across the lines of straighter darker trees,
> I like to think some boy's been swinging them.

Cinquain: Cinquain poems are five lines in length. There are syllable and word cinquain poems.

Syllable Cinquain

Line 1:	Title	2 syllables
Line 2:	Description of title	4 syllables
Line 3:	Action about the title	6 syllables
Line 4:	Feeling about the title	8 syllables
Line 5:	Synonym for title	2 syllables

Word Cinquain

Line 1:	Title	1 word
Line 2:	Description of title	2 words
Line 3:	Action about the title	3 words
Line 4:	Feeling about the title	4 words
Line 5:	Synonym for title	1 word

Couplet: A couplet is two lines of verse that usually rhyme and state one complete idea. (See "Stanza.")

Elegy: An elegy is a poem which states a poet's sadness about the death of an important person. In the famous elegy "O Captain, My Captain," Walt Whitman writes about the death of Abraham Lincoln.

Epic: An epic is a long story poem which describes the adventures of a hero. *The Odyssey* by Homer is a famous epic which describes the adventures of the Greek hero Odysseus.

Free Verse: Free verse is poetry which does not require meter or a rhyme scheme. (See 227.)

Haiku: Haiku is a type of Japanese poetry which presents a picture of nature. A haiku poem is three lines in length. The first line is five syllables; the second, seven; and the third, five.

> Water tumbles down
> In a gently flowing stream.
> Over rocks it trips.

Limerick: A limerick is a humorous verse of five lines. Lines one, two, and five rhyme, as do lines three and four. Lines one, two, and five have three stressed syllables; lines three and four have two.

> There once was a lady from Nantucket
> Who lived her whole life in a bucket.
> Her pleasures unknown,
> Were completely thrown,
> When in a mudhole her bucket got stuckit.

Lyric: A lyric is a short poem that expresses personal feeling.

> **My Heart Leaps Up When I Behold** (first 5 lines)
>
> My heart leaps up when I behold
> A rainbow in the sky;
> So was it when my life began;
> So is it now I am a man;
> So be it when I shall grow old.

Ode: An ode is a long lyric that is deep in feeling and rich in poetic devices and imagery. "Ode to a Grecian Urn" is a famous ode by John Keats.

Poetry: Poetry is a very concentrated form of writing which is imaginative, emotional, and thought-provoking. Words are chosen for their sound as well as their meaning.

Sonnet: A sonnet is a fourteen-line poem which states a poet's personal feelings. The Shakespearean sonnet follows the *abab / cdcd / efef / gg* rhyme scheme. Each line in a sonnet is 10 syllables in length; every other syllable is stressed, beginning with the second syllable.

The Forms of "Invented" Poetry

The nice thing about poetry is that you—the poet—can create not only the message but also the form. Many of the alternative forms listed below were "invented" by students like you. Don't be afraid to try something new the next time you sit down to write.

Alphabet Poetry: A form of poetry which states a creative or humorous idea using part of the alphabet. An alphabet poem is often written as a list.

> **H**ighly
> **I**gnorant
> **J**umping
> **K**angaroos
> **L**ove
> **M**aking
> **N**oise
> **O**bnoxiously

Clerihew Poetry: A form of humorous or light verse created by Edmund Clerihew. A clerihew poem consists of two rhyming couplets. The name of some well-known person creates one of the rhymes.

> The only way to pitch Pete Rose
> Is to throw the ball near his nose.
> Throw a pitch which he can hit
> And he'll blast a drive no one will get.

Concrete Poetry: A form of poetry in which the shape or design helps express the meaning or feeling of the poem.

pEAKs VALLEYs *LIFE!*

Contrast Couplet: A couplet in which the first line includes two words that are opposites. The second line makes a comment about the first.

> It really doesn't matter if you're young or old.
> There's always someone to say: "Do as you're told."

Definition Poetry: Poetry which defines a word or idea creatively.

> Styrofoam—
> a strange stuff
> which bends, dents, and rips
> when poked or pulled.

Headline Poetry: Poetry which is formed by creatively rearranging the words of newspaper or magazine headlines.

List Poetry: A form of poetry which lists words or phrases.

> **Rooms**
>
> There are rooms to start up in
> Rooms to start out in
> Rooms to start over in
> Rooms to lie in
> Rooms to lie about in
> Rooms to lay away in . . .
> — Ray Griffith

Name Poetry: A form of poetry in which the letters of a name are used to begin each line in the poem.

> **B**asically
> **A**ll kinds of activity and
> **R**eading a good book
> **B**ring out
> **A**ll that is
> **R**ight
> **A**bout me.

Phrase Poetry: A form of poetry which states an idea with a list of phrases.

> **Cross Country**
>
> Off with a bang
> around the bushes
> up the exhausting hill
> toward the finish
> without any breath

Riddle Poetry: Poetry which makes the reader guess the subject of the poem. "I Like to See It Lap the Miles" is an example of a riddle poem.

Terse Verse: A form of humorous verse made up of two words that rhyme and have the same number of syllables.

Old Flower	Worms	Braces
Lazy	Great	Tin
Daisy	Bait	Grin

Title-down Poetry: A form of poetry in which the letters that spell the subject of the poem are used to begin each line.

> **B**eing down is
> **L**ousy,
> **U**gh, but
> **E**veryone is down sometimes.

Story Writing

Each one of you is a born storyteller. Put something like "I'll never forget the time when . . ." or "Did she ever tell you about . . ." in front of you, and you're on your way. It's natural and easy to talk about your experiences. It's how you make sense out of your lives, how you confirm that you are a part of this world: "Hey, listen to me. I've got a story to tell."

237 From the Real World

You also like to invent stories, but it may not be as easy for you as it once was. That doesn't mean "Did you hear the one about . . ." or "Once there was . . ." wouldn't be enough to get some of you into a story right away. But most writers at your age would have to work hard at inventing a story. Why? Your imaginations might not be what they once were; they've gone south on you, so to speak. It's no fault of your own. You're simply at a point in your life in which you're much more focused on real-life experiences.

238 To the World of Your Imagination

The best way to feel more comfortable with the process of inventing is simple: Sit down and start writing stories. Write simple stories, crazy stories, stories modeled after the ones you read now and the ones you read when you were younger. (Reread a few of those to jog your memory.)

Write different endings for your favorite stories, and write a number of beginnings for new stories. Write the worst fairy tale ever told, a serious rewrite of a silly story, a story that begins: "And they all lived happily ever after." Write pass-around stories with friends and classmates. One of you thinks of an opening line and passes the paper on. Keep it going until a story is told.

> "When I'm asked how to write, I answer—'Tell me a story!'"
> —Anne McCaffrey

Dramatize or act out parts of stories. Tell your younger brother or sister a story, and make it up as you go along. Acquire a feel for inventing, and, in the process, recapture that rich imagination you had as a young child. (Use the advice and guidelines which follow to help you with your story writing.)

Inventing Stories:
A How-to Interview with a Real Story Writer

Bob Kann is a professional storyteller. He spends a lot of time not only searching for existing stories for his performances, but also writing a number of his own stories. He agreed to be "interviewed" by Trebor Nnak (who?) to share with you his insights into the story writing process. Be prepared. This is not your typical interview.

TN: Where do you suggest students look to find ideas for stories to write or to tell?

BK: Stories can be found in four different places. Some stories can come from your own experiences.

Objects like an interesting piece of clothing, a photograph or painting, an album or magazine cover, or even a motorcycle can be the source of a story idea.

Other stories you have heard or read in books, magazines, and comic strips can provide the seed for a story.

And finally, stories can be entirely invented in your imagination. Your mind plays with a particular idea, and before you know it, you have the makings of a story.

TN: Is there an easy way for a young writer to develop a story—maybe a plan to follow?

BK: Sure, developing a story idea is as easy as nailing chocolate pudding to a tree. I begin working with an idea by filling in four categories to organize my thoughts. These categories are people, place, activity, and conflict.

❖ In most stories, there are *people* (or creatures) in a place doing some activity and a conflict occurs.

❖ The *place* could be a home, school cafeteria, neighborhood, park, hangout, movie theater, shopping mall, another city, another planet.

❖ The main *activity* might be a problem within a family, a disagreement among friends, a picnic, a purchase, a loss, breaking up, or breaking out.

❖ The *conflict* is the main problem in the story. This is what keeps readers with the story. They want to know how things turn out.

For example, if you decide the story will be about two friends (people) in the school cafeteria (place) having a food fight (activity), the conflict could be a thief steals their wallets or all of their books during the fight, a flying tomato hits a teacher, or some other problem that has to be resolved.

240

TN: **Should a writer fill in all four categories before he or she starts writing?**

BK: Do fish swim in a car pool? Can you eat off the forks in the road? Of course not. But you really should know at least two of the categories (two friends having a disagreement). And there's nothing wrong with changing your mind about any of the categories. A better idea might come to mind once you start writing.

TN: **What do you do after you have an idea and a plan for a story?**

BK: I get to work immediately for fear that I'll wind up like the butcher I knew who had the accident. The butcher backed into his meat grinder. His body recovered, but he got a little behind in his orders. Pretty bad, huh?

TN: **The pits.**

BK: Anyway, once I know what the story is going to be about, I begin to think about the pot of gold at the end of the rainbow.

TN: **Is this going to be another terrible pun?**

BK: No, I'm not going to punish you like that again. What I mean is I begin by thinking about what I want to accomplish with my story.

❖ First, I want the opening of my story to introduce the main characters, set the scene, and catch my readers by surprise so they can't help but want to read on.

❖ Second, I want to clearly lead the reader in some direction but make the trip along the way as interesting as I can.

❖ Third, I want a strong ending. I want them to enjoy the journey and feel they got their money's worth when they get to the end.

❖ Fourth, I want my characters to be believable—to seem like they belong in my story. And I want my readers to enter the world of my characters—to get to know them through their words and actions.

❖ Finally, I want to give my story my best effort. If I feel good about my writing, there's a good bet my readers will too.

TN: **So now that you know what to do, how do you do it?**

BK: With a sense of humor. You can't take yourself too seriously.

TN: **Thanks for the suggestions, Mr. Kann. Any final tips for young writers?**

BK: Yes, if you get stuck when you're writing, if things aren't going very well, take a break. Eat a snack, play Nintendo, spike your hair. Then go back to your story. Read your story to friends or classmates; brainstorm for new ways to continue. This might help you work through trouble spots.

Note: Trebor Nnak is really Robert Kann spelled backwards.

Connecting: *Writing Your Story:*

How should you start? Most writers (and your teachers) would advise you to start right in the middle of the action. But you start wherever and whenever you want. Start with "Once upon a time . . ." if that's what feels right to you.

If you want to plan your opening before you start, consider how you want to introduce the main characters and conflict and how you want to get your readers interested in your story.

Keep it simple. Start with a few characters, one main problem to deal with, one basic setting, a limited span of time (it can be a matter of minutes), and see what you can make of it.

How should you continue? Tell your story in the most natural way—according to when things happened, unless there's good reason not to. Or, better yet, let the characters "tell" your story. If you do too much of the talking, your story will sound more like a report.

Frank slammed down his spoon and said, "Look Joe, either stop kicking my chair, or you're going to be wearing this jello!" (This sounds much more interesting than the following.) Joe kept kicking Frank's chair during lunch. At first, Frank just looked annoyed. Then he got mad and warned Joe to stop.

Don't fight your story if it starts taking charge while you're writing. Let it go where it wants to, at least for awhile. Who knows—you may end up with a far more interesting story than the one you originally planned. Expect the unexpected, and you'll seldom be disappointed.

How should you end? This may sound stupid, but end when you're satisfied that your story says what you want it to say from start to finish. Readers stick with your story because they expect an ending. They don't need (or necessarily want) a nice, neat "everybody lived happily ever after" ending. But give them something—even if it's nothing more than a natural stopping point to the action.

Close your story if you want to leave your readers with something special. **A closing** is an ending plus more to think about. Speakers often do this. They'll say, "In closing, I would like to leave you with this. . . ." A good closing leaves readers satisfied but not stuffed, looking forward to the next time they dine here.

244 **Connecting:** *Taking Inventory of Your Story*

The following checklist will help you and your classmates evaluate the progress of your story: (See "Plot Line," 386, for additional information.)

- Do the characters' words and actions make sense? (We wouldn't expect the neighborhood bully to talk like a college professor. Nor would we expect a high school coed to meet Tom Cruise on a blind date.)

- Is there a real problem that moves the story along? (A worthwhile problem would be one like the following: Mike just received a progress report in math and his mother is a math teacher. How about an earthquake or invasion of the Mole Men? Sorry. These problems are too big, too unmanageable for a short story.)

> "I keep the stories enjoyable for my readers by keeping them enjoyable for me."
>
> —Gordon Korman

- Is the main character influenced by the story's problem? (Things can't go too smoothly for your main character. His or her way should become increasingly more difficult. Generally, the main character undergoes some change in attitude or belief because of the problem.)

- Do all of the characters play an important role in the story? Are all of the conversations, explanations, and events important? (Make your story interesting, but also make sure that it moves along at a good clip. You don't have to tell your readers everything.)

- Does the story keep the readers guessing? (This is what makes stories fun to write and to read.)

- Does something important, something big happen near the end of the story? (The main character is really put to the test at this point.)

- Does the story come to a natural, surprising, or interesting stopping point? (This fulfills a story's destiny. It completes the circle.)

- Is the story told from one point of view? (Either someone within the story or someone outside of the story is the narrator—one or the other, not both. Personally, I like to see things from the main character's point of view.)

- Does the story read like a story? (What needs to be explained is explained; what needs to be described is described. The characters' words and actions should do the rest.)

- Does the story read smoothly? (Read the story out loud. If you don't have an audience, read it to yourself in front of a mirror. Change words, phrases, or ideas that cause you to stumble.)

Model Story

This model by a young writer proves what writer Ernest Hemingway said about good writing: Its power comes from the fact that, like an iceberg, nine-tenths of it rides underwater, out of sight. And there is a lot that is "out of sight" in this story. It's very short, compact, and leaves a lot to the reader's imagination. The action is played out in the mind of the main character.

Division Problem

The story starts right in the middle of the action.

As if in a dream, I hear my teacher's sharp voice calling my name as though condemning me to death. I approach the blackboard slowly, trembling. I seize my only weapon, one small piece of chalk. My hand shakes as I write the number of the problem on the blackboard. The teacher's unwavering voice calls other victims up to the board.

The reader follows the action as it happens.

I glance down at my paper and write. Calm down. How many times does seven go into fifty-four? Okay. Now bring down the one. I feel like the whole world is watching me. I hear the sound of chalk being put down. People sighing. Phew. Done.

Drama builds as the main character becomes confused.

But no, the remainder is too big. I'm on the edge of being totally confused. I'm the only one up at the board. Probably only the teacher is watching me, but it seems like 20,000 eyes are on me. Finally I finish. Better check to make sure. I check five times and get five different answers. I try to calm down. Still, something is wrong. Someone in the back of the class snickers. Someone else snores. The teacher yawns. My multiplication is right; my division must be wrong. I pick up the eraser and begin to erase my problem. Then I remember . . . oops! I forgot to add the remainder. Silly me. It comes out right. By now I forget how I got the right answer, so I have to do part of the problem over.

The action begins to wind down, but not for long.

Finally I finish and sit down. The teacher smiles. The class claps and the kids who fell asleep wake up. I smile to myself. Sure, it took a long time, but I did get it right.

I grin as the teacher calls more people to the board. Number eight, Lucy; number nine, Tom; number ten, Kelly; number eleven, Sharon; number twelve, *Sarah*.

The story comes to a surprising ending.

A groan goes up from the class. I stand and approach the blackboard. Brinnng! The bell. I grab my things and rush out of the room before the teacher can give me any extra work.

246   Start with a Pattern

There are a number of basic patterns that stories generally follow. One of these patterns may trigger an idea for a story, or it may help you shape a story idea that you already have.

- **The choice:** The main character must make a decision near the end of the story. Making (or failing to make) this decision is the high point of the story.
- **The reversal:** Something happens between two characters near the end of a story that changes their feelings toward each other.
- **The understanding:** Clues lead the main character to some truth or understanding. Again, the discovery is made near the end of the story.
- **The separation:** Events make the main character feel more and more confused and alone, until he or she feels completely isolated by the end of the story.
- **The return:** The main character returns to some significant place to get some answers, to find something out.

A Short Story Sampler

Here are some brief descriptions of a number of popular short story types. Use these as starting points for your own stories.

247   Scary Story

Write a story with one intention in mind: to scare your reader. You've probably read an Edgar Allan Poe story in school, so you know what a scary story is all about. Or, perhaps you have read an adventure story that has a scary part in it. And I'm sure some of you have seen a scary movie or two. Draw from these experiences when you create your own story.

248   Mystery

Think of a crime, a list of suspects, a criminal, a star detective, and you're ready to write your first who-dun-it. Pay close attention to the mysteries on TV like *Murder She Wrote* to see how screenwriters develop their stories. Think of the mystery stories like those in the Hardy Boys series you have probably already read. You might want to try some Sherlock Holmes stories. Or try reading books by Agatha Christie, Richard Peck, Tony Hillerman, Norma Johnston, or M. E. Kerr to see how professional writers develop their mysteries.

Fantasy

Add some fantastic elements to real world situations and create a fantasy. Think of some of your favorite childhood stories for ideas. Many of these stories contain fantastic elements: animals that talk, nightmares with feelings, bathtubs that become pirate ships. Also, think of some of your favorite movies for ideas: *Back to the Future* (I, II, and III) obviously is as much a fantasy as it is an adventure story. Joan Aiken, Lloyd Alexander, and Alan Garner are fantasy writers you might want to try.

Science Fiction

Imagine a world 100 years after a nuclear war. Who would be living? What would life be like? What would the people know about life as it was before the war? This is science fiction—when life as we know it is dramatically altered in some way. Read "By the Waters of Babylon" by Stephen Vincent Benét for a great story along these lines.

Or imagine a world in which a condition as we know it suddenly changes—all of the clocks have stopped, and we have no way to tell time. Imagine a world in which people can remember things for no longer than a minute.

Or imagine a futuristic world, one in which technology is far more advanced and different than ours. All of you science fiction buffs know all about this. Here are some sci-fi authors you might want to try: Isaac Asimov, Ray Bradbury, Michael Crichton, Madeleine L'Engle. (Ask your librarian for others.)

Myth

All of us have a fascination with myths. They are wonderful stories from past cultures that attempt to explain some natural phenomenon. For example, the story of Persephone's annual rebirth and death reflects the growing season from planting to harvesting. Other myths recount the incredible trials of great heroes like Hercules. Still others represent or symbolize characteristics of the human condition. The story of Icarus, for example, represents the impulsiveness or recklessness of youth.

Create your own myth. Describe why it is we cry, why early summer is tornado season, or, perhaps, why diamonds are so valued. See your school or community library for collections of myths from all cultures.

Fable

Write a brief story that makes a point, teaches, or advises. There are two basic ways you can go about fable writing: Start with a moral and develop a story that leads up to it. Or, develop a story, and decide afterwards what the story teaches or advises. For fable ideas, think of actual incidents that you've heard or read about which you feel teach something. Read Aesop's fables to become familiar with this story form.

Writing Dialogue

A story without dialogue would be like a basket-ball game without dribbling, a concert without drums. It simply wouldn't move or sound the way it should. Stories are about people, and people talk. We expect it in the stories we read. Dialogue makes a story seem real, makes a story come alive, makes a story unfold before our very eyes. Dialogue. Use it.

253   Now before some of you say, "Aha, caught you there . . . not all stories are about people," you're right. Some stories, especially children's stories, are about animals and other creatures; but don't forget, they almost always speak and act like real people.

And you're right again if you say that you've read some stories that don't contain any actual dialogue. One famous example that comes to mind is "To Build a Fire" by Jack London. But even in these stories, you'll find a special type of conversation going on between the main character and him- or herself. And this one-way conversation, sometimes called an **interior monologue**, can be just as engaging and entertaining as actual dialogue. (See the "Model Story," 245, for an example.)

 Helpful HINT   There's no one key to writing good dialogue. But it helps if you read a lot so you are used to seeing dialogue. It also helps if you are a little nosy and like to listen to snatches of conversations. And it's important to practice writing dialogue.

254 ## Imaginary Conversations:

For Practice and Ideas

You don't need to write a story to practice writing **dialogue**. I enjoy making up conversations for their own sake. Sometimes I'm in the conversation, and sometimes I'm not. There are times when I don't know either of the two speakers. Their identities only become known to me as I write.

Try it yourself. Start by saying something: "I said no talking." Have someone answer: "I know, but I just . . . ." Continue the dialogue and find out who the speakers are and the subject of their conversation. Keep the dialogue going as long as you can. In the process, you'll sharpen your skill as a dialogue writer and create a potential idea for a story. Or, by further shaping the dialogue, you can create a mini one-act play called a **duolog**. (See 257 for help with writing plays.)

Guidelines for Developing Dialogue

To develop good dialogues you do not have to follow any absolute rules. But here are some guidelines that may help you shape the conversations in your stories:

- Use words which your characters would actually use if they were able to speak. (Remember that people express what they have to say in different ways.)
- Get rid of any dialogue that just kills time. (There should always be a purpose for the dialogue—to reveal character, to set up a surprise, to intensify the action, or to lead toward a resolution.)
- Most of the dialogue should be about the speaker's beliefs or problems. (Generally one speaker's beliefs clash with another's. This adds drama to the story.)
- Write the dialogue as speakers actually speak. (People often interrupt each other in conversation, and, at other times, talk past or ignore each other.)
- Stop the conversation at the right spot. (The characters don't have to say everything. Leave some things to the reader's imagination.)
- Write and punctuate the dialogue so it is easy to read. (Indent every time someone new speaks and identify the speaker if it isn't clear who is talking. See "The Yellow Pages" for help punctuating.)

A Sample Dialogue

A portion of dialogue from a student narrative follows. Note how the conversation intensifies the action.

Junior and I entered a dark and dreary room at the end of the tunnel. It was full of cobwebs, old crates, and debris scattered all over the place. I could faintly hear water dripping.

After a few uneasy minutes, I said, "I think we better get out of here."

"Come on. Nothing is going to happen," Junior replied.

"I don't care. This place gives me the creeps!"

"All right, let's go."

As we were making our way out, Junior bumped into one of the supporting beams.

"We've got to move faster, Junior! I think this place might cave in!"

"I'm right behind you!"

Just as we reached the tunnel opening, the old place collapsed. There were rocks, mud, and splintered wood everywhere. Junior and I just looked at each other, knowing that if we had remained in that room just a few seconds longer, we would have been goners.

Writing Plays

Writing a play or script can be as simple as telling your friends what happened last night at the park. In fact, that may be exactly what your play is about—something that really did happen to you and your friends. At least that's the way you will want your play to sound. More than any other form of creative writing, a play can bring your personal experiences (or your imaginings) to life in a "dramatic" way. The tips which follow should help you transform your best ideas into exciting dramas worthy of any classroom or stage.

257 The Play-writing Process

The first thing you need to know about writing a play is that it truly is a process of discovery. You can't possibly imagine how your play is going to turn out before you write it. In fact, if you choose real-life characters based on people you know, they will actually write part of the play for you.

All you need to do is put these characters "on stage," give them a problem to overcome, and then watch and listen to what they say and do. You become as much a reporter taking notes and recording conversations as a struggling student playwright. Remember this as you write your play.

258 Selecting: *Choosing an Idea*

As you begin looking for an idea for your play, it is important to remember that a play is very much like a short story. And like a short story, very often the best ideas for a play are found in the everyday happenings and problems of real people: a narrow escape from trouble, a misunderstanding with a friend or parent, a need for something not easily gotten—you get the idea.

Consider, too, that most stories have a message (a theme, a point) in addition to a plot. What might the message or point of your story be? Well, like the idea for your play, the message should come from real life—things aren't always what they seem; harmless fun can sometimes backfire; strange things happen when certain people get together.

> "I start by thinking of characters and what they like and how they get along with each other. Then I think of a good first line and let the characters tell the rest of the story."
> — Janae, a student writer

Collecting: *Planning Ahead*

With a fairly clear idea of what your plot and message are going to be, you are ready to start collecting details. To help get you going and keep you on track, you should consider using some form of "collection sheet" or prewriting checklist. Probably the easiest way is to simply make a list of all the "elements" that go into a good play (see list below). Then fill in your list with as many details as you can. Actually writing down each part of your play can help you see the overall picture and figure out what still needs to be done.

Sample Collection Sheet

Main character #1: (List everything you feel is important for your audience to know about this character—name, age, occupation, personality traits, his or her place or role in the play, personal motives, etc.)

Main character #2: (Same as above)

Other characters: (List the role or relationship each character has to the others in the play, along with any other important information.)

Setting: (Describe where and when the story takes place.)

Main problem: (What is the main problem faced by the characters in the play? What do they have to do to overcome this problem?)

Complication: (What complication or added problem makes it difficult for the characters to find a solution to the main problem? How can this complication help you add humor or suspense to your play? What can your characters do or say to help solve or further complicate the situation?)

Solution: (How do they finally solve the problem and bring the play to an end?)

Message: (What, if anything, does your play have to "say" about life to your audience? Is there a moral, a lesson, a point?)

Please note: This list is just to get you started. Add or change questions as you need to.

✏ DIALOGUE-WRITING TIP

Write your dialogue out loud whenever possible and use simple, everyday language. Keep your characters "alive" by giving them lines in all scenes in which they are present. Often, the minor characters can be given questions to ask, like "What's going on?" This gives you a way to explain something to your audience which is otherwise difficult to work into your dialogue.

Connecting: *Writing the Script*

Getting Started

Once you have a good idea, a cast of interesting characters, and an overall plan or outline, you are ready to begin writing your play. As you know, a play looks quite different on the page than a short story. Here are some tips and a short sample which will help make your play look like a play.

- First, make a list of your characters and give their relationship to the other characters and a brief summary of their personal characteristics.
- Add a brief description of the setting (time and place) and situation the characters are in as the play begins.
- Begin the action of your play by first naming each character (in capital letters) before he or she speaks. Put parentheses around the voice and movement directions which tell your readers what each character is doing and how they are doing it (emotion in the voice, movement on the stage, props being used, and any other important information you cannot write into the dialogue).
- Skip a line between each exchange of dialogue.

MOTHER. (looking out the window) Mary! Mary!

MARY. (walks quickly into room) What is it? What's wrong?

MOTHER. (pointing to table) Quick, bring me my glasses! They're putting something into the trunk of their car. It's wrapped in a blanket.

MARY. (in a loud whisper) Mother, please . . . . They'll see you!

Keeping It Going

The best way to keep your play going is to simply let your characters talk things through. As the characters talk and act, they will reveal things about themselves and the situation they are in. Your job becomes mainly one of reacting to what each character says or does. Even though you are the one putting words into their mouths, it is more like reacting than writing. Each line or action leads naturally to the next. (For each action, there is a reaction.)

✏️ WRITING TIP

It is often a good idea to build the action in your play around one main character, the character who is most affected by the main problem or is most responsible for solving it. The other characters help (or hinder) this character. This character should have a distinct personality, one which may change as the play progresses. This personality will determine how the person talks (loudly, softly, boastfully), what the person says, and how the other characters react to him or her.

Your characters may also help you figure out when and how to work in the *complications*. (The first one should be fairly soon after your play begins.) Complications will not only make your play more believable, they will also add interest or suspense. In addition, they will give your audience a chance to see your characters in a variety of situations. If your characters are interesting (clever, weird, funny, lifelike), your audience will like and remember them—and your play.

Finishing It Off

Your play will come to an end when a final solution (*resolution*) is found to the main problem and each of the complications. Finding a good resolution may be your greatest challenge as a playwright. If you choose a resolution which is too obvious or predictable or one which is too far out of line, your audience will be disappointed. They will be looking forward to an ending which is at least a little bit surprising or unexpected, but also believable. End with a good closing line, one which brings it all together—and also brings a smile, a laugh, a groan.

Correcting: *Reviewing and Revising*

The most important thing to look for in a finished play is whether it works. Read your play out loud, by yourself at first. Make changes and corrections. Then get several friends or classmates to read it out loud (each taking a part) while you listen. Ask for their comments and change things as necessary. Finally, correct any spelling or mechanical errors.

Searching to Learn

Personal Research and Writing

I've never met Robert Fulghum, but I feel like I know a lot about him after reading his book *All I Really Need to Know I Learned in Kindergarten*. I'd like to share with you two things that I learned. And why? They will help you participate in a new and exciting type of research — the personal research project — described in this section.

First, Mr. Fulghum doesn't take himself too seriously. He writes, for example, about buying boxes of crayons as gifts for adults. And he'd love to have a party (a grown-up party, mind you) and pass crayons around and see what happens. That's not a sign of a serious man. **Secondly**, and most importantly, Mr. Fulghum is curious, and he is curious in a wonderful yet ordinary way. (The subtitle of his book is *Uncommon Thoughts on Common Things*.)

265

A wondering he will go . . .

266

He wonders about spiders and mushrooms and dandelions. He wonders why many people close their eyes when they brush their teeth and why many people put milk containers back in the refrigerator with just a tiny bit of milk left in them. He also wonders about "big-ticket" items like electricity and laughter and why you can't get to the end of a rainbow.

"All life is an experiment. The more experiments you make the better."

—Ralph Waldo Emerson

Sometimes his wondering leads to little adventures or mini research projects. He once searched his area of the country for the best chicken-fried steak. At another time, he celebrated the bicentennial of the first hot-air balloon ride by taking a balloon ride himself. And once he inquired about the lint and dust that naturally accumulated in his house, and he made some interesting discoveries. For example, did you know that meteorites which disintegrate when they hit the earth's atmosphere are one of the main sources of this stuff?

And did you know that sixty or seventy thousand spiders live in a typical suburban acre? Mr. Fulghum didn't either until he made this discovery during one of his little adventures.

267 A wondering you will go . . .

So why have I mentioned all of this? Well, I'd like you to nose around the ordinary occurrences in your own life, much like Mr. Fulghum, and see what there is that interests you, that arouses your curiosity, that gets you wondering. And why? This is how you will find subjects for your own mini research projects which I can guarantee you will be more personal, active, and interesting than most of the traditional research you have done in school.

> You know what I mean by traditional research—reading two or three encyclopedia articles and paging through one or two additional reference books on subjects like supercomputers, horses, apartheid, or Japan. And you know what this research leads to—the classroom report. Reports are fine. They give you firsthand experience using library resources. (See 271 for our chapter on the classroom report.) They just don't happen to be as active and exciting as personal research projects.

268 Where It Begins

Mr. Fulghum is able to pick up on any number of things to wonder and write about. And he makes it seem so easy, mainly because he spends a lot of time examining his life. It's not likely that you have this same type of experience, so we have developed this section to help you begin your own personal research adventures.

Personal research begins with your own natural curiosity about something. You might, for example, have something practical in mind, such as which bike to buy or which pair of tennis shoes makes the most sense or who makes the best pizza in your town or what would it be like to deliver pizzas?

Then again, you might wonder who lived in your house before you or what would it be like to design a house or tear one down? Or what happens to letters that you drop in your local mailbox or why are some people afraid of spiders and snakes or who's the best gardener in your neighborhood or why would anyone want to be a dentist? Or . . . you get the picture. There are a lot of things that might interest you. You just have to take the time to think about them.

✏️ WRITING TIP

Generate ideas by writing "I wonder . . ." statements as freely and rapidly as you can. Try working with a friend or classmate and alternate "I wonder . . ." statements. Or, in your writing group, list places and possible research ideas in your town that begin with each letter in the alphabet. What you'll end up with is quite an impressive list of research ideas.

Selecting and Collecting

Make sure that you select an idea that really interests you and is within your abilities to research. (I doubt, for example, that you have the ability to explore firsthand espionage as a career.) Then refer to the guidelines which follow to help you conduct your own personal research:

- **Share your research idea** with friends, classmates, parents, and teachers. Find out what they think of it, and ask for their help. They might know of people or other sources of information that will get you started.
- **Contact people**—in person, by telephone, by letter—knowledgeable about your idea.

Friends, friends of friends, classmates, neighbors, or relatives may be your best sources of information. They may also be able to suggest other people to talk to.

- **Plan carefully for interviews.** Most people will be more than willing to talk to you about their area of expertise if you approach them with meaningful questions and if you seem genuinely interested.
- **Take notes** or tape-record the interview. Request the names of other people to consult or other sources of information. This could include places to visit and activities to observe or participate in. It could also include brochures or literature that the person is willing to share with you.
- **Try sharing the ideas** of one interviewee with other people you interview: "Would you agree that . . . is important?" or "What do you think about . . . ?"
- **Refer to books or magazines** that have been recommended to you. (In personal research, the library shouldn't be your main source of information. It should be one of many sources, and often not the most important one. You may, in fact, not need to use the library at all in your research.)
- **Get as actively involved** in your research as you can. Carry out additional firsthand researching activities (visits, observations, questionnaires, experiments, etc.) whenever possible.

Before you tell your own story, see how the pros do it. It's not uncommon for stories in your favorite magazines and in special sections of your newspaper to be based on the personal research experiences of the writers.

270 **Connecting:** *Telling Your Research Story*

The end product of all of your collecting should be the story of your researching adventure.

■ Start your story at the beginning and share with your readers everything important that happened until your research was completed. (Eating a granola bar before your first interview is not important; how you felt before your first interview is.)

■ You might find it helpful to divide your paper into four parts:

1. **What I Knew:** Begin by explaining why you picked this topic and what you did and didn't know before you started.

2. **What I Wanted to Know:** Then explain what you hoped to find out from your research.

3. **What I Found Out:** Follow with the story of your research. Consider all important parts of the experience from setting up the first interview to the final article you read. *And tell it like it happened: That means include real feelings.* Include photographs with captions, sketches, charts, maps, and brochures if you wish.

4. **What I Learned:** Close by sharing with your reader what you learned (or didn't learn).

■ Try to tell your story much like you would in conversation with classmates or friends. Include dialogue, personal feelings, and good detail. Let us know, for example, something about the appearance of the person you interviewed, your impressions of him or her, how the interview progressed, how you felt after the interview. And let us know what you did with the information this person shared with you.

■ Check "The Classroom Report" (which follows) for additional tips. You might also check the "Story Writing" section for writing ideas. You are, after all, writing a research **story**.

The Classroom Report

When a teacher asks you to write a report, he or she is asking you to do two things. First, your teacher is asking you to learn facts and details about a specific subject. You will do this by asking questions, observing, and reading. Second, your teacher is asking you to share this information in a clear, organized written report. This section will help you develop a classroom report from start to finish, from selecting a subject to producing a neat final copy to share.

Writing the Classroom Report

Selecting: *Choosing a Subject*   271

Your teacher will identify the *general* subject for your report. It will be up to you to find a *specific* report subject that interests you. You will find it enjoyable to learn about a specific subject you are interested in.

Let's say you are assigned a report in your science class. The general subject is wildlife. Your teacher states that you must choose a specific wildlife mammal, bird, or fish which interests you as the specific subject or topic of your report. Check with your school library for books on wildlife. By paging through these books, you should be able to find a specific animal for your report. Keep in mind that when you select a topic, there must be enough information available to write a good report.

Collecting: *Gathering the Details*   272

Suppose you pick a certain bird of prey—the peregrine falcon—for the topic of your report. The next step is to find a good number of interesting facts and details about the topic. The books and magazines in your library will give you good background information to get you started.

You should, however, also look for other types of information. There are people you can talk to and places you can visit. A city museum, zoo, or nearby wildlife area would be good sources of information for a wildlife report since they usually employ wildlife experts and often feature special wildlife displays. There are many organizations which offer free material with valuable, up-to-date information. You simply have to write them a letter and ask for it.

Recording Your Information

Take notes: Once you have found the books and materials for your report, the next step is to read through all of them and take notes on important facts and details.

Ask questions: To help you organize your reading and note taking, it might be helpful to write some basic questions about your subject which you would like to answer in your report. Put each of these questions at the top of a separate note card. Anytime you find a fact that helps answer one of your questions, write this information on the note card with that question.

Example: In a report on the peregrine falcon, the following basic questions would be helpful in organizing the reading and note taking:

> What does the peregrine falcon look like?
> Where does the peregrine falcon live and mate?
> What does the peregrine falcon eat and how does it get its food?
> What are its natural enemies?
> How does it get along with man?
> How many peregrine falcons are there?
> What makes this bird interesting or different?

Sample Notes Cards

What does the peregrine falcon eat and how does it get its food?

Where does the peregrine falcon live and mate?

What does the peregrine falcon look like?
- usually between 15 and 20 inches in length
- wingspan - 43 inches
- hooked beak and razor-sharp talons for hunting
- top part of falcon is blue-gray
- the bottom part is white with black bars
- there are black stripes on the beak

Organizing Your Information

Select a main point: Once you have finished your reading and note taking, the next step is to begin arranging or organizing all the information you have found. Choose the information on one of your note cards to be the main point of your report. If you had done research on the peregrine falcon, for example, you would have learned that this bird is on the endangered species list. This information could certainly be the main point for a report.

Arrange your cards: Next, you should arrange the rest of your note cards. Keep in mind the main point of your report and put the rest of your note cards in the best possible order.

Outlining Your Information

Write a rough outline: The final step in the collecting stage of your report is to write an outline. Begin your outline by listing the headings (questions) that are written on the top of your note cards. List them in the same order that you have already organized them. Leave enough space between each heading to list the important facts or details which are written on each note card. Think of this as the first draft of your outline if you are required to develop a formal outline with your report. (Otherwise, this rough outline may be all you need.)

Rewrite your outline: Rewrite the first draft of your outline into a clear sentence outline. The headings or questions are the main ideas and should follow Roman numerals (I., II., III., IV., etc.). The details under each heading or main idea should follow capital letters (A., B., C., etc.). *Note:* The first two main ideas and supporting details for the model report on the peregrine falcon are outlined below.

I. The use of pesticides is the main reason the peregrine falcon is an endangered species.
  A. The falcons are infected when they eat other birds already infected with pesticides like DDT.
  B. Pesticides can affect the peregrine's ability to reproduce.
  C. They can cause falcon eggs to have very thin, weak shells.
  D. The pesticides can kill full-grown falcons.
II. Man's movement into the peregrine's natural habitat or home has also caused it to be an endangered species.
  A. The use of wilderness land for farming, game preserves, and parks has damaged the falcon's natural habitat.
  B. Sonic booms from modern aircraft may also be hurting the peregrine population.

276 **Connecting:** *Writing the First Draft*

Write your report: If you have a complete and organized outline, writing your report should be no problem. Each main idea could become the topic sentence for a paragraph in your report; the details under each main idea would be the sentences or supporting details for that paragraph. Don't be afraid to change your mind as you write your first draft. A new and better way of thinking about your subject may occur to you as you write.

Write an opening paragraph: This paragraph should say something interesting and catchy about the topic so that the reader will want to read your report. The introductory paragraph should also state the main point of your report. Whether you write this paragraph before or after you develop the body of your report is up to you. (See the "Model Report" at the end of this unit for an example.)

Write a closing paragraph: After you have written the main part or body of your report, add a closing paragraph, if needed. This paragraph should summarize the main points made in the report. Try to end with a strong closing sentence—one that will make a lasting impression.

✏ **WRITING TIP**

At some point as you are planning your outline or writing your first draft, you should see how well your writing matches up to your readers. If you're sure that all of the information you have gathered will be new to your readers, that's great. Give it all to them, in the best possible way. But if you're reporting on a fairly familiar subject, don't tell your readers things they already know. Give them what's new, what's different, what's important. Ask yourself the questions which follow.

---

277 **Questions to Consider**

■ Who am I writing for? Who are my readers? (You're probably writing for your teacher and classmates. But who knows, you might be involved in a special project in which your readers are younger children or, perhaps, a group of senior citizens.)

■ What do they want to know? (No one is interested in old information.)

■ What do they want to learn? (Readers most importantly want to learn something when they read a report. But they also like to be entertained, so think about including a few surprises.)

■ What do they need to know? (Your readers need to know anything that will help them understand and possibly react to the main point of your writing. Think of your report as more of a conversation starter than the last word on your subject.)

Improving the Writing

Revising a report takes time since there are many things to think about. Use the following checklist as a guide.

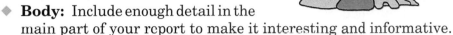

- ◆ **Introduction:** Your opening paragraph should get the reader's attention and introduce the topic.
- ◆ **Body:** Include enough detail in the main part of your report to make it interesting and informative.
- ◆ **Conclusion:** Your concluding paragraph should summarize the significant points in your report and leave your reader with a lasting impression.
- ◆ **Paragraphs:** Each paragraph should be clear and contain an important point about your topic; each sentence should be related, necessary, and clearly expressed. Your paragraphs should be arranged in the best possible order.
- ◆ **Wording:** Use your own words in your report. It should sound like it comes from you, a student report writer presenting his or her findings as clearly and sincerely as possible. (Use quotation marks when you use someone else's words.)
- ◆ **Color:** Use strong verbs and helpful comparisons in your text; add illustrations, charts, graphs, and other visual aids if they add interest to your report.

Correcting: *A Final Look*

- ◆ **Accuracy:** Make sure your report is accurate. Double-check for any missing information and any facts which seem fuzzy or hard to believe. Make sure your writing is accurate. Check the spelling, usage, capitalization, and punctuation of your report.
- ◆ **Giving Credit:** Give credit for an author's ideas or words if you are required to do so by your teacher. (Use "Giving Credit...," 280, as a guide.) If you are required to write a bibliography, follow the guidelines in your handbook. (See 281.)
- ◆ **Title Page and Outline:** Write the title page and outline for your report if they are required as part of your assignment. Follow the guidelines established by your teacher or the guidelines in your handbook. (See 282.)
- ◆ **Final Copy:** Write your final copy in ink on unlined paper. Number your pages in the upper right-hand corner starting with the second page. If you are typing your report, double-space the entire paper. Leave a 1 to 1-1/2 inch margin on all sides.

280 Giving Credit for Information Used in a Report

If you are required to give credit to the authors whose ideas or words you have used in your report, follow the guidelines set by your teacher. Your teacher may ask you to identify the authors on each page of your report or in a list at the end of your report.

Giving credit in the body: If your teacher asks you to give credit in the body of your report, you can do this by placing (in parentheses) the author's last name and the page number(s) on which you found the information. This reference is placed at the end of the last sentence or idea taken from that author. The sample reference below tells the reader that this information was originally written by the author *Allen* and was found on page 193. (For the author's full name and the title of the book, the reader can check the bibliography at the end of the report.)

> A peregrine's ability to reproduce may be upset by these pesticides. They can also cause falcon eggs to have very thin and weak shells (Allen 193).

If you use a book or material that doesn't have an author, use the title (or a shortened form of the title) in place of an author's last name. Also, page numbers are not required for one-page articles or articles in encyclopedias. The sample note given below tells the reader that the article about the peregrine in <u>Wildlife Notes</u> was only one page long.

> Mated pairs of falcons may hunt as a team. One floats high in the air while the other falcon flies at a lower level. The falcon at the lower level scares up prey and the other falcon dives and attacks it (<u>Wildlife Notes</u>).

Using common knowledge: It is not necessary to list an author or book for every single bit of information you use in your report. If the information is common knowledge—already known by many people—you do not have to list an author even though you may have just read this information as you were preparing your report.

✏ REPORT-WRITING TIP

You should give credit in your report (list an author and page number) for the following kinds of information:

- Information which is copied directly from another source. (You should not copy information directly unless the exact words of an expert or author are very important to your report.)
- Information which is written in your own words but contains key words, phrases, or ideas associated with an author or expert.

Adding a Bibliography

A **bibliography** is a page at the end of a report which lists in alphabetical order the books and materials you have used in your report. Follow your teacher's guidelines and those in this section.

 Double-space the information you include in your bibliography. The second line should be indented 1/2 inch (5 typed spaces).

■ **Books:** A typical listing for a book is written in the following way:

> *Author* (last name first). *Title*. *City where book is published: Publisher, copyright date.*

■ **Magazines:** A listing for a periodical or magazine follows:

> *Author* (last name first). *"Title of the article."* *Title of the magazine Date (day, month, year): Page numbers of the article.*

Adding a Title Page and Outline

If you are required to write a **title page**, make sure you follow the guidelines set by your teacher. Usually, the following information is placed on the title page: *title of your report, your name, your teacher's name, the name of the course,* and *the date.* This information should be centered on a separate sheet of paper. (*Note:* You may, however, be told to simply place this information on the top of the first page of your report.)

If you are required to include an **outline**, make sure it meets the requirements of the assignment and follows the written report. (*Note:* The outline for the "Model Report" contains only the main ideas.)

Model Outline

Introductory Paragraph
I. The use of pesticides is the main reason the peregrine falcon is an endangered species.
II. Man's movement into the peregrine's natural habitat or home has also caused it to be an endangered species.
III. Man has not always treated the peregrine falcon so harmfully.
IV. The peregrine falcon is built for hunting.
V. The peregrine falcon feeds mainly on pigeons, songbirds, and ducks.
VI. This bird of prey usually lives and breeds on the sides of high cliffs.
VII. Today, not many peregrine falcons are found in the United States.
VIII. Steps are being taken to save this bird of prey.
Concluding Statement

Model Works Cited Entries

One author	Allen, Thomas B. <u>Vanishing Wildlife of North America</u>. Washington, D.C.: National Geographic Society, 1974.
Two or three authors	Searles, Baird and Martin Last. <u>A Reader's Guide to Science Fiction</u>. New York: Facts on File, Inc., 1979.
More than three authors or editors	Brandes, Kathleen, et al., eds. <u>Vanishing Species</u>. NewYork: Time-Life Books, 1976. *Note:* For a book with more than three authors, simply drop *eds.* from the entry.
A single work from an anthology	Poe, Edgar Allen. "The Raven." <u>Selected Stories & Poems</u>. Ed. Joseph Wood Kruth. Danbury: Grolier Enterprises, 1978.
Encyclopedia article	Pettingill, Olin Sewall, Jr. "Falcon and Falconry." <u>World Book Encyclopedia</u>. 1980. *Note:* It is not necessary to give full publication information for encyclopedias. If the article is followed by the author's initials, check in the index of authors (usually located in the front of each volume) for the author's full name. If it is unsigned, give the title first.
Signed article in a weekly	Kanfer, Stefan. "Heard Any Good Books Lately?" <u>Time</u> 21 July 1986: 71.
Unsigned article in a weekly	"America on Drugs." <u>Newsweek</u> 28 July 1986: 48-50.
Signed article in a monthly	Heinrich, Bernd. "Why Is a Robin's Egg Blue?" <u>Audubon</u> July 1986: 64-71.
Signed news-paper article	Kalette, Denise. "California Town Counts Down to Big Quake." <u>USA Today</u> 21 July 1986, sec. A: 1.
Unsigned editorial or story	"A School Year Without a Strike." Editorial. <u>Chicago Tribune</u> 22 July 1986, sec. 1:10. *Note:* For an unsigned story, simply omit *Editorial.*
Signed pamphlet	Laird, Jean E. <u>The Metrics Are Coming</u>. Burlington, Iowa: National Research Bureau, 1976.
Pamphlet with no author, pub-lisher, or date	<u>Pedestrian Safety</u>. [United States]: n.p., n.d. *Note:* List the country of publication (in brackets) if known.
Filmstrips, slide programs, and videotape	<u>The Grizzlies</u>. Videotape. National Geographic Video, 1987. 60 min.
Radio or television program	"Latch-Key Kids." <u>Hour Magazine</u>. CBS, 15 Nov. 1983. *Note:* Other information (director, producer, narrator, writer) may be listed if appropriate.

Model Report

Tim Larsen
Mrs. Frenz
Life Science
May 3, 1986

The American Peregrine Falcon: A Vanishing Bird

Imagine something only 15 to 20 inches long dropping out of the sky at 200 miles an hour. It would be nothing but a blur. And that is what makes the peregrine falcon such an effective bird of prey. When it dives and attacks its prey, it can reach speeds of over 200 miles per hour. No wonder the United States Air Force Academy has made the falcon its official mascot. This lightning-quick bird of prey, however, may not fly and attack much longer. The peregrine falcon is an endangered species.

The use of pesticides is the main reason the peregrine falcon is an endangered species. Pesticides are chemicals sprayed on plants to kill insects. The falcons are infected when they eat other birds already infected with pesticides like DDT. A peregrine's ability to reproduce may be upset by these pesticides. They can also cause falcon eggs to have very thin and weak shells (Allen 193). These eggs break before they should, and the hatched falcons die. Sometimes the pesticides can kill full-grown falcons.

Man's movement into the peregrine's natural habitat or home has also caused it to be an endangered species. The use of wilderness land for farming and game preserves and parks has damaged the falcon's natural habitat. Also, the sonic booms from modern aircraft may be hurting the peregrine population. The power and sound of a sonic boom possibly upset nesting falcons and cause falcon eggs to crack too soon.

Man has not always treated the peregrine falcon so harmfully. The ancient Egyptians and Persians treated the falcon in a very special way. The Egyptians called the falcon "The Lofty One." During the Middle Ages, the very wealthy men of Europe used the falcon for hunting because of the bird's speed and intelligence. This type of hunting is called falconry. Falconry declined after the invention of guns. However, some people still hunt with falcons in England and the United States ("Falcon" 37).

Margin annotations:

An interesting opening line

A statement of the specific report topic

The first strong point

A second important point

Interesting historical information

A "note" giving credit for information

2

Important physical details about the falcon

The peregrine falcon is built for hunting. It is a large bird, usually between 15 and 20 inches in length. The falcon's long, pointed wings spread to around 43 inches in full flight. Its hooked beak and razor-sharp talons or claws can slice its prey when it attacks. The top part of a peregrine falcon is blue-gray in color, and the bottom part is white with black bars or stripes (Pettingill 14). The dull, natural colors of the falcon help keep it unnoticed when it is getting ready to attack.

Details about predators and prey

The peregrine falcon feeds mainly on pigeons, songbirds, and ducks. Prey is often killed in the air after a quick dive by a peregrine. The prey is struck suddenly with the peregrine's deadly claws. Mated pairs of falcons may hunt as a team. One floats high in the air while the other falcon flies at a lower level. The falcon at the lower level scares up prey and the other falcon dives and attacks it (Wildlife Notes).

This information was found on page 68 of Wilson's book

This bird of prey usually lives and breeds on the sides of high cliffs. Peregrine falcons have the same mate for life and produce three or four eggs each season. The young are hatched after about 32 days of nesting. They stay in the nest for five or six weeks. It takes another month before the young can fly and hunt for food. Normally, a falcon will live for four or five years, although they may live up to 12 years or longer (Wilson 68).

An update on falcons today

Today, not many peregrine falcons are found anywhere in the lower United States. As of 1978, only 31 pairs were known to have been nesting in the wild (Wildlife Notes). These birds were found in the southwestern part of our country. The remaining falcons in North America live mainly in Alaska, western Canada, and Mexico. At one time, peregrine falcons were common in the central Rocky Mountain region of the United States. They used to breed east of the Rockies as well.

Closing thoughts on the peregrine's future

Steps are being taken to save this bird of prey. Environmentalists are trying to limit the use of pesticides. Also, the Peregrine Fund at Cornell Laboratory of Ornithology in Ithaca, New York, has been created to breed peregrine falcons. A 10-year goal is to breed enough peregrines to populate its former habitats. Nearly 250 falcons have already been released (Brandes 82). Some of these birds must survive in the wild. It would be a tragedy to lose the peregrine falcon, one of the fastest and most spectacular birds in the air.

Works Cited

Allen, Thomas B.   <u>Vanishing Wildlife of North America</u>.

Washington, D.C.: National Geographic Society,

1974.

Brandes, Kathleen, et al., eds. ^(2 spaces)<u>Vanishing Species</u>. ^(2 spaces)New

York:^(1 space)Time-Life Books,^(1 space)1976.

"Falcon."   <u>The Audubon Nature Encyclopedia</u>.   The

Audubon Society.   12 vols.   Philadelphia: Cross,

1965.

Pettingill, Olin Sewall, Jr.   "Falcon and Falconry."

<u>World Book Encyclopedia</u>.   1980.

<u>Wildlife Notes: The American Peregrine Falcon</u>.

National Wildlife Federation, 1980.

Wilson, Ron.   <u>Vanishing Species</u>.   Secaucus, New

Jersey: Chartwell Books Inc., 1979.

"Works Cited" (or "Bibliography") one inch from the top

Double-space everything in bibliography.

Indent second and third lines 5 spaces.

Computers & Writing

What are the tools of the modern writer's trade? A notebook and some favorite pens and pencils, a few basic reference books like your handbook, maybe a trusty old typewriter, and a **personal computer**—all of these might be used during a writing project. None, however, will be more important than that number one time-saving device—the computer.

Those of you who have used a computer for writing already know why it has become such a valued piece of equipment. To the unacquainted, it is only a matter of time, and you too will see what an amazing tool the computer is. Even if you never own one of your own, your schools are (or soon will be) equipped with computers. And you can count on using a computer in the workplace since almost all businesses are already computerized.

287 Basic Bytes

Writers who are just getting into computers will find the following observations helpful. (You "users" will learn some things as well.)

- The computer is a medium for writing like pen and paper and the typewriter, nothing more. It can't think for you (as of yet), and it can't write for you. You still have to produce the words; the computer simply "captures" them more quickly and efficiently than other mediums.

- Don't put your pens and paper into storage once you start using a computer. You will still do plenty of old-fashioned longhand during most of your writing projects. Many writers feel most comfortable doing their initial collecting and writing on paper and their revising and correcting on the computer. Experience will tell you how best to utilize a computer.

- To hunt and peck with a computer is as tedious as it is with a typewriter, so you must learn how to keyboard. Most schools now offer keyboarding instruction. If your school doesn't offer it, find someone who has a keyboarding program you can use on your own.

 Helpful HINT

Practice keyboarding as often as you can—before, during, and after school. A person who can keyboard effectively is a person who can make full use of a computer as a writing tool. We have included two illustrations in your handbook to help you work on this important skill (see 846-847).

More Bytes

- You don't need to know (and probably shouldn't know) everything about a computer to write with it. Some people get so carried away with the technology that they forget that the computer is not an end in itself. It is a tool and should be used as a tool.

- Word processing programs make a computer the high-tech writing machine it is. All programs allow you to enter, delete, add, and move data. Some programs also allow you to check for spelling and punctuation errors when you are ready to correct your copy.

- Expect to lose one of the first few things you compose on a computer. It happens to everyone. It's best to work from a written copy of your composition until you get used to word processing, and it's always a good idea to save your work at regular intervals.

- You're all familiar with writer's cramp. Well, writing with a computer takes care of that, but it is not without a "cramp" of its own. Staring at a monitor for a long period of time can cause eyestrain. When your eyes begin to ache, save your text, turn off your machine, and come back to your work at another time.

Helpful HINT

Make sure that you adjust the contrast and brightness on your monitor so that it feels comfortable to your eyes. Also, adjust the lighting in the room. Brightness and glare lead to eyestrain.

Coming On-line

Anyone who regularly writes with a computer will tell you that it is most valuable for revising and proofreading. A computer will help you stay with your writing longer and develop it more thoroughly because you don't have to manually rewrite your paper after you make changes. You can do all of your adding, deleting, and moving right on the computer.

Have a printed copy of your writing on hand in case you want to make some quick notes or do some experimenting. You'll also find it helpful to have a copy of the original version of your writing to refer to after you make changes on the computer.

Note: Use pen and paper for collecting your initial thoughts and for your very first draft to ensure a free flow of ideas.

> "Writing with a computer will help you look for things to revise instead of wondering why you have to revise."

Using the Library

Suppose you are writing a story about "Joining a Club." As a student writer, you have two sources of information. The first source is yourself. You might write about clubs you've belonged to, clubs you will join in high school, or perhaps why you'd never join a club.

The second source of information is other people and their ideas, experiences, and knowledge. The best way to collect information from other people is to talk to them directly. You could interview your friends, parents, or teachers about their experiences with clubs.

Sometimes, however, people are too busy to talk with you, sometimes they live too far away, and sometimes they are strangers you're reluctant to approach. Then there are all of those people who have passed on before us. While we can't talk to these people, it is possible to "listen" to many of them. No, we're not talking about reincarnation. We're talking about a place you can go nearly any time to share in the past experiences of thousands of people—a place where you can read about the killer bees, learn about the O.K. Corral, or even find out which presidents like to eat broccoli— THE LIBRARY.

290 Only in a library . . .

Only in your library (or, I suppose, a well-stocked bookstore) can you find thousands upon thousands of stories just waiting to be shared. Researching the topic of *clubs* at the library might produce interesting information or a good quote about clubs or a club member which you could include as part of your story. For example, when the comedian Groucho Marx was invited to become a member of a certain club, he replied, "I do not wish to belong to the kind of club that accepts people like me as members."

> "There is more treasure in books than in all the pirates' loot on Treasure Island."
> —**Walt Disney**

Before you can find stories like Groucho Marx's, you have to know how and where to find them. Because there are so many books in your library, you can't simply walk up to the first shelf you come to and begin looking. It would be the same as going from house to house in a big city looking for a friend. You may know the name or the subject of the book, but without the book's "address," there is little chance you'll ever find it.

Searching for Materials   291

You can find the address or *call number* of each resource your library has by looking in the **card catalog** (or a computer file). The card catalog contains cards for each book and nearly all other materials located in the library. Each book is listed by *title, author,* and *subject*. This means you can find a book you are interested in even if you don't know the author or the exact title. All you really need to know is what the book is about.

Each drawer in the card catalog is labeled clearly so that you can see which cards are contained inside. The cards are arranged alphabetically. However, certain words, numbers, and abbreviations are handled in a special way when they come first in a title. Here are some guidelines:

Titles

■ If the first word in a title is an article (*a, an, the*), you should skip over the article and begin looking for the title under the second word. **Example:** The title card for *The Magnificent Seven* is placed in the *M* drawer under *Magnificent*.

■ If the title begins with an abbreviation, the title is filed as if the abbreviation were spelled out. **Example:** The title card for *Mr. Chips Takes a Vacation* is placed in the *M* drawer under *Mister*.

Authors

■ Authors are listed by last name first. **Example:** McCarthy, Mary.

■ Last names beginning with *Mc* are often filed as *Mac*.

Subjects

■ Subject cards are listed alphabetically and are placed before titles which begin with the same word. **Example:** The subject card MEDICINE—HISTORY comes before the title card *Medicine for All*.

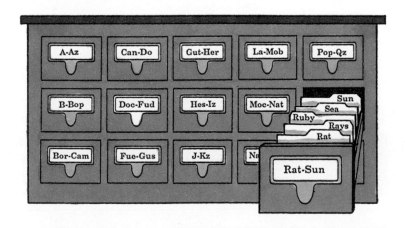

292 Inside the Card Catalog

To find out if your library contains a certain book, simply look in the drawer (or in the computer) for the *title* of the book. If you don't know the title, but do know the *author*, check for the author card. Finally, if you don't know the title or the author, look under the general *subject* of the book. Also look under the subject if you are interested in finding several books on your topic.

The catalog cards will give you the following information: the call number (address), the author, title, subject, publisher, illustrator, copyright date, number of pages, and information about the content (sometimes called an *annotation*) of the book. The sample cards below are the same kind of cards you will find in your school's card catalog.

293 Sample Catalog Cards

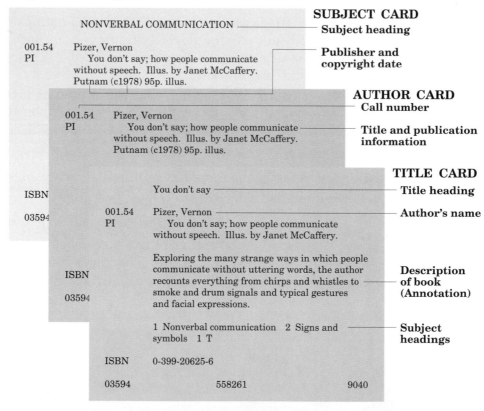

SUBJECT CARD
Subject heading

NONVERBAL COMMUNICATION

001.54 PI — Pizer, Vernon
You don't say; how people communicate without speech. Illus. by Janet McCaffery. Putnam (c1978) 95p. illus.

Publisher and copyright date

AUTHOR CARD
Call number

001.54 PI — Pizer, Vernon
You don't say; how people communicate without speech. Illus. by Janet McCaffery. Putnam (c1978) 95p. illus.

Title and publication information

TITLE CARD
Title heading

You don't say

001.54 PI — Pizer, Vernon
You don't say; how people communicate without speech. Illus. by Janet McCaffery.

Author's name

Exploring the many strange ways in which people communicate without uttering words, the author recounts everything from chirps and whistles to smoke and drum signals and typical gestures and facial expressions.

Description of book (Annotation)

1 Nonverbal communication   2 Signs and symbols   1 T

Subject headings

ISBN   0-399-20625-6

03594   558261   9040

Once you have found the card you are looking for in the card catalog, copy down the call number (and the title and author) of the book. This will save you the trouble of looking it up again later if you don't immediately find the book.

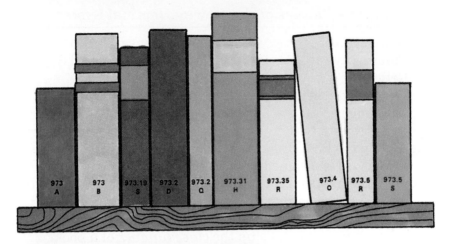

Finding a Book: The Call Number

Once you have found the call number, you can begin looking for your book on the shelf. As you look for your book, you must remember to read the call numbers very carefully because several books may have the same number *on the top line*. When this happens, you must look closely at the letters or numbers *on the second line*. In the illustration above, you will notice that the first two books have the same number on the top line. Therefore, the books are arranged in order by the letter in the second line. This is why $^{973}_{A}$ comes before $^{973}_{B}$.

Helpful HINT

Some call numbers contain several decimal places and are much longer than other call numbers. For example, number 973.198 might at first appear to be larger than 973.2. It is, in fact, a "longer" number but not a larger one. You must keep this in mind as you search for your book.

The Dewey Decimal System

At this point, you might well ask where the call number for each book comes from and why some books have longer numbers than others. To begin with, most call numbers are assigned according to the **Dewey Decimal System**, a system set up to help people arrange books more efficiently. Using this system, a librarian can give each book a separate number, a number which tells the reader what that book is about.

A history book, for example, is given a number in the 900's, while a language book is given a number in the 400's. This means that books on the same subject are given similar numbers and are placed together on the shelves. This makes your job of locating several books on the same topic much easier.

The Ten Classes of the Dewey Decimal System

000	Generalities	500	Pure Science
100	Philosophy	600	Technology (Applied Science)
200	Religion	700	The Arts
300	The Social Sciences	800	Language and Rhetoric
400	Language	900	Geography and History

In the Dewey Decimal System, all knowledge is divided into ten main classes. Each class is assigned a set of numbers from 000 to 900. (See the chart above.) Each class is further divided into divisions. (See the chart below.) Each division is then divided into sections, each with its own number. These sections are divided into as many subsections as necessary. Together these numbers make up the *class number* of a book.

Understanding the Dewey Decimal Class Number

900	History	Class
9**7**0	History of North America	Division
97**3**	History of the United States	Section
973.**7**	History of the U.S. Civil War	Subsection
973.**74**	History of Civil War Songs	Subsection

In addition to its class number, a call number contains the first letter of the author's last name. It may also contain a "cutter" number assigned by the librarian to help in shelving the book and the first letter of the title's first significant word.

Sample Call Number

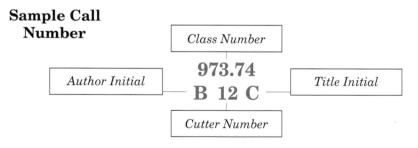

Class Number

Author Initial

973.74

B 12 C

Title Initial

Cutter Number

Helpful HINT

Fiction books (novels) and individual biographies are *not* classified by subject like other books. Fiction is usually kept in a separate section of the library where the books are arranged by the author's last name. Individual biographies and autobiographies are arranged on a separate shelf by the last name of the person written about.

The Reference Section

Another section of the library worth knowing about is the **reference section**. Students are usually familiar with the reference section because this is the area where the encyclopedias are kept. But there are a number of other reference books which can be just as helpful and often more up-to-date. Some of the most popular titles are listed below:

- The **Abridged Readers' Guide to Periodical Literature** is a list of articles from a select group of magazines. These lists are arranged alphabetically by subject in paperbound volumes published monthly during the school year. The monthly issues are bound together in a single volume once a year.

- **Bartlett's Familiar Quotations** contains 20,000 quotations arranged in chronological order from ancient times to the present.

- **Current Biography** is published monthly and annually. Each article includes a photo of the well-known individual, a biographical sketch, and information concerning his or her birth date, address, occupation, and so on.

- **Facts About the Presidents** is a single-volume reference book which contains important facts and dates about all the presidents in chronological order.

- The **Junior Authors** books contain biographical information on children's and young adult authors. Each volume is listed in alphabetical order with volumes three through five indexing all others.

- **Kane's Famous First Facts** is a large, single volume which lists "firsts" in all areas of life by event, year, and date.

- **Something About the Author:** *Facts and Pictures About Contemporary Authors and Illustrators of Books for Young People* contains about 200 biographical sketches. Each edition contains two volumes, and each volume contains an index.

- **Webster's Biographical Dictionary** is a collection of information about famous people.

- **Webster's New Geographical Dictionary** is a list of all the world's most important places. The names are listed in alphabetical order with important geographical and historical information given about each.

- The **World Almanac and Book of Facts** is published once a year. It contains facts and statistics about the following subjects: entertainment, sports, business, politics, history, religion, education, and social programs. In addition to this information, the book also includes a review of major events of the past year.

Readers' Guide to Periodical Literature

The *Readers' Guide to Periodical Literature* is another useful guide to finding information in the library. The *Readers' Guide* is an organized list of all the latest magazine articles, articles you may find useful for a number of classroom reports or writing assignments.

299 Using the *Readers' Guide*

To use the *Readers' Guide*, simply select the volume which covers the time period (month or year) you are interested in. If, for example, you hope to find a magazine article on a scientific discovery made in November of last year, select the volume covering November and possibly December of that year. You can locate any article by looking up either the author or the subject.

When you find an article you would like to read, fill out a request form (*call slip*). If no forms are available, simply put the title, date, and volume of the magazine on a piece of paper and take it to the librarian. The librarian will get the magazine for you. Look closely at the sample page from the *Readers' Guide*. Notice the following:

- The *Readers' Guide* is cross-referenced *(see* and *see also)*. This means you will find one or more subject headings listed along with each article. You can go to these other subjects in the *Readers' Guide* to find more information on the same topic.
- Magazine articles are arranged alphabetically **by subject and author**; the title is listed under both of these entries.
- Each subject entry is divided into subtopics whenever there are a large number of articles on the same subject listed together.

✏ SEARCHING TIP

The *Readers' Guide* is especially useful if you are looking for current information, information which has been reported during the last 12 to 18 months. You should also know that many libraries today have *Readers' Guide* on informational disks so that you can search for current information on a computer.

Sample Readers' Guide Page

ENGLER, PAUL
Oil Shortage today. Beef tomorrow? por Farm J 99:B16 Mr '89

	AUTHOR ENTRY

ENGLISH
ENVIRONMENTAL engineering (buildings)
Architecture, energy, economy, and efficiency. G. Soucie. Audubon 77:122 S '89
Autonomous living in the Ouroboros house. S.J. Marcovich. il Pop Sci 207:80-2+ D '89
Conditioned air gets used three times in an energy-conscious design. il Archit Rec 158:133-4 N '89

	NAME OF AUTHOR

Energy house from England aims at self-sufficiency. D. Scott. il Pop Sci 207:78-80 Ag '89
Houses designed with nature: their future is at hand; Ouroboros and integral projects. S. Love. bibl il Smithsonian 6:46-53 D '89

	DATE

OCF presents awards for energy conservation. il Archit Rec 158:34 D '89
PM visits a house full of energy-saving ideas. J.F. Pearson. il Pop Mech 144:59+ Ag '89
Profession and industry focus on solar energy. il Archit Rec 158:35 Ag '89

	NAME OF MAGAZINE

Round table: toward a rational policy for energy use in buildings; with introd by W. F. Wagner, Jr. il Archit Rec 158:8, 92-9 mid-Ag '89
Solar energy systems: the practical side. il Archit Rec 158:128-34 mid-Ag '89
ENVIRONMENTAL health
Environmental hazards and corporate profits. Chr Cent 92:404 Ap 23 '89

	VOLUME

See also
Environmental diseases

	"SEE ALSO" CROSS-REFERENCE

ENVIRONMENTAL impact statements. See Environmental policy
ENVIRONMENTAL indexes. See Environment–Statistics
ENVIRONMENTAL law
Capitol watch. G. Alderson Liv Wildn 38:60 Wint '88; 39:33 Spr; 42 Jl; 41 O '89
How to save a river; Bellport, N.T. high students, sponsoring Carmans River bill. A. Rubin, Sr Schol 105:4-7 Ja 16 '89
Overview: law. A. W. Reitze Jr and G. L. Reitze. See issues of Environment
See also
Air pollution – Laws and legislation
Land utilization – Laws and regulations

	SUBJECT ENTRY

ENVIRONMENTAL movement
After setbacks – new tactics in environmental crusade. J. McWethy. il U.S. News 78:62-3 Je 9 '89
Be a part of Food day every day. Org Gard & Farm 22:32+ Ap '89
Dialogue: C. Amory versus environmental groups on hunting issue. R. E. Hall. Conservationist 29:1 Ap '89

	TITLE OF ARTICLE

Ecological view. J. Marshall. Liv Wildn 39:5-10 Spr '89
Environment, a mature cause in need of a lift. L. J. Carter. Science 187:45-6+ Ja 10 '89
Junior leagues focus on community education; environmental projects. M. D. Poole, por Parks & Rec 10:21+ D '89
Obligation and opportunity. R. F. Hall. Conservationist 29:1 Je '89
Organic living almanac. See issues of Organic gardening and farming

	"SEE" CROSS-REFERENCE

Prophets of shortage; address, July 11, 1975. D. Hodel. Vital Speeches 41:621-5 Ag 1 '89
What conservationists think about conservation; results of questionnaire. H. Clepper. il Am For 81:28-9+ Ag '89

	PAGE NUMBER

See also
Canada-United States environmental council
Industry and the environmental movement

Exhibitions	**SUBTOPIC**

See also
International exposition on the environment. 1988.

Parts of a Book

If the book you have searched for and located in the library is a nonfiction book which you need for a research paper or assignment, it is necessary to understand how to use that book efficiently. It is especially important, for instance, to make full use of the index and special glossary and tables when using nonfiction books. Below you will find a brief description of each part of a book.

■ The **title page** is usually the first printed page in a book. It gives you (1) the full title of the book, (2) the author's name, (3) the publisher's name, and (4) the place of publication.

■ The **copyright page** is the page right after the title page. Here you will find the year in which the copyright was issued which is usually the same year the book was published. (If the book is too old, it may no longer be a good source of information.)

■ The **preface** (also called **foreward, introduction,** or **acknowledgment**) comes before the table of contents and is there to give you an idea of what the book is about and why it was written. (This can save you having to read several pages before discovering what the book is about.)

■ The **table of contents** is one section most of you are familiar with since it shows you the major divisions of the book (*units, chapters,* and *topics*). It comes right before the body of the book and is used to help locate major topics or areas covered in the book.

■ The **body** of the book, which comes right after the table of contents, is the main section or *text* of the book.

■ Following the body is the **appendix**. This supplementary section gives extra information, usually in the form of maps, charts, tables, diagrams, letters, or copies of official documents. (Any of these materials may be just what you need for your work.)

■ The **glossary** follows the appendix and is the dictionary portion of the book. It is an alphabetical listing of technical terms, foreign words, or special words, with an explanation or definition for each.

■ The **bibliography** is a list of books or articles used by the author when preparing to write the book; the list also serves as a suggestion for further reading on the same or related topics.

■ The **index** is probably the most useful part of a book. It is an alphabetical listing of all the important topics appearing in the book. It is similar to the table of contents, except that the index is much more detailed. It will tell you, first, whether the book contains the information you need and, second, on which page that information can be found.

Using the Thesaurus

> A **thesaurus** is, in a sense, the opposite of a dictionary. You go to a dictionary when you know the word but need the definition. You go to a thesaurus when you know the definition but need the word.

A thesaurus would come in handy, for example, if you needed to find a word that means *fear,* the kind of fear that causes a great deal of worry:

The new student suffered an _____ *attack in homeroom.*

If you have a thesaurus which is in "dictionary form," simply look up the word *fear* as you would in a dictionary. If, however, you have a more traditional thesaurus, you must first look up your word in the INDEX at the back of the thesaurus where you find this entry for *fear* :

FEAR 860

fearful *painful* 830

timid 862

The numbers after *fear* are GUIDE NUMBERS, not page numbers. (Guide numbers are similar to the topic numbers used in your handbook.) The guide numbers in dark type or boldface will always appear next to the key word for that particular group of synonyms. For instance, if you look up number 860 in the body of the thesaurus, you will find a long list of synonyms for the word *fear*. These include *anxiety, care, misgiving, mistrust,* and *suspicion.* You select the word *anxiety*:

The new student suffered an anxiety *attack in homeroom.*

Another feature of the traditional thesaurus is that the synonyms and antonyms for a word are directly before or after each other. Suppose you wanted a word that meant the opposite of *fear*. You could look up *fear* as you did above (guide number 860) and find that guide word 861 is *courage,* the opposite of fear. The guide word is then followed by a list of antonyms of fear such as *boldness, daring, heroism,* and *bravery.*

---

259   PERSONAL AFFECTIONS   *860-861*

860. FEAR.—*N.* **fear**, anxiety, care, misgiving, mistrust, suspicion, qualm; hesitation, apprehensiveness, fearfulness, apprehension.

   Fright, alarm, dread, awe, terror, horror, dismay, panic, scare; stampede [*of horses*].

   intimidation, bullying; terrorism, reign of terror; terrorist, bully.

   V. **fear**, be afraid, apprehend, dread, distrust; hesitate, falter, cower, crouch, skulk, take fright, take alarm; start, wince, flinch, shy, shrink, fly.

   tremble, shake, shiver, shudder, flutter, quake, quaver, quiver, quail.

   frighten, fright, terrify, inspire (*or* excite) fear, bulldoze [*colloq.*], alarm, startle, scare, dismay, astound; awe; strike terror, appall, petrify, horrify.

   Adj. **afraid**, frightened, alarmed, fearful, timid, nervous, fainthearted, shaky, afraid of one's shadow, apprehensive; aghast, awe-struck, awe-stricken, horror-stricken, panic-stricken.

   861. [absence of fear] COURAGE—*N.* courage, bravery, valor, resoluteness, boldness, spirit, daring, gallantry, nerve, backbone, prowess, heroism, chivalry, rashness.

Using the Dictionary

A dictionary can be used for much more than simply looking up the spelling or meaning of a word. Below are some of the most important ways. (Each is illustrated on the next page.)

■ **Spelling**: Not knowing how to spell a word does make it difficult to find in the dictionary, but not impossible. By following its *sounded-out* spelling, you can find most words.

■ **Capital Letters**: If you need to know whether a certain word is capitalized, simply look it up in a dictionary.

■ **Syllabication**: The dictionary is often used to check on where you can divide a word at the end of a line.

■ **Pronunciation**: To remember a word and its meaning, you must know its correct pronunciation. (The dictionary gives you a **Pronunciation Key** at the bottom of all right-side pages.)

■ The **Parts of Speech**: The dictionary uses nine abbreviations for the parts of speech:

> **n.**—noun, **pron.**—pronoun, **v.i.**—intransitive verb, **v.t.**—transitive verb, **interj.**—interjection, **conj.**—conjunction, **adj.**—adjective, **adv.**—adverb, **prep.**—preposition

■ **Etymology** (History): Just after the pronunciation and part of speech, you will find [in brackets] the history of each word. Knowing a little about its history can make a word easier to remember.

■ **Restrictive Labels**: There are three main types of labels used in a dictionary: **subject labels**, which tell you that a word has a special meaning when used in a particular field or subject (*mus.* for *music, med.* for *medicine*); **usage labels**, which tell you how a word is used (*slang, colloq.* for *colloquial*); and **geographical labels**, which tell you the region of the country where that word is mainly used (*N.E.* for *New England*, W. for *West*).

■ **Synonyms and Antonyms**: A good dictionary will list synonyms and antonyms after the meaning.

■ **Illustration**: Whenever a definition is difficult to make clear with words alone, a picture or drawing is used.

■ **Meaning**: It is important for you to know that most dictionaries list their meanings chronologically. This means the oldest meaning of the word is given first, then the newer or more technical versions. You can see why it is extremely dangerous to simply take the first meaning listed—it is quite possible that this first one is not the meaning you need. Remember to read all the meanings and then select the one which is best for you.

Main entry ——— **spark** [spärk] *n.*   **1.** A glowing particle, such as one thrown off or left over from a fire or one caused by friction.   **2. a.** A brief flash of light, especially one produced by electric discharge.   **b.** An electric discharge of this kind, especially a short one.   **c.** The current that flows in such a discharge. —*v.*   **1.** To produce or give off sparks.   **2.** To set in motion or rouse to action: *His speech sparked them into working harder.*

Definition with three closely related "senses" or meanings

Guide words

spar·kle [spär´kel] *v.* **spar·kled, spar·kling.**   1. To give off or produce sparks.   2. To release bubbles of gas; effervesce.   3. To be brilliant or witty; shine with animation: *The conversation sparkled at the dinner table.* —**spar´kling** *adj. sparkling lights; sparkling conversation.* —*n.*   1. A small spark or glowing particle.   2. The property or capacity of releasing bubbles of gas; effervescence.   3. Animation; vivacity.

Spelling of verb forms

Used in a sentence

Definition ——— **spark plug.**   A device that fits into a threaded hole extending into the combustion chamber of an internal-combustion engine, producing an electric spark to ignite the fuel mixture. [SEE PICTURE]

Syllable division

spar·row [spär´ō] *n.*   Any of several small brownish or grayish birds, such as the widespread **house sparrow** (or **English sparrow**), which is common in cities.

Spelling of adjective forms

sparse [spärs] *adj.* **spars·er, spars·est.**   Not dense or crowded: *sparse vegetation; a sparse population.* —**sparse´ly** *adv.* —**sparse´ness** *n.*

Other forms of the word

Geographic entry

Spar·ta [spär´te].   An ancient city-state in southern Greece, famous for its military might and the strict discipline of its soldiers.

Spelling and capital letters

Spar·tan [spär´tn] *n.*   1. A citizen of Sparta.   2. Someone of Spartan character. —*adj.*   1. Of Sparta or the Spartans.   2. Resembling the Spartans; austere.

spas·mod·ic [spăz mŏd´ĭk] *adj.*   1. Of, like, or affected by a spasm.   2. Happening intermittently; fitful: *spasmodic attempts to climb the mountain.* —**spas·mod´i·cal·ly** *adv.*

Pronunciation and accent marks

3 homographs: different words with same spelling

spat¹ [spăt].   A past tense and past participle of spit (eject saliva).

spat² [spăt] *n.*   Often **spats.** A cloth or leather covering for the ankle and the top part of the shoe, having buttons up the side and a strap under the instep; a gaiter.

spat³ [spăt] *n.*   A brief, petty quarrel. —*v.*   To engage in a brief, petty quarrel.

Part of speech label

Principal parts of the verb

speak (spēk) *v.* **spoke** (spōk), **spok·en** [spō´ken], **speak·ing.**   1. To utter words; talk: *They spoke about the weather.*   2. To express (thoughts or feelings): *He spoke his fears. Actions speak louder than words.*   3. To pronounce, recite, or say: *phrasal verb.*

Phrasal verb ——— **speak out.** 1. To talk loudly and clearly.   2. To talk freely and fearlessly.   **speak up.** 1. To raise the voice: *Speak up so we can hear you.*   2. To speak without hesitation or fear.

Pronunciation key

Usage label ——— *Idioms.* **so to speak.**   In a manner of speaking; as the saying goes.   **speak well for.**   to be good.

ă pat/ā pat/ä care/ä father/
ĕ pet/ē be/ĭ pit/ī pie/î fierce/
ŏ pot/ō go/ô paw, for/oi oil/
oo boot/ou out/ŭ cut/û fur/
th the/th thin/hw which/
zh vision/e ago, item, pencil,
atom, circus

spark plug

Thinking to Learn

Thinking Better

Would you like to be a faster thinker . . . more logical or creative? How about learning to keep more thoughts in mind and holding them in focus? Would you like to clear up your muddy thinking? Would you like to think longer and harder? How about some step-by-step help through some hard problems? Would you like to do better in school? Read on.

The Planet of Bad Thinkers

306

Suppose you're an astronaut and your space capsule accidentally slips out of orbit. You sail through the blackness of space and finally land on a planet called BLOK. While NASA sends out a rescue ship, you decide to look around. What you discover is astounding. The creatures on BLOK, who call themselves Chips, are *bad thinkers*. Every one of them. Everything they try fails. Everything they build falls down. It's a miracle they survive. They don't seem to understand anything.

You don't know if NASA will ever find you, but in case they ever do, you make a list of all the things the Chips do wrong when they try to think. Someday your list might save your fellow Earthlings from making a mess of their own planet.

What would you put on your list? Maybe something like this:

Why the Chips Are Down

---

1. Chips are in too big a hurry.
2. They never set goals.
3. They never ask questions.
4. They ignore the evidence.
5. They believe whatever they read.
6. They go with the crowd.
7. They stick with their first emotional reaction; they also talk in cliches and think in slogans.
8. They never connect what they've learned in one subject to another.
9. They never think about *how* they think.
10. They never write anything down.

■ Is it any wonder the planet BLOK is a mess? If you ever get home to Earth, don't be a Chip off the old BLOK. And warn your fellow Earthlings what can happen if they turn into bad thinkers.

Becoming a Better Thinker

Ironically, the lessons we learn about thinking from the planet of bad thinkers are the same lessons we need to learn in order to become better thinkers ourselves. Here are those lessons with a few added thoughts:

1. **Be patient** . . . don't expect quick, easy solutions to every problem or challenge you face; good thinking often takes time and requires you to plan, read, listen, discuss, etc.

2. **Set goals** . . . think about what you should (or can) do now (*short-term goals*) and what you have to patiently work on step by step to accomplish (*long-term goals*).

3. **Be curious** . . . gather all kinds of information, wonder about how things works, and consider the many possible solutions a problem may have.

4. **Think logically** . . . think beyond your "knee-jerk" emotions or the first answer that pops into your head; look at all sides of a question; propose reasonable and sensible solutions; then support these thoughts with good reasons, interesting examples, and solid evidence.

5. **Ask questions** . . . ask questions about what you read, what you hear, even what you see; if you think you know "what" it is, then ask "why, who, when, where, how, how much, why not"; ask "if" questions: "If this is true, then why . . . ."

6. **Think for yourself** . . . think carefully about each problem or issue and develop your own system for attacking a problem; listen to others and learn from (or build on) what they have to say.

7. **Be creative** . . . do not settle for the obvious answer or the usual way of doing things; experiment, invent, redesign, reenact, rewrite.

8. **Make connections** . . . learn from experience; use what you have learned to help you solve new problems; use comparisons, analogies, metaphors.

9. **Be aware of how you think** . . . "supervise" your thinking; watch yourself as you work through a thinking task and be prepared to steer your mind wherever you must to meet the challenge (slow down, speed up, zoom in, back up, switch tactics).

10. **Write things down** . . . writing can help you clarify thoughts and remember them longer; it can help you discover things you didn't know you knew; it can help you sort through your thoughts and "see" them in a new light; it can do more than you ever imagined.

Why Bother to Think?

There are lots of good reasons to think: 1) thinking saves time, 2) thinking prevents accidents, 3) thinking leads to success, 4) thinking can be fun, and so on. But, the most obvious reason for thinking is that *thinking helps you figure things out*. And if you're like everybody else, you have lots of . . .

■ **problems to solve**

How can I get this moped onto that tailgate without getting a hernia?

■ **decisions to make**

Should I invite Sharyn and Janelle to my party when I know they're jealous of each other?

■ **concepts to understand**

What does Ms. Farrar mean when she refers to "human rights"?

■ **things to evaluate**

Is being in the church choir worth three hours of my time every week?

■ **arguments to build**

I've got to convince my parents that a 9:30 bedtime is too early.

For all of these problems, if you think clearly, you'll find your own solutions. If you don't, you'll be stuck.

How to Think

When you "try to figure things out" for yourself, you use *clusters* of basic thinking skills or strategies. Luckily, you've been using some of these skills since you first began to walk and talk. Now you can do the easiest ones without any effort, the way a cat gathers itself for a leap or the way you ride a bicycle "no hands."

When you can do simpler tasks without struggling, your mind is free to focus on more complicated operations. If it gets hung up, it will circle back to a simpler task—like noticing a new detail or recalling a comment somebody made—to get the thinking process under control once again. It's the same as when your bicycle hits a pothole. Suddenly, you're very aware of your steering again, the way you were the first time your two-wheeler went wobbling down the walk.

| What's Ahead | **Your Basic Thinking and Writing Moves:** What follows on the next page is a "process chart" showing the kinds of thinking (from simple to complex) that go on when you write. Don't expect, however, to think in a straight line. No one can. Thinking takes our minds in and out, backward and forward, up and down. |

Your Basic Writing and Thinking Moves

OBSERVE

| Watch | Listen | Taste | Feel | Smell | Perceive (sense it) |

GATHER

| Collect observations | Use personal experiences | Free-write, cluster, list | Brainstorm with others | Interview others | Read, write, draw |

QUESTION

| Ask who, what, when, where, why? | Ask how? How much? | Wonder what if . . . Why not? | Look into, investigate, survey |

FOCUS

| Find a main point or center of interest | Identify or define the key problem or issue | Select a way to approach the issue | Set a simple goal or purpose |

ORGANIZE

| Distinguish the whole from the part | Put in meaningful order | Compare, contrast | Give reasons | Group, classify | Pro/Con (for/against) |

ANALYZE

| Select best idea(s) or feature(s) | Relate it to other things | What caused it? What did it cause? | See patterns, relationships, connections |

IMAGINE

| See from another point of view | Create new ideas, alternatives | Experiment, invent, design | Infer (draw conclusions) | Hypothesize (make an educated guess) | Predict, estimate |

RETHINK

| Restate ("What I really mean is . . ." | Reconsider (What are the consequences?) | Re-examine (Look for weaknesses) | Rearrange (Change the order) | Revise (Review rules, goals, models) | Restructure (See from new perspective) |

EVALUATE

| Judge (Is it understandable? Is it clear? accurate? concise?) | Criticize (Is it effective? workable? interesting?) | Persuade (Is it worthwhile? practical? logical?) | Argue (What are the advantages? disadvantages?) |

Thinking and Writing

When you are with friends, it is easy to talk about what you like and don't like about school, popular music, or television shows. It is a little different when you are talking to people you don't know very well, because you're never sure how they will react to something you say. If another person questions something you say, you might have to back up one of your ideas or opinions. And, as you already know, this is not always an easy thing to do.

Sharing Your Thoughts

311

It is especially difficult to share your ideas and opinions in one of your classes. Your teachers expect you to support or back up what you say or write with clear facts and details. They know that supporting ideas and opinions is a very special skill which requires careful thinking. This is why teachers give you so many assignments each year to practice this skill. Just remember: to become a better thinker, you must write; to become a better writer, you must think.

Levels of Thinking

312

You will use many different kinds of thinking in school. The levels of thinking are often divided into six general categories: **recalling, understanding, applying, analyzing, synthesizing,** and **evaluating**. *Recalling* is a very basic level of thinking; *evaluating* is a very advanced level. All of these levels of thinking are connected. That is, you never use just one level of thinking for an assignment, except if you are asked to simply recall or list information. For example, if you are asked in an assignment to use a very advanced level of thinking like *evaluating*, you must also be able to use some or all of the other types of thinking.

"Writing is the inking of our thinking."
—Robin Fogarty

| What's Ahead | An explanation of each of the six levels of thinking follows. These explanations will help you understand and use the different levels of thinking in your assignments, especially your writing. |

Recalling Information

The most basic type of thinking you practice in school is **recalling information**. This type of thinking is needed when you are asked to remember and repeat information which you discussed in class or read about in a textbook. Since your teachers expect you to recall the most important information, make sure that you listen carefully in class and that you read carefully in your textbook.

Recalling on Tests

Recalling is the level of thinking most often used when you answer multiple-choice, matching, and fill-in-the-blank questions on a test. Your teachers will give very few writing assignments in which they want you simply to recall information. Usually, this level of thinking is combined with other more advanced levels in writing assignments. However, some test questions might ask you simply to recall information.

Let's say you are studying the world hunger problem in your social studies class. As one part of this unit, you read about Live Aid, a project which was organized to save the lives of starving people in Africa. As a basic test question, your teacher might ask you to list (recall) in sentences five important facts you have learned about the concert organized by Live Aid officials. The sample answer below *recalls* this information.

Using Recall to Answer a Test Question

Test Question: List in sentences five important facts you have learned about the Live Aid concert.

Answer:

1. In 1985, the Live Aid concert was organized to raise money for hunger relief in Africa.
2. Over 60 rock stars like Bob Dylan and Sting performed at the concert for no charge.
3. There were really two Live Aid concerts held at the same time, one in Philadelphia and one in London.
4. The two concerts were televised throughout the world.
5. Live Aid earned over $70 million for relief aid.

Understanding Information

Your teachers will often ask you to do more than simply *recall* information in list form. You will be asked to show that you **understand** the information well enough to reword what you've learned into a paragraph or two. And, just as understanding is a more advanced level of thinking than recalling, a paragraph is a more advanced level of writing than a list of remembered information.

Reading, Studying, and Understanding

To understand information from a textbook, you must be a careful reader. Use a study-reading method (SQ3R, KWL) and take notes. To test whether you understand the material in your notes, try rewording it or "teaching" it to someone else. If you can do neither, ask for help.

Understanding in Paragraphs and Essay Tests

Understanding is often called for when you work on paragraphs and essay test questions. Anytime one of your teachers asks you to *describe, explain,* or *summarize* ideas or events, he or she is asking you first to understand information, and then, to retell what you've learned in a paragraph(s). Let's say your social studies teacher asks you to describe the Live Aid concert, a fund-raising event you talked about in class. Your teacher is really asking you to **understand** as well as **recall** clearly in your own words the important facts and details—the *who, what, when, where,* and *why*—about this event. The paragraph below is a sample of what you might have written. (Also see "The Essay Test," 421.)

Assignment: In a paragraph, describe the details concerning the Live Aid concert—the planning, the performance, and the results.

Model Understanding Paragraph

One important fund-raising event staged to help famine victims in Africa was the Live Aid concert. This concert was organized in London by a group of concerned people under the direction of Irish rock singer Bob Geldof. Live Aid took place in Philadelphia and London on July 13, 1985, and featured over sixty of the world's most famous rock stars. Older stars like Bob Dylan and Mick Jagger joined new stars like Sting and Lionel Richie. All of the musicians performed at no charge. Live Aid attracted 162,000 rock fans in person, and twelve television satellites showed the concert to over a billion viewers in 150 countries. More than $70 million was raised from ticket sales, television rights, and donations. Most of the money came from the donations of large corporations and from the donations of people who pledged money by phone during the concert. Live Aid ended up being the biggest money-making event staged to help the hunger victims in Africa.

315 Applying Information

When you are asked to **apply information**, you must be able to use what you've learned to *locate, select, organize, illustrate,* or *demonstrate.* You must be able to make connections between past learning and the current situation. If, for example, you have been learning to play an instrument, you may be asked to apply what you have learned by playing a scale or a short solo.

316 Thinking and Writing

You will often be asked to apply what you know in school. Let's say that as part of a world hunger unit, your social studies teacher asks you to apply all the information you have thus far learned. You are handed the following scenario: *You have been chosen chairman of the World Food Bank. Your first responsibility is to contact other corporate leaders and encourage them to make ongoing contributions to the World Food Bank.*

317

Assignment: Write a letter based on the above scenario, "choosing" the most crucial facts to "demonstrate" the need for contributions.

Dear Mr. Iacocca:

Isn't it time that you took someone out to dinner? A child in Yemen, a mother and child in Chad, a whole family in Brazil—any of the millions who have little or nothing for dinner? I know that you are a caring, well-informed individual and that you have probably already done something to help fight world hunger. But, as we both know, much more remains to be done.

Did you know . . .

*that every day of this past year 40,000 young children died of malnutrition and infection?

*that we can cut the child mortality rate in half by giving a local person three weeks of training and 10 cents worth of salts to administer to young victims of intestinal infections?

*the world spends $600 billion a year for arms, but balks at spending $15 to $18 billion for the aid that could make the poorest countries self-sufficient by the year 2000?

Thank you for reading my letter. The enclosed brochure will help you and your company make plans to help the World Food Bank.

Sincerely,

Analyzing Information

More and more, you will be asked to examine or **analyze information** you have learned about a topic in order to arrive at a general conclusion or a more meaningful understanding. You might, for example, use what you've learned in a geography class to compare and contrast two countries and show how they are very much alike—or not alike at all. Or you might use the information you've gathered in science to *tell why* light travels faster than sound.

Deciding the Purpose

Basically, you must answer three important questions when you are thinking and writing at this level. First, "What is the purpose of this writing assignment?" Is it to show how things are alike (*comparing*) or different (*contrasting*), to put similar ideas into groups (*grouping*), or to give reasons (*cause and effect*)? These are the most common purposes.

Selecting Facts and Details

The second important question you have to answer is "Which facts and details are the right ones to use for this writing assignment?" Let's say the purpose of an assignment is to *classify* or *categorize* what you've learned. You will want to select the information that fits into the general category and then break it down into several smaller groups according to what they have in common.

Organizing the Facts and Details

The third question you have to answer is "How should the facts and details for this writing assignment be organized?" Will you organize the details in the order in which they happened (chronological or time order), in the order of importance, in the order of location, or by cause and effect? To help you answer these questions, use the following sample as a guide:

- **Sample assignment:** In a paragraph, identify the important reasons for the hunger problem in Africa.
- **Purpose:** To identify the reasons or steps which "caused" (or led to) this condition. Or, at a more advanced level, to come to a better understanding of the hunger problem after thinking and writing about the reasons behind it.
- **Selecting details:** Choose good reasons and enough facts and details to make each reason clear to the reader.
- **Organizing:** Paragraphs which give reasons for something are organized chronologically or by order of importance.

322 Giving Reasons (Cause and Effect)

Let's say as part of a world hunger unit that your social studies teacher asks you to write a paragraph which gives the reasons for the hunger problem in Africa. After studying your class notes and reading carefully, you decide that there are four important reasons for the hunger problem in Africa. The model which follows is an example of what you might have written for this assignment.

323 **Assignment:** In a paragraph, identify the important reasons for the hunger problem in Africa.

Model Reasons Paragraph

Most areas in the world, except for Africa, have made progress in ending hunger. In Africa, there is less food per person today than there was in 1960. The most important reason for the hunger problem is the serious drought which has been going on in many parts of Africa. Some areas have not had a decent amount of rain for three years. Another important reason for the hunger problem is the lack of planning by many African nations for times of drought. For example, there are few food storage or irrigation systems in the drought-stricken areas. Without these systems, people have no chance to prepare for difficult times. The hunger problem has also been caused by the poorly run governments within certain African countries—especially Ethiopia and Chad. Governments in these countries are so concerned about staying in power that they spend very little time helping hunger victims. A final reason for the hunger problem is the lack of a good transportation system in most of the areas. Without good roads or railroads, transporting supplies to hunger victims who live in remote areas is almost impossible. Unless these conditions improve soon, it is estimated that over 35 million people will face starvation in Africa.

Most important reason is given first.

Facts and details support each reason.

The ending looks at the possible effects.

Synthesizing Information

If your teacher asked you to listen to a piece of music and write down what you "saw" or imagined while you listened, you would be **synthesizing**. You would be turning one form of material (music) into a new form (writing). You become a "synthesizer." (Did you ever wonder where the term "synthesizer," as in music synthesizer, came from?)

Design, Create, Predict . . .

What often separates the "advanced" thinker from the "basic" thinker is his or her ability to combine or synthesize information. Common ways to synthesize information are *inventing, predicting, redesigning, blending,* and *hypothesizing*. In each case, you have to "reshape" the information you already have.

Writing and Thinking Assignment

Suppose, for example, you are studying world hunger and your teacher asks you to "synthesize"—to take the information you have gathered and reshape it. One way to do this is to use a form not ordinarily used for this kind of topic—perhaps a title-down poem or paragraph (see sample below). Or you might decide to brainstorm using open-ended questions, which is a very good way to shape material into a new form. In the second example below, both imagination and knowledge are pushed and pulled in a number of new directions by asking, "What if . . . ?"

My Title-Down Paragraph (Hunger)

Hunger is a way of life for 1,000,000,000 people.

Uganda, Uruguay, and the United States

Need to address the hunger problem.

Global awareness could provide safe drinking water and basic sanitation, cut the child death rate in half to 7,300,000, and help banish world hunger by the year 2000.

Ethiopia, El Salvador, Ecuador also need to address hunger.

Respect the rights of the hungry. They have a "right" to a share of the world's food—just like you and me.

"What If . . . ?"

- **What if** one of the children who died today was another Einstein, Schweitzer, or Jonas Salk?
- **What would happen if** a long drought were to hit this country?
- **What if** the United States donated all its surplus grain and food?

327 | Judging Information

Judging is the most advanced level of thinking and writing you will be asked to use. Generally, when your teachers ask you to "judge," they are asking you to do one of two things: They are asking you to *evaluate* (rate the value or decide the worth of) the information you've learned. Or, your teachers are asking you to *persuade* the reader that one of your opinions is a good one.

328 | Studying and Evaluating a Subject

When you are asked to *evaluate* information, you are being asked to think like an "expert" on the topic. To become an expert, you must carefully think about all the facts and details you've learned. (Do these details reveal strengths or weaknesses about your subject?) When you "know" your subject well enough to judge its value, you are ready to begin. Start with a sentence or two which identifies your overall evaluation; then, add facts and details which prove your evaluation is a good one.

Let's say that as part of a unit on world hunger in your social studies class you are asked to evaluate the Live Aid project. After studying your notes and reading about this project, you feel you have enough information to judge its value. The model which follows is an example of what you might have written for this assignment.

329 | **Assignment:** In a paragraph, evaluate the Live Aid project.

Model Evaluating Paragraph

Live Aid has been a project with two main goals: first, to raise money for famine relief and, second, to get relief supplies to the famine victims in Africa. In terms of raising money, the project has been very successful since the Live Aid concert held in the summer of 1985 earned over $70 million for African famine relief. By the end of 1985, $32 million of this money had already been spent for food and medical supplies. But three problems are making it difficult to get these supplies to the famine victims. First, governments in some of the African countries are involved in civil wars and are not interested or able to work with Live Aid officials. Second, some of the worst famine conditions are occurring in hard-to-reach areas where there are few passable roads. Third, outdated railroads and the lack of available trucks make it difficult to even try to transport supplies. Even though these problems have not made things easy for Live Aid officials, they continue to ship supplies to Africa. They also have bought their own fleet of trucks and trailers to help transport the supplies. However, the number of starving people that they will be able to reach with life-saving aid—especially those in the remote areas—is still to be determined.

Thinking About Questions and Answers

Whenever you are asked to . . .	You should be ready to . . .
INPUT — **Know** recall label underline cluster list identify name memorize record define	**Recall what you've learned** ■ to list details ■ to identify or define ■ to collect information ■ to remember information
Comprehend understand show review restate cite explain summarize describe	**Show that you understand what you've learned** ■ by giving examples ■ by restating the important details ■ by explaining how something works
PROCESS — **Apply** apply utilize select choose model imitate organize illustrate demonstrate locate	**Use what you've learned** ■ to select the most important details ■ to organize information ■ to make something work ■ to show how something works
Analyze analyze classify compare divide contrast edit characterize tell why map examine break down	**Break material down to understand it better** ■ by examining and putting each part into the correct group ■ by making connections between this and other things: cause and effect, comparison, contrast
OUTPUT — **Synthesize** combine develop speculate invent design blend compose propose create formulate predict imagine	**Reshape material into a new form** ■ by inventing a better way of doing something ■ by redesigning or blending the old and the new ■ by predicting or hypothesizing (making an educated guess)
Evaluate judge rate recommend measure argue persuade evaluate assess criticize convince	**Judge the worth of the material** ■ by pointing out its strengths and weaknesses (pluses and minuses) ■ by evaluating its clearness, accuracy, value, etc. ■ by convincing others of its value/worth

Thinking Creatively

Successful short stories and poems offer readers something new, something unexpected, something—at times—even outrageous. They start with basic ideas which are then bent, twisted, played with, and eventually reworked into new and exciting shapes. The section which follows describes the creative "mind" which triggers these new shapes. Use it as your guide to creative thinking and writing.

331 What Is Creativity?

It's the power of a four-year-old to invent new words—her classmates are curled up on their rugs like "boa and arrow constrictors." Ginger ale, says another, "tastes like your foot's asleep."

It's your power to see a similarity between a toaster and the family's old car; your power to imagine what the school of tomorrow might be like; your power to turn a near-fight into new friendship.

332 The Creative Process

The creative process is not a step-by-step procedure. Instead, it is the use of many different methods for preparing the mind, stimulating the mind, opening the mind, and guiding the mind as it spins out bright ideas.

Where dull thinking (DT) plucks a sandbur off his socks and throws it away, creative thinking (CT) invents Velcro. DT stays angry because somebody ripped off his CD player. CT wins one hundred dollars in a literary contest with a story told from the point of view of the thief.

333 The Creative Mind in Action

Suppose you write a short paragraph describing the lamp beside your bed, and I give you back the paper with the comment, "You seem to like your lamp. How about describing it from a creative new angle?"

What do you think my comment means? What is a "creative new angle," and how can you find one?

| What's Ahead | A creative new angle could be just about anything—anything that's *creative*, and *new*. Be more specific? All right. How about a ten-point checklist of questions to help you see things from a new angle and a step-by-step description of the creative process? That's what you'll find on the next two pages. |

What if . . . ?

The best creative thinkers see things differently than the people around them. They see challenges rather than problems. They set aside all the rules, all the scorecards, all of what is usually expected, and begin to imagine "What would happen if . . . ?" If you sometimes find it hard to imagine, to go beyond the correct or obvious answer, maybe the suggestions below will help.

- **What if** a certain person, place, thing, or idea did not exist today? What if it suddenly appeared 100 years before its time? (What if the airplane had not yet been invented? What if it had been invented before the Civil War?)
- **What if** people did things differently than they do? (What if everyone spoke whenever they felt like it and said whatever they wanted? What if no one collected our garbage?)

- **What if** the world were different in some important way? (What if the sun were to shine only two hours a day? 20 hours a day? What if it rained only twice a year? every day?)
- **What if** two people, things, or ideas which are usually separate were brought together? (Parents and rock musicians? Tomatoes and ice cream?)
- **What if** you were to change just one important thing about an object or machine? (Change the ink in every pen to green? Cut the size of the gas tanks on all cars to one-fourth their current size?)

"Most people see things as they are and ask, 'Why?' I see things that never were and ask, 'Why not?'"
—Robert F. Kennedy

- **What if** a certain object could talk? (Your shoe? Your house? A newborn baby?)
- **What if** a certain object were made of another material? (Metal car tires? Grass clothes? Cardboard furniture?)
- **What if** a certain person, place, object, or idea were the "opposite" of what he, she, or it is now? (What if George Bush became Georgia Bush? Homes became schools? Cars became helicopters? Forward became backward?)
- **What if** a certain object were suddenly very scarce or plentiful? (What if there were suddenly very little paper? Plenty of money?)
- **What if** a certain object were a totally different size? (2-foot pens? 9-foot baskets?)
- **What if** . . .

An Overview of the Creative Process

Whenever you find a need to think creatively, follow the suggestions below. They should help you get your creative thoughts flowing.

335   **Look closely!** Creativity starts with sensory **perceptions:** seeing, hearing, smelling, tasting, and touching. But don't just look at something. Study it. Empty yourself of all ideas about it. Keep on studying until it gives you news about itself. That's the creative way of sensing the world. Sensory perceptions in turn trigger memories. The creative process is set in motion.

336   **Catch the stirrings.** The first **stirring** of a creative idea may come from a memory, a new way of seeing something, or a prompt from another person. Often the stirring will occur while your mind is occupied with something else. While the left brain is away, the right brain will play. But creative stirrings are of no use to you unless you are ready to catch them. A personal journal makes a good net.

337   **Explore freely and energetically.** Then a period of **exploring** and **gathering** may begin. Gather whatever comes your way. Save the shaping for later. This is the time to try out, have fun, make mistakes, act foolish, be surprised, ask *What if . . . ?* (See 334.)

338   **Don't become impatient.** Next, many creative thinkers go through a period of **resting** and waiting, sometimes called "incubation." The idea may seem to be forgotten, but the brain keeps working on it subconsciously, trying out different angles.

339   **The creativity begins!** After all that preparation, **inspiration** may strike. It is tempting to see inspiration as the destination and reward of thinking. But inspiration is more like a launching pad. The fun, the work, the real creativity begins there. Belt yourself in and take off.

340   **Catch new ideas.** As you work out the details of your creative idea, keep the spirit of creativity alive. Expect to catch new ideas as they stir up from your field of thought.

341   **Swerving along.** For inspiration to last, the creative thinker must soon begin **shaping** thought (through drawing, dancing, sculpting, or in this case, writing). But don't force yourself to work straight through from start to finish. Your inspiration may lead you from the center to the shores or from puddle to puddle. Work out connections later.

342   **Fine-tune your ideas.** The last phase of the creative process is **revising** or reworking your thoughts or writing in order to make it a more creative expression of the idea. Make the spirit of your imagination sparkle even in the tiniest details.

Thinking Logically

When you want to make (or prove) an important point in either speaking or writing, you must "connect" your ideas in just the right way—in a clear, logical way. The suggestions which follow will help you make these connections.

For your thinking to be logical, it has to make sense. It has to "hold up" under careful examination by your audience. It has to be **reasonable** (supported with good reasons) and **reliable** (supported with solid evidence). In short, your thinking has to be believable.

So how do you go about making your thinking believable and, therefore, acceptable to your audience? Generally speaking, you must organize, support, and present your points *so well* that your audience cannot disagree with or question what you've said or written. Specifically, you can follow the process or stages listed below. (These steps are especially useful when putting together debates, speeches, research papers, etc.)

Becoming a Logical Thinker

- **Decide** on your purpose and state it clearly on the top of your paper.
- **Gather** whatever information you can on the topic.
- **Focus** on a central "claim" or point which you feel you can logically support or prove.
- **Define** any terms which may be unclear.
- **Support** your point with evidence which is interesting and reliable.
- **Explain** why your audience should accept your evidence.
- **Consider** any objections your audience could have to your explanation.
- **Admit** that some arguments against your point may be true.
- **Point out** the weaknesses in those arguments you do not accept.
- **Restate** your central claim or point.
- **Urge** your audience to accept your viewpoint.

Helpful HINT   You will probably not use every one of these stages each time you set out to prove a point. Each situation is different and requires some creative thinking and common sense as well as logic and reason.

Using Logic to Persuade

One of the most common types of "logical" thinking you will have to use is persuasive thinking. When your teachers assign a persuasive thinking and writing assignment, they really are asking you to do two things. First, they are asking you to form an opinion—a personal feeling or belief—about some important or controversial subject. Second, they are asking you to judge, evaluate, or prove your opinion. You can do this by listing (and then studying) the important facts and details which you feel support your opinion.

344 ## Guidelines for Persuasive Writing and Thinking

When you "know" your opinion is a good one—that is, you have plenty of good facts to support it—you are ready to begin your persuasive writing assignment. If you find that your opinion is not a very strong one—that is, you don't have many facts to support it—modify or change it until you have an opinion which you can support effectively. Use the guidelines which follow to help you with persuasive thinking and writing assignments. (Also, see 074 and 080 for a model and additional guidelines for writing persuasively.)

345 ### 1. Know the Difference Between Fact and Opinion

Make sure you understand the difference between an opinion and a fact before you start a persuasive writing assignment. An *opinion* is a view or belief held by a person. A good opinion is based on fact, but it is not a fact itself. A *fact* is a specific statement which can be checked or proven to be true. Note below the difference between the opinion and the supporting facts. The opinion states a personal view about a teacher. The facts are specific and can be proven; they support the opinion.

Opinion: Mr. Brown might not be a popular teacher, but he has three qualities that make him a good teacher.

Facts: He is well organized for every class.
He is always concerned that we do our best.
He treats everyone fairly.

2. Form an Opinion

Make sure you understand and believe the opinion you are trying to support. It is difficult to write in a sincere, natural style if you don't really believe in your topic. *Note:* Don't be afraid to form an opinion about a controversial issue or topic. There is not much point in forming an opinion if everyone already agrees.

3. Write an Opinion Statement

Before an opinion can work well for a writing assignment, it must be well stated. After you have chosen a specific subject, follow the simple formula given below to help you write a good opinion statement.

Formula: A specific subject (Mr. Brown) + a specific opinion or feeling (might not be a popular teacher, but he has three qualities that make him a good teacher) = a good opinion statement.

Caution! Opinions including words which are strongly positive or negative like *all, best, every, never, none,* or *worst* may be difficult to support. For example, an exaggerated opinion statement like "All dogs chase mail carriers" would certainly be impossible to support.

4. Support Your Opinion

When you support or defend an opinion, make sure you do so with clear, provable facts. Otherwise, your reader probably won't believe your opinion. Let's say you are supporting the opinion that "The Live Aid concert was a huge success." Note the difference in the following supporting facts.

Provable Fact: "Twelve television satellites transmitted the Live Aid concert throughout the world." (You simply have to read different reports of the concert to prove that this statement is true.)

Not a Provable Fact: "Most people who watched the concert donated as much money as they could to Live Aid." (Certainly an exaggerated statement like this is untrue and impossible to prove.)

5. Organize Your Facts

You can develop a persuasive thinking and writing assignment in two basic ways. You can state your opinion or belief in the topic sentence and then support it with specific facts. Or, you can start your assignment by presenting a number of specific facts which lead to a believable concluding or ending statement. Your opinion or belief is made clear in this concluding statement. *Note:* In the "Model Persuasive Paragraph," 080, an opinion about a teacher is stated in the topic sentence, and the rest of the paragraph is made up of facts which support this opinion.

Avoid Fuzzy Thinking

Make sure that all of your ideas in a persuasive writing assignment are meaningful and well thought out. Often, young writers try to take shortcuts in persuasive thinking and writing assignments and include meaningless and misleading ideas. Avoid this kind of fuzzy thinking in your own writing.

350 ■ **Avoid statements which jump to a conclusion.**

"Because the Live Aid concert earned over $70 million, thousands of starving people in Africa will be saved."

Discussion: This statement jumps to a conclusion. It suggests that many people will be saved just because a concert earned a lot of money. However, there is much more to saving starving people than simply raising money.

351 ■ **Avoid statements which are supported with nothing more than the simple fact that the majority of the people also feel this way.**

"Mr. Brown is not a good teacher because most of the guys think he is really hard on them."

Discussion: This type of statement is based on the idea that if more than half the people believe something, it must be true. In other words, Mr. Brown can't possibly be a good teacher because most of the guys think he is hard on them. Certainly, there is more to judging the quality of a teacher than whether the majority of the students like him or not.

■ **Avoid statements which contain a weak or misleading comparison.**   `352`

"Mr. Brown is a good teacher because he is a lot like Vince Lombardi."

Discussion: This statement could be a weak or misleading comparison. Often, a comparison can be helpful in persuasive writing. However, make sure the comparison is a fair one; otherwise, it may hurt rather than help your argument. Comparing a teacher to a legendary professional football coach is probably not a fair comparison to make.

■ **Avoid statements which exaggerate the facts or mislead the reader.**   `353`

"Live Aid was a huge success in this country. The American people showed how generous and concerned they are by donating their hard-earned money to help the starving people in Africa."

Discussion: The second statement might be true, but it also could be an exaggeration which tricks us into believing that the majority of Americans donated to Live Aid. It could be that only a small part of the population actually contributed.

■ **Avoid statements which appeal only to the reader's feelings and contain no factual information.**   `354`

"Live Aid was very successful because anything done to help starving people is a good thing."

Discussion: This statement might appear to be factual, but it actually appeals to our feelings of sadness and pity. It is true that most efforts to fight world hunger are good. However, some efforts might give charities a bad name if they are poorly handled, especially if the money raised ends up in the wrong hands.

■ **Avoid statements which contain part of the truth, but not the whole truth. These statements are called half-truths.**   `355`

"Mr. Brown is not a good teacher because he leaves school the very minute school is out each day."

Discussion: Even though the last portion of this statement is true, it is misleading because it does not contain the whole truth. The statement does not tell the reader the reason Mr. Brown leaves is so that he can travel to the high school where the track team he coaches is waiting for him to arrive.

Using Your Brain

You don't have to *be* a brain to *use* your brain. In fact, as you read this page, you are already using the thinking skills a nuclear physicist, a fine artist, or a philosopher would use. You observe, name, add, compare, form general ideas, evaluate things, and solve problems. Moreover, you were using those skills already in first grade, without even thinking about it.

356 Opening Thoughts

Other than age and experience, what is the difference between a first grader and a thinker like you? You have become more skilled over the years. You did it by . . .

- using your brain more often,
- using more of your brain's potential,
- enlarging your aims or goals,
- doing more to control your thinking process, and
- learning helpful techniques.

Before you go on, remember one thing. Only a small portion of a person's thinking takes place on the conscious level. Most of it goes on in the dark caverns of the "subconscious" mind. No rules or techniques can ever capture the whole process. Thoughts have to fight their way upstream like salmon. They swarm toward their destination like bees. They churn like a potful of boiling soup. Formal guidelines may help you start, stop, or steer your thoughts, but when they begin to get in the way of subconscious thoughts, they have lost their usefulness. Don't put your genius behind bars. Stay flexible. Keep it fun.

357 Left Brain/Right Brain

From the top, the brain looks something like a shelled walnut. The two halves look like mirror opposites; they work that way, too. The right half handles nerve impulses to the left side of the body; the left half serves the right side of the body.

Researchers have shown that the two halves think in quite different ways. You need both ways to be a well-rounded thinker. In general, the left brain is a "splitter." In other words, it is best at breaking down thoughts into logical parts. The right brain, by contrast, is a "lumper"— it composes wholes and grasps them imaginatively.

Left Brain	Right Brain	358

Left Brain

- Recognizes parts: trees
- Processes items one by one: fries, root beer, hamburger
- Thinks logically: "If this flops, then we're in trouble, unless we go to plan B."
- Sees details: brush strokes
- Grasps information: "I have just stepped on a snail."
- Bounded by rules: "Subject must agree with verb in number."
- Remembers complicated sequences of actions: the motions required to spike a volleyball
- Uses language: apple
- Perceives words as verbal signs: "I" + "love" + "you"

Right Brain

- Recognizes wholes: forest
- Processes items all at once: supper
- Thinks in analogies and comparisons: "This is a time bomb."
- Sees overall designs: a landscape
- Grasps emotional subtlety: "Yuck!"
- Unbounded, open: "This essay is powerful, like a bull, a train, a thunderstorm."
- Remembers complex sequences of imagery: the appearance of a spike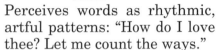
- Uses pictures:
- Perceives words as rhythmic, artful patterns: "How do I love thee? Let me count the ways."

Thinking Phase

Notice that the **right brain** specializes in the kind of thinking that makes children so fresh and creative: thinking in images, in comparisons, in emotions, in pictures, and in rhythms. But also notice that the **left brain** specializes in the kinds of thinking that are more and more emphasized in school as you grow older: information, analysis, detail, rules, logic, grammar, language.

According to Gabriele Lusser Rico, a noted researcher and writer, children go through three major phases as their minds develop:

1. **Innocent Phase** (ages 2-7): the right brain dominates. A child feels much wonder, emotion, curiosity, and delight in the patterns around him or her.

2. **Conventional Phase** (ages 8-16): the left brain begins to dominate. Thinking is more bound by rules, habits, realism, conventional patterns, cliché.

3. **Cultured Phase** (ages 17 and up): increased cooperation and "orchestration" between right and left hemispheres. Recovery of some right-brain, imaginative, intuitive functions.

Take stock of your own ways of thinking. If you discover weaknesses in either "half," try to bring the two types of thinking into better balance.

Reading to Learn

Study-Reading Skills

If you want to develop all your interests and talents to their fullest, you must be able to read—and read well. Being able to read well is a key to doing well in school and, later, doing well on the job. Luckily, it's never too late to become a better reader. The information in this section of your handbook will help you improve your reading, studying, and learning skills.

What Is a Good Reader?

361

A good reader is a careful, thoughtful reader who understands the reason he or she is reading. A good reader is always looking for ways to improve his vocabulary and knows when and how to use a dictionary or reference book. A good reader knows how to use "context clues" and read between the lines. And, perhaps most importantly, a good reader knows when to simply "enjoy" a good book, and when and how to "study" one.

Techniques for Reading to Learn

362

Much of the reading you will be asked to do in school will involve study-reading, reading which you are expected to remember for a discussion, test, or project. There are many techniques or strategies you can use for these types of reading assignments. Among the most popular are KWL, Mapping, Word Pictures, and SQ3R.

KWL

363

To use the KWL technique, all you need to do is set up a chart similar to the one below and fill it in each time you read. It may seem too simple to be of much help, but you will be surprised how helpful it can be.

K	W	L
List what you KNOW	List what you WANT to know	List what you LEARNED

Mapping

364

A second technique is called "mapping." As the name suggests, you actually draw a map of the reading material. Mapping is much like clustering, but in mapping the ideas come from the reading, not your personal experiences. (Refer to the clustering sample, 035.) Simply place the subject of your reading in the center and "map" out the details as you read.

365 Word Pictures

A third technique is called "word pictures." It is similar to mapping, but instead of developing your own map, you use one of the following "pre-designed" maps.

Describing

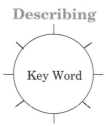

Key Word

■ Write the subject, idea, concept, person, etc. you want to describe in the circle. List the important details on the spokes as you read.

Finding Cause and Effect

Cause

_____

_____

_____

↓

Effect

_____

_____

_____

■ Again, as you read, fill in all the causes on the first set of lines and all the effects on the bottom set.

Finding Examples

Topic | Example

■ List the main topic in the center square and the examples which relate to it on all sides.

Comparing and Contrasting

_____   _____

similarities

_____

_____

_____

differences

_____ ←→

_____ ←→ _____

_____ ←→ _____

■ Write the two things you want to compare or contrast on the top lines. Then list all the ways they are similar; next list all the ways they differ.

Identifying a Problem/Solution

Problem   →   Solution

_____   _____

_____   _____

_____   _____

■ Simply list the problems on the left, the solutions on the right.

Finding Sequence

Topic _____

1 _____

2 _____

3 _____

■ If the material you are studying has a definite sequence to it, list the facts and details in order beneath it.

SQ3R

Another popular technique for reading to learn is the **SQ3R** method. SQ3R stands for the five steps in the study-reading process: *Survey, Question, Read, Recite,* and *Review*.

■ **Survey:** The first step in the SQ3R study method is **survey**. When you "survey" a reading assignment, you try to get a general picture of what the assignment is about. To do this, you must look briefly at each page, paying special attention to the headings, chapter titles, illustrations, and boldfaced type. It is also a good idea to read the first and last paragraphs. This should give you a good overall picture or survey.

■ **Question:** As you do your survey, you should begin to ask yourself **questions** about the reading material—questions which you hope to find the answers to as you read. One quick way to come up with questions to ask is to turn the headings and subheadings into questions. Asking questions will make you an "active" rather than "passive" reader. It will keep you involved in the subject and keep you thinking about what may be coming up next.

■ **Read: Read** the assignment carefully from start to finish. Look for main ideas in each paragraph or section. Take notes as you read, or stop from time to time to write a brief summary. Read the difficult parts slowly. (Reread them if necessary.) Use context clues to help you figure out some of the most difficult passages; look up unfamiliar words or ideas. Use your senses to imagine what each subject in your assignment looks, feels, sounds, tastes, or smells like.

■ **Recite:** One of the most valuable parts of the SQ3R method is the **reciting** step. It is very important that you recite out loud what you have learned from your reading. (Whisper quietly to yourself if you are in a public place.) It is best to stop at the end of each page, section, or chapter to answer the *who, what, when, where, why,* and *how* questions. By reciting this information out loud, you can test yourself on how well you understand what you have read. You can then go back and reread if necessary. Even if you understand the material well, reciting it out loud will help you remember it much longer.

■ **Review:** The final step in the SQ3R study method is the **review** step. You should review or summarize what you have read as soon as you finish. If you have been given some questions to answer about the assignment, do that immediately. If you have no questions to answer, summarize the assignment in a short writing. You can also make an outline, note cards, flash cards, illustrations, etc. to help you review and remember what you have read.

Guidelines for Reading to Learn

The guidelines which follow will help you bring together several related reading and study skills into a personal learning plan.

367 **Before you read . . .**

- Know exactly what the reading assignment is, when it is due, and what you have to do to complete it.
- Gather all the materials you may need to complete your assignment (notebook, handouts, reference books, etc.).
- Decide how much time you will need to complete the assignment and when and where (library, study hall, home) you will do it.
- Try to avoid doing your studying or reading when you are overly hungry or tired; take breaks only after completing an assignment or a major part of it.

368 **As you read . . .**

- Know your textbooks and what they contain; use the index, glossary, and special sections.
- Use a specific approach to your study-reading—KWL, SQ3R, Mapping, Word Pictures, for example. (See 363-366.)
- Preview each page before you begin reading to get an overall picture of what the selection is about; if there are questions which go with the assignment, look them over before you begin reading.
- Read the titles and headings and use them to ask yourself questions about what may be coming up next.
- Try to figure out the main idea of each paragraph and the supporting details which are worth remembering. Notice words or phrases which are in *italics* or **boldface**.
- Look closely at maps, charts, graphs, and other illustrations to help you understand and remember important information.
- Take good notes of everything you read—summarize, outline, star, underline, or highlight important information.
- Use all of your senses when you read. Try to imagine what something looks, feels, and tastes like; draw illustrations.
- Remember that some reading assignments are much more difficult than others. Read difficult material slowly; reread if necessary.

369 **After you read . . .**

- Try hard to figure out difficult material by rereading first; then ask someone for an explanation if necessary.
- Always summarize difficult material out loud (either to yourself or to someone else); make note cards or flash cards to study later.
- Keep a list of things you want to check on or ask your teacher about.

Use Context Clues

Each word you read or write, in order to make sense, depends on the other words in the sentence. These other words are called the **context** of a word. By looking closely at these surrounding words, you can pick up hints or clues which will help you figure out the meaning of a difficult word. Good readers use context clues regularly and are generally aware of the different types. Knowing something about these clues can help you sharpen your word-attack skills and improve your overall reading ability. Seven of the most common types of context clues are listed below.

Types of Context Clues

■ Clues supplied through **synonyms:**

Carol is fond of using *trite*, worn-out expressions in her writing. Her favorite is "You can lead a horse to water, but you can't make him drink."

■ Clues contained in **comparisons and contrasts:**

As the trial continued, the defendant's guilt became more and more obvious. With even the slightest bit of new evidence against him, there would be no chance of *acquittal*.

■ Clues contained in a **definition or description:**

Peggy is a *transcriptionist*, a person who makes a written copy of a recorded message.

■ Clues through **association** with other words in the sentence:

Jim is one of the most talented students ever to have attended Walker High. He has won many awards in art, music, and theatre. He also writes poetry and short stories for the school paper and creates video games on his computer. He is on the basketball and football teams and runs marathons in the summer. Jim's talents are *innumerable*.

■ Clues which appear in a **series**:

The *dulcimer*, fiddle, and banjo are all popular among the Appalachian Mountain people.

■ Clues provided by the **tone and setting**:

The streets filled instantly with *bellicose* protesters, who pushed and shoved their way through the frantic bystanders. The scene was no longer peaceful and calm as the marchers had promised it would be.

■ Clues derived from **cause and effect**:

Since nobody came to the first voluntary work session, attendance for the second one is *mandatory* for all the members.

Improving Vocabulary

One of the best things you can do to improve your reading skills is to improve your vocabulary. Unless you have a good vocabulary, it is very difficult to improve your reading. There are a number of methods which you can use for improving vocabulary.

371 Use a Dictionary and Thesaurus

Rather than guessing what an unfamiliar word means, it is usually a good idea to take some time and "look it up" in the dictionary. When you do, check over *all* the meanings listed, not just the first one. This will give you the best definition and expand your vocabulary at the same time. Also check the pronunciation of the words you look up. It is much easier to remember the definition of a word if you know how to pronounce it.

A thesaurus is a dictionary of synonyms and antonyms. It can be a great help to you as you work on your vocabulary improvement. The most efficient time to use a thesaurus is when you are writing a paper which calls for creativity as well as accuracy. Rather than using the same word over and over again, use your thesaurus to find a synonym for that word. (See 302.)

372 Use a Notebook or Journal

Maybe you are already keeping a notebook (or part of a notebook) for new words you are learning in science, social studies, or math. You can—and should—do the same thing for every new word you come across, especially if you suspect you may want to use that word again later.

373 Use Words Parts

By studying the "parts" of a word (the prefix, suffix, and root which make up a word), it is possible to understand the meaning of that word. Before you can use word parts, however, you must become familiar with the meanings of the most widely used prefixes, suffixes, and roots in our language. For instance, the root *aster* is found in the word *asterisk*, where it means *star*; it is also found in the words *astrology, asteroid, astrodome, astrolabe, astronaut,* and *astronomer* where, in each case, it also means *star*.

Not all roots are found in as many as seven different words. Many are, however; and some are found in as many as thirty or forty different words. On the next ten pages, you will find a list of the most common prefixes, suffixes, and roots in the English language. Look them over and see if you recognize any. Then learn as many as you can—a few at a time.

Prefixes

Prefixes are those "word parts" which come *before* the root word (pre=before). Prefixes often change the meaning of a word from positive to negative, or negative to positive. As a skilled reader, you will want to know the meaning of the most common prefixes and then watch for them when you read.

a, an [*not, without*] amoral (without a sense of moral responsibility), atypical, atom (not cutable), apathy (without feeling)

ab, abs, a [*from, away*] abnormal, avert (turn away), abduct

acro [*high*] acropolis (high city), acrobat, acronym, acrophobia (fear of height)

ad, ac, af, ag, al, an, ap, ar, as, at [*to, towards*] admire (look at with wonder), attract, admit, advance, allege, announce, assert, aggressive, accept

ambi, amb [*both, around*] ambidextrous (skilled with both hands), ambiguous, amble

amphi [*both*] amphibious (living on both land and water), amphitheater

ana [*on, up, backward*] analysis (loosening up or taking apart for study), anatomy

ante [*before*] antedate, anteroom, antebellum, antecedent (happening before)

anti, ant [*against*] anticommunist, antidote, anticlimax, antacid

apo [*from, off*] apostasy (standing from, abandoning a professed belief), apology, apothecary, apostle

be [*on, away*] bedeck, belabor, bequest, bestow, beloved

bene, bon [*well*] benefit, bonus, benefactor, benevolent, benediction, bonanza

bi, bis, bin [*both, double, twice*] bicycle, biweekly, binoculars, bilateral, biscuit

by [*side, close, near*] bypass, bystander, byproduct, bylaw, byline

cata [*down, against*] catalogue, catapult, catastrophe, cataclysm

cerebro [*brain*] cerebral, cerebrum, cerebellum

circum, circ [*around*] circumference, circumnavigate, circumspect

co, con, col, cor, com [*together, with*] compose, copilot, conspire, collect, concord

contra, counter [*against*] controversy, contradict, counterpart

de [*from, down*] demote, depress, degrade, deject, deprive

deca [*ten*] decade, decathlon, decapod (ten feet)

di [*two, twice*] divide, dilemma, dilute

dia [*through, between*] diameter, diagonal, diagram, dialogue (speech between people)

dis, dif [*apart, away, reverse*] dismiss, distort, distinguish, diffuse

dys [*badly, ill*] dyspepsia (digesting badly, indigestion), dystrophy, dysentery

em, en [*in, into*] embrace, enslave

eu, ev [*well*] eulogize (speak well of, praise), eupepsia, euphony, eugenics

epi [*upon*] epidermis (upon the skin, outer layer of skin), epitaph, epithet

ex, e, ec, ef [*out*] expel (drive out), ex-mayor, exit, exorcism, eccentric (out of the center position), eject, emit

extra, extro [*beyond, outside*] extraordinary (beyond the ordinary), extracurricular, extrovert

fore [*before in time*] forecast, foretell (to tell beforehand), foreshadow, foregone, forefather

hemi, demi, semi [*half*] hemisphere, hemicycle, semicircle (half of a circle), demitasse

hex [*six*] hexameter, hexagon

homo [*man*] Homo sapiens, homicide (killing man)

hyper [*over, above*] hypersensitive (overly sensitive), hypertensive, hyperactive

hypo [*under*] hypodermic (under the skin), hypothesis

idio [*private, personal*] idiom, idiosyncrasy, idiomatic

il, ir, in, im [*not*] incorrect, illegal, immoral, irregular

in, il, im [*into*] inject, inside, illuminate, impose, illustrate, implant, imprison

infra [*beneath*] infrared

inter [*between*] intercollegiate, interfere, intervene, interrupt (break between)

intra [*within*] intramural, intravenous (within the veins)

intro [*into, inward*] introduce, introvert (turn inward)

375

macro [*large, excessive*] macrodent (having large teeth), macrocosm

mal [*badly, poorly*] maladjusted, malnutrition, malfunction, malady

meta [*beyond, after, with*] metabolism (thrown beyond, literally; hence, chemical and physical change), metaphor, metamorphosis, metaphysical

mis [*incorrect, bad*] misuse, misprint

miso [*hating, wrong*] misanthropist, misogynist, miser

mono [*one*] monoplane, monotone, monochrome, monocle

multi [*many*] multiply, multiform

neo [*new*] neopaganism, neoclassic, neologism, neophyte

non [*not*] nontaxable (not taxed), nontoxic, nonexistent, nonsense

ob, of, op, oc [*towards, against*] obstruct, offend, oppose, occur

oct [*eight*] octagon, octameter, octave, octopus

paleo [*ancient*] paleoanthropology (pertaining to ancient man), paleontology (study of ancient life-forms)

para [*beside, almost*] parasite (one who eats beside or at the table of another), paraphrase, parody, parachute, paramedic, parallel

penta [*five*] pentagon (figure or building having five angles or sides), pentameter, pentathlon

per [*throughout, completely*] pervert (completely turn wrong, corrupt), perfect, perceive, permanent, persuade

peri [*around*] perimeter (measurement around an area), periphery, periscope, pericardium, period

poly [*many*] polygon (figure having many angles or sides), polygamy, polyglot, polychrome

post [*after*] postpone, postwar, postscript, posterity

pre [*before*] prewar, preview, precede, prevent, premonition

pro [*forward, in favor of*] project (throw forward), progress, promote, prohibition

pseudo [*false*] pseudonym (false or assumed name), pseudo, pseudopodia

quad [*four*] quadruple (four times as much), quadriplegic, quadratic, quadrant

quint [*five*] quintuplet, quintuple, quintet, quintile

re [*back, again*] reclaim, revive, revoke, rejuvenate, retard, reject, return

retro [*backwards*] retrospective (looking backwards), retroactive, retrorocket

se [*aside*] seduce (lead aside), secede, secrete, segregate

self [*by oneself*] self-determination, self-employed, self-service, selfish

sesqui [*one and a half*] sesquicentennial (one and one-half centuries)

sex, sest [*six*] sexagenarian (sixty years old), sexennial, sextant, sextuplet, sestet

sub [*under*] submerge (put under), submarine, subhuman, substitute, subsoil, suburb

suf, sug, sup, sus [*from under*] suffer, suggest, support, suspect, sufficient, suspend

super, supr [*above, over, more*] supervise, superman, supreme, supernatural, superior

syn, sym, sys, syl [*with, together*] sympathy, system, synthesis, symphony, syllable, synchronize (time together), synonym

trans, tra [*across, beyond*] transoceanic, transmit (send across land or sea), transfusion

tri [*three*] tricycle, triangle, tripod, tristate

ultra [*beyond, exceedingly*] ultramodern, ultraviolet, ultraconservative

un [*not, release*] unfair, unnatural, unbutton

under [*beneath*] underground, underlying

uni [*one*] unicycle, uniform, unify, universe, unique (one of a kind)

vice [*in place of*] vice president, vice admiral, viceroy

376

NUMERICAL PREFIXES

Prefix	Symbol	Multiples and Submultiples	Equivalent	Prefix	Symbol	Multiples and Submultiples	Equivalent
tera	T	10^{12}	trillionfold	centi	c	10^{-2}	hundredth part
giga	G	10^{9}	billionfold	milli	m	10^{-3}	thousandth part
mega	M	10^{6}	millionfold	micro	u	10^{-6}	millionth part
kilo	k	10^{3}	thousandfold	nano	n	10^{-9}	billionth part
hecto	h	10^{2}	hundredfold	pico	p	10^{-12}	trillionth part
deka	da	10	tenfold	femto	f	10^{-15}	quadrillionth part
deci	d	10^{-1}	tenth part	atto	a	10^{-18}	quintillionth part

Suffixes

Suffixes come at the end of a word. Very often a suffix will "tell" you what kind of word (noun, adverb, etc.) it is part of and how it should be used in a sentence. Study them carefully.

able, ible [*able, can do*] capable, agreeable, edible, visible (can be seen)

ade [*result of action*] blockade (the result of a blocking action), lemonade

age [*act of, state of, collection of*] salvage (act of saving), storage, forage

al [*relating to*] sensual, gradual, manual, natural (relating to nature)

an, ian [*native of, relating to*] Canadian (native of Canada), African

ance, ancy [*action, process, state*] assistance, allowance, defiance, resistance

ant [*performing, agent*] assistant, servant

ar, er, or [*one who, that which*] doctor, baker, miller, teacher, racer, amplifier

ary, ery, ory [*relating to, quality, place where*] dictionary, dietary, bravery, dormitory (a place where people sleep)

asis, esis, osis [*action, process, condition*] hypnosis, neurosis, osmosis

ate [*cause, make*] liquidate, segregate (cause a group to be set aside)

cian [*having a certain skill or art*] musician, beautician, magician, physician

cide [*kill*] homicide, pesticide, genocide (killing a race of people)

cule, ling [*very small*] molecule, ridicule, duckling (very small duck), sapling

cy [*action, function*] hesitancy, prophecy, normalcy (function in a normal way)

dom [*quality, realm, office*] boredom, freedom, kingdom, wisdom (quality of being wise)

ee [*one who receives the action*] employee, nominee (one who is nominated), refugee

en [*made of, make*] silken, frozen, oaken (made of oak), wooden, lighten

ence, ency [*action, state of, quality*] difference, conference, urgency (state of being urgent)

ese [*a native of, the language of*] Japanese, Vietnamese

ess [*female*] actress, goddess, lioness

et, ette [*a small one, group*] midget, octet, baronet, majorette

fic [*making, causing*] scientific, specific

ful [*full of*] frightful, careful, helpful (full of help)

fy [*make*] fortify (make strong), simplify, amplify

hood [*order, condition, quality*] manhood, womanhood, brotherhood

ic [*nature of, like*] metallic (of the nature of metal), heroic, poetic, acidic

ice [*condition, state, quality*] justice, malice

ile [*relating to, suited for, capable of*] juvenile, senile (related to being old), missile

ine [*nature of*] feminine, genuine, medicine

ion, sion, tion [*act of, state of, result of*] action, injection, infection (state of being infected)

ish [*origin, nature, resembling*] foolish, Irish, clownish (resembling a clown)

ism [*system, manner, condition, characteristic*] alcoholism, heroism, Communism

ist [*one who, that which*] artist, dentist, violinist

ite [*nature of, quality of, mineral product*] Israelite, dynamite, graphite, sulfite

ity, ty [*state of, quality*] captivity, clarity

ive [*causing, making*] abusive (causing abuse), exhaustive

ize [*make*] emphasize, publicize (make public), idolize, penalize

less [*without*] baseless, careless (without care), artless, fearless, helpless

ly [*like, manner of*] carelessly, fearlessly, hopelessly, shamelessly

ment [*act of, state of, result*] contentment, amendment (state of amending), achievement

ness [*state of*] carelessness, restlessness, lifelessness

oid [*like, resembling*] asteroid, spheroid, tabloid

ology [*study, science, theory*] biology, anthropology, geology, neurology

ous [*full of, having*] gracious, nervous, spacious, vivacious (full of life)

ship [*office, state, quality, skill*] friendship, authorship, dictatorship

some [*like, apt, tending to*] lonesome, threesome, gruesome

tude [*state of, condition of*] gratitude, aptitude, multitude (condition of being many), solitude

ure [*state of, act, process, rank*] culture, literature, rupture (state of being broken)

ward [*in the direction of*] eastward, forward, backward

y [*inclined to, tend to*] cheery, crafty, faulty, itchy

Roots

Knowing the **root** of a word—especially a difficult word—can help you understand and remember it much better. This can be very useful when learning new words in all your classes. Because vocabulary is so important to success in all areas, knowing the following roots will be very valuable.

acer, acid, acri [*bitter, sour, sharp*] acidity (sourness), acrid, acrimony

acu [*sharp*] acute, acupuncture

ag, agi, ig, act [*do, move, go*] agent (doer), agenda (things to do), navigate (move by sea), ambiguous (going both ways, not clear), retroactive, agitate

ali, allo, alter [*other*] alias (a person's other name), alternative, alibi, alien (from another country or planet), alter (change to another form)

altus [*high, deep*] altimeter (a device for measuring heights), altitude

am, amor [*love, liking*] amorous, enamored, amiable

anni, annu, enni [*year*] anniversary, annually (yearly), centennial (occurring once in 100 years)

anthrop [*man*] anthropology (study of mankind), misanthrope (hater of mankind), philanthropic (love of mankind)

arch [*chief, first, rule*] archangel (chief angel), architect (chief worker), archaic (first; very early), archives, monarchy (rule by one person), matriarchy (rule by the mother), patriarchy (rule by the father)

aster, astr [*star*] aster (star flower), asterisk, asteroid, astrology (lit., star-speaking; study of the influence by stars and planets), astronomy (star law), astronaut (lit., star traveler; space traveler)

aud, aus [*hear, listen*] audible (can be heard), auditorium, audio, audition, auditory, audience

aug, auc [*increase*] auction, augur, augment (add to; increase)

auto, aut [*self*] automobile (self-moving vehicle), autograph (self-writing; signature), automatic (self-acting), autobiography (lit., self-life writing)

belli [*war*] rebellion, belligerent (warlike or hostile)

bibl [*book*] Bible, bibliography (writing, list of books), bibliomania (craze for books), bibliophile (book lover)

bio [*life*] biology (study of life), biography, biopsy (cutting living tissue for examination), microbe (small, microscopic living thing)

breve [*short*] abbreviate, brief, brevity

calor [*heat*] calorie (a unit of heat), calorify (to make hot), caloric

cap, cip, cept [*take*] capable, capacity, capture, accept, except, forceps

capit, capt [*head*] decapitate (to remove the head from), capital, captain, caption

carn [*flesh*] carnivorous (flesh-eating), incarnate, reincarnation

caus, caut [*burn, heat*] cauterize (to make hot; burn), cauldron, caustic

cause, cuse, cus [*cause, motive*] because, excuse (to attempt to remove the blame or cause), accusation

ced, ceed, cede, cees [*move, yield, go, surrender*] proceed (move forward), cede (yield), accede, concede, intercede, precede, recede, secede (move aside from), success

centri [*center*] concentric, centrifugal, centripetal, eccentric (out of center)

chrom [*color*] chrome, chromosome (color body in genetics), Kodachrome, monochrome (one color), polychrome (many colors)

chron [*time*] chronological (in order of time), chronometer (time-measured), chronicle (record of events in time), synchronize (make time with, set time together)

cide [*kill*] suicide (self-killer), homicide (man, human killer), pesticide (pest killer), germicide (germ killer), insecticide (insect killer)

cise [*cut*] decide (cut off uncertainty), precise (cut exactly right), concise, incision, scissors

cit [*to call, start*] incite, citation, cite

civ [*citizen*] civic (relating to a citizen), civil, civilian, civilization

clam, claim [*cry out*] exclamation, clamor, proclamation, reclamation, acclaim

clud, clus, claus [*shut*] include (to take in), recluse (one who shuts himself away from others), claustrophobia (abnormal fear of being shut up, confined), conclude

cognosc, gnosi [*know*] prognosis (forward knowing), diagnosis (thorough knowledge), recognize (to know again), incognito (not known)

cord, cor, card [*heart*] cordial (hearty, heartfelt), accord, concord, discord, record, courage, encourage (put heart into), discourage (take heart out of), core, coronary, cardiac

corp [*body*] corporation (a legal body), corpse, corpulent

cosm [*universe, world*] cosmos (the universe), cosmic, cosmology, cosmopolitan (world citizen), cosmonaut, microcosm, macrocosm

crat [*rule, strength*] autocracy, democratic

crea [*create*] creature (anything created), recreation, creation, creator

cred [*believe*] creed (statement of beliefs), credo (a creed), credence (belief), credit (belief, trust), credulous (believing too readily, easily deceived), credentials (statements that promote belief, trust), incredible

cresc, cret, crease, cru [*rise, grow*] crescendo (growing in loudness or intensity), crescent (growing, like the moon in first quarter), concrete (grown together, solidified), increase, decrease, accrue (to grow)

crit [*separate, choose*] critical, criterion (that which is used in choosing), hypocrisy

cur, curs [*run*] current (running or flowing), concurrent, concur (run together, agree), curriculum (lit., a running, a course), incur (run into), precursor (forerunner), recur, occur, courier

cura [*care*] manicure (caring for the hands), curator, curative

cus, cuse (see *cause*)

cycl, cyclo [*wheel, circular*] Cyclops (a mythical giant with one eye in the middle of his forehead), cyclone (a wind blowing circularly; a tornado), unicycle, bicycle

deca [*ten*] decade, decalogue, decathlon

dem [*people*] democracy (people-rule), demography (vital statistics of the people: deaths, births, etc.), epidemic (on or among the people)

dent, dont [*tooth*] dental (relating to teeth), orthodontist, denture, dentifrice

derm [*skin*] hypodermic (under skin; injected under the skin), dermatology (skin study), epidermis (on skin; outer layer), taxidermy (arranging skin; mounting animals)

dic, dict [*say, speak*] diction (how one speaks, what one says), dictionary, dictate, dictator, dictaphone, dictatorial, edict, predict, verdict, contradict, benediction

doc [*teach*] indoctrinate, document, doctrine

domin [*master*] dominate, dominion, domain, predominant

don [*give*] donate (make a gift), condone

dorm [*sleep*] dormant, dormitory

dox [*opinion, praise*] doxy (belief, creed or ism), orthodox (having the correct, commonly accepted opinion), heterodox (differing opinion; contrary, self-contradictory), paradox

duc, duct [*lead*] duke (leader), induce (lead into, persuade), seduce (lead aside), aquaduct (water leader, artificial channel), subdue, viaduct, conduct, conduit, produce, reduce

dura [*hard, lasting*] durable, duration, endurance

dynam [*power*] dynamo (power producer), dynamic, dynamite, hydrodynamics (lit., water power)

end, endo [*within*] endoral (within the mouth), endocardial (within the heart), endoskeletal

equi [*equal*] equinox, equilibrium

erg [*work*] energy, erg (unit of work), allergy, ergophobia (morbid fear of work), ergometer, ergograph

fac, fact, fic, fect [*do, make*] factory (the place where workmen are employed in making goods of various kinds), fact (a thing done, a deed), manufacture, faculty, amplification

fall, fals [*deceive*] falsify, fallacy

fer [*bear, carry*] ferry (carry by water), coniferous (bearing cones, as a pine tree), fertile (bearing richly), defer, infer, refer, referee, referendum, circumference

fic, fect (see *fac*)

fid, fide, feder [*faith, trust*] fidelity, confident, confidante, infidelity, infidel, federal, confederacy, Fido

fila, fili [*thread*] filament (a threadlike conductor heated by electrical current), filter, filet

fin [*end, ended, finished*] final, finite, finish, confine, fine, refine, define, finale

fix [*fix*] fix, fixation (the state of being attached), fixture, affix, prefix, suffix

flex, flect [*bend*] flex (bend), reflex (bending back), flexible, flexor (muscle for bending), inflexibility, reflect, deflect, genuflect (bend the knee)

flu, fluc, fluv [*flowing*] influence (to flow in), fluctuate (to wave in an unsteady motion), fluviograph (instrument for measuring the flow of rivers), fluid, flue, flush, fluently

form [*form, shape*] form, uniform, conform, deform, reform, perform, formative, formation, formal, formula

fort, forc [*strong*] fort, fortress (a strong point, fortified), fortify (make strong), forte (one's strong point), forte (strong, loud in music), fortitude (strength for endurance), force

fract, frag [*break*] fracture (a break), infraction, fragile (easy to break), fraction (result of breaking a whole into equal parts), refract (to break or bend, as a light ray), fragment

fum [*smoke*] fume (smoke; odor), fumigate (destroy germs by smoking them out), perfume

gam [*marriage*] bigamy (two marriages), monogamy, polygamy (lit., many marriages)

gastro [*stomach*] gastric, gastronomic, gastritis (inflammation of the stomach)

gen [*birth, race, produce*] genesis (birth, beginning), genus, genetics (study of heredity), eugenics (lit., well-born), genealogy (lineage by race, stock), generate, genitals (the reproductive organs), congenital (existing as such at birth), indigenous (born, or produced naturally in a region or country), genetic

geo [*earth*] geometry (earth measurement), geography (lit., earth-writing), geocentric (earth centered), geology

germ [*vital part*] germination (to grow), germ (seed; living substance, as the germ of an idea), germane

gest [*carry, bear*] congest (bear together, clog), suggestion (mental process by which one thought leads to another), congestive (causing congestion), gestation, suggestion

gloss, glot [*tongue*] polyglot (many tongues), epiglottis, glossary

glu, glo [*lump, bond, glue*] glue, conglomerate (bond together), agglutinate (make to hold in a bond)

grad, gress [*step, go*] grade (step, degree), gradual (step by step), graduate (make all the steps, finish a course), graduated (in steps or degrees), aggressive (stepping toward, pushing), congress (a going together, assembly)

graph, gram [*write, written*] graph, graphic (written; vivid), autograph (self-writing; signature), photography (light-writing), graphite (carbon used for writing), phonograph (sound-writing), bibliography

grat [*pleasing*] congratulate (express pleasure over success), gratuitous (gratis), gratuity (mark of favor, a tip), grateful, gracious, ingrate (not thankful; hence, unpleasant)

grav [*heavy, weighty*] grave, gravity, aggravate, gravitate

greg [*herd, group, crowd*] gregarian (belonging to a herd), congregation (a group functioning together), segregate (tending to group aside or apart)

hab, habit [*have, live*] habitat (the place in which one lives), inhabit (to live in; to establish as residence), rehabilitate, habitual

helio [*sun*] heliograph (an instrument for using the sun's rays), heliotrope (a plant which turns to the sun)

hema, hemo [*blood*] hematid (red blood corpuscle), hemotoxic (causing blood poisoning), hemorrhage, hemoglobin, hemophilia

here, hes [*stick*] adhere, cohere, cohesion

hetero [*different*] heterogeneous (different in birth), heterosexual (with interest in opposite sex)

homo [*same*] homogeneous (of same birth or kind), homonyn (word with same name or pronunciation as another), homogenize

hum, human [*earth, ground, man*] humility (quality of lowliness), humane (marked by sympathy, compassion for other human beings and animals), humus, exhume (to take out of the ground)

hydr, hydro, hydra [*water*] dehydrate (take water out of; dry), hydrant (water faucet), hydraulic (pertaining to water or to liquids), hydraulics, hydrogen, hydrophobia (fear of water)

hypn [*sleep*] hypnosis, Hypnos (god of sleep), hypnotherapy (treatment of disease by hypnosis)

ignis [*fire*] ignite, igneous, ignition

ject [*throw*] deject, inject, project (throw forward), eject, object

join, junct [*join*] junction (act of joining), enjoin (to lay an order upon; to command), juncture, conjunction, adjoining, injunction

jud, judi, judic [*judge, lawyer*] judge (a public officer who has the authority to give a judgement), judicial (relating to administration of justice), judicious, prejudice

jur, jus [*law*] justice (a just judgement), conjure (to swear together), juror, jurisdiction

juven [*young*] juvenile, rejuvenate (to make young again)

later [*side, broad*] lateral, latitude

laut, lac, lot, lut [*wash*] dilute (to make a liquid thinner and weaker), launder (to wash and iron clothes), lavatory, laundry, lotion, deluge

leg [*law*] legal (lawful; according to law), legislate (to enact a law), legislature (a body of persons who can make laws), legitimize (make legal)

levis [*light*] alleviate (lighten a load), levitate, levity (light conversation; humor)

lic, licit [*permit*] license (freedom to act), licit (permitted; lawful), illicit (not permitted)

lit, liter [*letters*] literary (concerned with books and writing), literature, literal, alliteration, obliterate

lith [*stone*] monolith (one stone, a single mass), lithography (stone writing, printing from a flat stone or metal plate), neolithic (lit., new stone; of the latest period of the Stone Age)

liver, liber [*free*] liberal (relating to liberty), delivery (freedom; liberation), liberalize (to make more free: as, to liberalize the mind from prejudice), deliverance

loc, loco [*place*] locomotion (act of moving from place to place), locality (locale; neighborhood), allocate (to assign; to place), relocate (to put back into place)

log, logo, ology [*word, study, speech*] zoology (animal study), psychology (mind study), logic (orig., speech; then reasoning), prologue, epilogue, dialogue, catalogue, logorrhea (a flux of words; excessively wordy)

loqu, locut [*talk, speak*] eloquent (speaking out well and forcefully), loquacious (talkative), colloquial (talking together; conversational or informal), circumlocution (talking around a subject), soliloquy

luc, lum, lus, lun [*light*] Luna (the moon goddess), lumen (a unit of light), luminary (a heavenly body; someone who shines in his profession), translucent (letting light come through), luster (sparkle; gloss; glaze)

lude [*play*] ludicrous, prelude (before play), interlude

magn [*great*] magnify (make great, enlarge), magnificent, magnanimous (great of mind or spirit), magnate, magnitude, magnum

man [*hand*] manual, manage, manufacture, manacle, manicure, manifest, maneuver, emancipate

mand [*command*] mandatory (commanded), remand (order back), countermand (order against, cancelling a previous order), mandate

mania [*madness*] mania (insanity; craze), monomania (mania on one idea), kleptomania (thief mania; abnormal tendency to steal), pyromania (insane tendency to set fires), maniac

mar, mari, mer [*sea, pool*] mermaid (fabled marine creature, half fish), marine (a sailor serving on shipboard), marsh (wetland, swamp), maritime (relating to the sea and navigation)

matri, matro, matric [*mother*] matrimony (state of wedlock), maternal (relating to the mother), matriarchate (rulership of a woman), matron

medi [*half, middle, between, halfway*] mediate (come between, intervene), medieval (pertaining to the Middle Ages), mediterranean (lying between lands), medium (a person having the faculty to make contact with the supernatural), mediocre

mega [*great*] megaphone (great sound), megalopolis (great city; an extensive urban area including a number of cities), megacycle (a million cycles), megaton (force of a million tons of TNT), omega (great)

mem [*remember*] memo (a note; a reminder), commemoration (the act of remembering by a memorial or ceremony), memento, memoir, memorable

meter [*measure*] meter (a measure), voltameter (instrument to measure volts in an electric circuit), barometer, thermometer

micro [*small*] microscope, microfilm, microcard, microwave, micrometer (device for measuring very small distance), micron (a millionth of a meter), microbe (small living thing), omicron (small)

migra [*wander*] migrate (to wander), emigrant (one who leaves a country), immigrate (to come into the land to settle)

mit, miss [*send*] emit (send out, give off), remit (send back, as money due), submit, admit, commit, permit, transmit (send across), omit, intermittent (sending between, at intervals), mission, missile

mob, mot, mov [*move*] mobile (capable of moving), motionless (without motion), motor (that which imparts motion; source of mechanical power), emotional (moved strongly by feelings), motivate, promotion, demote

mon [*warn, remind*] monument (a reminder or memorial of a person or event), admonish (warn), monitor, premonition (forewarning)

monstr, mist [*show*] demonstrate (to display; show) muster (to gather together; collect; put on display) demonstration, monstrosity

mori, mort, mors [*mortal, death*] mortal (causing death or destined for death), immortal (not subject to death), mortality (rate of death), immortality, mortician (one who buries the dead), mortuary (place for the dead, a morgue)

morph [*form*] amorphous (with no form, shapeless), Morpheus (the shaper, god of dreams), metamorphosis (a change of form, as a caterpillar into a butterfly), morphology

multi, multus [*many, much*] multifold (folded many times), multilinguist (one who speaks many languages), multiped (an organism with many feet), multiply (to increase a number quickly by multiplication)

nasc, nat [*to be born, to spring forth*] nature (the essence of a person or a thing), innate (inborn, inherent in), renascence (a rebirth; a revival), natal, native, nativity

neur [*nerve*] neuritis (inflammation of a nerve), neuropathic (having a nerve disease), neurologist (one who practices neurology), neural, neurosis, neurotic

nom [*law, order*] autonomy (self-law, self-government), astronomy, gastronomy (lit., stomach law; art of good eating), economy (household law, management)

nomen, nomin [*name*] nomenclature, nominate (name someone for an office)

nounce, nunci [*warn, declare*] announcer (one who makes announcements publicly), enunciate (to declare carefully), pronounce (declare; articulate), renounce (retract; revoke), denounce

nov [*new*] novel (new; strange; not formerly known), renovate (to make like new again), novice, nova, innovate

nox, noc [*night*] nocturnal, equinox (equal nights), noctilucent (something which shines by night)

number, numer [*number*] numeral (a figure expressing a number), numeration (act of counting), enumerate (count out, one by one), innumerable

omni [*all, every*] omnipotent (all-powerful), omniscient (all-knowing), omnipresent (present everywhere), omnivorous (all-eating)

onym [*name*] anonymous (without a name), pseudonym (false name), antonym (against name; word of opposite meaning), synonym

oper [*work*] operate (to labor; function), opus (a musical composition or work), cooperate (work together)

ortho [*straight, correct*] orthodox (of the correct or accepted opinion), orthodontist (tooth straightener), orthopedic (originally pertaining to straightening a child), unorthodox

pac [*peace*] pacifist (one for peace only; opposed to war), pacify (make peace, quiet), Pacific Ocean (peaceful ocean)

pan [*all*] Pan American, panacea (cure-all), pandemonium (place of all the demons; wild disorder), pantheon (place of all the gods)

pater, patr [*father*] patriarch (head of the tribe, family), patron (a wealthy person who supports as would a father), paternity (fatherhood, responsibility, etc.), patriot

path, pathy [*feeling, suffering*] pathos (feeling of pity, sorrow), sympathy, antipathy (against feeling), apathy (without feeling), empathy (feeling or identifying with another), telepathy (far feeling; thought transference)

ped, pod [*foot*] pedal (lever for a foot), impede (get the feet in a trap, hinder), pedestal (foot or base of a statue), pedestrian (foot traveler), centipede, tripod (three-footed support), podiatry (care of the feet), antipodes (opposite feet)

pedo [*child*] orthopedic, pedagogue (child leader; teacher), pediatrics (medical care of children)

pel, puls [*drive, urge*] compel, dispel, expel, repel, propel, pulse, impulse, pulsate, compulsory, expulsion, repulsive

pend, pens, pond [*hang, weigh*] pendant (a hanging object), pendulum, depend, impend, suspend, perpendicular, pending, dispense, pensive (weighing thought), appendage

phil [*love*] philosophy (love of wisdom), philanthropy, philharmonic bibliophile, Philadelphia (city of brotherly love)

phobia [*fear*] claustrophobia (fear of closed spaces), acrophobia (fear of high places), aquaphobia (fear of water)

phon [*sound*] phonograph, phonetic (pertaining to sound), symphony (sounds with or together)

photo [*light*] photograph (light-writing), photoelectric, photogenic (artistically suitable for being photographed), photometer (light meter), photosynthesis (action of light on chlorophyll to make carbohydrates)

plac, plais [*please*] placid (calm, peaceful), placebo, placate, complacent (self-satisfied)

plenus [*full*] replenish (to fill again), plentiful, plenteous, plenary

plu, plur, plus [*more*] plus (indicating that something is to be added), plural (more than one), plurisyllabic (having more than one syllable)

pneuma, pneumon [*breath*] pneumatic (pertaining to air, wind or other gases), pneumonia (disease of the lungs)

pod (see *ped*)

poli [*city*] metropolis (mother city; main city), police, politics, Indianapolis, megalopolis, Acropolis (high city, upper part of Athens)

pon, pos, pound [*place, put*] postpone (put afterward), component, opponent (one put against), proponent, expose, impose, deposit, posture (how one places himself), position

pop [*people*] population (the number of people in an area), populous (full of people), popular

port [*carry*] porter (one who carries), portable, transport (carry across), report, export, import, support, transportation, port

portion [*part, share*] portion (a part; a share, as a portion of pie), proportion (the relation of one share to others)

posse, potent [*power*] posse (an armed band; a force of legal authority), possible, potent, omnipotent, impotent

prehend [*seize*] apprehend (seize a criminal), comprehend (seize with the mind), comprehensive (seizing much, extensive)

prim, prime [*first*] primacy (state of being first in rank), prima donna (the first lady of opera), primitive (from the earliest or first time), primary, primal

proto [*first*] prototype (the first model made), protocol, protagonist, protozoan

psych [*mind, soul*] psyche (soul, mind), psychic (sensitive to forces of the mind or soul), psychiatry (hearing of the mind), psychology, psychosis (serious mental disorder), psychotherapy (mind treatment)

punct [*poin, dot*] punctual (being exactly on time), punctuation, puncture, acupuncture

put [*think*] computer (a computer or thinking machine), dispute, repute

que, qui [*ask, seek*] question, inquire, acquire, querulous

quies [*be at rest*] quiet, acquiesce, quiescent

reg, recti [*straighten*] correct, direct, regular, rectify (make straight), regiment, rectangle

ri, ridi, risi [*laughter*] ridicule (laughter at the expense of another; mockery), deride (make mock of; jeer at), risible (likely to laugh at), ridiculous

rog, roga [*ask*] prerogative (privilege; asking before), interrogation (questioning; the act of questioning), derogatory

rupt [*break*] rupture (break), interrupt (break into), abrupt (broken off), disrupt (break apart), erupt (break out), incorruptible (unable to be broken down)

sacr, sanc, secr [*sacred*] sacred, sanction, consecrate, desecrate, sacrosanct

salv, salu [*safe, healthy*] salvation (act of being saved), salvage (that which is saved after appearing to be lost), salutary (promoting health), salute (wish health to)

sangui [*blood*] sanguine, sanguinity, sanguinaria (bloodroot)

sat, satis [*enough*] satisfy (to give pleasure to; to give as much as is needed), satient (giving pleasure, satisfying), saturate

sci [*know*] science (knowledge), conscious (knowing, aware), omniscient (knowing everything)

scope [*see, watch*] telescope, microscope, kaleidoscope (instrument for seeing beautiful forms), periscope, stethoscope

scrib, script [*write*] scribe (a writer), scribble, inscribe, describe, subscribe, prescribe, manuscript (written by hand)

sed, sess, sid [*sit*] preside (sit before), president, reside, subside, sediment (that which sits or settles out of a liquid), session (a sitting), obsession (an idea that sits stubbornly in the mind), possess

sen [*old*] senior, senator, senile (old; showing the weakness of old age)

sent, sens [*feel*] sentiment (feeling), consent, resent, dissent, sentimental (having strong feeling or emotion), sense, sensation, sensitive, sensory, dissension

sequ, secu, sue [*follow*] sequence (following of one thing after another), sequel, consequence, subsequent, prosecute, execute, consecutive (following in order), ensue, pursue, second (following first)

serv [*save, serve*] servant, service, subservient, servitude, reservation, preserve, conserve, deserve, observe, conservation

sign, signi [*sign, mark, seal*] signal (a gesture or sign to call attention), signature (the mark of a person written in his own handwriting), design, insignia (distinguishing marks)

simil, simul [*like, resembling*] similar (resembling in many respects), simulate (pretend; put on an act to make a certain impression), assimilate (to make similar to), simile

sist, sta, stit, stet [*stand*] assist (to stand by with help), circumstance, stamina (power to withstand, to endure), persist (stand firmly; unyielding; continue), substitute (to stand in for another), status (standing), state, static, stable, stationary

solus [*alone*] solo, soliloquy, solitaire, solitude

solv, solu [*loosen*] solvent (a loosener, a dissolver), solve, absolve (loosen from, free from), resolve, soluble, solution, resolution, resolute, dissolute (loosened morally)

somnus [*sleep*] insomnia (not being able to sleep), somnambulist (a sleepwalker)

soph [*wise*] sophomore (wise fool), philosophy (love of wisdom), sophisticated (world wise)

spec, spect, spic [*look*] specimen (an example to look at, study), specific, spectator (one who looks), spectacle, speculate, aspect, expect, inspect, respect, prospect, retrospective (looking backwards), introspective

sphere [*ball, sphere*] sphere (a planet; a ball), stratosphere (the upper portion of the atmosphere), hemisphere (half of the earth), spheroid

spir [*breath*] spirit (lit., breath), conspire (breathe together; plot), inspire (breathe into), aspire (breathe toward), expire (breathe out; die), perspire, respiration

spond, spons [*pledge, answer*] sponsor (one who pledges responsibility to a project), correspond (to communicate by letter; sending and receiving answers), irresponsible, respond

string, strict [*draw tight*] strict, restrict, stringent (draw tight; rigid), constrict (draw tightly together), boa constrictor (snake that constricts its prey)

stru, struct [*build*] structure, construct, instruct, obstruct, construe (build in the mind, interpret), destroy, destruction

sume, sump [*take, use, waste*] consume (to use up), assume (to take; to use), presume (to take upon oneself before knowing for sure), sump pump (a pump which takes up water)

tact, tang, tag, tig, ting [*touch*] contact (touch), contagious (transmission of disease by touching), intact (untouched, uninjured), intangible (not able to be touched), tangible, tactile

tele [*far*] telephone (far sound), telegraph (far writing), telegram, telescope (far look), television (far seeing), telephoto (far photography), telecast, telepathy (far feeling)

tempo [*time*] tempo (rate of speed), temporary, pro tem (for the time being), extemporaneously, contemporary (those who live at the same time)

ten, tin, tain [*hold*] contain, tenacious (holding fast), tenant, tenure, untenable, detention, retentive, content, pertinent, continent, obstinate, abstain, pertain, detain, obtain, maintain

tend, tent, tens [*stretch, strain*] tension (a stretching, strain), tendency (a stretching; leaning), extend, intend, contend, pretend, superintend, tender, tent

terra [*earth*] territory, terrestrial, terrain, terrarium

test [*to bear witness*] testament (a will; bearing witness to someone's wishes), detest, attest (certify; affirm; bear witness to), testimony

therm [*heat*] thermometer, therm (heat unit), thermal, thermos bottle, thermostat (heat plus stationary; a device for keeping heat constant), hypothermia (subnormal body temperature)

tom [*cut*] atom (not cutable; smallest particle of matter), appendectomy (cutting out an appendix), tonsillectomy, dichotomy (cutting in two; a division), anatomy (cutting, dissecting to study structure)

tort, tors [*twist*] torsion (act of twisting, as a torsion bar), torture (twisting to inflict pain), retort (twist back, reply sharply), extort (twist out), distort (twist out of shape), contort, tortuous (full of twists)

tox [*poison*] toxic (poisonous), intoxicate, antitoxin

tract, tra [*draw, pull*] tractor, attract, subtract, tractable (can be handled), abstract (to draw away), subtrahend (the number to be drawn away from another)

trib [*pay, bestow*] tribute (to pay honor to), contribute (to give money to a cause), attribute, retribution, tributary

tui, tuit, tut [*guard, teach*] tutor (one who teaches a pupil), tuition (payment for instruction or teaching fees), intuition

turbo [*disturb*] turbulent, turmoil, disturb, turbid

typ [*print*] type, prototype (first print, model), typical, typography, typewriter, typology (study of types, symbols), typify

uni [*one*] unicorn (a legendary creature with one horn), unify (make into one), university, unanimous, universal

vac [*empty*] vacate (to make empty), vacuum (a space entirely devoid of matter), evacuate (to remove troops or people), vacation, vacant

vale, vali, valu [*strength, worth*] valor, (value; worth), validity (truth; legal strength), equivalent (of equal worth), evaluate (find out the value; appraise actual worth), valiant, value

ven, vent [*come*] convene (come together, assemble), intervene (come between), circumvent (coming around), invent, convent, venture, venue, event, avenue, advent, convenient, prevent

vert, vers [*turn*] reverse (turn back), avert (turn away), divert (turn aside, amuse), invert (turn over), introvert (turn inward, one interested in his own reactions), controversy (a turning against; a dispute),

vict, vinc [*conquer*] victor (conqueror, winner), evict (conquer out, expel), convict (prove guilty), convince (conquer mentally, persuade), invincible (not able to be conquered)

vid, vis [*see*] video (television), vision, evident, provide, providence, visible, revise, supervise (oversee), vista, visit

viv, vita, vivi [*alive, life*] revive (make live again), survive (live beyond, outlive), vivid (full of life), vivisection (surgery on a living animal), vitality, vivacious (full of life)

voc [*call*] vocation (a calling), avocation (occupation not one's calling), convocation (a calling together), invocation (calling in), evoke, provoke, revoke, advocate, provocative, vocal, vocabulary

vol [*will*] malevolent, benevolent (one of goodwill), volunteer, volition

volcan, vulcan [*fire*] Vulcan (Roman god of fire), volcano (a mountain erupting fiery lava), volcanize (to undergo volcanic heat)

vor [*eat greedily*] voracious, carnivorous (flesh-eating), herbivorous (plant-eating), omnivorous (eating everything), devour (eating greedily)

zo [*animal*] zoo (short for zoological garden), zoology (study of animal life), zoomorphism (attributing animal form to God), zodiac (circle of animal constellations), protozoa (first animals; one-celled animals)

Kinds of Literature

As you know, literature comes in all different sizes, shapes, and forms. Below you will find a brief description of some of the most common kinds or forms. See your index for the location of additional information.

An **allegory** is a story in which the characters and action represent an idea or truth about life; often, a strong moral or lesson is taught.

An **autobiography** is the writer's story of his own life.

A **biography** is the writer's story or account of some other person's life.

Comedy is writing which deals with life in a light, humorous way, often poking fun at people's mistakes. *Slapstick* comedy uses exaggerated action to get laughs.

Drama is the form of literature commonly known as plays. The word *drama* often refers to serious plays written about man and his relationship to society. (See "Comedy" and "Tragedy.")

An **essay** is literature which expresses an individual's point of view, usually in prose (paragraph) form.

Farce is literature written for one purpose: to make the reader laugh.

A **gothic novel** is a special type of book in which a mysterious, sometimes scary story is told. The action usually takes place in a large, old mansion or castle and may include a ghost or two. *Frankenstein* by Mary Shelley is a well-known gothic novel.

A **historical novel** is a special form of literature which imaginatively recreates a time or place in history.

Impressionism is literature which contains impressions of its subject instead of just facts. It is writing which gives the reader a general impression or picture (much like a painting) rather than a true-to-life picture (like a photograph).

Melodrama is a drama written in an exaggerated way to produce strong feeling or excitement in the reader or viewer as in TV soap operas.

A **myth** is a story that tries to explain a certain belief, especially a belief about nature or religion. Hercules is a famous character in Greek myth.

A **novel** is a book-length prose story. It is also fictional, which means it is created by the author's imagination.

A **parable** is a short story which explains a certain belief or moral.

Poetry is writing which is imaginative and emotional. Poetry is written with words that are vivid and colorful. These words are then arranged so that they have pleasing sound and rhythm. (See 221-236.)

Realism is writing that shows life as it really is rather than as the author or reader might like it to be. This kind of writing often includes the everyday things of life—like spilling milk or getting a knot in your shoelaces.

Romance is writing that shows life as the author or reader might like it to be rather than as it really is. Often, a romance is full of adventure, evil spies, and superheroes.

A **tragedy** is literature in which the hero is destroyed by some tragic flaw within his or her character.

Elements of Literature

Like most people, you know a "good" story or book when you read one. But can you put into words why you liked it? If not, the following glossary of what "goes into" a story (the elements) will help you discuss or write about what you've read.

Action refers to everything that goes on or happens in a story.

The **antagonist** is the person or thing fighting against the hero of a story; the villain or "negative force."

A **character** is a person in a story.

Characterization is the author's special way of explaining the people in his story—telling us about their personalities and motives.

Conflict is the "problem" in a story which triggers the action. There are five basic types of conflict.

◆ *Man vs. Man:* One character in a story has a problem with one or more of the other characters.

◆ *Man vs. Society:* A character has a conflict or problem with society— the school, the law, tradition.

◆ *Man vs. Himself:* A character struggles with himself and has trouble deciding what to do.

◆ *Man vs. Nature:* A character has a problem with some natural happening: a snowstorm, an avalanche, the bitter cold—some element of nature.

◆ *Man vs. Fate* (God): A character has to battle what seems to be an uncontrollable problem.

Dialogue refers to the talking that goes on between characters in a story.

Mood is the feeling(s) a reader gets from a story: happy, sad, peaceful.

The **moral** is the lesson an author is trying to teach in his story. Children's stories often have obvious morals such as "Treat others as you would like to be treated."

The **narrator** is the person or character who is telling the story. For example, Black Beauty tells his own story in the book *Black Beauty*, so the narrator is actually a horse.

The **plot** is the action of the story. This action is usually made up of a series of events called the *plot line*.

The **plot line** shows the action or events in a story. It has five parts: *exposition, rising action, climax, falling action,* and *resolution*:

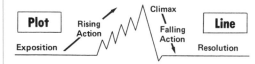

◆ The **exposition** is that part of a story (usually the beginning) which explains the background and setting of the story; the characters are often introduced in the exposition.

◆ The **rising action** is the central part of a story during which various problems arise, leading up to the climax.

◆ The **climax** is the highest point (turning point) in the action of a story.

◆ **Falling action** is that part of a story which follows the climax or turning point; it contains the action or dialogue necessary to lead the story to a resolution or ending.

◆ The **resolution** is the satisfying end of a play or story—that part in which the problems are solved.

Omniscient is a third-person point of view which allows the narrator to relate the thoughts and feelings of *all* the characters; a *godlike* intuition.

Limited omniscient allows the narrator to relate the thoughts and feelings of *only one* character.

Camera view (objective view) is seeing and recording the action from a *neutral* or unemotional point of view.

The **point of view** is the angle from which a story is told. This depends upon who is telling the story.

♦ A *first-person* point of view means that one of the characters is telling the story: "*I walked slowly, wishing I could turn and run instead of facing Mrs. Grunch.*"

♦ A *third-person* point of view means that someone outside of the story is telling it: "*She walked slowly, wishing she could turn and run instead of facing Mrs. Grunch.*" There are three third-person points of view: *omniscient, limited omniscient,* and *camera view.* (See illustration.)

The **protagonist** is the hero of the story.

The **setting** is the time and place of a story.

The **theme** is the *subject or message* being written about or discussed.

The **tone** is the author's attitude or feeling about a piece of writing. The author's tone may be *serious, humorous* (funny), *satiric,* and so on.

The **total effect** of a piece of writing is the overall influence it has on you, the reader—the way it makes you feel and the ideas it gives you.

Speaking and Listening to Learn

Preparing a Speech

When Barry Loco, the famous chain-saw juggler, came to our English class to talk about juggling, everyone—and I mean everyone— paid attention. As he was sharpening the teeth of the saw, he cautioned us, "Never, never look bored or turn your back on someone about to juggle CHAIN SAWS! If you do, your stay in this class could be—cut short."

For some kids and adults, delivering a speech in front of a group of people is as difficult and scary as juggling chain saws. Well, maybe not quite as scary, but in both cases your mouth may get dry, your knees may start shaking, and your palms may turn warm and slippery. And like a chain-saw juggler, you will need to go through a little trial and error before you are ready to perform.

Listening to a speech or a story or a lecture is rarely frightening, but it can be boring, difficult to follow, and frustrating. In this section, we'll offer you suggestions to improve your abilities to present speeches, read poems, tell stories, conduct interviews—and listen to others as they do the same. Then you, too, will be ready to dazzle your listeners—even without chain saws.

Why Am I Going to Speak?

389

The purpose behind all speaking is the same. It is to pass on ideas or feelings and get a favorable response in return. When you have to give a speech or an oral report, you must remember that the purpose is still the same. Below are a number of questions which you can ask yourself as you prepare your speech or report:

"Half the world is composed of people who have something to say and can't and the other half who have nothing to say and keep on saying it."

- What is the purpose of my speech? Is it to share information? Is it to show my classmates how to do something? Is it to persuade my audience?
- Who am I giving this speech for? My classmates? My teacher? Another class?
- Does my speech have to be about a particular topic, or may I select a topic I like and one which I think my audience will like as well?
- How long should the speech be?
- May I use visual aids?

390 What Should I Speak About?

If your speech may be on any subject, select a person, place, thing, or event which you are familiar with. This could be anything from taking photographs to a trip you took last summer. What's more important is that you like the topic, and you're pretty sure your audience will, too.

If your speech has to be on a current topic, you will need to find help from some other source. Possibly one of your teachers or a close friend will have some suggestions for you. If not, head for the library.

- Most libraries have some form of *vertical file* which contains hundreds of articles on current topics. Look through the articles and see if one would work as a speech topic.
- The *Readers' Guide to Periodical Literature* lists magazine articles by subject, providing hundreds of possible current topics.
- Every *newspaper* or *magazine* contains dozens of articles on the major issues in the world today.
- *Encyclopedias* and other reference books (even textbooks) can be very helpful tools when it comes to finding a speech topic.

Once you have found a possible topic, decide just how much of that topic you can cover in the *time limit* you've been given. You should now have a specific *topic* that will interest your *audience* and fit your *purpose*.

391 What Am I Going to Say?

After you have selected your topic, you are ready to gather details. You may begin by writing down your own thoughts on the topic, along with any personal experiences related to the topic. You may also ask friends and family members what their feelings or memories are about this topic and use these details to help you write your speech. If you need factual details, go to your library and use the material which is available there.

392 How Do I Say It?

Writing a speech is much the same as writing a paragraph or an essay. You must write in a clear, natural way so that your speech moves smoothly from one point to the next. Your information should be arranged into a beginning, a middle, and an end.

Helpful HINT

A speech is written to be *heard* rather than read. It must, therefore, *sound* good as well as look good on paper. It must be written using vivid, concrete words which create a clear, colorful picture for the audience. It must also be written with words that bounce and glide rather than plod along.

The Introduction   393

After you have collected enough information for your speech, you should arrange these details into an introduction, body, and conclusion. Your **introduction** should do the following: 1) gain the attention of your audience, 2) make it clear what your talk is going to be about, 3) get your audience to want to hear more about your topic, 4) lead into the main part of your speech. You may use one of these ideas in your introduction:

- an amazing fact or humorous story
- a series of interesting questions or a short history of the topic
- a short demonstration or a colorful visual aid
- a personal reason for picking the topic

The Body   394

In the **body** of the speech, you should move smoothly from one point to the next. You should cover the topic in an easy, natural way. You should use your own language—language which lets your audience feel like you're talking to each one of them personally.

Helpful HINT

Don't use big words just to try to impress your audience. They'd rather hear the real you, not some talking machine reciting facts, figures, and dates. You should, however, try to include enough "new" or little-known information to make your speech interesting.

Arrange your details in the best possible order—*order of importance, chronological order, comparison, cause and effect,* and so on. Explain or describe each part of your topic clearly so that your audience can follow along easily and enjoy what you have to say. If you are giving your opinion about something, make sure you support your point of view with enough reasons and facts to convince your audience.

The Conclusion   395

End your speech by reminding your audience what the purpose of your speech is. You might tell them why you feel your topic is important or why it may be important in the future. You may invite them to "get involved," "learn more," or "try it sometime." However you end your speech, always know *exactly* what your final two or three sentences are going to be—word for word. This is true even if you "make up" most of your speech as you go along. Otherwise, you may end up saying something corny like "That's the end of my report," "That's all," or "I guess that's it."

396 How Will I Give My Speech?

Preparing the Speech for Delivery

Once you are satisfied that your speech is well written, you can write your final copy. Follow the suggestions listed below:

- Always write or type your copy as neatly as possible and leave an extra-wide margin at the bottom of your card or paper.
- Never run a sentence from one page to another.
- Never abbreviate unless you plan to "say" the abbreviation. For example, YMCA and FBI may be abbreviated because you will actually read each letter; A.M. and P.M. should not be used when you intend to say *morning* or *afternoon*.
- Number each page.

397 Practicing the Delivery

After you have finished writing your speech, practice giving your speech (out loud) as often as you can. Try to get an audience of family or friends to listen to you. They can help you get used to "speaking" and can also offer suggestions for improvement. Practice until you feel comfortable or until you know your speech well enough to put the main points in your own words without looking at your paper or notes.

 If you are able to use a video recorder, practice your speech in front of it and review it for loudness, eye contact, posture, and so on. (Practicing in front of a mirror can also be helpful.)

---

398 Giving Your Speech

If you have practiced often and well, giving the actual speech should be easy. You may still feel a little nervous at first, but soon you will relax and enjoy sharing your "story" with your audience. Keep the following suggestions in mind as you give your speech:

- Speak loudly and clearly.
- Don't rush. Take your time and let your voice add color and interest to your topic.
- Use your hands. Sometimes you will need your hands to hold a chart or a poster. At the very least, let your hands hold your note cards or paper (if they are allowed). Never leave your hand movements to chance.
- Look at your audience as you speak.
- Keep both feet firmly on the floor. Don't slouch, sway, or teeter.
- Show enthusiasm for your topic from start to finish.

Reading to Others

Another common form of "speaking to learn" in the classroom is reading out loud. When you are first asked to read something for the class, it may scare you a bit. But if you go about it in the right way, it can be a positive, enjoyable experience for both you and the rest of the class. The guidelines which follow should be very helpful the next time you are asked to read to others.

Reading Poems, Plays, and Stories

400

Selecting and Studying . . .

1. Select a poem, play, or story you like and you think your audience will also like.
2. Read it aloud several times. Try to catch the general meaning.
3. Look between the lines for hidden meanings.
4. Think about the words and images (word pictures) and how each adds to the overall message of the poem, play, or story.
5. Think about the message, your personal feelings about it, and how you might read or "interpret" it for your audience.

Practicing . . .

6. Start with a clear, clean copy which is easy to read.
7. Look up any words you don't know how to pronounce and practice saying them out loud.
8. Practice "using" your voice to make the poem, play, or story sound real or exciting.
9. Think about where you want to emphasize a word or line, or where you want to pause, or where you want to raise your voice, or where you want to shout—you get the idea. (Mark your paper with lines or "symbols" to help you remember where to pause, shout, or look up.)

Reading . . .

10. ABOVE ALL ELSE . . . read slowly, clearly, and loudly enough to be heard by everyone in your audience.
11. Be enthusiastic—let yourself go.
12. Look at your audience; let each one of them think you are reading directly to him or her.
13. Relax and give it your best shot.

Reading Your Own Writing

If you were asked to tell about your worst injury or the most pain you've ever felt, you'd probably have no trouble thinking of a story. The trick to sharing your personal writing out loud is finding a story, poem, or topic that your audience will enjoy listening to.

Selecting a Story to Share

To select a story to tell, you need to decide what kind of story you enjoy telling. Do you like stories which make people laugh, stories which amaze or shock, stories with clever endings, or stories with audience participation? If you enjoy telling your story, your audience will enjoy hearing it.

The sample which follows was written by a girl who felt she had a "story" to tell. Like you, she had many memories to choose from, but chose a rather dramatic incident she felt would work well when read out loud.

One winter day in sixth grade, the rampaging our class was famous for came to an abrupt end, and I wince yet when I think about it. On that particular day, some of the girls decided to play "chicken" in the warm-up room, while some of the boys kept opening the door and throwing in snow. I wanted to go out and "get" someone, but just as I was stepping out, one of the boys threw another load of snow in and someone else slammed the door shut. Slamming a door shut is really no big deal—unless there are fingers in it. My fingers happened to be in it, and since they were, the door wouldn't shut all the way. Being the determined group they were, they didn't stop trying to get the door shut until they noticed I was screaming in agony.

The door was opened, and I got my fingers out, and everybody laughed—including me—until I took off my mitten. What I saw was no laughing matter; in fact, it was pretty ugly. The third and fourth fingers of my left hand were smashed into the shape of the door and whiter than the snow on the floor. The base of the nail on my fourth finger was sticking out. As we stood looking at it in disbelief, dark, red blood began to seep out and fill the depression.

Everyone was pretty scared by now, so they took me to the teacher, and she took me to the office, and they took me to the sickroom. They made me lie down and then scurried around wrapping up my finger. They didn't let me take off my coat, and when I said I was getting hot, they really panicked. They started packing my head in ice and asking me in loud voices if I was going to faint. I just thought, "I wonder if they know how foolish they look?"

I had to go to the doctor, and he took X rays to make sure nothing was broken. He pumped my finger full of painkiller and pulled the nail off. When I went back to school the next day, I heard all kinds of wild stories. Half the people thought my bone was sticking out, and the other half heard I fainted and went into convulsions in the sickroom. No one needed to add to the story—the truth was bad enough.

Listening Skills

Listening is one of the most valuable forms of learning we have. At the same time, listening is one of the most difficult of all the learning skills to improve. Why? First of all, to listen well you have to pay very close attention to the speaker. You have to concentrate on what he or she is saying and not let your mind wander away. You also have to listen "between the lines" and try to figure out what all of the information is adding up to. This isn't easy; it takes both time and patience.

Guidelines for Improving Listening Skills

Adjust your attitude . . .   402

- Have a positive attitude toward listening and learning; you have to "want" to improve before you can ever expect to.
- Avoid poor listening habits such as daydreaming, pretending to listen, or giving up when the material becomes difficult.

Listen carefully . . .   403

- Concentrate on the speaker and his tone of voice, facial expressions, and other gestures. This may help you figure out which points are most important as well as what the speaker is suggesting (saying between the lines).
- Listen for the speaker's use of signal words and phrases like *as a result, next, secondly,* etc. These signals can help you follow the speaker from one point to the next.

Think and write . . .   404

- Think about what is being said. What does this material mean to me? How might I use this information in the future?
- Listen with pen in hand. Take notes on any information you have to remember for tests or discussions; do not, however, take so many notes that you miss some of the important points or the main idea.
- Summarize each main point being made and decide why each point is important.
- Write down questions you would like to ask; ask them as soon as you get the chance.
- Find out how much of the information you will be expected to know in the future.
- Summarize the entire talk in one or two sentences as a final test of whether or not you understand what was said.

Interviewing

One of the most valuable sources of information available to people today is other people. And the best way to get good, current information from other people is to sit down and talk to them and listen to what they have to say. This is what newspaper, magazine, and television people do everyday. You, too, should consider interviewing others whenever you are asked to find information or research a topic. The tips which follow should help make your interview more comfortable and successful.

405 Tips for Better Interviewing

Before the Interview . . .

- Select a person to interview who has special knowledge or personal experiences to share.

- Write out all the questions you would like to ask. (Phrase your questions so that your subject cannot answer with just a "yes" or "no.")

- Make an appointment for a time and place which is convenient for the person you are going to interview.

- Let your subject know beforehand what kind of project you are working on and what topics you hope to cover. (You might even tell him or her some of the questions so he or she has time to think about them.)

- Study your topic as much as possible before the interview so that you are not likely to be overwhelmed with new information.

- Practice with your tape recorder beforehand so that you know how to change batteries, tapes, and sides of the tape. Label your tapes ahead of time.

- Also practice asking your questions and writing down responses. (A classmate or family member will be happy to let you practice your interview on him or her.)

During the Interview . . .

- Begin by introducing yourself and thanking your subject for the interview; also, ask if it's all right to take notes and/or use a tape recorder.

- Ask a good first question—then listen carefully. (If you ask good questions, you will end up listening far more than speaking.)

- Keep eye contact with your subject as much as possible, even while taking notes; notice the subject's facial expressions and gestures.

- Show that you are actively involved and interested in the topic by listening carefully, nodding, and adding an occasional "yes," "oh," or "um-humh."

- Don't interrupt your subject unless necessary. Wait with questions about spelling or points of fact until a natural pause in the conversation. (Mark the questions you hope to ask or put them in the margins of the notes.)

- Before you finish your interview, review your notes for any additional follow-up questions or points which need clarifying.

After the Interview . . .

- Thank your subject for the interview and offer to show him or her a copy of your finished work.

- As soon as possible after the interview, pull away by yourself and write like a maniac. Get down everything you remember before it slips away. Later, if you have time, type or write a transcript (a word-for-word copy) of the interview from the tape.

- Double-check any questionable facts or information with the subject or another authority before including it in your work.

- See to it that your subject gets a copy of your work if he or she wanted one.

MINI-lesson

Another way to collect information firsthand is to conduct a *poll* or *survey*. Instead of asking one important person a number of questions, you can ask a number of people one (or more) important questions. You can begin by surveying friends or classmates, or you can simply hit the streets and ask the first fifty people you meet. Either way, you should end up learning some interesting things about your topic.

Learning to Learn

Classroom Skills

Your teachers, your texts, and you—they all work together to make learning possible. Your teachers generally start the learning process by introducing or approving a new unit of study. Your texts—books, videos, discussions, etc.—provide you with learning material related to this unit. You then must supply the necessary enthusiasm and interest to make the learning happen. How do you do this? You must get actively involved by reading, writing, and talking about whatever it is you are studying. This is really the only way that you can make learning a meaningful experience.

This section includes three chapters, each of which will help you become an active and involved learner. "Classroom Skills" includes guidelines for keeping a learning log, plus guidelines for note taking and test taking. "Group Skills" provides insights into working and learning cooperatively. "Individual Skills" concludes the section with advice for developing long-range and short-term learning goals.

Writing in a Learning Log

409

A man named Samuel Crothers once said, "The trouble with facts is that there are so many of them." I'm sure many of you agree with him. Every day in your classes you are presented with any number of new facts and concepts that you are expected to remember and understand. It oftentimes becomes next to impossible to keep all of this new information under control, unless you really work at it. One of the most effective and enjoyable ways to work at learning is to keep a learning log.

"Learning makes man fit company for himself."
—**Thomas Fuller**

A learning log (or subject journal) gets you actively involved in your class work, and, more specifically, it gives you the opportunity to make sense of new concepts and facts presented in your classes. You can explore your thoughts and feelings about class discussions and group work in your learning log. You can react to reading assignments. You can evaluate your progress as you work on long-range projects and reports. You can keep track of important facts, concepts, and vocabulary words. You can review for major tests. A learning log is your all-purpose personal learning tool.

Guidelines for Keeping a Learning Log

The guidelines which follow will provide you with all of the how-to advice you need to begin your own learning log. Keep in mind that a learning log works best if you think and write as freely as possible about your course work, "personalizing" each piece of information.

410 Getting Started

- **Reserve** a section of a notebook for each class you would like to write about in your log; date your log entries.
- **Try** to maintain a writing schedule. The more difficult the course work, the more often you will want to write.
- **Write** nonstop in short bursts. Some of your entries may take you no more than three to five minutes. If, however, you're really on to something, keep going as long as you care to.
- **Discuss** new ideas and concepts in your learning log. Consider how this new information relates to what you already know.

411 Keeping It Going

- **Evaluate** your progress in a particular class. Consider your strengths, weaknesses, and relationship with members of the class.
- **Question** what you are learning. Dig deeply into the importance of new ideas; describe class assignments in your own words.
- **Argue** for or against something that came up in your class. Consider writing this in the form of a dialogue.
- **Confront** concepts that confuse you. Back them into a corner until you better understand the problem. (Share this with your teacher so he or she can see if you're on the right track.)

412 Writing-to-Learn Activities

You might be perfectly satisfied with writing freely in a learning log. If, however, you want a little variety, try one of the following activities:

First Thoughts: List your first impressions about something you are studying or reading. These thoughts will help you focus on your work.

Nutshelling: Try writing down in one sentence the importance of something you are studying or reading.

Stop-n-Write: Stop whatever you are studying or reading and start writing about it. This will help you keep on task.

Admit Slips/Exit Slips: Submit brief writings to your teacher before or after class. Write about an idea that confuses you, interests you, makes you angry, etc. Ask your teacher to react to your comments.

Synergizing: Generate ideas in pairs. Alternate statements or questions and answers with a classmate (especially effective when reviewing).

Taking Notes

Isn't it easier to understand or remember something you have actually done or seen than something you have only heard about? Taking notes is both doing and seeing. It changes information you have only heard or read about into information you have done something with. You not only hear the information, you also "see" it as you write it down. This "personalizes" the information and makes it much easier to remember and use.

The most important thing to know about note taking is that it's not simply writing down what you read or hear: it's *listening, thinking, questioning, summarizing, organizing, listing, illustrating*—and *writing*.

Why Take Notes?

413

Well, one good reason to take notes is that you will forget about half of what the teacher says before the class period ends if you don't. After two weeks, you will have forgotten more than 80 percent of the lesson.

Another good reason is that your "understanding" of the topic will be improved if you listen carefully AND take notes.

And, if you learn to take good notes now—you'll be developing a life-long skill that will benefit you in the future, especially if you plan to go to college or technical school (where many instructors spend the entire class period lecturing).

Guidelines for Improving Note-Taking Skills

414

The guidelines which follow will help you understand better what you must do to improve your note-taking skills. Read and follow each suggestion carefully. (Also read the "Listening Skills" section, 402.)

Be Attentive . . .

- Listen for and follow the special rules or guidelines your classroom teacher wants you to follow when you take notes.
- Place the date and the topic of each lesson at the top of each page of notes.
- Write your notes in ink, on one side of the paper, and as neatly as time will allow; leave space in the margin for revising or adding to your notes later. (See 417.)
- Begin taking notes immediately. Don't wait for something amazing or earthshaking before you write your first note.

415 **Be Concise . . .**

- Remember, taking good notes does not mean writing down everything; it means summarizing the main ideas and listing only the important supporting details.

- Write as concisely as you can. Leave out words that are not necessary; write your notes in phrases rather than complete sentences.

- Use as many abbreviations, acronyms, and symbols (U.S., avg., in., ea., lb., vs., @, #, $, %, &, +, =, etc.) as you can.

- Always copy down (or summarize) what the teacher puts on the board or on an overhead projector.

- Draw simple illustrations in your notes whenever it helps make a point clearer.

416 **Be Organized . . .**

- Write a title or heading for each new topic covered in your notes and skip lines between different points and ideas.

- Look for transitions or signal words to help you organize your notes (*first, second . . . before, after . . .*).

- Number all items presented in a list or in a time order.

- Circle those words or ideas which you will need to ask about or look up later.

- Read over the notes you have taken and recopy, highlight, or summarize them as needed. (Consider using a colored marker or pen to highlight those notes which you feel are especially important.)

- Review your notes within one day. Continue to review them at least once a week until you are through discussing that topic or unit in class.

417 ## Active Note Taking

To make note taking a more active, stimulating process, try the following form of learning log. Divide each page of your notebook in half. Use one side for traditional notes from discussions and readings. Use the other side to react to these notes. Your responses could include the following:

- ❖ a **comment** on what memory or feeling a particular concept brings to mind,
- ❖ a **reaction** to a particular point you strongly agree or disagree with,
- ❖ a **question** about a concept that confuses you,
- ❖ a **paraphrase** or rewording of a difficult concept,
- ❖ or a **discussion** of material presented in class.

Taking Tests

The key to doing well in school is simple—be involved and be prepared. This is never more true than when you are about to be tested on what you have learned. The guidelines which follow should help as you begin your preparation.

Test-Taking Skills

Organizing and Preparing Test Material ▬▬▬▬▬ 418

Ask questions . . .

- What will be on the test? Ask the teacher to be as specific as possible.
- How will the material be tested? (multiple choice? essay?)

Organize your notes . . .

- Review your class notes carefully.
- Get any notes or materials you may have missed from the teacher or another student.

Think about the test . . .

- Gather old quizzes and exams.
- Prepare an outline of everything to be covered on the test.
- Set aside a list of any questions you need to ask the teacher or another student.

Reviewing and Remembering Test Material ▬▬▬▬▬ 419

Begin studying early . . .

- Set up a specific time to study for an exam and stick to it.
- Begin reviewing early. Don't wait until the night before a test.
- Skim the material in your textbooks and make a list of special terms and ideas to study; copy over notes of the most important areas.

Use study aids . . .

- Use maps, lists, diagrams, acronyms, rhymes, or any other special memory aids.
- Use flash cards or note cards and review with them whenever time becomes available.

Test yourself . . .

- Try to imagine what questions will be on the test and write practice answers for them. (This is especially important for essay questions.)
- Recite material *out loud* whenever possible as you review; also, test yourself by teaching or explaining it to someone else.
- Study with others only *after* you have studied well by yourself.
- Go over your material at least once on the day of the exam.

420 Taking the Test

Before you begin . . .

- Check to see that you have all the materials (paper, pens or pencils, books, etc.) you need to take the test.

 Listen carefully to the final instructions of the teacher. How much time do you have to complete the test? Do all the questions count equally? Can you use a dictionary or handbook? Are there any corrections or additions to the test?

During the test . . .

- Skim the entire test quickly and estimate how much time you have for each question, problem, section. Then begin the test immediately and watch the time carefully.
- Read the directions carefully, underlining or marking special instructions. Follow all special instructions, like showing your work on math tests.
- Read all questions carefully, paying attention to words like *always, only, all,* and *never.*
- Answer the questions you are sure of first; move on to the next question when you are really stuck.

Before you finish . . .

- Double-check each section or page to make sure you have answered all the questions; check your work (and handwriting) thoroughly.
- Ask your teacher about any questions which still confuse you.

The Essay Test

Writing a good essay answer is not an easy task; yet it is one you will be called on to do over and over again, especially in high school. It is, therefore, very important for you to realize that when you take an essay test, you are doing much more than simply writing an answer to a question. You are *reading*—carefully—*thinking, planning, organizing, judging*, etc. If any one of these steps is missing or weak, your answer (and grade) will suffer.

Understanding the Essay Test Question

421

Understanding what the teacher is asking for in an essay test question is very important. Too many students make the error of thinking that the best way to answer an essay question is to write down everything they know about the topic as fast as they can. But this is not the best way. The best way is to think carefully and plan before you write.

The first step in planning your essay answer is to read the question several times or until you are sure you know what the question is asking. For example, if the question asks you to *evaluate* an event or idea, but you simply *explain* what it is, you have not answered the question correctly. You have not thought "deeply" enough about the question. Your grade will probably be disappointing.

 As you read the essay question, you must pay special attention to the "key words" that are found in every essay question. These key words will tell you what kind of thinking and writing are needed to answer the question correctly.

Key Words

422

The list which follows includes the most common key words used on essay tests. It also includes a definition of each word. Study these words carefully: It is the first step to improving your essay test scores.

Compare: To *compare*, you must use examples to show how two things are alike; usually they will be alike in several important ways. (You may also need to point out important differences.)

Contrast: To *contrast*, you must use examples to show how two things are different; you should concentrate on the important differences.

Define: To *define*, you must tell what the word or subject in the question means, what group or category it belongs to, what its function is, and how it is different from the others in that group.

Describe: To *describe*, you must tell in "story" form how something or someone looks, feels, sounds, etc. You should use enough vivid details to create a clear word picture of the subject.

Discuss: To *discuss*, you must look at the topic from all sides and try to come to some conclusion about the importance of the topic. A discussion answer can get quite long, so plan carefully.

Helpful HINT

Because this list of "key words" is too long to memorize all at once, concentrate on the first five in the list: *compare, contrast, define, describe,* and *discuss*. These five are the most commonly used terms on essay tests.

Evaluate: To *evaluate*, you must give your opinion (or an expert's opinion) of the value or worth of the subject. You must write about both the good points (advantages) and bad points (disadvantages).

Explain: To *explain*, you must tell how something happens or show how something works. Use reasons, causes, or step-by-step details when you explain.

Identify: To *identify*, you must answer the *who, what, when, where, why,* and *how* questions in an organized paragraph or essay.

List: To *list*, you must include a specific number of examples, reasons, causes, or other details in "list" form. You will number the parts of your answer in some way: *first, second, finally,* etc.

Outline: To *outline*, you must organize your answer (facts and details) into main points (or ideas) and subpoints. In some cases, you will use an actual outline to do this; other times, you will present your main points and subpoints in paragraph form.

Prove: To *prove*, you must present facts and details (proof) which show clearly that something is true.

Relate: To *relate*, you must show how two or more things are connected; *relate* can also mean to tell in story form.

Review: To *review*, you must give an overall picture or summary of the most important points about the subject.

State: To *state,* you must present your ideas about the subject using sentences which are brief and to the point.

Summarize: To *summarize*, you must present the main points in a clear, concise form. Details, illustrations, and examples are seldom included in a summary.

Trace: To *trace*, you must present (one step at a time) those details or events which show the history or progress of the subject.

Planning and Writing the Essay Answer

In addition to a good understanding of the key words used in essay questions, you must also understand how to actually write the essay answer. The following steps should help:

- **Read the question** several times or until you clearly understand what you are being asked to write. (Pay special attention to the "key word.")

MINI-lesson

Reword the question into a topic sentence. *Note:* One way to change your question into a topic sentence is to drop the key word and add a word (or words) which states the overall point or topic you are going to cover in your answer. (Notice these changes in the following example.)

Question: *Explain* the immediate effects of the atomic bomb on Hiroshima. **Topic sentence:** The immediate effects of the atomic bomb on Hiroshima were devastating. (The key word *explain* has been dropped; the main topic, *the devastating effects*, has been added.)

- **Stop and think** about the question and what you might include in your answer. List, cluster, or gather in some other way all the thoughts and details you can recall on the topic.

- **Outline the main points** you plan to cover in your answer and arrange them in the best possible order (time, order of importance, cause and effect, etc.). Don't try to include too many details in your outline—you may run short on time. (The outline below is a student sample taken from an essay test on *Hiroshima*, an award-winning book about the effects of the atomic bomb that was dropped on Hiroshima, Japan, at the end of World War II.)

Sample Outline

I. The Explosion
   A. 62,000 buildings destroyed
   B. Trains and bridges toppled
II. The Fire
   A. Ignited by bomb
   B. Ignited by debris
III. The Fallout
   A. Black rain
   B. Contamination

- **Write your essay.** Your opening sentence will be your topic sentence (the reworded question). Then include any additional information needed to make the rest of your answer clear. Use connecting words (*first, second, third,* etc.) to keep you on track.

425 **One-Paragraph Answer**

If you feel that only one paragraph is needed to answer the "essay" question, use all of your main points and important supporting details in this one paragraph. Arrange the information in the best possible way. Your arrangement will depend on the question being asked (chronological, order of importance, comparison, etc.).

Question: Explain the immediate effects of the atomic bomb on Hiroshima.

One-Paragraph Answer:

Essay question becomes topic sentence.	*The immediate effects of the atomic bomb on Hiroshima were devastating.* The initial explosion and violent wind which followed toppled train cars, stone walls, and bridges as far as two miles away from the impact area. Of the 90,000 buildings in Hiroshima, an estimated 62,000 were destroyed in an instant. Buildings near the center of the explosion were ignited at once by the tremendous heat (estimated at 6,000 degrees C) which was gener-
All main points and supporting details included in same paragraph.	ated by the splitting atoms. Away from the impact area, the splintered wreckage was ignited by exposed wiring and overturned cooking stoves. By late afternoon of the first day, very nearly every building in Hiroshima was burning. As the fires raged, huge drops of "black rain," created by heat, dust, and radiation, began to fall on the city. The radioactive "fallout" polluted the air and water adding to the problems of those who had survived the blast and fires. Before the day had ended, the
Summary or closing sentence	devastation from the bomb was nearly complete. *Very little of Hiroshima remained.*

426 **Multi-Paragraph Answer**

If the question is too complicated to be answered in a single para-graph, use your topic sentence in the first paragraph. Also include one of your main points in the first paragraph. Use facts, examples, reasons, or other details to back up your first point.

Begin your second paragraph with another one of your main points and add supporting details. Do the same for a third and fourth paragraph if one is necessary. End your essay with a sentence(s) which summarizes the overall point you are trying to make. (See the sample on the next page.)

Question: Explain the immediate effects of the atomic bomb on Hiroshima.

Multi-Paragraph Answer:

Question reworded into controlling sentence of essay answer.

The immediate effects of the atomic bomb on Hiroshima were devastating. The initial explosion of the atomic bomb on Hiroshima has often been described by those who survived it as a "noiseless flash." The bomb which was dropped on this island city was equal in power to 13,000 tons of TNT; incredibly, no explosion was heard by the residents of Hiroshima. Instead, they recall an enormous flash of blinding light followed by a tremendous wave of pressure. The wave and the violent wind which followed did an unbelievable amount of damage. Train cars, stone walls, and bridges as far as two miles away from the impact area were toppled. Of the 90,000 buildings in Hiroshima, an estimated 62,000 were destroyed in an instant. In that same instant, the smoke and dust carried by the wind turned day into night.

First main point explained in first paragraph: the initial explosion.

Second main point: fires sprang up throughout the city

The darkness quickly gave way to light as fires sprang up throughout the city. Buildings near the center of the explosion were ignited at once by the tremendous heat (estimated at 6,000 degrees C) which was generated by the splitting atoms. Away from the impact area, it was simply a matter of time before the splintered wreckage was ignited by exposed wiring and overturned cooking stoves. By late afternoon of the first day, very nearly every building in Hiroshima was burning.

Third main point: the additional effects of the bomb

As the fires raged, additional effects of the bomb became evident. Huge drops of "black rain" began to fall. The explosion had lifted tremendous amounts of smoke, dust, and fission fragments high into the atmosphere over Hiroshima. Soon a condensed moisture, blackened by the smoke and dust and contaminated with radiation, began to fall like rain on the city. The radioactive "fallout" polluted the air and water adding to the problems of those who had survived the blast and fires.

Closing or summary sentences

Before the day had ended, the devastation from the bomb was nearly complete. Very little of Hiroshima remained.

The Objective Test

One of the most common errors made by students on objective tests is that they don't carefully read the entire question before they answer. Keep that and the other guidelines listed below in mind the next time you take an objective exam.

428 True/False Test

■ Read the entire question before answering. Often one half of a statement will be true or false, while the other half is just the opposite. For an answer to be true, *the entire statement must be true.*

■ Be especially careful of true/false statements which contain words like *all, every, always, never*. Often these statements will be false simply because there is an exception to nearly every rule.

■ Watch for statements which contain more than one negative word. *Remember*: Two negatives make a positive.

429 Matching Test

■ Read through both lists quickly before you begin answering. (*Helpful Hint:* When matching word to phrase, *read the phrase first* and look for the word it describes.)

■ Cross out each answer as you find it—*unless* you are told that the answers can be used more than once.

■ If you get stuck when matching word to word, figure out the part of speech of each word. (If one word is a verb, match it to a verb.)

430 Multiple Choice Test

■ Read the directions very carefully to determine whether you are looking for the *correct* answer or the *best* answer. Also check to see if some questions can have more than one correct answer.

■ Read the first part of the question very carefully, looking for negative words like *not, never, except, unless,* etc.

■ Answer each question in your mind before looking at the choices; then read all the choices before selecting an answer. This is very important in tests where you have to select the "best" answer.

■ As you read through the choices, try to rule out those which are obviously incorrect; then choose from the remaining answers.

431 Fill in the Blanks

■ If the word before the blank is *a*, the word you need *probably* begins with a consonant; if the word before the blank is *an*, your answer should begin with a vowel.

■ If there are several blanks in a row, they *could* represent the number of words which are needed in your answer.

Group Skills

Collaborative means "to work together." You have probably collaborated on many school projects in the past, and will certainly collaborate on many more in the future. But, as you know, working in small groups or teams can sometimes be difficult—not everything always goes smoothly.

The following skills will help you work and learn better in groups: **listening, observing, cooperating, responding,** and **clarifying**. These skills are often called "people skills" because they help people work together successfully in groups, teams, and families. Sometimes these skills are called "interactive skills," because they help us interact or cooperate effectively with those around us. A more common term is "team skills" or "group skills."

Whatever name they go by, it is now obvious that the ability to use these skills in teams or groups is becoming more and more important for success in school and later on the job.

How Groups Are Formed

Groping . . . Griping . . . Grasping . . . Grouping

Groups don't just happen. Like most things, it takes much time and effort to form a good working group. Each group must go through several stages of development before everyone begins to truly work together.

1. **Groping:** During the groping stage, there is a general lack of understanding about the purpose and direction of the group. Each individual tries to find his or her place in the group; the group is "individual centered."

2. **Griping:** This is a period of discouragement, conflict, and frustration; members find it difficult to adjust to their places and roles in the group.

3. **Grasping:** The group begins to develop harmony, first by avoiding conflict. Members begin listening and observing and soon begin feeling more comfortable.

4. **Grouping:** The group develops a sense of purpose and begins working together. Members begin responding to and clarifying one another's ideas. Leaders emerge and efficient work begins.

Skills for Listening

Listening is not an easy skill to master. Like all other people, you listen in spurts. A spurt may last from a few seconds to a few minutes, but no one can listen with complete attention for a full hour. This is why it is so important to know how to listen as effectively as possible whenever you work in a group.

433 ■ **Listen actively.**

To be a good listener, you must be an "active" listener. This means you should let the speaker know you are listening. You should make eye contact, nod your head, and remain attentive. You can let the speaker know you have listened by asking a good question, summarizing, or by offering a compliment or comment. Finally, think about what the speaker is saying and restate it inside your mind or on paper.

434 ■ **Listen accurately.**

Hearing is not the same as listening. Listen with your ears AND your mind. Think about what is being said, not about what you are going to say as soon as you get a chance. Listen with pen in hand. Jot down a word, phrase, or question to help you remember what is being said and what you want to add. Then, when the speaker stops, you can offer your ideas.

Keep an open mind about the speaker and the topic; do not conclude beforehand that you are not going to like what is about to be said.

---

435 ■ **Know when—and how—to interrupt.**

If you are a good listener, you will sooner or later have a burning question to ask or an important fact to add. Even so, interrupting someone who is speaking is not usually a good idea. If you do feel you must interrupt to add important information to the discussion, say, "Excuse me, Janet, when you finish I have something to add."

Sometimes it is also necessary to interrupt a group member who has wandered off the topic. When that happens, you are right to say, "Excuse me, Bert, but I think we should get back to the main point of our discussion." Or if someone is "hogging" the discussion, try to interrupt on someone else's behalf by saying, "Excuse me, Bert, but yesterday Ernie said something about this. Ernie, could you add your thoughts?"

436 ■ **Learn how to respond when you are interrupted.**

When you are interrupted without good reason by a group member, you can say, "I wasn't finished making my point yet" or "Could you please wait until I'm finished?" Whatever you say, say it courteously. You can discourage interruptions by keeping what you say short and to the point.

Skills for Observing

Being observant is also an important group skill. People "say" as much with their actions and tone of voice as with their words.

■ Watch body language.   437

Sometimes you can "see" what a person is saying. This is called *body language*, and it includes facial expressions, the position of the hands, and any other gesture which tells us something about the attitude of that person. Is someone leaning away from the group? This may mean he or she is withdrawing from the group. Is the speaker leaning toward the group? This may mean the next point is very important. Body language can tell you what a speaker is "saying between the lines."

■ Offer words of encouragement.   438

When you encourage another person, you demonstrate your appreciation of that person's ideas. All of us are more likely to participate in groups if we feel that what we say will be accepted. You can say, "I like that idea" or "Let's talk more about that." To someone who has not been participating, you can say, "Hank, what do you think?" or "Jo, you often have good ideas. What can you add?"

Skills for Cooperating

Cooperating means "working together." The only way people can successfully cooperate is if they use common sense, common courtesy, and share a common goal. (It also helps to be patient.)

■ Offer compliments or thanks.   439

We too often forget to offer compliments or thanks when we work in groups. Simply say, "Thank you, John, for keeping notes for our group" or "I really like your suggestion to . . . ." Likewise, don't hesitate to offer an apology if you put someone down or if you aren't doing your fair share of the work. All of this helps to build stronger groups.

■ Never use put-downs.   440

Put-downs come in many shapes and sizes. Let's hope you've never heard a group member say, "Jon, let Suzy talk. She always has the best ideas" or "That's really a dumb idea!" Such put-downs disrupt the group and cause members to lose their self-confidence.

■ Do not unintentionally disturb others.   441

Sometimes we unintentionally cause harm, pain, or discomfort to another person. Invading another's space is one example. To avoid this, keep your arms and legs out of the space occupied by other members. Ignoring one or more of the members also hurts the overall group effort.

Skills for Responding

When you work in a group, nearly everything you say and do is a response to what someone else has said or done. Responding is actually a three-part process: **First**, you hear another person's statement or observe his behavior. **Second**, you take a moment to think about the ways you could respond. **Third**, you choose your response. There are five ways for you to respond: you can simply **tell** what you know, you can **sell** your ideas to the group, you can **test** or challenge an idea, you can **agree** with or support an idea, or you can **advise** when someone asks you to.

442 ■ **Respond to a person when they put you down.**

When someone uses a put-down, you should respond to it. Ignoring put-downs will only encourage people to continue their insensitive behavior. Say something like, "If our group is going to work together, we can't be putting each other down all the time."

Inappropriate responses include making a face, sticking out your tongue, walking away, calling names, and pretending you didn't hear or notice the put-down.

443 ■ **Think before responding.**

For example, a classmate says to you, "New Kids on the Block is a dumb group." You may think 1) This person is challenging me to defend this group, 2) He hasn't given any reasons to support his opinion, or 3) I wonder what he means by "dumb"?

You can then choose how you will respond. You can avoid the discussion by saying, "Everyone is entitled to his own opinion." You can look for some details by asking, "Why do you feel they're dumb?" Or you can seek clarification by asking, "What do you mean by 'dumb'?"

Before knowing anything about group skills you may have said, "Yeah, well I think you're dumb" or "You obviously don't know anything about music." If you respond in this manner, the other person has dragged you into a dead-end argument instead of a discussion.

444 ■ **Learn how to disagree.**

Never say, "I disagree with you." Say instead, "I disagree. I don't think George Washington was the greatest president." This is disagreeing with the idea, not the speaker. You should continue by listing some reasons why you disagree. Or instead of saying "I disagree," you can ask the speaker a few questions, questions which will show that some important points have been left out. After trying to answer the questions, the speaker may change his position.

■ **Learn from disagreements.**   445

Always make good eye contact when expressing disagreement. Don't lean away from the other person(s). Don't get angry. Keep your voice calm and interested. Listen carefully . . . it may be you will want to change *your* position.

Remember that disagreements are often helpful. They increase your ability to challenge appropriately, to think, to defend your viewpoint, and to combine your ideas with those of another person.

■ **Use "I" statements.**   446

Using "I" statements is one of the best group skills you can develop. "I" statements often begin with *how you feel* and conclude with *why you feel* or think that way. Some samples of "I" statements are "I feel uncomfortable when you . . . because . . . ," "I appreciate it when you . . . because . . . ," and "I feel a little left out when you . . . ."

When you express a negative feeling with an "I" statement, you are telling your listener exactly how you think and feel; but you are also showing him or her that you are accepting responsibility for how you feel and are not trying to pass on the blame.

 "I" statements are the opposite of "you" statements. ("You are responsible for this mess.") Needless to say, "I" statements help groups work together more effectively.

Skills for Clarifying

■ **Offer to explain or clarify.**   447

A thoughtful group member observes her or his listeners. Do they look puzzled? Are they looking out the window? Do they avoid eye contact with you? It is sometimes hard to observe your listeners and still remember what you want to say. So after you have finished speaking, you can ask, "Are there any questions?" *Note:* If you offer to explain or clarify and your offer is rejected, let it go at that.

■ **Request help or clarification when needed.**   448

You can request help if necessary by saying, "I want to be sure I understand this. What happens if . . . ?" Or summarize the material in question and end with, "Is that about it, or did I miss something?"

■ **Help your group reach a decision.**   449

❑ Continue to discuss choices until everyone in the group agrees. (This can take time.)

❑ Agree to get more information before a decision is made.

❑ Vote on the list of choices or ask an "expert" to make the decision.

Individual Skills

Throughout your handbook, we encourage you to take risks, to explore, to let yourself go, so to speak, in your writing and learning. We want you to see possibilities as much as we want you to come up with right answers. But that doesn't mean we want you to approach learning without any goals in mind or without concern for deadlines or due dates. We know these are very important issues, and that's why we've included this chapter on individual learning skills in your handbook. We begin with information on setting goals and follow with guidelines for managing your time and completing assignments. We conclude this section with information on managing stress in your daily life.

450 Setting Goals

People who set goals and follow through with them are generally confident and independent individuals. They are, by their nature, active people interested in all that life has to offer. They are the type of people who inspire us. A story about one of my former students follows. His accomplishment was an inspiration to all of us in the class.

A Goal Setter in Action

Mike wanted to do something a little different for his short story assignment. He wanted to write, direct, and produce his own movie. As a teacher, I was more than a little skeptical. Writing a short story was challenge enough for most of my students, yet Mike had it in his mind to make a movie. To make a long and involved story short, Mike did make his movie, and it took him most of the final quarter to do so. He showed it to us the last day of school, and it was a wonderful "creature feature" along the lines of *Invasion of the Killer Tomatoes*.

After we saw his movie, Mike shared with us the story behind the final product. We were amazed with what he had done all on his own. He wrote the script, held auditions for parts, created all of his own special effects, and filmed and edited the entire movie himself. Nothing Mike had done in my class that year could compare with what he gained from this experience. He had challenged himself with a major undertaking, and he had succeeded (well beyond his own expectations, I'm sure). His classmates benefited as well. They not only saw a good movie, but they also saw firsthand what it means to establish a long-range goal and follow through with it.

Guidelines for Setting Goals

Can you think of any projects you would like to undertake, any skills you would like to improve, any resolutions you would like to keep? The guidelines which follow will give you insights into planning long-range goals and help you in carrying them out.

■ **Be realistic about the goals you set for yourself.** Mike had access to a video camera, had done a lot of reading about movies, and had done some movie making on a smaller scale in the past. So producing a movie, although a big challenge, was not an unrealistic goal for him. (See the story about Mike on the preceding page.)

What would be a realistic goal for you? Are you capable of writing a novel or setting out to break the state record in the mile run? I doubt it, unless you're a very gifted individual. Try these on for size: Plan to write one full page each day in a personal journal—maybe for six months or even longer. Or, each time you run in a track meet, plan to run a faster race than the time before. These seem to be reasonable goals.

■ **Do whatever you can to work toward your goal or plan but be flexible enough to accept occasional setbacks.** There will be times when you just can't write—although, there should almost always be time for at least one page of writing. And there will be track meets when it will be next to impossible for you to run your best time—perhaps you're running in a monsoon or you're just not feeling well.

■ **Plan how you expect to accomplish your goal.** Set aside a specific time to write and stick to it. And make it a point to talk to your coach after every race. Find out from him or her what you can do to improve your time, and then work on that aspect of your running between meets.

■ **If you set a goal which covers an extended period of time, divide it into more manageable parts.** Treat yourself to an ice-cream cone if you stick to your writing schedule for two straight weeks. Rent one of your favorite videos if you improve your time for two consecutive races.

■ **Give each of your goals a chance.** There's a lot to be gained by dedicating yourself to a long-range goal. If you write one page every day for six months, you'll have written 183 pages. That's quite an accomplishment. If you write in your journal for a year, you'll have filled 365 pages. Most of the books you read don't have that many pages. And think of the sense of accomplishment you will feel if you do make steady improvements in your running—and the respect you will gain.

> *"The world stands aside to let anyone pass who knows where he is going."*
> —**Jordan Allister**

Managing Your Time

If you can't seem to get things done, or if you *procrastinate*—put off doing what you should do—you may want to practice time management. Time management is probably not a skill you'll learn in school, so it's up to you to make it part of your own learning style. Here's how you do it.

Steps in the Process

- **Turn big jobs into smaller jobs.** When you're faced with a major project or some other important task, don't look at it as one big job. Break it down into smaller, more manageable parts. Spread your project over a period of time and work on it in smaller time slots. Studying or working 15 minutes a day for two weeks beats two or three hours of work the night before your science project is due.

- **Keep a weekly schedule.** A weekly planner shows you at a glance what you have coming up and helps you plan time for activities, studying, and fun. A model weekly planner follows. Design your own planner to meet your personal needs.

WEEKLY PLANNER

Day/Date	Assignments	Due Date	Activities, Meetings	Study Schedule	Fun Time
Monday 10/30					

- **Make a "Daily List."** Write down things you need to do today and must do tomorrow. Number them in order of importance; then cross each item off as it is completed.

- **Plan your study time realistically.** Fifteen- to twenty-minute time slots followed by a five-minute break works well for most students.

- **Keep a flexible schedule.** Plans change and new things pop up daily. Be realistic and willing to change those events that can be changed.

Helpful HINT

Find out when you are the most productive. Reserve this time for your most challenging assignments and projects. Also, make time for relaxation and exercise. They are important elements in a well-balanced work schedule.

Completing Assignments

One of the challenges you and your classmates face each day is completing your assignments correctly and on time. If you have good study habits, it's a challenge you've probably already met, something you do without thinking. Or maybe it's a constant problem for you. Maybe you need to organize your thinking much more carefully. If so, the guidelines which follow should help.

Planning ahead . . .

453

- First of all, know exactly what the assignment is, when it is due, and what you must do to complete it successfully.
- Decide how much time you will need to complete the assignment and set aside that time in your daily schedule.
- Decide when and where (library, study hall, home) you will do your assignment; work in a quiet, comfortable place whenever possible.
- Gather any materials you may need to complete your assignment (journal, notebook, handouts, dictionary, handbook).

Helpful
HINT

If you are having trouble getting started on your assignments, try doing them at the same time and place each day. This will help you control the urge to wait until you are "in the mood" before starting. Also, try to avoid doing your assignments when you are overly hungry or tired.

Getting it done . . .

454

- Go over all the directions your teacher has given you for this assignment. Look up any words you are unsure of and write down the meaning of each.
- Plan to take breaks only after completing a certain amount of each assignment and stick to that schedule. If necessary, ask your family not to disturb you and hold any phone calls you may get.
- Keep a list of things you need to check on or ask your teacher about. (Remember, all learning is an attempt to solve a problem. You must clearly understand a problem before you can solve it.)
- Use a study method (KWL, SQ3R) to help you complete the reading and studying parts of your assignment. Follow the suggestions in "Writing to Learn," "The Classroom Report," or any other helpful section of your handbook.
- Turn your assignment in on time and welcome any suggestions your teacher may give you for future improvement. (Make sure your assignment is neat and free of careless errors.)

Managing Stress

You are the best person to identify signs and causes of stress or pressure in your daily life, and only you can decide whether or not your stress is becoming unmanageable. Stress can produce any number of symptoms from simply feeling uptight to feeling angry, from experiencing headaches to eating too little or too much. The information below will help you recognize the causes and symptoms of stress in your life.

455 ## Causes of Stress

- Moving
- Divorce of parents
- Performing in front of others
- Doing something you know is wrong
- Peer pressure
- Birth of a sibling
- High expectations
- Doing poorly in school

456 ## Symptoms of Stress Overload

- ❑ unusual mood swings
- ❑ withdrawal from family or friends
- ❑ withdrawal from activities
- ❑ overdoing an activity
- ❑ disinterest in school
- ❑ loss of concentration
- ❑ low self-esteem
- ❑ sleeping too much

457 ## Reducing Stress

There are a number of things you can do. First you must identify the things in your life that are causing you stress, and then you should create a plan for dealing with them.

1. **Eliminate the problem that is causing stress:** Getting to the root of the problem is one of the best long-term solutions for dealing with stress. Working on a plan to improve your grades or change your attitude are both good examples of long-term solutions.

2. **Avoid the problem:** While this is not an ideal solution, it can be temporarily useful. Going to a movie, reading a good book, playing piano, or going for a walk or run are all good ways to "put off" stressful situations. "Temporarily" avoiding a problem can sometimes give you the space you need to come up with a long-term solution.

   "I get by with a little help from my friends."
   —**Paul McCartney**

3. **Stress-reducing activities:** Most people find that much of the stress they experience will have to be faced each day. Following a healthy diet, exercising regularly, talking to a friend, and doing something you enjoy are good ways to keep your stress level low.

The Yellow Pages Guide to
Marking
Punctuation

PUNCTUATIONMARKSWERENTDESIGNEDTODRIVEYOU CRAZYTHATHONORHASBEENGIVENTOYOURENGLISHTEACHERS

PUNCTUATIONMARKS:AREPARTOFYOURLANGUAGESYSTEM: THEYHELPYOUMANAGE:THEWORDSANDIDEAS:YOUWRITE: THEYHELPYOUCOMMUNICATE

AND•THEY•HELP•READERS•APPRECIATE•WHAT•YOU• WRITE•PUNCTUATION•MARKS•SERVE•AS•THEIR•ROAD• MARKERS•DIRECTING•THEIR•WAY•SO•THEY•DONT•GET• LOST•WHILE•TRAVELING•ALONG•THIS•STRETCH•OF•ROAD

What you've just read or tried to read are examples of how early manuscripts and inscriptions were written. Very early on, manuscripts were written in all capital letters with no space between the words and no punctuation marks. This way of writing is next to impossible to read as you can tell by the first example. Later, a mark like our colon (see the second example) was added between phrases to make the writing easier to read. At one point, centered dots were even added between each word for the sake of readability (see the last example).

These changes were made a long time ago (around 260 B.C.) in ancient Greece. Between that time and now, the way we punctuate our sentences has changed a great deal. And our system of punctuation will continue to change, just as other aspects of our language system will continue to change.

The guidelines which follow obviously reflect the language of the 1990's. They are meant to help you punctuate all of your writing—be it a report for your science class, a story you want to submit for publication, or a letter you would like to fax to a friend.

The example sentences punctuated "1990 style" read as follows: *Punctuation marks weren't designed to drive you crazy (that honor has been given to your English teachers). Punctuation marks are part of your language system. They help you manage the words and ideas you write. They help you communicate. And they help readers appreciate what you write. Punctuation marks serve as their road markers— directing their way, so they don't get lost while traveling along this stretch of road.*

Period
459

A **period** is used to end a sentence which makes a statement or a request, or which gives a command which is not used as an exclamation.

> **Try these car facts on for size.** [Command]
>
> **Cars of the future will come with electronic navigation systems.** [Statement]
>
> **Video rearview mirrors will relay the "rear view" on an in-dash video screen.** [Statement]
>
> **Relax.** [Request]
>
> **In-car radar systems (they can scan up to 400 feet) will help you avoid head-on collisions.** [Statement]

Note: It is not necessary to place a period after a statement which has parentheses around it and is part of another sentence.

460 ....After an Initial

◆ A period should be placed after an initial.

> **M.E. Kerr** [writer]
>
> **Steven P. Jobs** [founder of Apple computers]

461 ....As a Decimal

◆ Use a period as a decimal point and to separate dollars and cents.

> **Experts are 69.9 percent sure (okay 70 percent) that a pill now under development will prevent cavities and cost about $9.50 each.**

At the End of a Sentence 462

◆ When an abbreviation is the last word in a sentence, only one period should be used at the end of the sentence.

> **By the year 2030, a 65-year-old individual may be as fit as a 45-year-old person today because of advances in nutrition, exercise, preventative medicine, etc.**

After Abbreviations 463

◆ A period is placed after each part of an abbreviation—unless the abbreviation is an acronym. An acronym is a word formed from the first (or first few) letters of words in a set phrase. (See 556.)

> **Abbreviations ....Mr., Mrs., Ms., Dr., A.D., B.C.**
>
> **Acronyms ....BASIC, DOS, Laser, Modem**

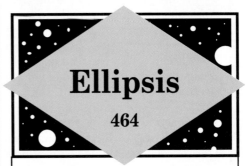

Ellipsis
464

An **ellipsis** (three periods) may be used to indicate a pause in dialogue or to show omitted words or sentences. (When typing, leave one space before, after, and between each period.)

To Show a Pause 465

◆ An ellipsis is used to indicate a pause in dialogue.

> **"Why did I get home late, Dad? Well, Jill and I . . . ah . . . yeah, were in another galaxy. Well, I . . . ah . . . mean we were watching *2001: A Space Odyssey* on Jill's new 3-D TV."**

466 .... To Show Omitted Words

◆ An ellipsis is used to show that one or more words have been left out of a quotation. Read below a segment of a magazine article in which Trip Hawkins, president of Electronic Arts, describes a video space game of tomorrow.

> **"The game would start with a terrific stereo sound track, like a science-fiction movie. Then you'd blast off, with realistic animated sequences, in full color, on screen, as if you were looking out the window of a spaceship."**

Note: Here's how you would type part of this quote, leaving some words out.

> **"Then you'd blast off . . . on screen, as if you were looking out . . . of a spaceship."**

467 .... At the End of a Sentence

◆ If the words left out are at the end of a sentence, use a period followed by three dots.

> **"The game would start with a terrific stereo sound track. . . . Then you'd blast off, with realistic animated sequences, in full color, on screen, as if you were looking out the window of a spaceship."**

Comma
468

Commas are used to indicate a pause or a change in thought. Commas are used to keep words and ideas from running together, making our writing easier to read. No other form of punctuation is more important to understand than the comma.

Items in a Series 469

◆ Commas are used between words, phrases, or clauses in a series. (A series contains at least three items.)

> **Computers of tomorrow will be fun, attractive, and chatty.** [words]

> **Turn your computer on with the sound of your voice, dial your computer when away from home, and hear it read the day's mail out loud.** [clauses]

SCHOOL DAZE

470 .... To Keep Numbers Clear

◆ Commas are used to separate the digits in a number in order to distinguish hundreds, thousands, millions, etc.

> By the year 2000, nearly 7,500,000 Americans could be working in their homes on computer-related jobs.

Note: Commas are not used in years. Also, it is often easier to write out unusually large numbers in the millions and billions (7.5 million, 16 billion).

471 .... In Dates and Addresses

◆ Commas are used to distinguish items in an address and items in a date.

> In June our family is moving to 2727 Telluride Avenue, Denver, Colorado 81435.

> In August 1989 my father designed a totally computerized house which we hope to occupy by July 4, 1995.

Note: Do not use a comma to separate the state from the zip code. Also, if only the month and year are written, no comma is needed to separate the two.

472 .... To Set Off Dialogue

◆ Commas are used to set off the exact words of the speaker from the rest of the sentence.

> The electronics executive said, "Did you know that computers can now speak with a Texas drawl?"

Note: When reporting rather than quoting what someone said, use no comma (or quotation marks) as in the example below.

> The electronics executive said that computers can now speak with a Texas drawl.

To Set Off Interruptions 473

◆ Commas are used to set off a word, phrase, or clause that interrupts the main thought of a sentence. Such expressions usually can be identified through the following tests:

1. They may be omitted without changing the substance or meaning of a sentence.

2. They may be placed nearly anywhere in the sentence without changing the meaning of the sentence.

> Computers will definitely become smaller. You can, *for example*, already buy a lap-top model that will fit in a standard pocket folder.

To Set Off Interjections 474

◆ A comma is used to separate an interjection or weak exclamation from the rest of the sentence.

> *No kidding*, you mean computers may be sewn into clothing someday?

> *Yes,* and don't be surprised if that piece of clothing reminds you of your dentist appointment and homework assignments.

In Direct Address 475

◆ Commas are used to separate a noun of direct address from the rest of the sentence. (A noun of direct address is the noun which names the person spoken to in the sentence.)

> *Jill*, listen to this. With a touch of a key an interior decorator can change fabrics and wallpaper on her computer screen.

> That's nothing, *Jack*. An architect can design a building on her computer and, by the touch of a key, see how light will fall in different parts of the building.

476 .... To Enclose Information

◆ Commas are used to enclose a title, name, or initials which follow a person's last name.

> Melanie Prokat, M.D., and Gerald Zahn, Ph.D., admitted that they can't program their VCR's. Then Merrick, B., Abrams, J.D., and Hendricks, J., confessed that they were "VCR illiterate."

Note: If an initial comes at the end of a statement, use only one period.

477 .... Between Two Independent Clauses

◆ A comma may be used between two independent clauses which are joined by coordinate conjunctions such as these: *and, but, or, nor, for,* and *yet.*

> There will always be a number of steps involved in programming a VCR, but the process will be made easier on new machines. Instructions for each step will be shown on the TV screen.

Avoid comma splices! A comma splice results when two independent clauses are "spliced" or pasted together with only a comma—and without a conjunction. (See 092.)

478 .... To Separate Clauses and Phrases

◆ A comma should separate an adverb clause or a long modifying phrase from the independent clause which follows it.

> In libraries of the future, books will not reside on shelves but on special disks. [long modifying phrase]

> After a student calls up a text on a computer screen, he will print the pages he wants to take home and study. [adverb clause]

> *In time* students will be able to use all of the library's resources without setting foot in the library. [No comma is needed after a short phrase.]

To Separate Adjectives 479

◆ Commas are used to separate two or more adjectives which equally modify the same noun.

> Many *intelligent, well-educated* scientists are convinced we will pick up signals from another galaxy around the year 2000.

Note: Intelligent and *well-educated* are separated by a comma because they modify *scientists* equally.

> Is it possible that I will wake up some *cold December* morning to learn that Earth has been contacted by aliens from outer space?

Note: Cold and *December* do not modify *morning* equally; therefore, no comma separates the two.

◆ **Use these tests** to help you decide if adjectives modify equally: (1) **Switch the order** of the adjectives; if the sentence is clear, the adjectives modify equally. *Well-educated* and *intelligent* can be switched; *cold* and *December* cannot. (2) **Insert *and*** between the adjectives; if the sentence reads well, use a comma when *and* is omitted.

Caution: No comma separates the last adjective from the noun.

> Will our scientists know what to do when and if the unidentified, *extraterrestrial signal* reaches earth?

480 .... To Set Off Phrases

◆ Commas are used to separate an explanatory phrase from the rest of the sentence.

> English, *the language which computers speak worldwide,* is also the most widely used language in all fields of science and medicine.

481 .... To Set Off Appositives

◆ An appositive, a specific kind of explanatory word or phrase, identifies or renames a noun or pronoun. (Do not use commas with single-word appositives.)

> Acid rain, *a form of pollution caused by burning coal,* affects most of North America. [The appositive phrase, *a form of pollution caused by burning coal,* is set off with commas.]

> The pollutant *sulfur* contributes greatly to the problem of acid rain. [The single-word appositive *sulfur* is not set off.]

482 .... Separate Nonrestrictive Phrases and Clauses

◆ Commas are used to punctuate **nonrestrictive** phrases and clauses (those phrases or clauses which **are not** necessary to the basic meaning of the sentence).

> Ninety-seven percent of the Earth's water supply is contained in our oceans, and 2 percent is frozen. We get our water from the 1 percent that is left, *which comes from the Earth's surface or groundwater.*

Note: The clause—*which comes from the Earth's surface* or *groundwater*—is additional information; it is **nonrestrictive** (not required). If the clause were left out, the meaning of the sentence would remain clear.

◆ **Restrictive** phrases or clauses (those which **are** needed in the sentence) restrict or limit the meaning of the sentence and are **not** set off with commas.

> Groundwater *which is free from harmful liquids and chemicals* is a rare commodity.

Note: The clause—*which is free from harmful liquids and chemicals*—is **restrictive**; it is needed to complete the meaning in the basic sentence and is not, therefore, set off with commas.

Semicolon
483

A **semicolon** is a cross between a period and a comma. It is sometimes used in place of a period; other times, it serves the same function as a comma.

To Join Two Independent Clauses 484

◆ A semicolon is used to join two independent clauses which are not connected with a coordinate conjunction. (This means that each of the two clauses could stand alone as a separate sentence.)

> My dad bought a robot-operated lawnmower; I was anxious to see the thing work.

 See 710 for an explanation and examples of independent clauses.

485 ....To Set Off Independent Clauses

◆ Use a semicolon to separate independent clauses if they are long, or if they have internal commas.

> After "setting the course" by guiding the mower around the perimeter of our lawn, it was set to cut the grass; but when I checked on it later, I discovered that our hi-tech "work saver" had also cut Mrs. Crabb's yard— and all of her flowers.

486 ....Used with Conjunctive Adverbs

◆ A semicolon is also used to join two independent clauses when the clauses are connected only by a conjunctive adverb (*also, as a result, for example, however, therefore, instead.*)

> I apologized for the "robot's slipup"; however, Mrs. Crabb continued to scream about "careless teenagers" and "dumb machines."

487 ....To Separate Groups Which Contain Commas

◆ A semicolon is used to distinguish groups of items within a list.

> Here's a list of things we should be recycling: aluminum cans; cardboard, newspapers, and other paper products; glass bottles, jars, and other glass items.

> There are also those items which are still difficult to recycle: styrofoam cups, plates, and cartons; plastic bags, diapers, and packaging; used tires and chemicals.

Colon
488

A **colon** may be used to introduce a list, letter, or important point. Colons are also used between the numbers in time.

After a Salutation 489

◆ A colon may be used after the salutation of a business letter.

> ■ **Dear Ms. Manners:**

As a Formal Introduction......490

◆ A colon may be used to formally introduce a sentence, a question, or a quotation.

> The author of *The Nature Conservancy* makes this alarming claim: "By the year 2000, 20% of all the Earth's species could be lost forever."

For Emphasis 491

◆ A colon is used to emphasize a word or phrase.

> By the year 2000, immunologists say it may be possible to prevent one of our most chronic and painful diseases: rheumatoid arthritis.

Between Numerals Indicating Time 492

◆ A colon is used between the parts of a number which indicate time.

> During a beach cleanup along 300 miles of the Gulf shoreline in 1988, 15,600 plastic six-pack rings were found in the three hours between 9:00 and 12:00.

493 .... To Introduce a List

◆ A colon is used to introduce a list.

> We produce enough styrofoam cups annually to circle the earth 436 times. And these things are nonbiodegradable. That means they're with us forever.
>
> Here's how we can begin to control this problem: buy paper picnic products, purchase eggs in paper cartons, and request a paper plate or container for food in your favorite fast food restaurant.

Note: When introducing a list, the colon usually comes after a "summary" word(s)—*the following, these, things*—or words describing the subject of the list.

> To conserve water you should: install a "low flow" shower head, turn the water off while brushing your teeth, and fix drippy faucets. [incorrect—no summary word]
>
> To conserve water you should do the *following three things:* install a "low flow" shower head, turn the water off while brushing your teeth, and fix drippy faucets. [correct—a summary word comes before the colon]

Dash
494

The **dash** can be used to indicate a sudden break in a sentence, to emphasize a word or clause, and to show that someone's speech is being interrupted.

To Indicate a Sudden Break 495

◆ A dash can be used to show a sudden break in a sentence.

> There is one thing—actually several things—that I find hard to believe about the superphone of the future. Push a few buttons and it will print out everything from the news to sports scores to concert information.

For Emphasis 496

◆ A dash may be used to emphasize a word, series of words, a phrase, or a clause.

> In the future, tiny TV cameras mounted on eyeglasses will transmit electronic images directly to the brain—giving limited vision to the blind.
>
> Hopefully one of three service options—military service, VISTA, or the Peace Corps—will interest you. According to futurist Marvin J. Cetron, young people may be required to serve their country in one of these areas by the year 2000.

To Indicate Interrupted Speech 497

◆ A dash is used to show that someone's speech is being interrupted by another person.

> Why, hello—yes, I understand—no, I remember—oh—of course, I won't—why, no, I—why, yes, I—why don't I just fax it to you.

Note: A dash is indicated by two hyphens--without spacing before or after--in all handwritten and typed material.

Hyphen
498

The **hyphen** is used to join the words in compound numbers from twenty-one to ninety-nine, to form compound words, and to divide words at the end of a line. The hyphen is also used to join numbers which indicate the life span of an individual, the scores of a game, and so on.

499 .... To Divide a Word

◆ The hyphen is used to divide a word when you run out of room at the end of a line. A word may be divided only between syllables. Here are some additional guidelines.

❖ Never divide a one-syllable word: *raised, through*.

❖ Avoid dividing a word of five letters or less: *paper, study*.

❖ Never divide a one-letter syllable from the rest of the word: *omit-ted,* not *o-mitted*.

❖ Never divide abbreviations or contractions.

❖ Never divide the last word in more than two lines in a row or the last word in a paragraph.

❖ When a vowel is a syllable by itself, divide the word after the vowel: *epi-sode*, not *ep-isode*.

In a Compound Word 500

◆ The hyphen is used to make a compound word.

> **dot-matrix printer**
>
> **three-dimensional television**
>
> **in-dash microwave oven**
>
> **14-year-old Nintendo wizard**
>
> **80-column screen display**

Between Numbers
In a Fraction 501

◆ A hyphen is used between the numbers in a fraction, but not between the numerator and denominator when one or both are already hyphenated.

> **four-tenths, five-sixteenths, (7/32) seven thirty-seconds**

To Join Letters and Words ... 502

◆ A hyphen is used to join a capital letter to a noun or participle.

> **G-rated, T-bar lift, X-ray therapy, T-bone steak**

SCHOOL DAZE

Sarah, we've completed **two-thirds** of the quarter, and you haven't turned in one assignment. What do you have to say for yourself?

Ahh ... is there anything I can do for extra credit?

503 ....To Create New Words

◆ A hyphen is used to form new words beginning with the prefixes *self, ex, all, great,* etc. A hyphen is also used with suffixes such as *elect* and *free.*

> A special mesh seeded with live cells may induce *self-generating* skin for burn victims.
>
> In the future, the telephone, TV set, VCR, fax machine, and personal computer will be part of one *all-purpose* workstation.
>
> We should use *phosphate-free* laundry and dish soaps.

504 ....To Avoid Confusion or Awkward Spelling

◆ Use a hyphen with other prefixes or suffixes to avoid confusion or awkward spelling.

> Rc-collect (not recollect) the reports we distributed last week.
>
> It has a shell-like (not shelllike) texture.

505 ....To Form an Adjective

◆ Use the hyphen to join two or more words which work together to form a single adjective (a *single-thought* adjective) before a noun.

> voice-recognition software
>
> on-screen directions
>
> last-ditch effort

Note: When words forming the adjective come after the noun, do not hyphenate them.

> *Easy-to-use* digital shortwave radios are becoming popular. [before the noun]
>
> Digital shortwave radios are *easy to use.* [after the noun]

Caution: When the first of the words ends in *ly,* do **not** use a hyphen; also, do not use a hyphen when a number or letter is the final part of a one-thought adjective.

> newly designed dryer
>
> grade B movie (a movie made on a low budget)

Question Mark
506

A **question mark** is used after an interrogative sentence and to show doubt about the correctness of a fact or figure.

Direct Question 507

◆ A question mark is used at the end of a direct question (an interrogative sentence).

> How long will it be before deep-diving vehicles will be able to search the deepest ocean floor for deposits of silver, manganese, and cobalt?

Indirect Quotation 508

◆ No question mark is used after an indirect quotation.

> Because I love seals and dolphins, my father always asks me if I want to be a marine biologist.
>
> I asked if marine biologists will be required to live on the ocean floor.

509 ....In Parentheses

◆ The question mark is placed within parentheses to show that the writer isn't sure a fact or figure is correct.

> By the year 2050 (?) we will be able to explore the ocean floor without attachment to any support vehicle.

Exclamation Point

510

The **exclamation point** is used to express strong feeling. It may be placed after a word, a phrase, or an exclamatory sentence. (The exclamation points should not be overused.)

> Cowabunga, dudes!
>
> I'm going to the U-2 concert!
>
> Cool!
>
> Americans produce over 150 million tons of garbage every year!

Caution: Never write more than one exclamation point; such punctuation is incorrect and looks foolish.

> Isn't the Eagle a great roller coaster!!!
>
> Who even thinks about going upside down!!!

Quotation Marks

511

Quotation marks are used to set off the exact words of a speaker, to show what a writer has "borrowed" from another book or magazine, to set off the titles of publications, and to show that certain words are used in a special way.

To Set Off Direct Quotations **512**

Quotation marks are placed before and after direct quotations. Only the exact words quoted are placed within quotation marks.

> A noted sociologist recently remarked, "You can say goodbye to your key rings. By the turn of the century, plastic cards that open electronic locks will be commonplace."

For a Quote Within a Quote **513**

◆ Single quotation marks are used to punctuate a quotation within a quotation. Double and single quotation marks are then alternated in order to distinguish a quotation within a quotation within a quotation.

> "I loved reading Poe's 'The Raven'!" exclaimed Sung Kim.
>
> My English teacher smiled proudly and said, "Did you hear Mr. Kim say, 'I loved reading Poe's "The Raven"'?"

514 ....For Long Quotations

◆ If more than one paragraph is quoted (as in a report or research paper), quotation marks are placed before each paragraph and at the end of the last paragraph (Example A). Quotations which are more than four lines on a page are usually set off from the rest of the paper by indenting ten spaces from the left. No quotation marks are placed either before or after the quoted material unless they appear in the orginal copy (Example B).

Sample A

Sample B

515 ....Placement of Punctuation

◆ Periods and commas are always placed *inside* quotation marks.

> "I don't know," said Albert. Albert said, "I don't know."

◆ An exclamation point or a question mark is placed *inside* the quotation marks when it punctuates the quotation; it is placed *outside* when it punctuates the main sentence.

> John said, "Mom, will you zap me a cheeseburger?"

> Did Ms. Wiley really say, "You can tour an art museum on a computer"?

◆ Semicolons or colons are placed *outside* quotation marks.

> First, I will read "The Masque of the Red Death"; then I will read "The Raven."

Special Words 516

◆ Quotation marks also may be used (1) to set apart a word which is being discussed, (2) to indicate that a word is slang, or (3) to point out that a word or phrase is being used in a special way.

> New home computers will be able to store information on an "optical disk," which can hold 100,000 pages of text.

> I'd say that group was really "bad."

> This electronic lure is really going to "light up" some fish's life.

To Punctuate Titles 517

◆ Quotation marks are used to punctuate titles of songs, poems, short stories, lectures, courses, episodes of radio or television programs, one-act plays, short films, chapters of books, and articles found in magazines, newspapers, or encyclopedias.

> "Vogue" [song]
>
> "Thank You, Ma'am." [short story]
>
> "The Creature from the Pit" [a television episode—*Dr. Who*]
>
> "We'll Never Conquer Space" [a chapter in a book]
>
> "Beginning Photography and Printing" [course title]
>
> "VCR Still Stumps the Smarties" [newspaper article]

Note: When you punctuate a title, capitalize the first word, last word, and every word in between except for articles, short prepositions, and short conjunctions.

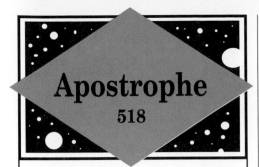

Apostrophe
518

An **apostrophe** is used to show possession, to form plurals, or to show that a letter(s) has been left out of a word.

519 ....In Contractions

An apostrophe is used to show that one or more letters have been left out of a word to form a contraction.

> **don't** [*o* is left out]
>
> **she'd** [*woul* is left out]
>
> **it's** [*i* is left out]

520 ....To Form Plurals

◆ An apostrophe and *s* are used to form the plural of a letter, a number, a sign, or a word discussed as a word.

> **A's, 8's, +'s, six nay's**

521 ....In Place of Omitted Letters or Numbers

◆ An apostrophe is also used to show that one or more letters or numbers have been left out of numerals or words which are spelled as if they were actually spoken.

> **class of '99** [*19* is left out]
>
> **I'm fixin' to fax that first thing tomorrow.** [*g* is left out]

Note: Letters and numbers are usually not omitted in formal writing.

To Form Singular Possessives 522

◆ The possessive form of singular nouns is usually made by adding an apostrophe and *s*.

> **The world's population will double or triple by the year 2050.**
>
> **Did Mr. Strandberg's last lecture have to do with endangered species?**

◆ When a singular noun ends with an *s* or *z* sound, the possessive may be formed by adding just an apostrophe. When the singular noun is a one-syllable word, however, the possessive is usually formed by adding both an apostrophe and *s*.

> **Texas' resources (or) Texas's resources**
>
> **boss's request** [one-syllable noun ending in *s*]

To Form Plural Possessives 523

◆ The possessive form of plural nouns ending in *s* is usually made by adding just an apostrophe. For plural nouns not ending in *s*, an apostrophe and *s* must be added.

> **Joneses' great-grandfather**
>
> **children's book**

Remember! The word immediately before the apostrophe is the owner.

> **the kid's custom-designed sneakers** [kid is the owner]
>
> **the girls' wide-leg riding pants** [girls are the owners]
>
> **boss's office** [boss is the owner]
>
> **bosses' office** [bosses are the owners]

524 .... To Show Shared Possession

◆ When possession is shared by more than one noun, add an apostrophe and *s* to the last noun in the series.

> VanClumpin, VanDiken, and VanTulip's air band. [All three are members of the band.]

> VanClumpin's, VanDiken's, and VanTulip's air guitars. [Each guy owns an air guitar.]

525 .... In Compound Nouns

◆ The possessive of a compound noun is formed by placing the possessive ending after the last word.

> her sister-in-law's pop-funk music [singular]

> the secretary of state's wife [singular]

> their sisters-in-law's tastes in music [plural]

> the secretaries of state's wives [plural]

526 .... With Indefinite Pronouns

◆ The possessive of an indefinite pronoun is formed by placing an apostrophe and *s* on the last word.

> everyone's, anyone's, somebody else's

527 .... To Express Time or Amount

◆ An apostrophe is used with an adjective which is part of an expression indicating time or amount.

> Tomorrow's schools will be much more plugged into technology than today's schools.

> My father lost an entire day's work when that thunderstorm knocked our power out.

Italics
528

Italics is a printer's term for a style of type which is slightly slanted. In this sentence the word *happiness* is typed in italics. In handwritten or typed material, each word or letter which should be in italics is underlined.

> In <u>2001: A Space Odyssey</u> the destination of <u>Discovery</u> is a planet on the farthest edge of the solar system. [typed]

> In *2001: A Space Odyssey* the destination of *Discovery* is a planet on the farthest edge of the solar system. [printed]

Note: Discovery is italicized (underlined when typed) because it is the name of an aircraft.

In Titles 529

◆ Underline the titles of books, plays, book-length poems, magazines, radio and television programs, movies (videos), record albums (cassettes, CD's), pamphlets, manuals, the names of ships and aircraft, and newspapers.

> <u>The Lord of the Rings</u> [novel]

> <u>Discover</u> [magazine]

> <u>Dr. Who</u> [television program]

> <u>Back to the Future</u> [movie]

> <u>I'm Breathless</u> [album]

> <u>U.S.S. Arizona</u> [ship]

> <u>Columbia</u> [space shuttle]

<u>New York Times</u> or New York <u>Times</u> [newspaper]

Note: When the name of a city is used as part of the name of a newspaper, the name of the city need *not* be underlined.

Exceptions: Do not underline or put in quotation marks your own title at the top of your page.

530 ....Foreign Words

◆ Underline foreign words which are not commonly used in everyday English. Also underline scientific names.

> **<u>E Pluribus Unum</u> appears on most U.S. currency.**
>
> **Mankind is also known as <u>Homo sapiens</u>.**

531 ....For Special Uses

◆ Underline any word, number, or letter which is being discussed or being used in a special way. (Sometimes quotation marks are used for this same reason. See 516.)

> I got an <u>A</u> on my test because I could explain <u>brain tuning</u>.

Parentheses
532

Parentheses are used around words which are included in a sentence to add information or to help make an idea clearer.

> Enclosed shopping malls are encouraging people of all ages to visit and stay for a wide range of activities in addition to shopping. These uses include exercise (from health clubs to indoor walking circuits), events (from political campaigning to rock concerts), and entertainment (from video arcades to movies).
> [Taken from *The American Forecaster*: 1990, 83.]

Note: Punctuation is placed within parentheses to mark the material within the parentheses. Punctuation is placed outside the parentheses when it is needed for the entire sentence. *Also note:* For a parentheses within a parentheses, use brackets.

PUNCTUATION MARKS

´	Accent	,	Comma	.	Period
'	Apostrophe	—	Dash	?	Question mark
*	Asterisk	/	Diagonal/Slash	" "	Quotation marks
{ }	Brace	¨	Dieresis	;	Semicolon
[ ]	Brackets	...	Ellipsis	~	Tilde
^	Caret	!	Exclamation Point	_	Underscore
Ç	Cedilla	-	Hyphen		

The Yellow Pages Guide to
The Mechanics of Writing

When you finally finish writing your first novel, be sure you take it to an editor and a proofreader before you send it off to a publisher. *Writing* a novel is one thing—*preparing* it for the publisher is another.

However, for the writing you do now, you will have to fill all three roles—you will have to be a writer, editor, and proofreader. That's part of what makes writing such a challenging process. At the same time, it also helps make it an exciting, rewarding challenge. Are you best at writing the original? editing the first draft? proofreading the final copy? Whatever you're best at, and whatever your needs may be, you should find many helpful suggestions throughout this handbook. In the following section, you'll find rules and guidelines to help you proofread your capitalization, plurals, abbreviations, numbers, and spelling.

Capitalization
533

Capitalize all proper nouns and all proper adjectives. A proper noun is the name of a particular person, place, thing, or idea. A proper adjective is an adjective formed from a proper noun.

> Common Noun .... country, president, continent
> Proper Noun .... Canada, Andrew Jackson, Asia
> Proper Adjective ...... Canadian, Jacksonian, Asian

◆ Capitalize the names of people and also the initials or abbreviations that stand for those names.

> Margaret Thatcher; Martin Luther King, Jr.; Saddam Hussein; Toshiki Kaifu; Sinead O'Connor; Wendy Wasserstein

Note: If a woman uses both her maiden name and married name, the maiden name is listed first, and both are capitalized.

> Martha Ulferts Meyer, Kimberly Yashiki Smith, Jenny Du Clos Hart

◆ Capitalize the names of historical events, documents, and periods of time.

> Word War I, the Bill of Rights, the Magna Carta, the Middle Ages, the Paleozoic Era

CAPITALIZE GEOGRAPHIC NAMES

Planets and heavenly bodies	Earth, Jupiter, Milky Way
Continents	Europe, Asia, South America, Australia, Africa
Countries	Morocco, Haiti, Greece, Chile, United Arab Emirates
States	New Mexico, Alabama, West Virginia, Delaware, Iowa
Provinces	Alberta, British Columbia, Quebec, Ontario
Counties	Sioux County, Kandiyohi County, Wade County
Cities	Montreal, Baton Rouge, Prinsburg, Albuquerque, Portland
Bodies of water	Delaware Bay, Chickamunga Lake, Saskatchewan River, Indian Ocean, Gulf of Mexico, Skunk Creek
Landforms	Appalachian Mountains, Bitterfoot Range, Capitol Reef
Public areas	Tiananmen Square, Sequoia National Forest, Pipe Spring National Monument, Eiffel Tower, Statue of Liberty, Mount Rushmore, Open Space Park, Vietnam Memorial
Roads and highways	New Jersey Turnpike, Kairn Highway, Interstate 80, Central Avenue, Chisholm Trail, Mutt's Road
Buildings	Pentagon, Te Paske Theatre, Empire State Building

536 .... Abbreviations

■ Capitalize abbreviations of titles and organizations.

> **U.S.A., M.D., FBI, B.C., B.A., NATO (North Atlantic Treaty Organization), M.A., Ph.D.**

537 .... Organizations

◆ Capitalize the name of an organization, association, or a team and its members.

> **New York State Historical Society, the Red Cross, General Motors Corporation, the Miami Dolphins, a Republican, the Democratic Party**

538 .... Names of Subjects

■ Capitalize the name of a specific course, but not the name of a general subject. (Exception—the names of all languages are proper nouns and are always capitalized: French, German, Latin.)

> **My brother flunked *Family Living* because he exploded an egg in the microwave oven.** [specific course]

> **The *home economics* teacher said that she could forgive all his mistakes, but she was fed up with his pranks.** [general subject]

First Words 539

◆ Capitalize the first word of every sentence and the first word in a direct quotation. Do not capitalize the first word in an indirect quotation.

> ***That's* when my dad took my brother to visit the teacher.** [sentence]

> **My brother explained to Dad and the home ec. teacher *that* the egg was no prank—it was a natural science experiment.** [indirect quotation]

> **Then Dad said, "*Well* son, I think it's time you try a social science experiment: being grounded for one month with no TV or music."** [direct quotation]

> **"But Dad," squealed my brother, "it was only a joke!"** [Notice that *it* begins a new phrase, but is not capitalized because the word does not begin a new sentence.]

> **"I understand that," replied Dad. "Natural science is a funny discipline. But I think you'll find social science to be a good deal more serious."** [Notice that *natural* is capitalized because it begins a new sentence.]

540 .... Particular Sections of the Country

◆ Capitalize words which indicate particular sections of the country; words which simply indicate direction are not capitalized.

> Having grown up on the hectic *West Coast*, I find life in the *South* to be refreshing. My little block in *northern* Los Angeles had more residents than my entire county located *east* of Memphis.

◆ Also capitalize proper adjectives formed from names of specific sections of a country. Do not capitalize adjectives formed from words which simply indicate direction.

> Here in *western* Tennessee, *Southern* hospitality is a way of life.

541 .... Names of Languages, Races, Nationalities, Religions

◆ Capitalize the names of languages, races, nationalities, and religions, as well as the proper adjectives formed from them.

> Spanish, Yiddish, Dutch, Arab, Iranian, Judaism, Catholicism, Protestantism, African art, Irish linen, Swedish meatballs, Methodist

Words Used as Names 542

◆ Capitalize words such as *mother, father, aunt,* and *uncle* when these words are used as names.

> *Uncle* George started to sit on the couch. [*Uncle* is a name; the speaker commonly calls this person "Uncle George."]

> Then *Uncle* stopped in midair. [*Uncle* is a name; the speaker commonly calls this person "Uncle."]

> My *aunt* had just found him. [The word *aunt* is not used as a name, but to describe this person.]

> Then my *dad* and *mom* walked into the room. [The words *dad* and *mom* are not used as names in this sentence.]

> *"Mom,* what is everyone doing in here?" I asked. [*Mom* is used as a name.]

Note: Words such as *mom, dad, grandma,* etc. are not usually capitalized if they come after a possessive pronoun (*my, his, our*).

Days of the Week 543

◆ Capitalize the names of days of the week, months of the year, and special holidays. (Do not capitalize the names of seasons.)

> Thursday, July, Independence Day, Labor Day, New Year's Day, Arbor Day, winter, spring

Capitalize	Do Not Capitalize
American	*un*-American
January, February	*winter, spring*
Lakes Erie and Michigan	Missouri and Ohio *rivers*
The South is quite conservative.	Turn *south* at the stop sign.
Duluth Central High School	a Duluth *high school*
Governor Douglas Wilder	Douglas Wilder, our *governor*
President George Bush	George Bush, our *president*
Ford Mustang GT	a Ford *automobile*
The planet Earth is egg shaped.	The *earth* we live on is good.
I'm taking History 101.	I'm taking *history*.

544 .... Official Names

◆ Capitalize the names of businesses and the official names of their products. (These are called trade names.) Do not, however, capitalize a general descriptive word like *toothpaste* when it follows the product name.

> **Post Sugar Crisps, Memorex tape, Ford Probe GT, Pioneer sound system, Crest toothpaste, Pizza Hut, Tombstone pizza**

545 ...... Titles Used with Names

◆ Capitalize titles used with names of persons and abbreviations standing for those titles.

> **Mayor Andrew Young, President George Bush, Senator Helms, Chairman Mao, Premier Li Ping, Representative Plasier, Prof. Lorna Van Gilst, Dr. Karen De Mol**

546 .... Titles

◆ Capitalize the first word of a title, the last word, and every word in between except articles (*a, an, the*), short prepositions, and short conjunctions. Follow this rule for titles of books, newspapers, magazines, poems, plays, songs, articles, movies, works of art, pictures, stories, and essays.

> *The Adventures of Tom Sawyer* [book]
>
> *The Las Vegas Tribune* [newspaper]
>
> *Field and Stream* [magazine]
>
> "Jeremiah Was a Bullfrog" [song]
>
> "The Death of the Hired Man" [poem]
>
> *Phantom of the Opera* [play]
>
> *Back to the Future* [movie]

Plurals
547

The **plurals** of most nouns are formed by adding *s* to the singular.

> **cheerleader — cheerleaders, wheel — wheels**

The plural form of nouns ending in *sh, ch, x, s,* and *z* are made by adding *es* to the singular.

> **lunch — lunches, dish — dishes, mess — messes, buzz — buzzes, fox — foxes**

Words Ending in *o* 548

◆ The plurals of words ending in *o* (with a vowel just before the *o*) are formed by adding *s*.

> **radio — radios, rodeo — rodeos, studio — studios**

◆ The plurals of most nouns ending in *o* (with a consonant letter just before the *o*) are formed by adding *es*.

> **echo — echoes, hero — heroes, tomato — tomatoes**

Exception: Musical terms always form plurals by adding *s*; consult a dictionary for other words of this type.

> **alto — altos, banjo — banjos, solo — solos, piano — pianos**

Words Ending in *ful* 549

◆ The plurals of nouns which end with *ful* are formed by adding an *s* at the end of the word.

> **three platefuls, six tankfuls, four cupfuls, five pailfuls**

550.......Nouns Ending in *f* or *fe*

◆ The plurals of nouns that end in *f* or *fe* are formed in one of two ways: If the final *f* sound is still heard in the plural form of the word, simply add *s;* if the final sound is a *v* sound, change the *f* to *ve* and add *s.*

> **roof** —**roofs, chief** — **chief***s*
> [plural ends with *f* sound]
>
> **wife** — **wi***ves*, **loaf** — **loa***ves*
> [plural ends with *v* sound]

551................Nouns Ending in *y*

◆ The plurals of common nouns which end in *y* (with a consonant letter just before the *y*) are formed by changing the *y* to *i* and adding *es.*

> **fly** — **fl***ies*, **jalopy** — **jalop***ies*

◆ The plurals of nouns which end in *y* (with a vowel before the *y*) are formed by adding only *s.*

> **donkey** — **donkeys**
> **monkey** —**monkeys**

◆ The plurals of proper nouns ending in *y* are formed by adding *s:*

> **Two new Open Pantrys are being built in our town.**

552 ....Compound Nouns

◆ The plurals of compound nouns are usually formed by adding *s* or *es* to the important word in the compound.

> **brothers-in-law**
> **maid***s* **of honor**
> **secretaries of state**

553 ....Irregular Spelling

◆ Some words (including many foreign words) form a plural by taking on an *irregular* spelling; others are now acceptable with the commonly used *s* or *es* ending.

> **child**—**children, goose**—**geese, cactus** — **cacti** or **cactuses**

Adding an *'s* 554

◆ The plurals of symbols, letters, figures, and words discussed as words are formed by adding an *apostrophe* and an *s.*

> As a clown in the Rose Bowl parade, I liked yelling "Hello's" and "Hi there's" to perfect strangers. But I got dizzy from doing *figure-8's* on my tricycle. So first I tried S's, and then I tried O's. And that's when it happened.

Abbreviations
555

An **abbreviation** is the shortened form of a word or phrase. The following abbreviations are always acceptable in both formal and informal writing:

> *Mr., Mrs., Miss, Ms., Dr., a.m., p.m., (A.M., P.M.), A.D., B.C., B.A., M.A., Ph. D., M.D.*

Caution: Do **not** abbreviate the names of states, countries, months, days, units of measure, or courses of study in formal writing. Do **not** abbreviate the words *Street, Road, Avenue, Company,* and similar words when they are part of a proper name. Also, do **not** use signs or symbols (%, &, $, #, @) in place of words. The dollar sign is, however, appropriate when using numerals to express an amount of money ($325).

556 ....Acronyms

◆ Most abbreviations are followed by a period. Acronyms are exceptions. An acronym is a word formed from the first (or first few) letters of words in a phrase.

> **radar** [**ra**dio **d**etecting **and** **r**anging]
>
> **CARE** [**C**ooperative for **A**merican **R**elief **E**verywhere]
>
> **VISTA** [**V**olunteers **I**n **S**ervice **T**o **A**merica]

557 ....Initialism

◆ An initialism is similar to an acronym except that the initials used to form this abbreviation cannot be pronounced as a word. Initialisms are not usually followed by periods.

> **CIA — Central Intelligence Agency**
>
> **PLO — Palestine Liberation Army**
>
> **IRA — Irish Republican Army**

Numbers
558

Numbers from one to nine are usually written as words; all numbers 10 and over are usually written as numerals.

> ■ **two, seven, nine, 10, 25, 106**

Note: Numbers being compared or contrasted should be kept in the same style.

> **8 to 11 years old** *or* **eight to eleven years old**

Very Large Numbers 559

◆ You may use a combination of numbers and words for very large numbers.

> ■ **1.3 million, 17 million**

◆ You may spell out large numbers that can be written as two words.

> ■ **two thousand; but 2001**

Sentence Beginnings 560

◆ Use words, not numerals, to begin a sentence.

> ■ *Eleven* **students said they were unable to finish the assignment.**

Numerals Only 561

◆ Use numerals for any numbers in the following forms: money, decimal, percentage, chapter, page, address, telephone, zip code, dates, time, identification numbers, and statistics.

> ■ **$2.39, 26.2, 8 percent, chapter 7, pages 287-89, 2125 Cairn Road, July 6, 44 B.C., A.D. 79, 4:30 P.M., Highway 36, a vote of 23 to 4, 34 mph**

Numerals in Compound Modifiers 562

◆ Numbers which come before a compound modifier which includes a figure should be written as words.

> **The class has been working on** *two* **7-page reports.**
>
> **By today, each student should have finished the research and recorded the information on** *twenty* **5 x 10-inch cards.**
>
> **But the boys said that all the information they could find about the Civil War filled the backs of only** *two* **3 Musketeers candy bar wrappers.**

Spelling
563

564 .... i before e

◆ Write *i* before *e* except after *c*, or when sounded like *a* as in *neighbor* and *weigh*.

Exceptions: Eight of the exceptions are in this sentence:

> *Neither sheik* dared *leisurely seize either weird species* of *financiers.*

Note: Other exceptions to the *i before e* rule are *their, height, counterfeit, foreign,* and *heir.*

565 .... Silent e

◆ If a word ends with a silent *e*, drop the *e* before adding a suffix which begins with a vowel.

> state — stating — statement
> like — liking — likeness
> use — using — useful
> nine — ninety — nineteen

(Notice that you do *not* drop the *e* when the suffix begins with a consonant. Exceptions include *truly, argument,* and *ninth.*)

Words Ending in Y 566

◆ When *y* is the last letter in a word and the *y* comes just after a consonant, change the *y* to *i* before adding any suffix except those beginning with *i*.

> fry — fries, hurry — hurried,
> lady — ladies, ply — pliable,
> happy — happiness, beauty —
> beautiful

◆ When forming the plural of a word which ends with a *y* that comes just after a vowel, add *s*.

> toy — toys, play — plays,
> monkey — monkeys

Consonant Ending 567

◆ When a one-syllable word (bat) ends in a consonant (ba**t**) preceded by one vowel (b**a**t), double the final consonant before adding a suffix which begins with a vowel (batt**ing**).

◆ When a multi-syllable word (con trol) ends in a consonant (**l**) preceded by one vowel (**o**), the accent is on the last syllable (con **trol**), and the suffix begins with a vowel (**ing**)—the same rule holds true: double the final consonant (contro**l**ling).

> sum — summary
> god — goddess
> prefer — preferred
> begin — beginning

SCHOOL DAZE

> Gee Ms. Roberts, if I have to cut any more **misspelled** words, the only thing left will be my name!

The Yellow Pages Guide to
Improved Spelling

1. First of all, be patient. Learning to become a good speller takes time.
2. **Check your spelling** by using a dictionary or list of commonly misspelled words (like the list which follows).
3. **Check the correct pronunciation** of each word you are attempting to spell. Knowing the correct pronunciation of each word is important to remembering its spelling.
4. **Also check the meaning of each word** as you are checking the dictionary for pronunciation. (Knowing how to spell a word is of little use if you don't know what it means.)
5. **Practice spelling the word** before you close the dictionary. You can do this by looking away from the page and trying to "see" the word in your "mind's eye." Write the word on a piece of paper. Check the spelling in the dictionary and repeat the process until you are able to spell the word correctly.
6. **Keep a list** of the words which you misspell.
7. **Write often.** As noted educator Frank Smith said, "There is little point in learning to spell if you have little intention of writing."

A

ab-bre-vi-ate
a-board
a-bout
a-bove
ab-sence
ab-sent
ab-so-lute (-ly)
a-bun-dance
ac-cel-er-ate
ac-ci-dent
ac-ci-den-tal (-ly)
ac-com-pa-ny
ac-com-plice
ac-com-plish
ac-cord-ing
ac-count
ac-cu-rate
ac-cus-tom (ed)

ache
a-chieve (-ment)
a-cre
a-cross
ac-tu-al
a-dapt
ad-di-tion (-al)
ad-dress
ad-e-quate
ad-just (-ment)
ad-mire
ad-ven-ture
ad-ver-tise (-ment)
ad-ver-tis-ing
a-fraid
af-ter
af-ter-noon
af-ter-ward
a-gain
a-gainst
a-gree-able
a-gree (-ment)
ah

aid
air-y
aisle
a-larm
al-co-hol
a-like
a-live
al-ley
al-low-ance
all right
al-most
al-ready
al-though
al-to-geth-er
a-lu-mi-num
al-ways
am-a-teur
am-bu-lance
a-mend-ment
a-mong
a-mount
an-a-lyze
an-cient

an-gel
an-ger
an-gle
an-gry
an-i-mal
an-ni-ver-sa-ry
an-nounce
an-noy-ance
an-nu-al
a-non-y-mous
an-oth-er
an-swer
ant-arc-tic
an-tic-i-pate
anx-i-ety
anx-ious
any-body
any-how
any-one
any-thing
any-way
any-where
a-part-ment

a-piece
a-pol-o-gize
ap-par-ent (-ly)
ap-peal
ap-pear-ance
ap-pe-tite
ap-pli-ance
ap-pli-ca-tion
ap-point-ment
ap-pre-ci-ate
ap-proach
ap-pro-pri-ate
ap-prov-al
ap-prox-i-mate
ar-chi-tect
arc-tic
aren't
ar-gu-ment
a-rith-me-tic
a-round
a-rouse
ar-range (-ment)
ar-riv-al
ar-ti-cle
ar-ti-fi-cial
a-sleep
as-sas-sin
as-sign (-ment)
as-sis-tance
as-so-ci-ate
as-so-ci-a-tion
as-sume
ath-lete
ath-let-ic
at-tach
at-tack (ed)
at-tempt
at-ten-dance
at-ten-tion
at-ti-tude
at-tor-ney
at-trac-tive
au-di-ence
Au-gust
au-thor
au-thor-i-ty
au-to-mo-bile
au-tumn
a-vail-a-ble
av-e-nue

av-er-age
aw-ful (-ly)
awk-ward

B

bag-gage
bak-ing
bal-ance
bal-loon
bal-lot
ba-nan-a
ban-dage
bank-rupt
bar-ber
bar-gain
bar-rel
base-ment
ba-sis
bas-ket
bat-tery
beau-ti-ful
beau-ty
be-cause
be-come
be-com-ing
be-fore
be-gan
beg-gar
be-gin-ning
be-have
be-hav-ior
be-ing
be-lief
be-lieve
be-long
be-neath
ben-e-fit (-ed)
be-tween
bi-cy-cle
bis-cuit
black-board
blan-ket
bliz-zard
both-er
bot-tle
bot-tom
bough
bought

bounce
bound-a-ry
break-fast
breast
breath (n.)
breathe (v.)
breeze
bridge
brief
bright
bril-liant
broth-er
brought
bruise
bub-ble
buck-et
buck-le
bud-get
build-ing
bul-le-tin
buoy-ant
bu-reau
bur-glar
bury
busi-ness
busy
but-ton

C

cab-bage
caf-e-te-ria
cal-en-dar
cam-paign
ca-nal
can-celed
can-di-date
can-dle
can-is-ter
can-non
can-not
ca-noe
can't
can-yon
ca-pac-i-ty
cap-tain
car-bu-re-tor
card-board
ca-reer

care-ful
care-less
car-pen-ter
car-riage
car-rot
cash-ier
cas-se-role
cas-u-al-ty
cat-a-log
ca-tas-tro-phe
catch-er
cat-er-pil-lar
cat-sup
ceil-ing
cel-e-bra-tion
cem-e-ter-y
cen-sus
cen-tu-ry
cer-tain
cer-tain (-ly)
cer-tif-i-cate
chal-lenge
cham-pi-on
change-a-ble
char-ac-ter (-is-tic)
chief
chil-dren
chim-ney
choc-o-late
choice
cho-rus
cir-cum-stance
cit-i-zen
civ-i-li-za-tion
class-mates
class-room
cli-mate
climb
clos-et
cloth-ing
coach
co-coa
co-coon
cof-fee
col-lar
col-lege
colo-nel
col-or
co-los-sal
col-umn

com-e-dy
com-ing
com-mer-cial
com-mis-sion
com-mit
com-mit-ment
com-mit-ted
com-mit-tee
com-mu-ni-cate
com-mu-nity
com-pan-y
com-par-i-son
com-pe-ti-tion
com-pet-i-tive (-ly)
com-plain
com-plete (-ly)
com-plex-ion
com-pro-mise
con-ceive
con-cern-ing
con-cert
con-ces-sion
con-crete
con-demn
con-di-tion
con-duc-tor
con-fer-ence
con-fi-dence
con-grat-u-late
con-nect
con-science
con-scious
con-ser-va-tive
con-sti-tu-tion
con-tin-ue
con-tin-u-ous
con-trol
con-tro-ver-sy
con-ve-nience
con-vince
cool-ly
co-op-er-ate
cor-po-ra-tion
cor-re-spond
cough
couldn't
coun-ter
coun-ter-feit
coun-try
coun-ty

cour-age
cou-ra-geous
court
cour-te-ous
cour-te-sy
cous-in
cov-er-age
co-zy
crack-er
crank-y
crawl
cred-i-tor
cried
crit-i-cize
cru-el
crumb
crum-ble
cup-board
cu-ri-os-i-ty
cu-ri-ous
cur-rent
cus-tom
cus-tom-er
cyl-in-der

D

dai-ly
dair-y
dam-age
dan-ger (-ous)
daugh-ter
dealt
de-ceive
de-cided
de-ci-sion
dec-la-ra-tion
dec-o-rate
de-fense
def-i-nite (-ly)
def-i-ni-tion
de-li-cious
de-pen-dent
de-pot
de-scribe
de-scrip-tion
de-sert
de-serve
de-sign

de-sir-able
de-spair
des-sert
de-te-ri-o-rate
de-ter-mine
de-vel-op (-ment)
de-vice
de-vise
di-a-mond
di-a-phragm
di-a-ry
dic-tio-nary
dif-fer-ence
dif-fer-ent
dif-fi-cul-ty
din-ing
di-plo-ma
di-rec-tor
dis-agree-able
dis-ap-pear
dis-ap-point
dis-ap-prove
dis-as-trous
dis-ci-pline
dis-cov-er
dis-cuss
dis-cus-sion
dis-ease
dis-sat-is-fied
dis-tin-guish
dis-trib-ute
di-vide
di-vine
di-vis-i-ble
di-vi-sion
doc-tor
doesn't
dol-lar
dor-mi-to-ry
doubt
dough
du-al
du-pli-cate

E

ea-ger (-ly)
econ-o-my
edge

e-di-tion
ef-fi-cien-cy
eight
eighth
ei-ther
e-lab-o-rate
e-lec-tric-i-ty
el-e-phant
el-i-gi-ble
el-lipse
em-bar-rass
e-mer-gen-cy
em-pha-size
em-ploy-ee
em-ploy-ment
en-close
en-cour-age
en-gi-neer
e-nor-mous
e-nough
en-ter-tain
en-thu-si-as-tic
en-tire-ly
en-trance
en-vel-op (v.)
en-ve-lope (n.)
en-vi-ron-ment
equip-ment
equipped
e-quiv-a-lent
es-cape
es-pe-cial-ly
es-sen-tial
es-tab-lish
ev-ery
ev-i-dence
ex-ag-ger-ate
ex-ceed
ex-cel-lent
ex-cept
ex-cep-tion-al (-ly)
ex-cite
ex-er-cise
ex-haust (-ed)
ex-hi-bi-tion
ex-is-tence
ex-pect
ex-pen-sive
ex-pe-ri-ence
ex-plain

ex-pla-na-tion
ex-pres-sion
ex-ten-sion
ex-tinct
ex-traor-di-nar-y
ex-treme (-ly)

fa-cil-i-ties
fa-mil-iar
fam-i-ly
fa-mous
fas-ci-nate
fash-ion
fa-tigue (d)
fau-cet
fa-vor-ite
fea-ture
Feb-ru-ar-y
fed-er-al
fer-tile
field
fierce
fi-ery
fif-ty
fi-nal-ly
fi-nan-cial (-ly)
fo-li-age
for-ci-ble
for-eign
for-feit
for-mal (-ly)
for-mer (-ly)
forth
for-tu-nate
for-ty
for-ward
foun-tain
fourth
frag-ile
freight
friend (-ly)
fright-en
ful-fill
fun-da-men-tal
fur-ther
fur-ther-more

gad-get
gauge
gen-er-al-ly
gen-er-ous
ge-nius
gen-tle
gen-u-ine
ge-og-ra-phy
ghet-to
ghost
gnaw
gov-ern-ment
gov-er-nor
grad-u-a-tion
gram-mar
grate-ful
grease
grief
gro-cery
grudge
grue-some
guar-an-tee
guard
guard-i-an
guess
guid-ance
guide
guilt-y
gym-na-sium

ham-mer
hand-ker-chief
han-dle (d)
hand-some
hap-haz-ard
hap-pen
hap-pi-ness
ha-rass
hast-i-ly
hav-ing
haz-ard-ous
head-ache
height

hem-or-rhage
hes-i-tate
his-to-ry
hoarse
hol-i-day
hon-or
hop-ing
hop-ping
hor-ri-ble
hos-pi-tal
hu-mor-ous
hur-ried-ly
hy-drau-lic
hy-giene
hymn

i-ci-cle
i-den-ti-cal
il-leg-i-ble
il-lit-er-ate
il-lus-trate
im-ag-i-nary
im-ag-i-na-tive
im-ag-ine
im-i-ta-tion
im-me-di-ate (-ly)
im-mense
im-mi-grant
im-mor-tal
im-pa-tient
im-por-tance
im-pos-si-ble
im-prove-ment
in-con-ve-nience
in-cred-i-ble
in-def-i-nite-ly
in-de-pen-dence
in-de-pen-dent
in-di-vid-u-al
in-dus-tri-al
in-fe-ri-or
in-fi-nite
in-flam-ma-ble
in-flu-en-tial
in-i-tial
ini-ti-a-tion
in-no-cence

in-no-cent
in-stal-la-tion
in-stance
in-stead
in-sur-ance
in-tel-li-gence
in-ten-tion
in-ter-est-ed
in-ter-est-ing
in-ter-fere
in-ter-pret
in-ter-rupt
in-ter-view
in-ves-ti-gate
in-vi-ta-tion
ir-ri-gate
is-land
is-sue

jeal-ous (-y)
jew-el-ry
jour-nal
jour-ney
judg-ment
juic-y

K

kitch-en
knew
knife
knives
knock
knowl-edge
knuck-les

L

la-bel
lab-o-ra-to-ry
la-dies
lan-guage
laugh
laun-dry
law-yer

league
lec-ture
le-gal
leg-i-ble
leg-is-la-ture
lei-sure
length
li-a-ble
li-brar-y
li-cense
lieu-ten-ant
light-ning
lik-able
like-ly
li-quid
lis-ten
lit-er-a-ture
liv-ing
loaves
lone-li-ness
loose
lose
los-er
los-ing
lov-able
love-ly

M

ma-chin-er-y
mag-a-zine
mag-nif-i-cent
main-tain
ma-jor-i-ty
mak-ing
man-u-al
man-u-fac-ture
mar-riage
ma-te-ri-al
math-e-mat-ics
max-i-mum
may-or
meant
mea-sure
med-i-cine
me-di-um
mes-sage
mile-age
min-i-a-ture

min-i-mum
min-ute
mir-ror
mis-cel-la-neous
mis-chie-vous
mis-er-a-ble
mis-sile
mis-spell
mois-ture
mol-e-cule
mo-not-o-nous
mon-u-ment
mort-gage
moun-tain
mus-cle
mu-si-cian
mys-te-ri-ous

N

na-ive
nat-u-ral (-ly)
nec-es-sary
ne-go-ti-ate
neigh-bor (-hood)
nei-ther
nick-el
niece
nine-teen
nine-teenth
nine-ty
nois-y
no-tice-able
nu-cle-ar
nui-sance

O

o-be-di-ence
o-bey
ob-sta-cle
oc-ca-sion
oc-ca-sion-al (-ly)
oc-cur
oc-curred
of-fense
of-fi-cial
of-ten

o-mis-sion
o-mit-ted
o-pin-ion
op-er-ate
op-po-nent
op-por-tu-ni-ty
op-po-site
or-di-nar-i-ly
orig-i-nal
out-ra-geous

P

pack-age
paid
pam-phlet
par-a-dise
para-graph
par-al-lel
par-a-lyze
pa-ren-the-ses
par-tial
par-tic-i-pant
par-tic-i-pate
par-tic-u-lar (-ly)
pas-ture
pa-tience
pe-cu-liar
peo-ple
per-haps
per-ma-nent
per-pen-dic-u-lar
per-sis-tent
per-son-al (-ly)
per-son-nel
per-spi-ra-tion
per-suade
phase
phy-si-cian
piece
pitch-er
planned
pla-teau
play-wright
pleas-ant
plea-sure
pneu-mo-nia
pol-i-ti-cian
pos-sess

pos-si-ble
prac-ti-cal (-ly)
prai-rie
pre-cede
pre-cious
pre-cise (-ly)
pre-ci-sion
pref-er-a-ble
pre-ferred
prej-u-dice
prep-a-ra-tion
pres-ence
pre-vi-ous
prim-i-tive
prin-ci-pal
prin-ci-ple
pris-on-er
priv-i-lege
prob-a-bly
pro-ce-dure
pro-ceed
pro-fes-sor
prom-i-nent
pro-nounce
pro-nun-ci-a-tion
pro-tein
psy-chol-o-gy
pump-kin
pure

Q

quar-ter
ques-tion-naire
qui-et
quite
quo-tient

R

raise
re-al-ize
re-al-ly
re-ceipt
re-ceive
re-ceived
rec-i-pe
rec-og-nize

rec-om-mend
reign
re-lieve
re-li-gious
re-mem-ber
rep-e-ti-tion
rep-re-sen-ta-tive
res-er-voir
re-sis-tance
re-spect-ful-ly
re-spon-si-bil-i-ty
res-tau-rant
re-view
rhyme
rhythm
ri-dic-u-lous
route

S

safe-ty
sal-ad
sal-a-ry
sand-wich
sat-is-fac-to-ry
Sat-ur-day
scene
sce-ner-y
sched-ule
sci-ence
scis-sors
scream
screen
sea-son
sec-re-tary
seize
sen-si-ble
sen-tence
sep-a-rate
sev-er-al
sher-iff
shin-ing
sim-i-lar
since
sin-cere (-ly)
ski-ing
sleigh
sol-dier
sou-ve-nir

spa-ghet-ti
spe-cif-ic
sphere
sprin-kle
squeeze
squir-rel
stat-ue
stat-ure
stat-ute
stom-ach
stopped
straight
strength
stretched
study-ing
sub-tle
suc-ceed
suc-cess
suf-fi-cient
sum-ma-rize
sup-ple-ment
sup-pose
sure-ly
sur-prise
syl-la-ble
sym-pa-thy
symp-tom

T

tar-iff
tech-nique
tem-per-a-ture
tem-po-rary
ter-ri-ble
ter-ri-to-ry
thank-ful
the-ater
their
there
there-fore
thief
thor-ough (-ly)
though
through-out
tired
to-bac-co
to-geth-er
to-mor-row

tongue
touch
tour-na-ment
to-ward
trag-e-dy
trea-sur-er
tried
tries
tru-ly
Tues-day
typ-i-cal

U

un-con-scious
un-for-tu-nate (-ly)
unique
uni-ver-si-ty
un-nec-es-sary
un-til
us-able
use-ful
using
usu-al (-ly)
u-ten-sil

V

va-ca-tion
vac-u-um
valu-able
va-ri-ety
var-i-ous
veg-e-ta-ble
ve-hi-cle
very
vi-cin-i-ty
view
vil-lain
vi-o-lence
vis-i-ble
vis-i-tor
voice
vol-ume
vol-un-tary
vol-un-teer

W

wan-der
weath-er
Wednes-day
weigh
weird
wel-come
wel-fare
whale
where
wheth-er
which
whole
whol-ly
whose
width
wom-en
worth-while
wreck-age
writ-ing
writ-ten

Y

yel-low

The Yellow Pages Guide to
Using the Right Word

Here are some tips which will help you "use the right word" whenever you write. **First,** it won't take you long to realize that proper word choice is more important in some situations than in others: for example, it is important in a letter to the editor of the local paper, in a formal essay or research paper, and in a presentation to a local church or civic group. **Second**, you should become familiar with the words which are commonly misused by looking through this section in your handbook. **Third**, you should refer to this section whenever you have a question about which word is the correct one to use. (*Note:* If your handbook doesn't answer your question, refer to a dictionary.) **Finally**, you should make every effort to keep your writing both correct and natural.

574 ....**a, an**

◆ *A* is used before words which begin with a consonant sound; *an* is used before words which begin with a vowel sound.

> *a* heap, *a* cat, *an* idol, *an* elephant, *an* honor, *a* historian

575 ....**accept, except**

◆ The verb *accept* means "to receive"; the preposition *except* means "other than."

> Melissa graciously *accepted* defeat [verb]. All the boys *except* Zach were here [preposition].

576............................**affect, effect**

◆ *Affect* is always a verb; it means "to influence." *Effect* can be a verb, but it is most often used as a noun. As a verb, *effect* means "to produce or make happen."

> Mark's giggle *affected* the preacher. Mark's giggle *effected* a pinch from his mother.

◆ The noun *effect* means "the result."

> The *effect* of the pinch was a sore leg.

allowed, aloud........................**577**

◆ The verb *allowed* means "permitted" or "let happen"; *aloud* is an adverb which means "in a normal voice."

> We weren't *allowed* to read *aloud* in the library.

allusion, illusion...................**578**

◆ An *allusion* is a brief reference or mention of a famous person, place, thing, or idea. An *illusion* is a false impression or idea.

> As he made an *allusion* to the great magicians of the past, Houdini created the *illusion* of having sawed his assistant in half.

a lot **579**

◆ *A lot* is not one word; *a lot* (two words) is a very general descriptive phrase which should be avoided in formal writing.

580 .... already, all ready

◆ *Already* is an adverb which tells when. *All ready* is a phrase meaning "completely ready."

> By 9:00 a.m. *already*, the class was *all ready* to try out the substitute.

581 .... alright, all right

◆ *Alright* is the incorrect spelling of *all right*. *All right* is a phrase meaning "correct." (Please note, the following are spelled correctly: *always, altogether, already, almost*.)

582 .... altogether, all together

◆ *Altogether* is always an adverb meaning "completely." *All together* is used to describe people or things which are gathered in one place at one time.

> "No," said the principal. "There is *altogether* too much goofing around whenever seventh graders have assemblies *all together*."

583 .... among, between

◆ *Among* is used when speaking of more than two persons or things. *Between* is used when speaking of only two.

> Putrid socks were scattered *among* the sweaty uniforms. A single streamer dangled *between* the goalposts.

amount, number 584

◆ *Number* is used when you can actually count the persons or things. *Amount* is used to describe things which can be weighed or measured, but not counted.

> The liquid produced a large *number* of burps. The burps were the result of a large *amount* of gas.

annual, biannual,
semiannual, biennial,
perennial 585

◆ An *annual* event happens once every year. A *biannual* event happens twice a year (*semiannual* means the same as *biannual*). A *biennial* event happens every two years. A *perennial* event is active throughout the year and continues to happen year after year.

ant, aunt 586

◆ *Aunt* is a relative. *Ant* is an insect.

> The tiny *ant's aunt* scolded him for calling her, "Old Spider Legs."

ascent, assent 587

◆ *Ascent* is "the act of rising"; *assent* is "agreement."

> The pilot *assented* that the plane's *ascent* was unusually bumpy.

SCHOOL DAZE

John, I've got the projects **all together**. Now which one is yours?

I'm not **altogether** sure. See if there's one with a missing piece.

588 .... bare, bear

◆ The adjective *bare* means "to be na-ked." A *bear* is a large, furry ani-mal.

> He chased the polar *bear* across the snow though his feet were *bare*.

◆ The verb *bear* means "to put up with" or "to carry."

> Dwayne could not *bear* another of his older brother's lectures.

589 .... base, bass

◆ *Base* is the foundation or the lower part of something. *Bass* is a deep sound or tone. *Bass* (*a* pronounced as in *fast*) is a fish.

590 .... be, bee

◆ *Be* is the verb. *Bee* is the insect.

591 .... beat, beet

◆ The verb *beat* means "to strike, to defeat"; a *beet* is a carrot-like vege-table (often red).

> After our team *beat* Tom's team, four games to one, I was as red as a *beet*.

592 .... berth, birth

◆ *Berth* is a space or compartment. *Birth* is the process of being born.

> We give up our most comfortable *berths* through *birth*.

593 .... beside, besides

◆ *Beside* means "by the side of." *Be-sides* means "in addition to."

> Jeff laid his gum *beside* his plate. *Besides* some burned toast, Ber-nice fed him some warm lemon-ade.

594 .... billed, build

◆ *Billed* means either "to be given a bill" or "to have a beak." The verb *build* means "to construct."

blew, blue 595

◆ *Blew* is the past tense of *blow*. *Blue* is a color; *blue* is also used to mean "feeling low in spirits."

boar, bore 596

◆ A *boar* is a wild pig. *Bore* is a verb that means "to tire with dullness" or "to make a hole by drilling."

board, bored 597

◆ A *board* is a piece of wood. *Board* also means "a group or council which helps run an organization."

> The school *board* approved the purchase of fifty 1" x 6" pine *boards*.

◆ *Bored* may mean "to make a hole by drilling" or "to become weary or tired of something."

> Dissecting fish *bored* Joe, so he took his tweezers and *bored* a hole in the tail of the perch.

brake, break 598

◆ A *brake* is a device used to stop a vehicle. *Break* means "to split, crack, or destroy."

> I hope my *brakes* never *break*.

bring, take 599

◆ Use *bring* when the action is mov-ing toward the speaker; use *take* when the action is moving away from the speaker.

> Humpty Dumpty rubbed his sore yoke and bellowed, "*Bring* me some glue, and *take* that spatula out of here!"

by, buy 600

◆ *By* is a preposition meaning "near or through." *Buy* is a verb meaning "to purchase."

> On the side of her lemonade stand Rosa had painted: "Smart people *buy*; the others walk *by*!"

601 ....can, may

◆ *Can* means "able to" while *may* means "permitted to."

> "*Can* I go to the library?" actually means, "Do you think my mind and body are tough enough to get me there?" "*May* I go?" means, "Do I have your permission to go?"

602 ....cannon, canon

◆ A *cannon* is a big gun; a *canon* is a rule or law made by an authority in a church or organization.

603 ....canvas, canvass

◆ *Canvas* is a heavy cloth; *canvass* means "to go among the people asking them for votes or opinions."

604 ....capital, capitol

◆ *Capital* can be either a noun or an adjective. The noun *capital* refers to a city or to money. The adjective *capital* means "major or important." *Capitol* is used only when talking about a building.

> The *capitol* building is in the *capital* city for a *capital* reason. The city government contributed the *capital* for the building project.

605 ....cell, sell

◆ *Cell* means "a small room or a small unit of life which makes up all plants and animals." *Sell* is a verb meaning "to give up for a price."

606 ....cent, sent, scent

◆ *Cent* is a coin; *sent* is the past tense of the verb "send"; *scent* is an odor or smell.

> For twenty-two *cents*, I *sent* my girlfriend a mushy love poem in a perfumed envelope. She loved the *scent* but hated the poem.

chord, cord 607

◆ *Chord* may be used to mean "an emotion or feeling," but it is more often used to mean "the sound when three or more musical tones are played at the same time," as with a piano *chord*. A *cord* is a string or rope.

> The band struck a *chord* at the exact moment the mayor pulled the *cord* on the drape covering the new statue.

chose, choose 608

◆ *Chose* (choz) is the past tense of the verb *choose* (chooz).

> This afternoon Mom *chose* tacos and hot sauce; this evening she will *choose* Alka-Seltzer.

coarse, course 609

◆ *Coarse* means "rough or crude." *Course* means "a path or direction taken"; *course* also means "a class or series of studies."

> Heidi took a *course* up the mountain which was very *coarse*.

complement, compliment 610

◆ *Complement* means "completes or goes with." *Compliment* is an expression of admiration or praise.

> I *complimented* Aunt Betty by saying that her hat *complemented* her coat and dress.

continual, continuous 611

◆ *Continual* refers to something which happens again and again; *continuous* refers to something which doesn't stop happening.

> Sunlight hits Peoria, Iowa, on a *continual* basis; but sunlight hits the world *continuously*.

612 .... counsel, council

◆ When used as a noun, *counsel* means "advice"; when used as a verb, *counsel* means "to advise." *Council* refers to a group which advises.

> The jackrabbit *council counseled* all bunnies to keep their tails out of the old man's garden. That's good *counsel*.

613 .... creak, creek

◆ A *creak* is a squeaking sound; a *creek* is a stream.

> The old willow leaning over the *creek*, *creaks* in the wind.

614 .... cymbal, symbol

◆ A *cymbal* is a metal instrument shaped like a plate. A *symbol* is something (usually visible) that stands for or represents another thing or idea (usually invisible).

> The cracked *cymbal* lying on the stage was a *symbol* of the band's final concert.

615 .... dear, deer

◆ *Dear* means "loved or valued"; *deer* are animals.

> My *dear*, people will think you're strange if you write that you kissed your *deer* in the moonlight.

616 .... desert, dessert

◆ A *desert* is a barren wilderness. *Dessert* is a food served at the end of a meal.

> The scorpion tiptoed through the moonlit *desert*, searching for *dessert*.

◆ The verb *desert* means "to abandon"; the noun *desert* also may mean "deserving reward or punishment."

> The frightened rabbit *deserted* the boy; the loss of his pet was the cruel boy's just *desert*.

die, dye 617

◆ *Die (dying)* means "to stop living." *Dye (dyeing)* is used to change the color of something.

faint, feign, feint 618

◆ *Faint* means "to be feeble, without strength." *Feign* is a verb which means "to pretend or make up." *Feint* is a noun which means "a move or activity which is pretended or false."

> The little boy *feigned* a bruised, blood-spattered face and fell to the floor in a *feint*. His teacher, who didn't notice that the blood smelled like catsup, *fainted* beside him.

farther, further 619

◆ *Farther* is used when you are writing about a physical distance. *Further* is used when you are not referring to distances; it can also mean "additional."

> Alaska is *farther* north than Iceland. *Further* information can be obtained at your local library.

fewer, less 620

◆ *Fewer* refers to the number of separate units; *less* refers to bulk quantity.

> There is *less* sand to play with, so we have *fewer* sandboxes to make.

fir, fur 621

◆ *Fir* refers to a type of evergreen tree; *fur* is animal hair.

flair, flare 622

◆ *Flair* means "a natural talent"; *flare* means "to light up quickly or burst out."

> Hotheads have a *flair* for tempers which *flare*.

623 ....**for, fore, four**

◆ *For* is a preposition meaning "because" or "directed to"; *fore* means "earlier" or "the front." *Four* is the number 4.

> The dog had stolen one of the *four* steaks Mary had grilled *for* the party and was holding the bone in his *fore*paws when she found him.

624 ....**good, well**

◆ *Good* is an adjective; *well* is nearly always an adverb.

> The strange flying machines flew *well*. (The adverb *well* modifies *flew*.) They looked *good* as they flew overhead. (The adjective *good* modifies *they*.)

◆ When used in writing about health, *well* is an adjective.

> The pilots looked *good* at the start of the race. Not all of them felt so *well* at the finish.

625 ....**hare, hair**

◆ *Hair* refers to the growth covering the head and body of animals and human beings; *hare* refers to an animal similar to a rabbit.

> The *hair* on my head stood up as the *hare* darted out in front of our car.

heal, heel **626**

◆ *Heal* means "to mend or restore to health." *Heel* is the back part of a human foot.

> The arrow pierced Achilles' *heel*, and the wound would not *heal*.

hear, here **627**

◆ You *hear* with your *ears*. *Here* is the opposite of *there* and means "nearby."

heard, herd **628**

◆ *Heard* is the past tense of the verb *hear; herd* is a large group of animals.

> The *herd* of grazing cows raised their heads when they *heard* the collie barking in the distance.

heir, air **629**

◆ *Heir* is a person who inherits something; *air* is the stuff we breathe.

> Will the next generation be *heir* to terminally polluted *air*?

hole, whole **630**

◆ A *hole* is a cavity or hollow place. *Whole* means "entire or complete."

> The *hole* in the ozone layer is a serious problem requiring the attention of the *whole* world.

School Daze

631 ....immigrate, emigrate

◆ *Immigrate* means "to *come into* a new country or area." *Emigrate* means "to *go out* of one country to live in another."

> Martin Ulferts *immigrated* to this country in 1882. He was only three years old when he *emigrated* from Germany.

632 ....imply, infer

◆ *Imply* means "to suggest indirectly"; *infer* means "to draw a conclusion from facts." (A writer or speaker *implies*; a reader or listener *infers*.)

633 ....it's, its

◆ *It's* is the contraction of *it is*. *Its* is the possessive form of *it*.

> *It's* noisiest in the zoo when the giraffe gargles *its* mouthwash.

634 ....kernel, colonel

◆ A *kernel* is a seed or core; a *colonel* is a military officer.

> The *colonel* hates unpopped *kernels* in his microwave popcorn.

635 ....knew, new

◆ *Knew* is the past tense of the verb *know*. *New* means "recent or modern."

> She *knew* that a *new* life began with graduation from kindergarten.

636 ....know, no

◆ *Know* means "to understand." *No* means "the opposite of *yes*."

> Don't you *know* that *no* means *no*?

637 ....later, latter

◆ *Later* means "after a period of time." *Latter* refers to the second of two things mentioned.

> *Later* in the year 1965, Galen married Sam; the *latter*, Sam, is a lady.

lay, lie 638

◆ *Lay* means "to place." (*Lay* is a transitive verb; that means it needs a word to complete the meaning.)

> I *lay* the cigar down today. I *laid* it down yesterday. I had *laid* it down before. (*Cigar* and *it* complete the meaning by answering the question *what*.)

◆ *Lie* means "to recline." (*Lie* is an intransitive verb.)

> The mutt *lies* down. It *lay* down yesterday. It has *lain* down before.

lead, led 639

◆ *Lead* is a present tense verb meaning "to guide." The past tense of the verb is *led*. When the words are pronounced the same, then *lead* is the metal.

> "Hey, Nat, get the *lead* out!"
> "Hey, cool it, man! Who gave you a ticket to *lead* me around?"

learn, teach 640

◆ *Learn* means "to get information"; *teach* means "to give information."

> If you want to test yourself on something you've just *learned*, try *teaching* it to others.

leave, let 641

◆ *Leave* means "to allow something to remain behind." *Let* means "to permit."

> Rozi wanted to *leave* her boots at home, but George wouldn't *let* her.

like, as 642

◆ *Like* is a preposition meaning "similar to"; *as* is a conjunction meaning "such as." *Like* usually introduces a phrase; *as* usually introduces a clause.

> The glider floated *like* a bird. The glider floated *as* he had hoped.

643 ....loose, lose, loss

◆ *Loose* (loos) means "free or untied"; *lose* (looz) means "to misplace or fail to win"; *loss* means "something lost."

> Even though he didn't want to *lose* the *loose* tooth, it was no big *loss*.

644 ....made, maid

◆ *Made* is the past tense of *make* which means "to create." A *maid* is a female servant; *maid* is also used to describe an unmarried girl or young woman.

> The *maid* asked if our beds needed to be *made*.

645 ....mail, male

◆ *Mail* refers to letters or packages handled by the postal service. *Male* refers to the masculine sex.

646 ....main, mane

◆ *Main* refers to the principal or most important part or point. *Mane* is the long hair growing from the top or sides of the neck of certain animals such as the horse, lion, etc.

647 ....meat, meet

◆ *Meat* is food or flesh; *meet* means "to come upon or encounter."

648 ....metal, meddle, medal, mettle

◆ *Metal* is an element like iron or gold. *Meddle* means "to interfere." *Medal* is an award. *Mettle*, a noun, refers to quality of character.

> The golden snoop cup is a *metal medal* which is awarded to the greatest *meddler*. Snooping is a habit of people of low *mettle*.

649 ....miner, minor

◆ A *miner* digs in the ground for valuable ore. A *minor* is a person who is not legally an adult. A *minor* problem is one of no great importance.

> The use of *minors* as *miners* is no *minor* problem.

moral, morale 650

◆ *Moral* relates to what is right or wrong. *Morale* refers to a person's attitude or mental condition.

> "I don't care whether hunting deer is *moral*," she said. "I care about my *morale*."

morning, mourning 651

◆ *Morning* refers to the first part of the day before noon; *mourning* means "showing sorrow."

> Abby was *mourning* her test grades all *morning*.

oar, or, ore 652

◆ An *oar* is a paddle used in rowing or steering a boat. *Or* is a conjunction indicating choice. *Ore* refers to a mineral made up of several different kinds of material, as in iron ore.

pain, pane 653

◆ *Pain* is the feeling of being hurt. *Pane* is a section or part of something, as in a framed section of glass in a window or door.

pair, pare, pear 654

◆ A *pair* is a couple (two); *pare* is a verb meaning "to peel"; *pear* is the fruit.

past, passed 655

◆ *Passed* is always a verb. *Past* can be used as a noun, as an adjective, or as a preposition.

> That Geo *passed* my 'Vette [verb]. The old man won't forget the *past* [noun]. I'm sorry, but I'd rather not talk about my *past* life [adjective]. Old Blue walked *past* us and never saw it [preposition].

656 .... **peace, piece**

◆ *Peace* means "harmony or freedom from war." *Piece* is a part or fragment.

> Someone once observed that *peace* is not a condition, but a process—a process of building goodwill one *piece* or one person at a time.

657 .... **personal, personnel**

◆ *Personal* means "private." *Personnel* are people working at a job.

658 .... **plain, plane**

◆ *Plain* means "an area of land which is flat or level"; it also means "clearly seen or clearly understood."

> My teacher told me to "check the map" after I said that it was *plain* to me why the early settlers had trouble crossing the Rockies on their way to the Great *Plains*.

◆ *Plane* means "flat, level, and even"; it is also a tool used to smooth the surface of wood.

> I used a *plane* to make the board *plane* and smooth.

659 .... **pore, pour, poor**

◆ A *pore* is an opening in the skin. *Pour* means "a constant flow or stream." *Poor* means "needy."

> Long math tests on warm spring days make my *poor pores pour*.

principal, principle **660**

◆ As an adjective, *principal* means "primary." As a noun, it can mean "a school administrator" or "a sum of money." *Principle* means "idea or doctrine."

> His *principal* gripe is lack of freedom.

> "Hey, Charlie, I hear the *principal* chewed you out!"

> After twenty years, the amount of interest was higher than the *principal*.

> The *principle* of freedom is based on the *principle* of self-discipline.

quiet, quit, quite **661**

◆ *Quiet* is the opposite of noisy. *Quit* means "to stop." *Quite* means "completely or entirely."

raise, rays, raze **662**

◆ *Raise* is a verb meaning "to lift or elevate." *Rays* are thin lines or beams, as in rays of sunlight. *Raze* is a verb which means "to tear down completely."

> As I *raised* the shade, bright *rays* of sunlight shot across the room and bounced to the ceiling. Across the street I could see the old theater which they plan to *raze* soon to build a parking lot.

SCHOOL DAZE

At first Mrs. Warren was really **quiet**.

She couldn't **quit** looking at my project. Finally, she said, "Gloria, I've never seen sardines used in **quite** that way before."

663 .... real, very, really

◆ Do not use *real* in place of the adverbs *very* or *really*.

> Pimples are *very* (not *real*) embarrassing. Her nose is *really* (not *real*) long.

664 .... red, read

◆ *Red* is a color; *read* is a verb meaning "to understand the meaning of written words and symbols."

665 .... right, write, wright, rite

◆ *Right* means "correct or proper"; it also refers to anything which a person has a legal claim to, as in copyright. *Write* means "to record in print." *Wright* is a person who makes or builds something. *Rite* is a ritual or ceremonial act.

> Did you *write* that it is the *right* of the ship*wright* to perform the *rite* of christening—breaking a bottle of champagne on the stern of the ship?

666 .... scene, seen

◆ *Scene* refers to the setting or location where something happens; it also may mean "sight or spectacle." *Seen* is a part of the verb "see."

> An actor likes to be *seen* making a *scene*.

667 .... seam, seem

◆ *Seam* is a line formed by connecting two pieces of material. *Seem* means "to appear to exist."

> The ragged *seams* in the old man's coat *seem* to match the creases in his face.

668 .... sew, so, sow

◆ *Sew* is a verb meaning "to stitch"; *so* is a conjunction meaning "in order that." The verb *sow* means "to plant."

sight, cite, site 669

◆ *Sight* means "the act of seeing." *Cite* means "to quote or refer to." *Site* means "location or position."

> Mark's *sight* was destroyed when a guy's cigarette ignited a gas can on the building *site*. The judge *cited* the man for careless use of smoking materials.

sit, set 670

◆ *Sit* means "to put the body in a seated position." *Set* means "to place."

> "How can you just *sit* there and watch as I *set* all these chairs in place?"

sole, soul 671

◆ *Sole* means "single, only one"; *sole* also refers to the bottom surface of a foot or shoe. *Soul* refers to the spiritual part of a person.

> A person's *sole* develops blisters on a two-mile hike while his *soul* walks on eternally.

some, sum 672

◆ *Some* means "a certain unknown number or part." *Sum* means "an amount."

> The total *sum* was stolen by *some* thieves.

sore, soar 673

◆ *Sore* means "painful"; to *soar* means "to rise or fly high into the air."

> Craning to watch the eagle *soar* overhead, our necks soon grew *sore*.

stationary,
stationery 674

◆ *Stationary* means "not movable"; *stationery* is the paper and envelopes used to write letters.

675 ....**steal, steel**

◆ *Steal* means "to take something without permission"; *steel* is a metal.

> He lived in constant fear that someone would *steal* the *steel* wheels from his car.

676 ....**than, then**

◆ *Than* is used in a comparison; *then* tells when.

> *Then* he cried and said that his big brother was bigger *than* my big brother. *Then* I cried.

677 ....**their, there, they're**

◆ *Their* is a possessive pronoun, one which shows ownership. *There* is a pronoun used to point out a location. *They're* is the contraction for *they are*.

> *They're* upset because *their* son dumped garbage over *there*.

678 ....**threw, through**

◆ *Threw* is the past tense of "throw." *Through* means "passing from one side of something to the other."

> The bride *threw* her bouquet *through* their outstretched hands and into . . . the cake.

679 ....**to, at**

◆ *To* should not be used in place of *at* in a sentence.

> He is *at* (not *to*) school.

680 ....**to, too, two**

◆ *To* is the preposition which can mean "in the direction of." (*To* also is used to form an infinitive.) *Too* is an adverb meaning "very or excessive." (*Too* is often used to mean *also*.) *Two* is the number.

> The *two* divers were careful not *to* swim *to* the sunken ship *too* quickly.

vain, vane, vein **681**

◆ *Vain* means "worthless." It may also mean "thinking too highly of one's self; stuck-up." *Vane* is a flat piece of material set up to show which way the wind blows. *Vein* refers to a blood vessel or a mineral deposit.

> The weather *vane* indicates the direction of wind; the blood *vein* determines the direction of flowing blood; the *vain* mind moves in no particular direction and is satisfied to think only about itself.

vary, very **682**

◆ *Vary* is a verb that means "to change." (The weather can *vary* from snow to sleet to sunshine in a single day.) *Very* can be an adjective meaning "in the fullest sense" or "complete." (His story was the *very* opposite of the truth.) *Very* can also be an adverb meaning "extremely." (The story was *very* interesting.)

waist, waste **683**

◆ *Waist* is the part of the body just above the hips. The verb *waste* means "to wear away, decay"; the noun *waste* refers to material which is unused or useless.

wait, weight **684**

◆ *Wait* means "to stay somewhere expecting something." *Weight* is the measure of heaviness.

ware, wear, where **685**

◆ *Ware* means "a product which is sold"; *wear* means "to have on or to carry on one's body"; *where* asks the question, "in what place? or in what situation?"

> The little boy who sold pet fleas boasted, "Anybody can *wear* my *ware* any*where*, and he'll always know right *where* it is."

686 .... **way, weigh**

◆ *Way* means "path or route." *Weigh* means "to measure weight."

> After being *weighed* at Weight Watchers club, the two sad friends walked the long *way* home . . . past the malt shop.

687 .... **weather, whether**

◆ *Weather* refers to the condition of the atmosphere. *Whether* refers to a possibility.

> The *weather* will determine *whether* I go fishing.

688 .... **week, weak**

◆ A *week* is a period of 7 days; *weak* means "not strong."

689 .... **which, witch**

◆ *Which* is a pronoun used to refer to or point out something. In ancient tales, *witches* are older women believed to cast spells and keep company with black cats.

> The *witch* drives a broomstick *which* has a tachometer.

690 .... **who, which, that**

◆ *Which* refers to nonliving objects or to animals; *which* should never refer to people. *Who* is used to refer to people. *That* may refer to animals, people, or nonliving objects.

who, whom **691**

◆ *Who* is used as the subject in a sentence; *whom* is used as the object of a preposition or as a direct object.

> *Who* ordered this pizza? The pizza was ordered by *whom*?

Note: To test for *who/whom*, arrange the parts of the clause in a subject-verb-object order. (*Who* works as the subject, *whom* as the object.)

who's, whose **692**

◆ *Who's* is the contraction for *who is*. *Whose* is a possessive pronoun, one which shows ownership.

> "*Who's* that kid with the red ears?" "*Whose* ears are you talking about, fella?"

wood, would **693**

◆ *Wood* is the stuff which trees are made of; *would* is a part of the verb "will."

> The captain who had a *wooden* leg *would* always be shortening his trousers whenever termites were on board.

your, you're **694**

◆ *Your* is a possessive pronoun, one which shows ownership. *You're* is the contraction for *you are*.

School Daze

David, **you** know **you're** supposed to be doing **your** homework.

I am, Mom. I'm doing firsthand research on energy conservation.

The Yellow Pages Guide to
Understanding
Sentences

There is little doubt that the sentence is the cornerstone of all writing. Whether we like it or not, we are expected to use *sentences*—not sentence fragments, run-ons, or spliced sentences—but complete, colorful, concise, correct sentences in a variety of shapes and sizes. As you practice and experiment with your sentences, it might be helpful for you to know how different kinds of sentences are put together and what the various sentence "elements" are. The information in this section should help.

Sentence
695

A **sentence** is made up of one or more words which express a complete thought. (*Note:* A sentence begins with a capital letter; it ends with a period, question mark, or exclamation point.)

> This book should help you write. It explains many things.

> How do you plan to use it? I hope you find it helpful!

For more information on sentences, turn to "Composing Sentences," 090-114, in your handbook.

WORDS IN A SENTENCE

Subject & Predicate 696
◆ A sentence must have a subject and predicate in order to express a complete thought. Either the subject or the predicate (or both) may *not* be stated, but both must be clearly understood.

> [*You*] **Join our union!** [*You* is the understood subject.]

> **Who needs independence? People.** [*do*] [*Do* is the understood predicate.]

> **What can you lose by joining?** [*We can lose*] **Freedom.** [*We* is the understood subject, and *can lose* is the understood predicate.]

Subject 697
◆ A subject is the part of a sentence which is doing something or about which something is said.

> In 1939 *Russia* took away the independence and identities of the Baltic states. Since then *they* have been prisoners in the union.

698 ....Simple Subject

◆ The simple subject is the subject without the words which describe or modify it.

> Today, the Latvian, Estonian, and Lithuanian *people* want what they lost.

699 ....Complete Subject

◆ The complete subject is the simple subject and all the words which modify it.

> Today, *the Latvian, Estonian, and Lithuanian people* want what they lost.

700...................Compound Subject

◆ A compound subject has two or more simple subjects.

> *Students* and *teachers* need school.

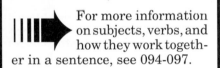 For more information on subjects, verbs, and how they work together in a sentence, see 094-097.

701 ....Predicate

◆ The predicate is the part of the sentence which says something about the subject.

> Principals *remember.*

702 ....Simple Predicate

◆ The simple predicate is the predicate (verb) without the words which describe or modify it.

> Little people *can talk* faster than big people. [*Can talk* is the simple predicate; *faster than big people* describes how little people *can talk.*]

703 ....Complete Predicate

◆ The complete predicate is the simple predicate with all the words which modify or describe it.

> Little people *can talk faster than big people.*

Compound Predicate 704

◆ A compound predicate is composed of two or more simple predicates.

> Big people *talk* slowly but *eat* fast.

Compound Subject & Predicate 705

◆ A sentence may have a compound subject and a compound predicate.

> Sturdy *tongues* and thick *teeth* *say* sentences slowly but *chew* food quickly.

Direct Object 706

◆ Whatever receives the action of the simple predicate is the direct object.

> The guy in the back row builds paper *airplanes.* He has developed a tremendous *fleet.*

◆ The direct object may be compound.

> Chickens eat oyster *shells* and *grit.*

 For additional examples and information on direct and indirect objects, see 762-764.

Modifier 707

◆ A modifier is a word or a group of words which changes or adds to the meaning of another word.

> Estonia, Lithuania, and Latvia are *the small, Baltic* states searching for independence. [*The, small,* and *Baltic* modify *states.*]

> After World War II, Russia *firmly* pulled *the tiny* countries into *the* Soviet Union. [*Firmly* modifies *pulled, the* and *tiny* modify *countries,* and *the* modifies *Soviet Union.*]

PHRASE

708 ....Phrase

◆ A phrase is a group of related words which lacks either a subject or a predicate (or both).

> **has nothing on it** [The predicate lacks a subject.]
>
> **This guy's desk** [The subject lacks a predicate.]
>
> **except two dead plants** [The phrase lacks both a subject and a predicate.]
>
> **This guy's desk has nothing on it except two dead plants.** [Together, the three phrases present a complete thought.]

709 ....Types of Phrases

◆ Phrases usually take their names from the main words which introduce them (prepositional phrase, verb phrase, etc.). They can also be named for the function they serve in a sentence (adverb phrase, adjective phrase).

> The ancient oak *tree*
> [noun phrase]
> *with* crooked old limbs
> [prepositional phrase]
> *has stood* its guard,
> [verb phrase]
> *very* determined,
> [adverb phrase]
> *protecting* the little house.
> [verbal phrase]

CLAUSE

> A clause is a group of related words which has both a subject and a predicate.

Independent & Dependent Clauses 710

◆ An **independent clause** presents a complete thought and can stand as a sentence; a **dependent clause** does not present a complete thought and cannot stand as a sentence.

In the following sentences, the dependent clauses are in boldface *italics* and the independent clauses are in **boldface**.

> **A small pony can attack a large horse** *if it kicks its heels in the horse's belly.*
>
> **Sparrows make nests in cattle barns** *so they can stay warm during the winter.*

CONTROLLING SENTENCES

Need help making your clauses and phrases work together?

WE CAN HELP!

See our complete display of clear, concise, agreeable sentences.

‖‖⮕ **090-114**

SCHOOL DAZE

Boy, are you guys in for a real block-buster next hour!

Ya . . . Mr. Runge is showing a movie called **A Day in the Life of a Dependent Clause**.

TYPES OF SENTENCES

711.....................Simple Sentence

◆ A simple sentence is a sentence with only one independent clause (one complete thought). It may have either a simple subject or a compound subject. It may also have either a simple predicate or a compound predicate.

◆ A simple sentence may contain one or more phrases, but no dependent clauses.

> My *back aches*. [simple subject; simple predicate]
>
> My *muscles* and my *eyes hurt*. [compound subject; simple predicate]
>
> My *face* and *hair look* and *feel terrible*. [compound subject; compound predicate]
>
> I must be getting a case of the flu. [simple subject: *I;* simple predicate: *must be getting;* phrase: *a case of the flu]*

712...............Compound Sentence

◆ A compound sentence is made up of two or more simple sentences (also called *independent clauses*) which are joined by a coordinate conjunction, punctuation, or both.

> I try to avoid illness, but the flu bug always finds me.
>
> I drink plenty of liquids; I get plenty of sleep.

713...................Complex Sentence

◆ A complex sentence contains one independent clause (in **boldface**) and one or more dependent clauses (in ***boldface italics***).

> *Even though I feel down,* **I plan to carry on.** [dependent clause followed by independent clause]
>
> **It isn't easy, though,** *when my nose runs until it turns red.* [independent clause followed by two dependent clauses]

Compound-Complex Sentence 714

◆ These sentences contain two or more independent clauses (in **boldface**) and one or more dependent clauses (in ***boldface italics***).

> *If I really hope to outsmart this bug,* **maybe I should consider exercising every day, and maybe it's even time to begin eating breakfast regularly.** [dependent clause followed by two independent clauses]

KINDS OF SENTENCES

Declarative Sentence 715

◆ Declarative sentences make statements. They tell us something about a person, place, thing, or idea.

> The Statue of Liberty is a grand, old lady who stands in New York harbor as a symbol of our freedom.

Interrogative Sentence 716

◆ Interrogative sentences ask questions.

> Did you know that some tourists choose to write on her skirts and to scratch on her eyes? Why doesn't she scream out?

Imperative Sentence 717

◆ Imperative sentences make commands. They often contain an understood subject (you).

> Look at that scribbling. Consider what it says about our understanding and misuse of the freedom the statue stands for.

Exclamatory Sentence 718

◆ Exclamatory sentences communicate strong emotion or surprise.

> What! You're twelve years old and you don't understand! You're thirty years old and you don't care!

The Yellow Pages Guide to
Understanding Our Language

Do chickens have lips? Do snakes have shoulders? Does the English language have a way to make it easier to understand words and how to use them? Give up? The answers are maybe, maybe, and yes. We'll let you stew on the chicken and snake questions even though you probably think it's a fowl idea. Meanwhile, it might be handy for you to know that all words in the English language have been put into one of eight groups. (No, they're not called Miami Sound Machine or the Rolling Stones or the New Kids on the Block.)

These eight groups are called the **Parts of Speech,** and they can be heard at your favorite concert, on your favorite TV show, and they're even staring at you right now. Not only that, but they're reliable, trustworthy, and usually do just what you expect them to do. Each part of speech contains words which are used basically the same way in sentences. You can count on a drummer to play the drums, and you can count on a noun to act like a noun. Because words can be used in eight different ways, the **Parts of Speech** is an eight-member band featuring *noun, pronoun, verb, adjective, adverb, preposition, conjunction,* and *interjection.* Now let's check out each of the players and see what they do, what they say, how they move, and how they play.

Noun
719

A **noun** is a word which is the name of something: a person, place, thing, or idea.

> **Grandma Ulferts, uncle; Lake Michigan, river; "Star-Spangled Banner," song; Labor Day, holiday**

◆ A proper noun is the name of a specific person, place, thing, or idea. Proper nouns are always capitalized.

> **Sandra Day O'Connor, Fido, Grand Ole Opry, Corvette, Friday,** *Call of the Wild,* **North (meaning specific area of the country)**

◆ A common noun is any noun which does not name a specific person, place, thing, or idea. Common nouns are not capitalized.

> **child, country, rainbow, blockhead, winter, happiness, north (meaning direction)**

722 ....Concrete Noun
◆ A concrete noun names a thing that is tangible or physical (can be touched or seen). Concrete nouns are either proper or common.

> **Chevrolet, White House, car, guitar, drums, book, author,** *Back to the Future: Part XXVIII*

723 ....Abstract Noun
◆ An abstract noun names something you can think about but which you cannot see or touch. Abstract nouns are either common or proper.

> **Christianity, Judaism, satisfaction, poverty, illness, love, excellence, courage**

724 ....Collective Noun
◆ A collective noun names a *collection* of persons, animals, places, or things.

> **PERSONS** ....**tribe, congregation, class, team**
>
> **ANIMALS** ....**flock, herd, gaggle, clutch, litter**
>
> **PLACES**..............**United States, United Nations, Philippines**
>
> **THINGS** ....**batch, cluster, bunch**

Specific Nouns

Use specific nouns when you write—they add color and clarity.

See our display in "The Art of Writing" for additional tips and helpful hints.

THE NUMBER OF NOUNS

> Nouns are also grouped according to their **number**. The number of a noun tells us whether the noun is *singular* or *plural*.

Singular Noun 725
◆ A singular noun names one person, place, thing, or idea.

> **boy, stage, rock concert, group, audience**

Plural Noun 726
◆ A plural noun names more than one person, place, thing, or idea.

> **boys, stages, rock concerts, groups, audiences**

Compound Noun 727
◆ A compound noun is made up of two or more words.

> **football**
> [written as one word]
>
> **high school**
> [written as two words]
>
> **brother-in-law**
> [written as a hyphenated word]

THE GENDER OF NOUNS

> Nouns have **gender**; that is, they are grouped according to sex: *feminine, masculine, neuter,* and *indefinite*.

Types of Gender 728

> **FEMININE** .....**mother, hostess, women, cow, hen** [female]
>
> **MASCULINE** ....**uncle, brother, men, bull, rooster** [male]
>
> **NEUTER** ....**tree, cobweb, closet** [without sex]
>
> **INDEFINITE**.............**president, duckling, doctor, lawyer, assistant** [male or female]

THE USE OF NOUNS

> Nouns are also grouped according to where they are used and how they are related to the other words in the sentence: *subject, predicate, possessive, object.*

729 ....Subject Nouns

◆ A noun becomes the subject of a sentence when it does something or is being talked about.

> The guidance *counselor* looked the eighth-grade student in the eye and warned him, "The high school *principal* won't allow you to take more than one study hall."

730 ....Predicate Nouns

◆ A noun is also considered a predicate noun when it follows a form of the *be* verb *(is, are, was, were, been)* and repeats or renames the subject. In the examples below, *place* renames *study hall* and *waste* renames *hours.*

> "A *study hall* is a good *place* to work on your assignments, but two *hours* of study hall is a *waste* of your valuable time."

731.....................Possessive Nouns

◆ A noun becomes a possessive noun when it shows possession or ownership.

> The *student's* face showed concern. "But I need an *hour's* rest every day in order to do well in my classes."

732 ....Object Nouns

◆ A noun becomes an object noun when it is used as the direct object, the indirect object, or the object of the preposition.

> "Don't worry. You'll enjoy *high school* with only one study hall."
> [*High school* is a direct object.]

> "High school teachers give every *student* plenty of *time* to finish his or her assignments."
> [*Student* is an indirect object; *time* is the object of the preposition *of.*]

Pronoun
733

A **pronoun** is a word used in place of a noun.

> MOST COMMON.............I, you, he, she, it, we, they
>
> ADDITIONAL FORMS ....his, hers, her, its, me, myself, us, yours, etc.
>
> Amanda tweaked *her* uncle's nose after *he* teased the kids about *their* dancing to rock "noise."

Antecedent.................................734

◆ An antecedent is the noun which the pronoun refers to or replaces. All pronouns have antecedents.

> The *speaker* coughed and reached for the glass of water. When the glass reached his lips, he noticed a *fly* which was "swimming" in the water.
> [*Speaker* is the antecedent of *his* and *he; fly* is the antecedent of *which.*]

 All pronouns must agree with their antecedents in number, person, and gender. See "Problems with Pronouns," 098, for additional information.

PERSONAL PRONOUNS

735 .... Personal Pronouns

◆ Personal pronouns take the place of nouns in a sentence; they come in many shapes and sizes.

> SIMPLE ....I, you, he, she, it, we, they
>
> COMPOUND .... myself, yourself, himself, herself, ourselves
>
> PHRASAL.............one another, each other

NUMBER OF A PRONOUN

> Pronouns can be either singular or plural in **number**.

736 .... Singular/Plural Pronoun

> SINGULAR ....I, you, he, she, it
>
> PLURAL ....we, you, they

Notice that the pronouns *you, your,* and *yours* may be singular or plural.

PERSON OF A PRONOUN

> The **person** of a pronoun tells us whether the pronoun is speaking, being spoken to, or being spoken about.

First Person 737

◆ A first person pronoun is used in place of the name of the speaker.

> *I* am speaking.
>
> *We* are speaking.

Second Person 738

◆ A second person pronoun is used to name the person or thing spoken to.

> Eliza, will *you* please listen.
>
> *You* dogs better stop growling and listen, too.

Third Person 739

◆ A third person pronoun is used to name the person or thing spoken about.

> And *he* better listen if *he* ever wants to use the car again.

SINGULAR PRONOUNS

	Subject Pronouns	Possessive Pronouns	Object Pronouns
1st Person	I	my, mine	me
2nd Person	you	your, yours	you
3rd Person	he	his	him
	she	her, hers	her
	it	its	it

PLURAL PRONOUNS

	Subject Pronouns	Possessive Pronouns	Object Pronouns
1st Person	we	our, ours	us
2nd Person	you	your, yours	you
3rd Person	they	their, theirs	them

USE OF A PRONOUN

> A pronoun can be used as a subject, an object, or to show possession.

740 ....Subject Pronouns

◆ Subject pronouns are used as the subjects of a sentence *(I, you, he, she, it, we, they)*.

> *I* like myself when things go well.

◆ A subject pronoun is also used after a form of the *be* verb *(am, is, are, was, were, been)* if it repeats the subject.

> "It is *I*," growled the big wolf from under Grandmother's bonnet.

> "It is *he*!" shrieked Little Red as she twisted his snout into a corkscrew.

741 ....Possessive Pronouns

◆ A possessive pronoun shows possession or ownership. (*Note*: You do not use an apostrophe with a personal pronoun to show possession.)

> *my, mine, our, ours, his, her, hers, their, its, yours*

742......................Object Pronouns

◆ An object pronoun can be used as the object of a verb or preposition *(me, you, him, her, it, us, them)*.

> My five-year-old son hugged *me*. [*Me* is the direct object of the verb *hugged* because it receives the action of the verb.]

> My two-year-old son told *me* a story. [*Me* is the indirect object of the verb *told* because it indirectly receives the action of the verb.]

> Our one-year-old dog listened because the story was about *him*. [*Him* is the object of the preposition *about*.]

OTHER TYPES OF PRONOUNS

> In addition to the commonly used personal pronouns, there are several other types of pronouns. (See the chart on the next page.)

Reflexive Pronouns 743

◆ A reflexive pronoun is a pronoun which throws the action back upon the subject of a sentence.

> The young skunk never washed *himself.* [direct object]

> He never bought *himself* deodorant. [indirect object]

> He was never unhappy about *himself.* [object of the preposition]

Note: These sentences would *not* be complete without the reflexive pronouns.

Intensive Pronoun 744

◆ An intensive pronoun intensifies or emphasizes the noun or pronoun it refers to.

> He, *himself,* decided to stink . . . and to smile about it.

Note: The sentence *would be complete* without its intensive pronoun.

Relative Pronoun 745

◆ A relative pronoun is both a pronoun and a connecting word. It connects a subordinate clause to the main clause.

> *Candid Camera* once showed a horse *that appeared to be able to talk.* [*that* relates to *horse*]

> An actor, *who was hidden in the horse's stall*, did the talking. [*who* relates to *actor*]

> A woman, *who stopped to reply to the horse's greeting,* solemnly wrote down the betting tips *that he gave her.* [*who* relates to *woman*; *that* relates to *tips*]

746 ....Indefinite Pronoun

◆ An indefinite pronoun is a pronoun that does not specifically name its antecedent (the noun or pronoun it replaces).

> While we were fishing, *somebody* made me a sardine sandwich.
>
> The "sardines" wiggled in my sandwich, and *anybody* could see there were fewer minnows in the minnow pail.

 For more information on indefinite pronouns, see the chart below. Also see 096 for details on using indefinite pronouns properly in a sentence.

747 ....Interrogative Pronoun

◆ An interrogative pronoun asks a question.

> "*Who* is here, and *what* do you want?" asked my friend from inside the door.
>
> "*Whose* friendly voice is rattling this door with such unfriendly questions?" I replied.

Demonstrative Pronoun 748

◆ A demonstrative pronoun points out or identifies a noun without naming the noun. When used together in a sentence, *this* and *that* distinguish one item from another, and *these* and *those* distinguish one group from another.

> *This* was a wonderful experience; *that* was a nightmare.

Caution: To add *here* or *there* to a demonstrative pronoun is **incorrect**.

> The little girl pointed to the candy and said, "Now *this here* is yours, and *that there* is mine."

KINDS OF PRONOUNS

Relative
who, whose, which, what, that, whoever, whatever, whichever

Demonstrative
this, that, these, those

Interrogative
who, whose, whom, which, what

Intensive and Reflexive
myself, himself, herself, yourself, themselves, ourselves

Indefinite Pronouns

all	both	everything	nobody	several
another	each	few	none	some
any	each one	many	no one	somebody
anybody	either	most	nothing	someone
anyone	everybody	much	one	something
anything	everyone	neither	other	such

Verb

749

A **verb** is a word which expresses action or existence (state of being).

> **Stevie Wonder** *hosted* **the show.** [action]
>
> **Many famous people** *joined* **him on stage.** [action]
>
> **They** *were* **present to honor Dr. Martin Luther King, Jr.** [existence]

THE NUMBER OF A VERB

> Verbs have **number** which means they are *singular* (one) or *plural* (more than one). The number of a verb depends on the number of its subject. A singular subject needs a singular verb, and a plural subject needs a plural verb.

750 .... Singular Verbs

◆ A singular subject needs a singular verb.

> **In 1963, the Berlin Wall** *stood* **as a new symbol of communism's strength.** [singular]
>
> **Today it** *stands* **in pieces as a new symbol of communism's weakness.** [Notice that *stands*, with an "s," is singular.]

Plural Verbs 751

◆ A plural subject needs a plural verb.

> **In 1963, two ten-year-old girls** *were* **pushed apart by the wall.** [plural]
>
> **Today, the thirty-seven-year-old women** *stand* **together on top of it.** [Notice that *stand*, without an "s," is plural.]

THE PERSON OF A VERB

Point of View 752

◆ Verbs will also differ in form depending upon the point of view or *person* of the pronouns being used with them: **first person** *(I)*, **second person** *(you)*, and **third person** *(he, she, it)*. [See chart below.]

THE VOICE OF A VERB

> The **voice** of a verb tells you whether the subject is doing the action or is receiving the action.

Active Voice 753

◆ A verb is in the active voice if the subject is doing the action in a sentence.

> **The** *baseball hit* **the batter.**

Passive Voice 754

◆ A verb is in the **passive voice** if the subject is receiving the action or not personally doing the action.

> **The** *batter was hit* **by the baseball.**

Point of View	Singular	Plural
1st Person	I sniff	we sniff
2nd Person	you sniff	you sniff
3rd Person	he/she/it *sniffs*	they sniff

THE TENSE OF A VERB

> A verb has three principal parts: the **present, past,** and **past participle.** All six of the tenses are formed from these principal parts. The past and past participle of regular verbs are formed by adding *-ed* to the present form. (See the chart on the next page.)

755 ....Present Tense

◆ A verb is in the **present tense** when it expresses action (or existence) which is happening *now* or which happens *continually, regularly.*

> My stomach *tightens* into a knot sometimes.
>
> My breaths *are* shorter, and my palms *sweat.*

756 ....Past Tense

◆ A verb is in the **past tense** when it expresses action (or existence) which is completed at a *particular* time in the past.

> Yesterday my stomach tightened into a knot, and my palms "perspired" before the game.

Future Tense 757

■ A verb is in the **future tense** when it expresses action that *will* take place.

> Anxiety *will visit* you too some day, and he *will be* tough! But you *will be* tougher.

Present Perfect Tense 758

■ A verb is in the **present perfect tense** when it expresses action which *began in the past* but *continues* or *is completed in the present.* (To form the present perfect tense, add *has* or *have* to the past participle.)

> She *has screamed* at her friends many times, and they *have ignored* it.

Past Perfect Tense 759

■ A verb is in the **past perfect tense** when it expresses action which *began in the past* and *was completed in the past.* (To form the past perfect tense, add *had* to the past participle.)

> Then, last Friday at the Pizza Hut, they *had eaten* more than their share of the pizza, and she *had called* them "greedy pigs."

TENSE	ACTIVE VOICE		PASSIVE VOICE	
	Singular	Plural	Singular	Plural
Present Tense	I find	we find	I am found	we are found
	you find	you find	you are found	you are found
	he/she/it finds	they find	he/she/it is found	they are found
Past Tense	I found	we found	I was found	we were found
	you found	you found	you were found	you were found
	he found	they found	he was found	they were found
Future Tense	I shall find	we shall find	I shall be found	we shall be found
	you will find	you will find	you will be found	you will be found
	he will find	they will find	he will be found	they will be found
Present Perfect	I have found	we have found	I have been found	we have been found
	you have found	you have found	you have been found	you have been found
	he has found	they have found	he has been found	they have been found
Past Perfect	I had found	we had found	I had been found	we had been found
	you had found	you had found	you had been found	you had been found
	he had found	they had found	he had been found	they had been found
Future Perfect	I shall have found	we shall have found	I shall have been found	we shall have been found
	you will have found	you will have found	you will have been found	you will have been found
	he will have found	they will have found	he will have been found	they will have been found

760 ....Future Perfect Tense

■ A verb is in the **future perfect tense** when it expresses action or existence which *will begin in the future* and *will be completed by a specific time in the future*. (To form the future perfect tense, add *shall have* or *will have* to the past participle.)

> By next Friday, she *will have* forgotten the pizza, but they *will have remembered* the name-calling.

HELPING/AUXILIARY VERBS

761..........................Helping Verbs

◆ **Helping verbs** *help* to form some of the tenses and voice of the main verb. (Helping verbs are also called *auxiliary verbs.)*

> Elmer *was* using super-strength, slow-drying glue. For ten minutes he *had been* holding the two broken parts together. He *should have* bought a C-clamp for a glue job like this.

> **Common helping verbs are these:** *shall, will, could, would, should, must, can, may, have, had, has, do, did,* and the forms of the verb *be—is, are, was, were, am, been.*

TRANSITIVE VERBS

Transitive Verbs 762

◆ **Transitive verbs** are verbs which *transfer* their action to an object. An object must receive the action of a transitive verb for the meaning of the verb to be complete.

> **The earthquake *shook* San Francisco with a fury.** [*Note: Shook* transfers its action to *San Francisco.* Without the word *San Francisco* the meaning of the verb *shook* is incomplete.]

> **San Francisco *was shaken* by the earthquake.** [*Note:* The subject of the sentence, *San Francisco,* receives the action of the verb, *was shaken.*]

Common Irregular Verbs and Their Principal Parts

Present Tense	Past Tense	Past Participle	Present Tense	Past Tense	Past Participle	Present Tense	Past Tense	Past Participle
am, be	was, were	been	fly	flew	flown	shine		
begin	began	begun	forsake	forsook	forsaken	(light)	shone	shone
bid (offer)	bid	bid	freeze	froze	frozen	(polish)	shined	shined
bid (order)	bade	bidden	give	gave	given	shrink	shrank	shrunk
bite	bit	bitten	go	went	gone	sing	sang, sung	sung
blow	blew	blown	grow	grew	grown	sink	sank, sunk	sunk
break	broke	broken	hang			sit	sat	sat
bring	brought	brought	(execute)	hanged	hanged	slay	slew	slain
burst	burst	burst	(dangle)	hung	hung	speak	spoke	spoken
catch	caught	caught	hide	hid	hidden, hid	spring	sprang, sprung	sprung
come	came	come	know	knew	known	steal	stole	stolen
dive	dived	dived	lay	laid	laid	strive	strove	striven
do	did	done	lead	led	led	swear	swore	sworn
drag	dragged	dragged	lie (recline)	lay	lain	swim	swam	swum
draw	drew	drawn	lie (deceive)	lied	lied	swing	swung	swung
drink	drank	drunk	raise	raised	raised	take	took	taken
drown	drowned	drowned	ride	rode	ridden	tear	tore	torn
drive	drove	driven	ring	rang	rung	throw	threw	thrown
eat	ate	eaten	rise	rose	risen	wake	woke, waked	waked
fall	fell	fallen	run	ran	run	wear	wore	worn
fight	fought	fought	see	saw	seen	weave	wove	woven
flee	fled	fled	set	set	set	wring	wrung	wrung
flow	flowed	flowed	shake	shook	shaken	write	wrote	written

◆ A transitive verb throws the action directly to a **direct object** and indirectly to an **indirect object.** For a sentence to have an indirect object, it must have a direct object. A sentence can, however, have only a direct object. (Direct objects and indirect objects are always nouns or pronouns.)

> **My teacher wanted my *essay.*** [direct object: *essay*]

> **But I didn't write *one.*** [direct object: *one*]

> **So I gave *her* a big *smile* instead.** [indirect object: *her*; direct object: *smile*]

> **And she gave *me* an "*F.*"** [indirect object: *me*; direct object: "*F*"]

763 ....Direct Object

◆ The direct object is the noun or pronoun which receives the action directly from the subject. (The direct object answers the question *what* or *whom?*)

> **After class I wrote a *note.*** [*Note* is the direct object; it answers the question, "I wrote a *what?*"]

764 ....Indirect Object

◆ An **indirect object** is the noun or pronoun which receives the action of a transitive verb, *indirectly.* An indirect object names the person *to whom* or *for whom* something is done.

> **After class I wrote *her* a note.** [*Her* is the indirect object because it names the person to whom the note was written.]

◆ When the indirect object follows a preposition, it becomes the object of the preposition, and is no longer considered an indirect object.

> **After class I wrote a note *to her.*** [*Her* is the object of the preposition *to.*]

INTRANSITIVE VERBS

Intransitive Verb 765

◆ An **intransitive verb** completes its action without an object.

> **I *apologized* for my late assignment.** [*Assignment* is the object of the preposition *for;* there is no direct object.]

> **Then I *explained* about my sore toe.** [Again, *toe* is the object of the preposition *about*; there is no direct object.]

Special Verbs. 766

◆ Many verbs can be either **transitive** or **intransitive.**

> **She *read* my note.** [transitive]

> **She *read* about my toe.** [intransitive]

Linking Verb 767

◆ A linking verb *links* a subject to a noun or adjective in the predicate. Because it does not express an action, a linking verb is intransitive.

> **Apologies *are* wonderful.** [*Wonderful* is a predicate adjective because it is linked by the verb *are* to the subject *apologies.*]

> **But my explanation *was* a failure. A sore toe *is* a lousy excuse.** [*Failure* is a predicate noun because it is linked by the verb *was* to the subject *explanation. Excuse* is a predicate noun because it is linked by the verb *is* to the subject *toe.*]

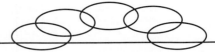

The most **common linking verbs** are forms of the verb *be— is, are, was, were, been, am* —and verbs such as *smell, look, taste, remain, feel, appear, sound, seem, become, grow, stand, turn.*

VERBAL

A **verbal** is a word which is made from a verb, has the power of a verb, but acts as another part of speech. Verbals can be **gerunds, participles,** and **infinitives.**

768 ....Gerund

◆ A **gerund** is a verb form which ends in -*ing* and is used as a noun.

> **Smoking** rots your lungs. [The noun *smoking* is the subject.]
>
> You should quit *smoking*. [The noun *smoking* is the direct object.]

769 ....Participle

◆ A **participle** is a verb form ending in -*ing* or -*ed*. A participle functions as an adjective.

> Those kids *digging* for China are already tired. Those *tired* kids will probably lose interest before they make it. [*Digging* and *tired* modify *kids.*]

770 ....Infinitive

◆ An **infinitive** is a verb form introduced by *to*; it may be used as a *noun, adjective,* or *adverb.*

> **To scream** in class was her secret wish. [The noun, *to scream*, is the subject.]
>
> But the last student *to scream* was sent away. [*To scream* is an adjective modifying *student.*]

Adjective
771

An **adjective** is a word used to describe a noun or pronoun.

> Why did *ancient* dinosaurs become *an extinct* species?
>
> Were they wiped out by *a catastrophic* flood or *a deadly* epidemic?

Articles 772

◆ The articles *a, an,* and *the* are adjectives.

> *A* brontosaurus was *an* animal about seventy feet long.
>
> *The* huge dinosaur lived on land and ate plants.

Proper Adjective 773

◆ A **proper adjective** is formed from a proper noun, and it is always capitalized.

> The *Chicago* museum is home to a skeleton of one of these ancient beasts. [*Chicago* functions as a proper adjective describing the noun *museum*.]

SCHOOL DAZE

Who can give me an example of a **gerund** used as a subject?

Hanging upside down refreshes my brain.

774.................Common Adjective

◆ A **common adjective** is any adjective which is not proper, and it is not capitalized (unless it is the first word in a sentence).

> *The mammoth* critter peers down at *tiny* thieves, daring them to mess with *his* home. [Notice that the pronoun *his* functions as a common adjective.]

SPECIAL TYPES OF ADJECTIVES

775 ....Compound Adjective

◆ A **compound adjective** is made up of more than one word. (Sometimes it is hyphenated.)

> *Scar-faced* Bronty is no *scarecrow* guard. The big guy finds *knee-high* thugs no more threatening than *wide-eyed* kids.

776 ....Demonstrative Adjective

◆ A demonstrative adjective is one which points out a particular noun. Common demonstrative adjectives are *this* and *these* (which point out something nearby) and *that* and *those* (which point out something at a distance).

> *This* kitten is mean, but *that* cat is meaner.

Note: When a noun does not follow *this, these, that,* or *those,* they are pronouns, not adjectives.

777 ....Indefinite Adjective

◆ An **indefinite adjective** is one which gives us an approximate number or quantity. It does not tell *exactly* how many or how much. (See *indefinite pronoun.*)

> *Some* cats enjoy having *many* mice around so there are *more* choices on the menu. A menu with *fewer* choices frustrates cats.

Predicate Adjective 778

◆ A **predicate adjective** is an adjective which follows a linking verb and describes the subject.

> A frustrated kitten is *unpleasant.* [*unpleasant* kitten]

> But frustrated cats are *dangerous.* [*dangerous* cats]

THE FORMS OF ADJECTIVES

Positive Form 779

◆ The **positive form** describes a noun or pronoun without comparing it to anyone or anything else.

> Superman is *tough.*

> Superman is *wonderful.*

Comparative Form 780

◆ The **comparative form** (*-er*) compares two persons, places, things, or ideas.

> Tarzan is *tougher* than Superman.

> Tarzan is *more wonderful* than Superman.

Superlative Form 781

◆ The **superlative form** (*-est*) compares three or more persons, places, things, or ideas.

> But I, Big Bird, am the *toughest* of all!

> But I, Big Bird, am the *most wonderful* of all!

Two-Syllable Adjective 782

◆ Some adjectives which are *two or more syllables long* show comparisons either by their *er/est* suffixes, or by modifiers like *more* and *most.*

> For example, you may say, "*clumsy, clumsier, clumsiest.*"

> But, you may also say, "*clumsy, more clumsy, most clumsy.*"

783 ....Three- (or More)
Syllable Adjective

◆ When adjectives are three or more syllables long, they usually require the words *more/most, less/least* to express comparison.

| **ridiculous, less ridiculous, least ridiculous.**

Note: You would NOT say, "ridiculous, ridiculousless, ridiculousleast."

784 ....Exceptions

◆ Some adjectives use completely different words to express comparison.

| **good, better, best**
| **bad, worse, worst**

Adverb

785

An **adverb** is a word used to modify a verb, an adjective, or another adverb. An adverb tells *how, when, where, why, how often,* and *how much.*

| **Dad snores *loudly*.** [*Loudly* modifies the verb *snores*.]

| **His snores are *really* explosive.** [*Really* modifies the adjective *explosive*.]

| **Dad snores *very* loudly.** [*Very* modifies the adverb *loudly*.]

"ly" Endings **786**

◆ Adverbs often end in *-ly*, but not always. Words like *very, quite,* and *always* are adverbs also, modifying other adverbs or adjectives.

Caution: Not all words ending in *-ly* are adverbs. A word like "lovely" is an adjective.

❖ **TIME** — Adverbs of time tell *when, how often,* and *how long.*

| **tomorrow, often, never**

❖ **PLACE** — Adverbs of place tell *where, to where,* or *from where.*

| **there, backward, outside**

❖ **MANNER** — Adverbs of manner often end in *-ly* and tell *how* something is done.

| **unkindly, gently, well**

Note: Some adverbs can be written with or without the *-ly* ending. When in doubt, use the *-ly* form.

| **slow, slowly; deep, deeply; quick, quickly**

❖ **DEGREE** — Adverbs of degree tell *how much* or *how little.*

| **scarcely, entirely, generally**

Forms of Adverbs **787**

◆ Adverbs, like adjectives, have three forms: **positive, comparative,** and **superlative.** (See the chart below.)

 Do not confuse *good* and *well*. *Good* is an adjective; *well* is usually an adverb. (See 624.)

Positive	Comparative	Superlative
well	better	best
badly	worse	worst
fast	faster	fastest
loudly	more loudly	most loudly
dramatically	less dramatically	least dramatically

Preposition
788

A **preposition** is a word (or group of words) which shows how two words or ideas arc related to each other. Specifically, a preposition shows the relationship between its object (a noun or a pronoun that follows the preposition) and some other word in the sentence.

> **The caterpillar hung *under* Natasha's nose.** [*Under* shows the relationship between the verb, *hung*, and the object of the preposition, *nose*.]

789 .... Prepositional Phrase
◆ A prepositional phrase includes the *preposition*, the *object* of the preposition, and the *modifiers* of the object.

> **Little kids often run *away from* big caterpillars.** [preposition: *away from*—object: *caterpillars*—modifier: *big*]

◆ A prepositional phrase may function as an adjective or as an adverb.

> **But little kids *with wiggly mustaches* enjoy the hairy critters.** [The prepositional phrase, *with wiggly mustaches,* functions as an adjective and modifies *kids*.]

Object of Preposition 790
◆ A preposition never appears alone—it needs an object. If a word found in the list of prepositions appears in a sentence, but has no object, it is not a preposition. It is probably an adverb.

> **Natasha never had a mustache *before*.** [*Before* is used as an adverb in this sentence because it modifies *had*, a verb.]

LIST OF PREPOSITIONS

aboard	at	despite	in regard to	opposite	throughout
about	away from	down	in spite of	out	till
above	back of	down from	inside	out of	to
according to	because of	during	inside of	outside	together with
across	before	except	instead of	outside of	toward
across from	behind	exept for	into	over	under
after	below	excepting	like	over to	underneath
against	beneath	for	near	owing to	until
along	beside	from	near to	past	unto
alongside	besides	from among	notwithstanding	prior	up
alongside of	between	from between	of	regarding	up to
along with	beyond	from under	off	round	upon
amid	but	in	on	round about	with
among	by	in addition to	on account of	save	within
apart from	by means of	in behalf of	on behalf of	since	without
around	concerning	in front of	on top of	subsequent to	
aside from	considering	in place of	onto	through	

Interjection

791

An **interjection** is a word or phrase used to express strong emotion or surprise. Punctuation (usually an exclamation point) is used to separate an interjection from the rest of the sentence.

> **Wow! Would you look at that!**
>
> **Oh, no! He actually did it!**

Conjunction

792

A **conjunction** connects individual words or groups of words. There are three kinds of conjunctions: *coordinate, correlative,* and *subordinate*.

> **A puffer fish is short *and* fat.** [The conjunction *and* connects the word *short* to the word *fat*.]

Coordinate Conjunction 793

◆ A coordinate conjunction connects a word to a word, a phrase to a phrase, or a clause to a clause. The words, phrases, or clauses joined by a coordinate conjunction must be *equal* or of the *same type*.

> **A puffer rarely worries *about calories* or *about dieting*.** [Two equal phrases are connected by *or*.]
>
> **He simply *puts his lips on a snail* and *sucks out his next meal*.** [The conjunction *and* connects the phrase *puts his lips on a snail* to the phrase *sucks out his next meal*.]

Correlative Conjunction 794

◆ Correlative conjunctions are conjunctions used in pairs.

> ***Neither* pickles *nor* sauerkraut should be put on a chocolate sundae.**

Subordinate Conjunction......795

◆ A subordinate conjunction is a word or group of words that connects two clauses which are *not* equally important. A subordinate conjunction connects a dependent clause to an independent clause in order to complete the meaning of the dependent clause.

> **A chocolate sundae tastes best *when* it is topped with chopped nuts.** [The clause, *when it is topped with chopped nuts,* is dependent. It cannot stand alone.]

KINDS OF CONJUNCTIONS

Coordinate: and, but, or, nor, for, yet

Correlative: either, or; neither, nor; not only, but also; both, and; whether, or; just, as; just, so; as, so

Subordinate: after, although, as, as if, as long as, as though, because, before, if, in order that, provided that, since, so, so that, that, though, till, unless, until, when, where, whereas, while

Note: **Relative pronouns** and **conjunctive adverbs** can also connect clauses.

The Student Almanac

Tables and Lists

The **tables, charts,** and **lists** which follow should be both interesting to use and helpful to have at your fingertips. Everything from "Animal Crackers" to the "Periodic Table of the Elements" is worth knowing and may be expected of you in some class at some time. We hope the variety of information is both useful and fun.

Animal Crackers

Animal	Male	Female	Young	Collective	Gestation	Longevity
Ass	Jack	Jenny	Foal	Herd	340-385	18-20 (63)*
Bear	He-bear	She-bear	Cub	Sleuth	180-240	18-20 (34)
Cat	Tom	Queen	Kitten	Clutter/Clowder	52-65	10-12 (27)
Cattle	Bull	Cow	Calf	Drove/Herd	280	9-12 (25)
Chicken	Rooster	Hen	Chick	Brood/Clutch	21	7-8 (14)
Deer	Buck	Doe	Fawn	Herd	140-250	10-15 (26)
Dog	Dog	Bitch	Pup	Pack	55-70	10-12 (24)
Duck	Drake	Duck	Duckling	Brace/Herd	21-35	10 (15)
Elephant	Bull	Cow	Calf	Herd	515-760	30-40 (98)
Fox	Dog	Vixen	Cub/Kit	Skulk	51-60	8-10 (14)
Goat	Billy	Nanny	Kid	Tribe, Trip	135-163	12 (17)
Goose	Gander	Goose	Gosling	Flock/Gaggle	30	
Horse	Stallion	Mare	Filly/Colt	Herd	304-419	20-25 (50+)
Lion	Lion	Lioness	Cub	Pride	105-111	10 (29)
Monkey	Male	Female	Boy/Girl	Band/Troop	149-179	12-15 (29)
Rabbit	Buck	Doe	Bunny		27-36	6-8 (15)
Sheep	Ram	Ewe	Lamb	Flock/Drove	121-180	12 (16)
Swan	Cob	Pen	Cygnet	Bevy	30	
Swine	Boar	Sow	Piglet	Litter	101-130	10 (15)
Tiger	Tiger	Tigress	Cub		105	19
Whale	Bull	Cow	Calf	Gam/Pod	276-365	37
Wolf	Dog	Bitch	Pup	Pack	63	10-12 (16)

* ( ) Record for oldest animal of this type

Manual Alphabet (Sign Language)

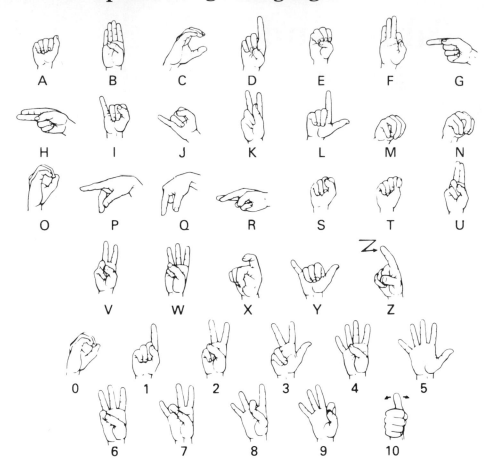

Braille Alphabet and Braille Numbers

a	b	c	d	e	f	g	h	i	j
1	2	3	4	5	6	7	8	9	0

k	l	m	n	o	p	q	r	s	t

u	v	w	x	y	z	Capital Sign	Numeral Sign

International Radio Alphabet and Morse Code

1: ·————	period: ·—·—·—	A: Alpha ·—
2: ··———	comma: ——··——	B: Bravo —···
3: ···——	question mark: ··——··	C: Charlie —·—·
4: ····—	semicolon: —·—·—·	D: Delta —··
5: ·····	colon: ———···	E: Echo ·
6: —····	hyphen: —····—	F: Foxtrot ··—·
7: ——···	apostrophe: ·————·	G: Golf ——·
8: ———··		H: Hotel ····
9: ————·		I: India ··
10: —————		J: Juliet ·———

R: Romeo ·—·
S: Sierra ···
T: Tango —
U: Uniform ··—
V: Victor ···—
W: Whiskey ·——
X: X-ray —··—
Y: Yankee —·——
Z: Zulu ——··

K: Kilo —·—
L: Lima (leema) ·—··
M: Mike ——
N: November —·
O: Oscar ———
P: Papa ·——·
Q: Quebec (kaybec) ——·—

How to Write in Cuneiform

A		N	
B		O	
C		P	
D		Q	
E		R	
F		S	
G		T	
H		U	
I		V	
J		W	
K		X	
L		Y	
M		Z	

Semaphore Code

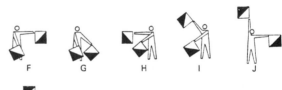

A   B   C   D   E

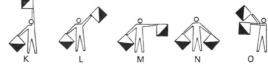

F   G   H   I   J

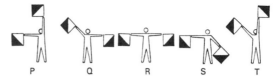

K   L   M   N   O

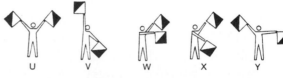

P   Q   R   S   T

U   V   W   X   Y

Z   ATTENTION   INTERVAL   NUMERAL

803 The Metric System

Linear Measure

1 centimeter	= 10 millimeters	= 0.3937 inch
1 decimeter	= 10 centimeters	= 3.937 inches
1 meter	= 10 decimeters	= 39.37 inches or 3.28 feet
1 decameter	= 10 meters	= 393.7 inches
1 hectometer	= 10 decameters	= 328 feet 1 inch
1 kilometer	= 10 hectometers	= 0.621 mile
1 myriameter	= 10 kilometers	= 6.21 miles

Square Measure

1 square centimeter	= 10 square millimeters	= 0.15499 square inch
1 square decimeter	= 100 square centimeters	= 15.499 square inches
1 square meter	= 100 square decimeters	= 1,549.9 sq. inches or 1.196 sq. yards
1 square decameter	= 100 square meters	= 119.6 square yards
1 square hectometer	= 100 square decameters	= 2.471 acres
1 square kilometer	= 100 square hectometers	= 0.386 square mile

Capacity Measure

1 centiliter	= 10 milliliters	= 0.338 fluid ounce
1 deciliter	= 10 centiliters	= 3.38 fluid ounces
1 liter	= 10 deciliters	= 1.0567 liquid qts. or 0.9081 dry qt.
1 decaliter	= 10 liters	= 2.64 gallons or 0.284 bushel
1 hectoliter	= 10 decaliters	= 26.418 gallons or 2.838 bushels
1 kiloliter	= 10 hectoliters	= 264.18 gallons or 35.315 cubic feet

Land Measure

1 centare	= 1 square meter	= 1,549.9 square inches
1 are	= 100 centares	= 119.6 square yards
1 hectare	= 100 ares	= 2,471 acres
1 square kilometer	= 100 hectares	= 0.386 square mile

Volume Measure

1 cubic centimeter	= 1,000 cubic millimeters	= .06102 cubic inch
1 cubic decimeter	= 1,000 cubic centimeters	= 61.02 cubic inches
1 cubic meter	= 1,000 cubic decimeters	= 35.314 cubic feet

Weights

1 centigram	= 10 milligrams	= 0.1543 grain
1 decigram	= 10 centigrams	= 1.5432 grains
1 gram	= 10 decigrams	= 15,432 grains
1 decagram	= 10 grams	= 0.3527 ounce
1 hectogram	= 10 decagrams	= 3.5274 ounces
1 kilogram	= 10 hectograms	= 2.2046 pounds
1 myriagram	= 10 kilograms	= 22.046 pounds
1 quintal	= 10 myriagrams	= 220.46 pounds
1 metric ton	= 10 quintals	= 2,204.6 pounds

804   In 1975, the United States signed the **Metric Conversion Act**, declaring a national policy of encouraging voluntary use of the metric system. Today, the metric system exists side by side with the U.S. customary system. The debate on whether the United States should adopt the metric system has been going on for nearly 200 years, leaving the United States the only country in the world not totally committed to adopting the system.

The metric system is considered a simpler form of measurement. It is based on the decimal system (units of ten) and eliminates the need to deal with fractions as we currently use them.

Handy Conversion Factors

To change	to	multiply by
acres	hectares	0.4047
acres	square feet	43,560
acres	square miles	.001562
Celsius	Fahrenheit	*9/5
*(Multiply Celsius by 9/5; then add 32)		
centimeters	inches	0.3937
centimeters	feet	.03281
cubic meters	cubic feet	35.3145
cubic meters	cubic yards	1.3079
cubic yards	cubic meters	0.7646
degrees	radians	.01745
Fahrenheit	Celsius	*5/9
*(Multiply Fahrenheit by 5/9 after subtracting 32)		
feet	meters	0.3048
feet	miles (nautical)	.0001645
feet	miles (statute)	.0001894
feet/sec.	miles/hr.	0.6818
furlongs	feet	660.0
furlongs	miles	0.125
gallons (U.S.)	liters	3.7853
grains	grams	0.648
grams	grains	15.4324
grams	ounces avdp.	.0353
grams	pounds	.002205
hectares	acres	2.4710
horsepower	watts	745.7
hours	days	.04167
inches	millimeters	25.4000
inches	centimeters	2.5400
kilograms	pounds avdp. or t.	2.2046
kilometers	miles	0.6214
kilowatts	horsepower	1.341
knots	nautical miles/hr.	1.0
knots	statute miles/hr.	1.151
liters	gallons (U.S.)	0.2642
liters	pecks	0.1135
liters	pints (dry)	1.8162
liters	pints (liquid)	2.1134
liters	quarts (dry)	0.9081

To change	to	multiply by
liters	quarts (liquid)	1.0567
meters	feet	3.2808
meters	miles	.0006214
meters	yards	1.0936
metric tons	tons (long)	0.9842
metric tons	tons (short)	1.1023
miles	kilometers	1.6093
miles	feet	5,280
miles (nautical)	miles (statute)	1.1516
miles (statute)	miles (nautical)	0.8684
miles/hr.	feet/min.	88
millimeters	inches	.0394
ounces avdp.	grams	28.3495
ounces	pounds	.0625
ounces (troy)	ounces (avdp.)	1.09714
pecks	liters	8.8096
pints (dry)	liters	0.5506
pints (liquid)	liters	1.4732
pounds ap. or t.	kilograms	0.3782
pounds avdp.	kilograms	0.4536
pounds	ounces	16
quarts (dry)	liters	1.1012
quarts (liquid)	liters	0.9463
rods	meters	5.029
rods	feet	16.5
square feet	square meters	.0929
square kilometers	square miles	0.3861
square meters	square feet	10.7639
square meters	square yards	1.1960
square miles	square kilometers	2.5900
square yards	square meters	0.8361
tons (long)	metric tons	1.1060
tons (short)	metric tons	0.9072
tons (long)	pounds	2,240
tons (short)	pounds	2,000
watts	BTU/hr.	3.4129
watts	horsepower	.001341
yards	meters	0.9144
yards	miles	.0005682

Ten Ways to Measure When You Don't Have a Ruler

1. Use the rulers printed on the inside covers of this handbook.
2. Floor tiles are usually manufactured in 12-inch by 12-inch squares.
3. U.S. paper currency is 6-1/8 inches long by 2-5/8 inches wide.
4. The diameter of a quarter is approximately 1 inch, and the diameter of a penny is approximately three-quarters of an inch.
5. A standard sheet of paper is 8-1/2 inches wide and 11 inches long.

Each of the following five items can be used as a measuring device by multiplying its length by the number of times it is used to measure an area in question.

6. A shoelace   7. A tie   8. A belt
9. Your feet—placing one in front of the other to measure floor area
10. Your outstretched arms from fingertip to fingertip

Table of Weights and Measures

Linear Measure (Length or Distance)

1 inch		=	2.54 centimeters
1 foot	= 12 inches	=	0.3048 meter
1 yard	= 3 feet	=	0.9144 meter
1 rod (or pole or perch)	= 5-1/2 yards or 16-1/2 feet	=	5.029 meters
1 furlong	= 40 rods	=	201.17 meters
1 (statute) mile	= 8 furlongs or 1,760 yards or 5,280 feet	=	1,609.3 meters
1 (land) league	= 3 miles	=	4.83 kilometers

Square Measure (Area)

1 square inch		=	6.452 square centimeters
1 square foot	= 144 square inches	=	929 square centimeters
1 square yard	= 9 square feet	=	0.8361 square meter
1 square rod	= 30-1/4 square yards	=	25.29 square meters
1 acre	= 160 square rods or 4,840 sq. yards or 43,560 square feet	=	0.4047 hectare
1 square mile	= 640 acres	=	259 hectares or 2.59 sq. kilometers

Cubic Measure

1 cubic inch		=	16.387 cubic centimeters
1 cubic foot	= 1,728 cubic inches	=	0.0283 cubic meter
1 cubic yard	= 27 cubic feet	=	0.7646 cubic meter
1 cord foot	= 16 cubic feet		
1 cord	= 8 cord feet	=	3.625 cubic meters

Chain Measure
(Gunter's or surveyor's chain)

1 link	= 7.92 inches	=	20.12 centimeters
1 chain	= 100 links or 66 feet	=	20.12 meters
1 furlong	= 10 chains	=	201.17 meters
1 mile	= 80 chains	=	1,609.3 meters

(Engineer's chain)

1 link	= 1 foot	=	0.3048 meter
1 chain	= 100 feet	=	30.48 meters
1 mile	= 52.8 chains	=	1,609.3 meters

Surveyor's (Square) Measure

1 square pole	= 625 square links	=	25.29 square meters
1 square chain	= 16 square poles	=	404.7 square meters
1 acre	= 10 square chains	=	0.4047 hectare
1 square mile or 1 section	= 640 acres	=	259 hectares or 2.59 sq. kilometers
1 township	= 36 square miles	=	9,324 hectares or 93.24 sq. kilometers

Nautical Measure

1 fathom	= 6 feet	=	1.829 meters
1 cable's length (ordinary)	= 100 fathoms		

(In the U.S. Navy 120 fathoms or 720 feet = 1 cable's length;
in the British Navy 608 feet = 1 cable's length)

1 nautical mile (6,076.10333 ft. by international agreement in 1954)	= 10 cables' length	=	1.852 kilometers

1.1508 statute miles (length
of a minute of longitude at the equator) .... 1 nautical mile

1 marine league (3.45 statute miles)	= 3 nautical miles	=	5.56 kilometers

1 degree of a great circle of the earth .... 60 nautical miles

Dry Measure

1 pint		= 33.60 cubic inches	=	0.5505 liter
1 quart	= 2 pints	= 67.20 cubic inches	=	1.1012 liters
1 peck	= 8 quarts	= 537.61 cubic inches	=	8.8096 liters
1 bushel	= 4 pecks	= 2,150.42 cubic inches	=	35.2383 liters

Liquid Measure

4 fluid ounces	= 1 gill	= 7.219 cubic inches	=	0.1183 liter
(see next table)				
1 pint	= 4 gills	= 28.875 cubic inches	=	0.4732 liter
1 quart	= 2 pints	= 57.75 cubic inches	=	0.9463 liter
1 gallon	= 4 quarts	= 231 cubic inches	=	3.7853 liters

Apothecaries' Fluid Measure

1 minim		= 0.0038 cubic inch	= 0.0616 milliliter
1 fluid dram	= 60 minims	= 0.2256 cubic inch	= 3.6966 milliliters
1 fluid ounce	= 8 fluid drams	= 1.8047 cubic inches	= 0.0296 liter
1 pint	= 16 fluid ounces	= 28.875 cubic inches	= 0.4732 liter

Circular (or Angular) Measure

60 seconds (")	=	1 minute (')
60 minutes	=	1 degree (°)
90 degrees	=	1 quadrant or 1 right angle
4 quadrants or 360 degrees	=	1 circle

Avoirdupois Weight

(The grain, equal to 0.0648 gram, is the same in all three tables of weight)

1 dram or 27.3 grains	=	1.772 grams
1 ounce	= 16 drams or 437.5 grains	= 28.3495 grams
1 pound	= 16 ounces or 7,000 grains	= 453.59 grams
1 hundredweight	= 100 pounds	= 45.36 kilograms
1 ton	= 2,000 pounds	= 907.18 kilograms

Troy Weight

(The grain, equal to 0.0648 gram, is the same in all three tables of weight)

1 carat	= 3.086 grains	= 200 milligrams
1 pennyweight	= 24 grains	= 1.5552 grams
1 ounce	= 20 pennyweights or 480 grains	= 31.1035 grams
1 pound	= 12 ounces or 5,760 grains	= 373.24 grams

Apothecaries' Weight

(The grain, equal to 0.0648 gram, is the same in all three tables of weight)

1 scruple	= 20 grains	= 1.296 grams
1 dram	= 3 scruples	= 3.888 grams
1 ounce	= 8 drams or 480 grains	= 31.1035 grams
1 pound	= 12 ounces or 5,760 grains	= 373.24 grams

Miscellaneous

3 inches	=	1 palm
4 inches	=	1 hand
6 inches	=	1 span
18 inches	=	1 cubit
21.8 inches	=	1 Bible cubit
2-1/2 feet	=	1 military pace

ADDITIONAL UNITS OF MEASURE

Astronomical Unit (A.U.): 93,000,000 miles, the average distance of the earth from the sun. Used in astronomy.

Board Foot (bd. ft.): 144 cubic inches (12 in. x 12 in. x 1 in.). Used for lumber.

Bolt: 40 yards. Used for measuring cloth.

Btu: British thermal unit. Amount of heat needed to increase the temperature of one pound of water by one degree Fahrenheit (252 calories).

Gross: 12 dozen or 144.

Knot: Not a distance, but the rate of speed of one nautical mile per hour.

Light, Speed of: 186,281.7 miles per second.

Light-year: 5,880,000,000,000 miles, the distance light travels in a year at the rate of 186,281.7 miles/second.

Pi (π): 3.14159265+. The ratio of the circumference of a circle to its diameter. For all practical purposes: 3.1416.

Roentgen: Dosage unit of radiation exposure produced by X rays.

Score: 20 units.

Sound, Speed of: Usually placed at 1,088 ft. per second at 32° F at sea level.

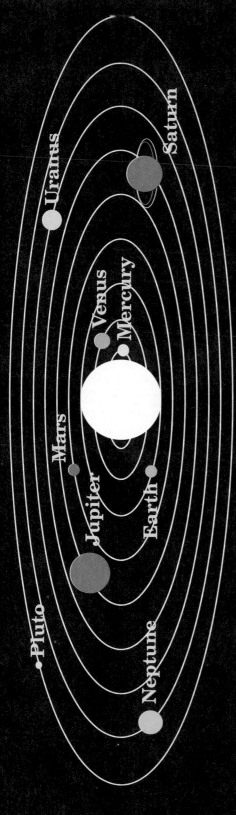

Planet Profusion

Our solar system is located in the Milky Way Galaxy. Even though this galaxy contains approximately 100 billion stars, our solar system contains only one star—the sun. The sun, which is the center of our solar system, has 9 planets and a myriad of asteroids, meteors, and comets orbiting it. The planets are large, nonluminous bodies which follow fixed elliptical orbits about the sun. (See the illustration above.) The planets are divided into two categories: the terrestrial planets—Mercury, Venus, Earth, Mars, and Pluto—which resemble the Earth in size, chemical composition, and density; and the Jovian planets—Jupiter, Saturn, Uranus, and Neptune—which are much larger in size and have thick, gaseous atmospheres and low densities. (See the table below.)

	Sun	Moon	Mercury	Venus	Earth	Mars	Jupiter	Saturn	Uranus	Neptune	Pluto
Orbital Speed (in miles per second)		.6	29.8	21.8	18.5	15.0	8.1	6.0	4.1	3.4	2.9
Rotation on Axis	24 days 16 hrs. 48 min.	27 days 7 hrs. 38 min.	59 days	243 days	23 hrs. 56 min.	1 day 37 min.	9 hrs. 55 min.	10 hrs. 39 min.	16 to 28 hours	16 hrs.	6 days
Mean Surface Gravity (Earth = 1.00)		0.16	0.38	0.87	1.00	0.38	2.87	1.32	.93	1.23	0.063
Density (times that of water)	100 (core)	3.3	5.4	5.3	5.5	3.9	1.3	0.7	1.2	1.6	1.0
Mass (times that of earth)	333,000	0.012	0.055	0.82	6 x 10^{21} metric tons	0.11	318	95	14.6	17.2	0.0026
Approx. Weight of a Human (in pounds)		25	49	130	150	55	396	172	148	190	75
Number of Satellites	9 planets	0	0	0	1	2	16	23	15	8	1
Mean Distance to Sun (in millions of miles)		93.0	36.0	67.23	92.96	141.7	483.7	886.2	1,781	2,793	3,660
Revolution Around Sun		365.25 days	88.0 days	224.7 days	365.25 days	686.99 days	11.86 years	29.46 years	84.0 years	164.8 years	247.6 years
Approximate Surface Temperature (degrees Fahrenheit)	10,000° (surface) 27,000,000° (center)	lighted side 200° dark side -230°	-315° to 648°	850°	-126.9° to 136°	-191° to -24°	-236°	-285°	-357°	-400°	-342° to -369°
Diameter (in miles)	867,000	2,155	3,031	7,520	7,926	4,200	88,700	74,600	31,570	30,800	1,420

Periodic Table of the Elements

Legend (box example):
Atomic Number — 2
Symbol — He
Atomic Weight (or Mass Number of most stable isotope in parentheses) — Helium 4.00260

Color key:
- Alkali metals
- Alkaline earth metals
- Transition metals
- Lanthanide series
- Actinide series
- Other metals
- Nonmetals
- Noble gases

1a	2a	3b	4b	5b	6b	7b	8	8	8	1b	2b	3a	4a	5a	6a	7a	0
1 H Hydrogen 1.00797																	2 He Helium 4.00260
3 Li Lithium 6.941	4 Be Beryllium 9.0128											5 B Boron 10.811	6 C Carbon 12.01115	7 N Nitrogen 14.0067	8 O Oxygen 15.9994	9 F Fluorine 18.9984	10 Ne Neon 20.179
11 Na Sodium 22.9898	12 Mg Magnesium 24.305											13 Al Aluminum 26.9815	14 Si Silicon 28.0855	15 P Phosphorus 30.9738	16 S Sulfur 32.064	17 Cl Chlorine 35.453	18 Ar Argon 35.948
19 K Potassium 39.0983	20 Ca Calcium 40.08	21 Sc Scandium 44.9559	22 Ti Titanium 47.88	23 V Vanadium 50.94	24 Cr Chromium 51.996	25 Mn Manganese 54.9380	26 Fe Iron 55.847	27 Co Cobalt 58.9332	28 Ni Nickel 58.69	29 Cu Copper 63.546	30 Zn Zinc 65.39	31 Ga Gallium 69.72	32 Ge Germanium 72.59	33 As Arsenic 74.9216	34 Se Selenium 78.96	35 Br Bromine 79.904	36 Kr Krypton 83.80
37 Rb Rubidium 85.4678	38 Sr Strontium 87.62	39 Y Yttrium 88.905	40 Zr Zirconium 91.224	41 Nb Niobium 92.906	42 Mo Molybdenum 95.94	43 Tc Technetium (98)	44 Ru Ruthenium 101.07	45 Rh Rhodium 102.906	46 Pd Palladium 106.42	47 Ag Silver 107.868	48 Cd Cadmium 112.41	49 In Indium 114.82	50 Sn Tin 118.71	51 Sb Antimony 121.75	52 Te Tellurium 127.60	53 I Iodine 126.905	54 Xe Xenon 131.29
55 Cs Cesium 132.905	56 Ba Barium 137.33	57-71* Lanthanides	72 Hf Hafnium 178.49	73 Ta Tantalum 180.948	74 W Tungsten 183.85	75 Re Rhenium 186.207	76 Os Osmium 190.2	77 Ir Iridium 192.22	78 Pt Platinum 195.08	79 Au Gold 196.967	80 Hg Mercury 200.59	81 Tl Thallium 204.383	82 Pb Lead 207.19	83 Bi Bismuth 208.980	84 Po Polonium (209)	85 At Astatine (210)	86 Rn Radon (222)
87 Fr Francium (223)	88 Ra Radium 226.025	89-103** Actinides (227)	104 Unq† Unnilquadium (261)	105 Unp†† Unnilpentium (262)	106 Unh Unnilhexium (263)	107 Uns Unnilseptium (262)		109 Une Unnilennium (266)									

*Lanthanides

57 La Lanthanum 138.906	58 Ce Cerium 140.12	59 Pr Praseodymium 140.908	60 Nd Neodymium 144.24	61 Pm Promethium (145)	62 Sm Samarium 150.36	63 Eu Europium 151.96	64 Gd Gadolinium 157.25	65 Tb Terbium 158.925	66 Dy Dysprosium 162.50	67 Ho Holmium 164.930	68 Er Erbium 167.26	69 Tm Thulium 168.934	70 Yb Ytterbium 173.04	71 Lu Lutetium 174.967

**Actinides

89 Ac Actinium 227.028	90 Th Thorium 232.038	91 Pa Protactinium 231.036	92 U Uranium 238.029	93 Np Neptunium 237.048	94 Pu Plutonium (244)	95 Am Americium (243)	96 Cm Curium (247)	97 Bk Berkelium (247)	98 Cf Californium (251)	99 Es Einsteinium (252)	100 Fm Fermium (257)	101 Md Mendelevium (258)	102 No Nobelium (259)	103 Lw Lawrencium (260)

†Other proposed names are kurchatovium (USSR) and hahnium (U.S.)
††Other proposed names are nielsbohrium (USSR) and rutherfordium (U.S.)

All About Maps

As you know, the world has changed dramatically in the past several years. As global citizens it is up to each of us to stay on top of those changes. Just as we once tried to understand something about each of the 50 states, we must now work to understand each of the 170 countries in the world. The section which follows will give you the map skills you need to begin your work.

Kinds of Maps

811

Maps have many uses, and there are as many different kinds of maps as there are uses. Your handbook uses one kind of map, the *political map*. Political maps show how the Earth is divided into countries and states. Often they also show the capitals and major cities. The different sizes and styles of the print (or type) used for names on the maps are also important. These are clues to help make the map information clear. Usually, the most important names are typed in the largest print. Different kinds of type are used for countries, cities, rivers, lakes, and other places.

Using the Maps

812

Mapmakers use special marks and symbols to show where things are or to give other useful information. Among other things, these marks and symbols show direction (north, south, east, and west).

On most maps, north is at the top. But you should always check the *compass rose* or *directional finder* to make sure you know where north is. If there is no symbol, you can assume that north is at the top.

The Legend

813

Other important marks and symbols are explained in a box printed on each map. This box is called the *legend* or *key*. It is included to make it easier for you to understand and use the map. Below is the United States map legend. This legend also includes symbols for state capitals and state boundaries.

UNITED STATES
POLYCONIC PROJECTION
SCALE OF MILES
0   100   200   300   400
SCALE OF KILOMETERS
0 100 200 300 400
Capitals of Countries _____⊛   State Capitals _____◉
International Boundaries _ __..   State Boundaries _ _ __.
Copyright by C. S. HAMMOND & Co., N. Y.

814 The Map Scale

Legends also explain the map scale. The purpose of a map scale is to show how far it really is between places. For example, a scale might show that one inch on the map equals one hundred miles on the Earth. If two cities are shown five inches apart, then they are really five hundred miles apart. A ruler makes using a scale easy, but even an index card or piece of paper will work. Here is the scale from the map of the United States.

SCALE OF MILES

0   100   200   300   400

Line up an index card or piece of paper under it. Put a dot on the card at "0." Now put another dot on your card at the right end of the scale. You've just marked off 400 miles. This can be used to judge the distance between points on the map. Don't forget that scales differ from map to map. Always refer to the scale on the map you are using.

815 Latitude and Longitude

Latitude and longitude lines are another feature of most maps which can be very useful. Latitude and longitude refer to imaginary lines that mapmakers use. When used together, these lines can be used to locate any point on Earth.

Latitude: The imaginary lines that go from east to west around the Earth are called lines of latitude. The line of latitude that goes around the Earth exactly halfway between the North Pole and the South Pole is called the equator. Latitude is measured in degrees, with the equator being 0 degrees (0°). Above the equator, the lines are called north latitude and measure from 0° to 90° North (the North Pole). Below the equator, the lines are called south latitude and measure from 0° to 90° South (the South Pole). On a map, latitude numbers are printed along the left- and right-hand sides.

Longitude: The imaginary lines that run from the North Pole to the South Pole are lines of longitude. Longitude is also measured in degrees, beginning with 0 degrees. The north-south line measuring 0° passes through Greenwich, England. This line is called the prime meridian. Lines east of the prime meridian are called east longitude. Lines west of the prime meridian are called west longitude. On a map, longitude numbers are printed at the top and bottom.

The latitude and longitude numbers of a place are sometimes called its coordinates. In each set of coordinates, latitude is given first, then longitude. To locate a certain place on a map using its coordinates, find the point where the two lines cross. The place you are looking for will be at or near this point.

Index to World Maps

Country	Latitude	Longitude	Country	Latitude	Longitude
Afghanistan	33° N	65° E	Guatemala	15° N	90° W
Albania	41° N	20° E	Guinea	11° N	10° W
Algeria	28° N	3° E	Guinea-Bissau	12° N	15° W
Andorra	42° N	1° E	Guyana	5° N	59° W
Angola	12° S	18° E	Haiti	19° N	72° W
Antigua and Barbuda	17° N	61° W	Honduras	15° N	86° W
Argentina	34° S	64° W	Hungary	47° N	20° E
Australia	25° S	135° E	Iceland	65° N	18° W
Austria	47° N	13° E	India	20° N	77° E
Bahamas	24° N	76° W	Indonesia	5° S	120° E
Bahrain	26° N	50° E	Iran	32° N	53° E
Bangladesh	24° N	90° E	Iraq	33° N	44° E
Barbados	13° N	59° W	Ireland	53° N	8° W
Belgium	50° N	4° E	Israel	31° N	35° E
Belize	17° N	88° W	Italy	42° N	12° E
Benin	9° N	2° E	Ivory Coast	8° N	5° W
Bhutan	27° N	90° E	Jamaica	18° N	77° W
Bolivia	17° S	65° W	Japan	36° N	138° E
Botswana	22° S	24° E	Jordan	31° N	36° E
Brazil	10° S	55° W	Kenya	1° N	38° E
Brunei	4° N	114° E	Kiribati	0° N	175° E
Bulgaria	43° N	25° E	North Korea	40° N	127° E
Burkina Faso	13° N	2° W	South Korea	36° N	128° E
Burma	22° N	98° E	Kuwait	29° N	47° E
Burundi	3° S	30° E	Laos	18° N	105° E
Cambodia	13° N	105° E	Lebanon	34° N	36° E
Cameroon	6° N	12° E	Lesotho	29° S	28° E
Canada	60° N	95° W	Liberia	6° N	10° W
Cape Verde	16° N	24° W	Libya	27° N	17° E
Central African			Liechtenstein	47° N	9° E
Republic	7° N	21° E	Luxembourg	49° N	6° E
Chad	15° N	19° E	Madagascar	19° S	46° E
Chile	30° S	71° W	Malawi	13° S	34° E
China	35° N	105° E	Malaysia	2° N	112° E
Colombia	4° N	72° W	Maldives	2° N	70° E
Comoros	12° S	44° E	Mali	17° N	4° W
Congo	1° S	15° E	Malta	36° N	14° E
Costa Rica	10° N	84° W	Mauritania	20° N	12° W
Cuba	21° N	80° W	Mauritius	20° S	57° E
Cyprus	35° N	33° E	Mexico	23° N	102° W
Czechoslovakia	49° N	17° E	Monaco	43° N	7° E
Denmark	56° N	10° E	Mongolia	46° N	105° E
Djibouti	11° N	43° E	Morocco	32° N	5° W
Dominica	15° N	61° W	Mozambique	18° S	35° E
Dominican Republic	19° N	70° W	Namibia	22° S	17° E
Ecuador	2° S	77° W	Nauru	1° S	166° E
Egypt	27° N	30° E	Nepal	28° N	84° E
El Salvador	14° N	89° W	Netherlands	52° N	5° E
Equatorial Guinea	2° N	9° E	New Zealand	41° S	174° E
Ethiopia	8° N	38° E	Nicaragua	13° N	85° W
Fiji	19° S	174° E	Niger	16° N	8° E
Finland	64° N	26° E	Nigeria	10° N	8° E
France	46° N	2° E	Northern Ireland	55° N	7° W
Gabon	1° S	11° E	Norway	62° N	10° E
The Gambia	13° N	16° W	Oman	22° N	58° E
Germany	51° N	10° E	Pakistan	30° N	70° E
Ghana	8° N	2° W	Panama	9° N	80° W
Greece	39° N	22° E	Papua New Guinea	6° S	147° E
Greenland	70° N	40° W	Paraguay	23° S	58° W
Grenada	12° N	61° W	Peru	10° S	76° W

Country	Latitude	Longitude	Country	Latitude	Longitude
Philippines	13° N	122° E	Switzerland	47° N	8° E
Poland	52° N	19° E	Syria	35° N	38° E
Portugal	39° N	8° W	Taiwan	23° N	121° E
Qatar	25° N	51° E	Tanzania	6° S	35° E
Romania	46° N	25° E	Thailand	15° N	100° E
Rwanda	2° S	30° E	Togo	8° N	1° E
St. Kitts & Nevis	17° N	62° W	Tonga	20° S	173° W
Saint Lucia	14° N	61° W	Trinidad/Tobago	11° N	61° W
Saint Vincent			Tunisia	34° N	9° E
and the Grenadines	13° N	61° W	Turkey	39° N	35° E
San Marino	44° N	12° E	Tuvala	8° S	179° E
Sao Tome and Principe	1° N	7° E	Uganda	1° N	32° E
Saudi Arabia	25° N	45° E	USSR	60° N	80° E
Scotland	57° N	5° W	United Arab Emirates	24° N	54° E
Senegal	14° N	14° W	United Kingdom	54° N	2° W
Seychelles	5° S	55° E	United States	38° N	97° W
Sierra Leone	8° N	11° E	Uruguay	33° S	56° W
Singapore	1° N	103° E	Vanuatu	17° S	170° E
Solomon Islands	8° S	159° E	Venezuela	8° N	66° W
Somalia	10° N	49° E	Vietnam	17° N	106° E
South Africa	30° S	26° E	Wales	53° N	3° W
Spain	40° N	4° W	Western Samoa	10° S	173° W
Sri Lanka	7° N	81° E	Yemen	15° N	44° E
Sudan	15° N	30° E	Yugoslavia	44° N	19° E
Suriname	4° N	56° W	Zaire	4° S	25° E
Swaziland	26° S	31° E	Zambia	15° S	30° E
Sweden	62° N	15° E	Zimbabwe	20° S	30° E

Topographic Tally Table

THE CONTINENTS

	Area (Sq Km)	Percent of Earth's Land
Asia	44,026,000	29.7
Africa	30,271,000	20.4
North America	24,258,000	16.3
South America	17,823,000	12.0
Antarctica	13,209,000	8.9
Europe	10,404,000	7.0
Australia	7,682,000	5.2

MAJOR ISLANDS

	Area (Sq Km)
Greenland	2,175,600
New Guinea	792,500
Borneo	725,500
Madagascar	587,000
Baffin	507,500
Sumatra	427,300
Honshu	227,400
Great Britain	218,100
Victoria	217,300
Ellesmere	196,200
Celebes	178,700
South (New Zealand)	151,000
Java	126,700

THE OCEANS

	Area (Sq Km)	Percent of Earth's Water Area
Pacific	166,241,000	46.0
Atlantic	86,557,000	23.9
Indian	73,427,000	20.3
Arctic	9,485,000	2.6

MAJOR LAKES

	Area (Sq Km)	Greatest Depth (Meters)
Caspian Sea, *Europe-Asia*	371,000	1,025
Superior, *North America*	82,100	406
Victoria, *Africa*	69,500	82
Aral Sea, *Asia*	64,500	67
Huron, *North America*	59,600	229
Michigan, *North America*	57,800	281

LONGEST RIVERS

	Length (Km)
Nile, *Africa*	6,671
Amazon, *South America*	6,437
Chang Jiang (Yangtze), *Asia*	6,380
Mississippi-Missouri, *North America*	5,971
Ob-Irtysk, *Asia*	5,410
Huang (Yellow), *Asia*	4,672
Congo, *Africa*	4,667
Amur, *Asia*	4,416
Lena, *Asia*	4,400
Mackenzie-Peace, *North America*	4,241

MAJOR SEAS

	Area (Sq Km)	Avg. Depth (Meters)
South China	2,974,600	1,464
Caribbean	2,515,900	2,575
Mediterranean	2,510,000	1,501
Bering	2,261,000	1,491
Gulf of Mexico	1,507,600	1,615
Sea of Okhotsk	1,392,100	973
Sea of Japan	1,012,900	1,667
Hudson Bay	730,100	93

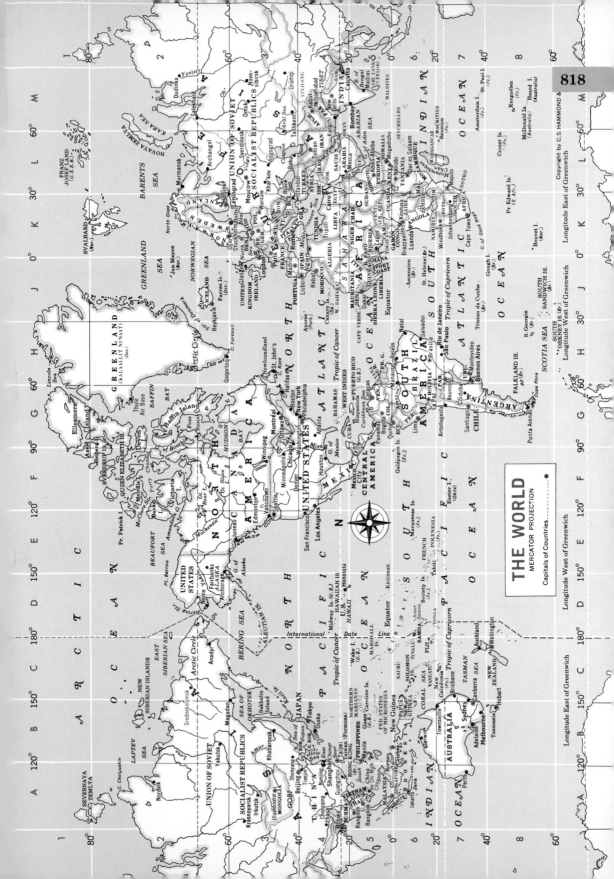

818

NORTH AMERICA

LAMBERT AZIMUTHAL EQUAL-AREA PROJECTION

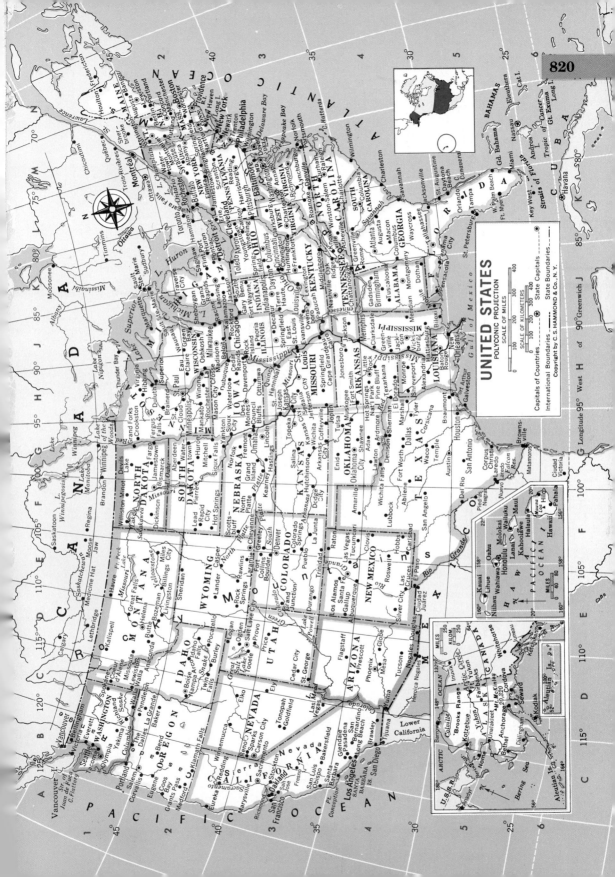

UNITED STATES
POLYCONIC PROJECTION

SCALE OF MILES
0   100   200   300   400

SCALE OF KILOMETERS
0   100   200   300   400

Capitals of Countries .... ⊛
International Boundaries ....

State Capitals .... ⊛
State Boundaries ....

Copyright by C. S. HAMMOND & Co., N.Y.

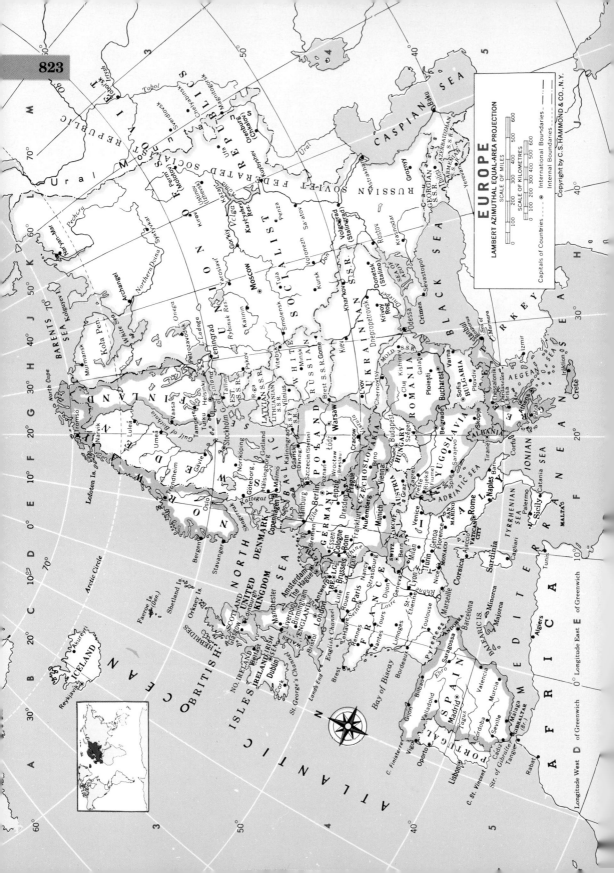

EUROPE

LAMBERT AZIMUTHAL EQUAL-AREA PROJECTION

SCALE OF MILES

100 200 300 400 500 600

SCALE OF KILOMETRES

0 100 200 300 400 500 600

Capitals of Countries .... ⊛

International Boundaries ------

Internal Boundaries ----------

Copyright by C. S. HAMMOND & CO., N.Y.

ASIA
LAMBERT AZIMUTHAL
EQUAL-AREA PROJECTION

SCALE OF MILES
0   300   600   900   1200

SCALE OF KILOMETERS
0   300   600   900   1200

Capitals of Countries .... ◉
International Boundaries .... ——
Canals .... ▲▲▲▲

© Copyright HAMMOND INCORPORATED, Maplewood, N. J.

E   60°   F   Longitude 80° East of   G   Greenwich 100°   H   120°   J

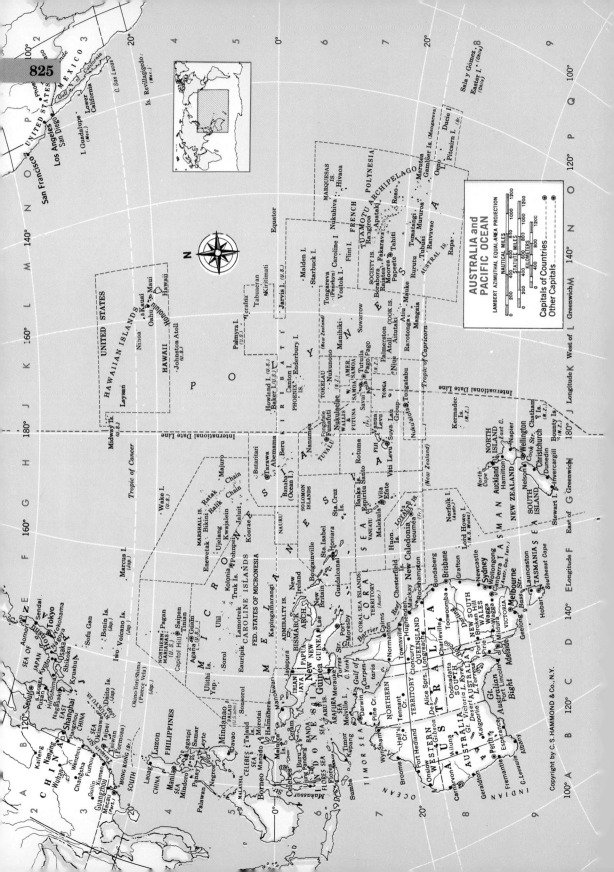

Improving Math Skills

Mathematics has its own special language. To "speak" or understand the language of mathematics, you must know its symbols or signs. Two lists of mathematical symbols follow. The first list includes common symbols and their meanings; the second list includes symbols which are used in more advanced math classes.

The charts include those for *prime numbers, multiplication facts, decimal equivalents,* and *Roman numerals.* Hopefully, each will come in handy at one time or another.

Common Math Symbols

+	plus (addition)
−	minus (subtraction)
×	multiplied by
÷	divided by
=	is equal to
≠	is not equal to
<	is less than
>	is greater than
±	plus or minus
%	percent
¢	cents
$	dollars
°	degree
′	minute (also foot)
″	second (also inch)
:	is to (ratio)
π	pi

Advanced Math Symbols

$\sqrt[2]{}$ or $\sqrt{}$	square root
$\sqrt[3]{}$	cube root
≥	is greater than or equal to
≤	is less than or equal to
{ }	set
∩	intersection
∪	union
⊂	is a subset of
∈	is an element of
⊄	is not a subset of
∉	is not an element of
∅	the empty set
≅	is congruent to
∠	angle
⊥	is perpendicular to
∥	is parallel to
∴	therefore

A Chart of Prime Numbers Less Than 500

2,	3,	5,	7,	11,	13,	17,	19,	23,	29,
31,	37,	41,	43,	47,	53,	59,	61,	67,	71,
73,	79,	83,	89,	97,	101,	103,	107,	109,	113,
127,	131,	137,	139,	149,	151,	157,	163,	167,	173,
179,	181,	191,	193,	197,	199,	211,	223,	227,	229,
233,	239,	241,	251,	257,	263,	269,	271,	277,	281,
283,	293,	307,	311,	313,	317,	331,	337,	347,	349,
353,	359,	367,	373,	379,	383,	389,	397,	401,	409,
419,	421,	431,	433,	439,	443,	449,	457,	461,	463,
467,	479,	487,	491,	499					

829 Table of Basic Multiplication Facts

X	0	1	2	3	4	5	6	7	8	9	10
0	0	0	0	0	0	0	0	0	0	0	0
1	0	1	2	3	4	5	6	7	8	9	10
2	0	2	4	6	8	10	12	14	16	18	20
3	0	3	6	9	12	15	18	21	24	27	30
4	0	4	8	12	16	20	24	28	32	36	40
5	0	5	10	15	20	25	30	35	40	45	50
6	0	6	12	18	24	30	36	42	48	54	60
7	0	7	14	21	28	35	42	49	56	63	70
8	0	8	16	24	32	40	48	56	64	72	80
9	0	9	18	27	36	45	54	63	72	81	90
10	0	10	20	30	40	50	60	70	80	90	100

830 Decimal Equivalents of Common Fractions

Fraction	Decimal	Fraction	Decimal	Fraction	Decimal	Fraction	Decimal
1/2	.5000	1/32	.0313	3/11	.2727	6/11	.5455
1/3	.3333	1/64	.0156	4/5	.8000	7/8	.8750
1/4	.2500	2/3	.6667	4/7	.5714	7/9	.7778
1/5	.2000	2/5	.4000	4/9	.4444	7/10	.7000
1/6	.1667	2/7	.2857	4/11	.3636	7/11	.6364
1/7	.1429	2/9	.2222	5/6	.8333	7/12	.5833
1/8	.1250	2/11	.1818	5/7	.7143	8/9	.8889
1/9	.1111	3/4	.7500	5/8	.6250	8/11	.7273
1/10	.1000	3/5	.6000	5/9	.5556	9/10	.9000
1/11	.0909	3/7	.4286	5/11	.4545	9/11	.8182
1/12	.0833	3/8	.3750	5/12	.4167	10/11	.9091
1/16	.0625	3/10	.3000	6/7	.8571	11/12	.9167

831 Roman Numerals

I	1	VIII	8	LX	60	$\overline{V}$	5,000
II	2	IX	9	LXX	70	$\overline{X}$	10,000
III	3	X	10	LXXX	80	$\overline{L}$	50,000
IV	4	XX	20	XC	90	$\overline{C}$	100,000
V	5	XXX	30	C	100	$\overline{D}$	500,000
VI	6	XL	40	D	500	$\overline{M}$	1,000,000
VII	7	L	50	M	1,000		

Word Problems

Solving word problems requires careful reading, thinking, and planning. If you try to take shortcuts, you will probably not solve them correctly. Given in the following guidelines are the important steps you should follow when you carefully work on word problems. With enough practice and with the help of these guidelines, you can train yourself to work through even the most difficult word problems.

Guidelines for Solving Word Problems

1. Read the problem carefully. This may mean that you have to read each word and phrase several times to understand all parts of the problem. (Try restating the problem in your own words, or get a little "crazy" and act out the problem. Your goal is to understand what is being asked.)

2. Identify the information you will need to solve the problem. Find all the numbers, for instance; sometimes they are written as numerals, sometimes as words. Make sure you find all of the numbers that may be "disguised"; dozen (12), gross (144), one half as many (divide by 2), twice as many (multiply by 2), etc.

3. Study any illustrations—maps, charts, graphs—which go along with the problem. They often contain important information.

4. Read the problem again, out loud; draw a picture or a diagram (if necessary) to help you figure out what is being asked.

5. Find out exactly what you have to do to solve the problem. Pay special attention to the key words and phrases.

   ❑ "In all," "in total," or "altogether" tell you to use addition or multiplication.

   ❑ "How many more than," "how many less than," "how many are left," or "how much younger than" tell you to use subtraction.

   ❑ "How much . . . each" and "how many . . . each" show a need for division.

6. After you've identified which basic operations (addition, subtraction, multiplication, division) you'll have to use to solve the problem, put the steps in the correct order. (Sometimes, you will have only one step to do.)

7. Solve the problem, showing all of your work so you can check your answer later.

8. Check your answer.

Sample Word Problems

Six sample word problems follow. Each of the first four problems deals with one of the basic operations—addition, subtraction, multiplication, and division. The last two problems deal with mixed numbers and fractions. Take special note of the discussion or explanation which goes along with the planning and solving of each word problem.

833 Addition ———————————————

Example: A shirt costs $8.79, a pair of pants costs $13.47, and a sweater costs $12.50. What would be the total cost if someone bought all three items?

Solution:

Step 1: **Set up the problem**

$ 8.79
13.47
+12.50

Discussion: This is a one-step problem in which you must add three numbers. (The word "total" is a key word which tells you to add.)

Step 2: **Solve the problem**

1 1 1
$ 8.79
13.47
+12.50
$34.76

Discussion: Drop the decimal point which separates the dollars from the cents down to your answer.

Step 3: **Check your answer**

1 1 1
$12.50
8.79
+13.47
$34.76

Discussion: Check your answer by adding the three numbers in a different order. Make sure that you have copied the numbers correctly and that your answer makes sense.

Answer: $34.76 is the amount of money to pay for the three items of clothing.

Subtraction ———————————————— 834

Example: The student council bought 48 chocolate donuts, 36 sugared donuts, and 36 powdered donuts for the school bake sale. Only 42 of the donuts were sold. How many donuts were left?

Solution:

Step 1: **Set up the problem**

$$48$$
$$36$$
$$+36$$
$$120$$

$$120$$
$$-42$$

Discussion: This is really a two-step problem. Before you can find out how many donuts were left, you have to find out how many donuts there were to begin with. Then subtract the 42 donuts sold in order to find out the number of donuts remaining.

Step 2: **Solve the problem**

$$1\,10$$
$$120$$
$$-42$$
$$78$$

Discussion: Check all of your calculating. You can check a subtraction problem by adding your answer to the second number in the subtraction problem. Also, make sure that your answer makes sense.

Step 3: **Check your answer**

$$78$$
$$+42$$
$$120$$

Answer: 78 donuts were left.

Multiplication ———————————————— 835

Example: Rent-A-Junker, a "new" car rental company, repaired 13 junkers each day in July in preparation for its grand opening in August. How many cars in total did this company prepare for its grand opening?

Solution:

Step 1: **Set up the problem**

$$31$$
$$\times 13$$

Discussion: This problem has some missing information. In order to solve the problem, you would need to know the number of days in July (31). Then, since the company repaired the same number of cars each day, you can multiply that number (13) times the number of days in July (31).

Step 2: **Solve the problem**

$$\begin{array}{r} 31 \\ \times\ 13 \\ \hline 93 \\ 31\ \ \\ \hline 403 \end{array}$$

Discussion: To check, divide the product, 403, by one of the numbers in the multiplication problem. Your answer should be the other number in the multiplication problem. Also, make sure your answer makes sense.

Step 3: **Check your answer**

$$\begin{array}{r} 13 \\ 31\overline{)403} \\ \underline{31}\ \ \\ 93 \\ \underline{93} \\ 0 \end{array}$$

Answer: Rent-A-Junker fixed up 403 cars in July.

836 Division ———————————————————

Example: The eighth grade class at Pilgrim Junior High School wants to go to a new amusement park for a class trip. The total cost for this trip—transportation, tickets, lunch—would be $1,164.00 if all 97 students in the class decide to go. How much would each student have to pay if they equally shared the total cost?

Solution:

Step 1: **Set up the problem**

$$97\overline{)1164}$$

Discussion: This is a one-step problem in which you must divide. (The phrase "each student" is a key phrase which tells you to divide.) Divide the total cost for the trip by the number of students in the class to solve the problem. You might want to round the numbers off to get an idea of what your answer might be—1,200 ÷ 100 = 12.

Step 2: **Solve the problem**

$$\begin{array}{r} 12 \\ 97\overline{)1164} \\ \underline{97}\ \ \\ 194 \\ \underline{194} \\ 0 \end{array}$$

Step 3: **Check your
          answer**

$$97$$
$$\times\ 12$$
$$194$$
$$97$$
$$1164$$

Discussion: To check your answer, multiply the divisor by the quotient of the division problem. Also, make sure that your answer makes sense. Compare it to the estimate you made with simpler numbers.

Answer: Each student would have to pay $12.00.

Mixed Numbers ———————————————— 837

Example: A carpenter needs to cut an eight-foot board into pieces that are each 2-2/3 feet long. How many pieces will the carpenter be able to cut from the eight-foot board?

Solution:

Step 1: **Set up the
          problem**

$$8 \div 2\frac{2}{3} = 8 \div \frac{8}{3}$$

Discussion: Since you are asked to find how many smaller pieces you can get from a large piece, you will need to divide. To divide eight by 2-2/3, you should first change the mixed number into a fraction. (Remember that dividing by a number is the same as multiplying by its reciprocal.)

Step 2: **Solve the
          problem**

$$\frac{\overset{1}{\cancel{8}}}{1} \times \frac{3}{\underset{1}{\cancel{8}}} = \frac{3}{1}$$

Discussion: You can simplify before you multiply.

Step 3: **Check your
          answer**

$$\begin{array}{r} 2\frac{2}{3} \\ 3\overline{)\ 8} \\ 6 \\ \hline 2 \end{array}$$

Discussion: To check your answer, divide the eight by the three to see if it equals 2-2/3. Also, make sure your answer makes sense.

Answer: The carpenter can cut three pieces of wood from the eight-foot board.

Fractions ————————————————————————

Example: One-quarter of the actors from the community play attend Park High School. One-third of the actors attend Jefferson Junior High School. What fraction of the entire cast for the spring play attend the two schools?

Solution:

Step 1: **Set up the problem**

$$\frac{1}{4} + \frac{1}{3} =$$

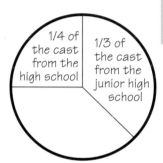

Discussion: To solve this problem, you will have to add the two fractions. You might want to draw a picture which illustrates the information given in the problem. (A picture can help you understand the problem.)

Step 2: **Solve the problem**

$$\frac{1 \times 3}{4 \times 3} = \frac{3}{12}$$

$$+ \frac{1 \times 4}{3 \times 4} = \frac{4}{12}$$

$$\frac{7}{12}$$

Discussion: To add fractions, you must have common denominators. As a result, you must find the least common multiple (LCM) of the numbers 3 and 4—the denominators of the two fractions. The LCM is 12.

Step 3: **Check your answer**

$$\frac{7}{12}$$

Discussion: Check your answer to make sure it is written in its simplest terms. (7/12 cannot be simplified any further.) Also, check your answer to see if it makes sense when you compare it to your picture. Since 7/12 and the picture both represent a little more than half, the answer makes sense.

Answer: 7/12 of the cast attend the two schools.

Using the Computer

If you haven't had any experience using a computer, it might seem like a very complex or difficult machine which knows a lot more than you do. Well, nothing could be further from the truth. A computer doesn't know anything. All it does is store information. Luckily, it stores it in a way that lets you use, add, and organize this information in new and creative ways.

Those of you who have worked with computers already know this. You also know that it is necessary to know at least the basic computer vocabulary to use one effectively. (Since a computer offers so many new ways to use information, it has a vocabulary of its own.) A glossary of basic computer terms follows. Use this list to help you understand, operate, and program a computer.

839

Also, a basic computer keyboard is illustrated. Use this illustration to help you practice typing. Knowing how to use a keyboard properly is important when you use a word processing program in your computer. Notice the illustration of the left and right hands which identifies the keys each finger can and should hit when you keyboard (847). Keep your fingers right above the home row (shaded in this illustration) as you practice.

COMPUTER TERMS

Address: A number used to identify where a piece of information is located in the computer's memory.

Algorithm: The computer programmer's "plan of attack" showing each step used in the solution of a problem.

Array: A group of variables called by the same name, but having different subscripts.

Back-up: A copy of data or programs used to protect the original copy if it is lost, stolen, or destroyed.

BASIC: *(Beginners All-purpose Symbolic Instruction Code)* A computer language specifically designed to be easy to learn and use. It is commonly used with smaller computers.

840

Binary: The number system commonly used by computers because the values 0 and 1 can easily be represented electronically in the computer.

Bit: *(BInary digiT)* The smallest piece of information understood by a computer consisting of either a 0 or a 1.

Boot: To start up a computer system by loading a program into the memory.

Bug: An error in a computer program.

Byte: A string of eight bits commonly acting as a single piece of information.

Character: A letter or digit used to display information.

Chip: A small piece of silicon containing thousands of electrical elements. Also referred to as an integrated circuit.

Command: An instruction to a computer to perform a special task

Compiler: A program which translates an instruction written in a high-level language into machine language so that the instruction can be understood by the computer.

Computer: An electronic device for performing programmed computations quickly and accurately. A computer is made up of five basic blocks: memory, control, arithmetic logic unit (ALU), input, and output.

Computer program: A list of statements, commands, and instructions written in computer language which, when executed correctly, will perform a task or function.

Control character: A character that is entered by holding down the control key while hitting another key. The control character "controls" or changes information which is printed or displayed.

CPU: *(Central Processing Unit)* The hardware portion of a computer which executes instructions. This "brain" of the computer controls all other devices.

CRT: *(Cathode Ray Tube)* An electronic vacuum tube, such as that found in a TV, which is used to display information.

Cursor: A symbol on a computer screen which points out where the next character typed from the keyboard will appear.

Data: Information used or produced by a computer program.

Data base: A collection of information which is organized in such a way that a computer can process it efficiently.

Debug: Removing errors from a computer program.

Device: A hardware component of a computer system designed to perform a certain task. A CRT, printer, or disk drive are examples of computer devices.

Digit: A character used to express numbers in a number system. For instance, 0 and 1 are digits in base 2; 0 to 7 are digits in base 8; 0 to 9 are digits in base 10; and 0 to 9, A, B, C, D, E, and F are digits in base 16.

Digital: A class of computers which process information which is in binary form. It is also used to describe information which is in binary form.

Dimension: A statement in a program which tells a computer how large an array is and to set aside memory for that array.

Disk: A magnetic storage device used to record computer information. Each disk appears flat and square on the outside; inside, the disk is circular and rotates so that information can be stored on its many circular tracks.

Disk drive: The device that writes and reads information onto the disk.

Documentation: A practice used by all good programmers in which comments are inserted into a computer program so that someone else can look at the program and understand what a program is supposed to do and how it does it.

DOS: *(Disk Operating System)* A software system that allows a computer to communicate with and control one or more disk drives.

Edit: To change an original document or program by adding, deleting, or replacing parts of it, thus creating a new document or program.

Error: A programming mistake which will cause the program to run incorrectly or not run at all.

Error message: A message, displayed or printed, which tells you an error or problem is in a program.

Execute: To run a computer program.

File: A collection of information stored on a computer device.

Floppy disk: A storage device made of a thin, magnetically coated plastic.

Flowchart: A diagram which shows the steps in a computer program.

Format: To prepare a blank disk for use (also *initialize).*

Graphics: Information which is displayed as pictures or images rather than by characters.

Hardcopy: A printed copy of a program, data, or results.

Hardware: The actual electronic and mechanical components of a computer system. A floppy disk is *hardware,* while a program stored on it is *software.*

Input: Information taken from a disk drive, keyboard, or other device and transported into a computer.

Instruction: Machine language which commands an action to be taken by the CPU *(central processing unit)* of a computer.

Interactive: A computer system in which the operator and computer frequently exchange information.

Interface: The hardware, software, and firmware which is used to link one computer or computer device to another.

K: A term used when describing the capacity of a computer memory or storage device. For example, 16K equals 16x1024 or 16,384 memory addresses.

Keyboard: An input device used to enter information into a computer by striking keys which are labeled much like those on a typewriter.

Letter-quality printer: A printer that produces type quality similar to that of an electric typewriter.

Library: A collection of programs which may be referred to often.

List: A display or printout of a computer program or file.

Load: To take information from an external storage device and *load* it into a computer's memory.

LOGO: A language which combines pictures and words to teach programming to children.

Loop: A series of instructions which is repeated, usually with different data on each pass.

Machine language: The language used to directly instruct computer hardware. The computer uses this language to process data and instructions in binary form.

Mainframe computer: A large computer generally with many operators using it at one time.

Main memory: The memory that is built into a computer.

Memory: The part of the computer which stores information and program instructions until they are needed.

Menu: A detailed list of choices presented in a program from which a user can select.

Microcomputer: A small, inexpensive computer using a microprocessor as its processing unit.

Minicomputer: A computer larger than a microcomputer whose CPU cannot be contained on a single chip; generally used in small business, science, and engineering.

Modem: *(MOdulator DEModulator)* A device which allows computers to communicate over telephone lines.

Monitor: A video screen on which information from a computer can be displayed. By viewing the displayed information, the user can visualize and control the operation of a program.

Output: Information sent from a computer to a disk drive, monitor, printer, or any other external device.

PASCAL: A high-level language designed to teach the principles of structured programming. (Named after Blaise Pascal, a 17th century mathematician.)

Peripheral device: An external device such as a plotter, disk drive, or printer added to a computer system to increase the capabilities of the system.

PILOT: *(Programmed Inquiry, Learning, Or Teaching)* A high-level language used for computer-aided instruction.

Printed circuit board: A flat, rigid board commonly made of fiberglass. It is used to hold and electronically connect computer chips and other electrical elements.

Printer: A peripheral device (similar to a typewriter) used to produce printed copies of computer data or programs.

Printout: A copy of computer output produced on paper by a printer.

Processor: The portion of computer hardware that performs machine-language instructions and controls all other parts of the computer.

Program: A step-by-step list of instructions which a computer will follow in order to accomplish a specific task.

Programmer: A person involved in the writing, editing, and production of a computer program.

Programming language: A set of guidelines and rules for writing a program which will perform a task on a computer.

Prompt: A question which asks the user to input information to be processed or to tell the computer which part of a program to branch to.

Resolution: Describes the quality of a video image displayed on a computer monitor or graphics screen.

Save: To take a program or file from main memory and store it on a device (disk, cassette, etc.) for later use.

Sector: A fraction of the recording surface on a disk; a sector is a fraction of a *track*.

Software: Programs which instruct a computer how to perform a desired task.

Spreadsheet: A program used to organize numbers and figures into a worksheet form.

Statement: An instruction in a program which will perform a desired operation.

Storage: Describes the main memory or external devices where information or programs can be stored.

String: A group of consecutive letters, numbers, and characters which are not used for computational purposes.

Subroutine: A group of statements which can be found and used from several different places in a main program.

System: The collection of hardware, software, and firmware that forms a functioning computer.

Telecommunications: Sending and receiving information from one computer to another over long distances via phone lines, satellites, or other forms of communication equipment.

Terminal: A peripheral device which contains a keyboard for putting information into a computer and a monitor to receive output from a computer.

Text: Information in the form of characters which can be read by an individual.

Track: A fraction of the recording surface on a disk. (A track can be compared to the space used by each song on an album.) The number of tracks on a disk varies.

User: A person *using* a computer.

Variable: A place in the computer's memory which can be assigned a value or have that value read, changed, or deleted from memory by the programmer.

Virus: A set of instructions, hidden in a computer system, that wipes out stored information.

Word: A string of bits treated as a single unit by a computer.

Word processor: A program designed to assist a user in writing letters, memos, and other kinds of text.

Write-enable notch: The small, rectangular cutout in the edge of a disk's jacket used to protect the contents of a disk. If the notch is not present, or is covered by a write-protect tab, information cannot be written on the disk.

Write-protect: To apply a write-protect tab to a disk, making it impossible for new information to be written on the disk. The information on the disk is now protected from being overwritten.

Write-protect tab: A sticker used to cover the write-enable notch on a disk.

COMMAND STATEMENTS

DATA: Allows data to be stored in a computer program. This data can be retrieved during the running of the program by the READ statement.

DIM: Saves space in memory for the size of an array you select.

END: The last statement in a program which stops the program and returns control of the computer to the user.

FOR: Allows the programmer to set up a loop which is to be repeated a specified number of times.

GOSUB: Causes the program to go to a subroutine. When a RETURN statement is made in the subroutine, the program returns to the line following the GOSUB statement.

GOTO: Causes the computer to go to a particular line in the program.

IF: A statement which tells the computer to go to the next line in the program if the argument following the IF statement is false or to go to a given line number if the argument is true.

INPUT: Allows the user to input information from the keyboard for use in a program.

LET: An optional instruction which can be used when a variable in a program is assigned a value. (Example: Let A=25.)

LIST: Displays or prints a copy of the program presently in the computer.

NEXT: Used with the FOR statement. When a NEXT statement is used in a program, the computer branches back to the FOR statement until the loop has been repeated a specific number of times.

PRINT: Instructs the computer to type or display information from a program.

READ: Instructs the computer to read the information in a DATA statement; takes information from a DATA statement and assigns the information to the variable(s) immediately following the READ statement.

REM: Allows the programmer to insert remarks and comments into a program which are used to make the program easier to understand.

RETURN: This command will instruct the computer to go back to the main part of the program. When encountered in a subroutine, this statement will cause the computer to branch to the first statement after the GOSUB command which sent the computer to the subroutine.

RUN: Causes the computer to "run" the program in memory.

THEN: Used with the IF statement. When the argument between the IF and THEN is true, the statements following the THEN statement are performed.

Computer Keyboard

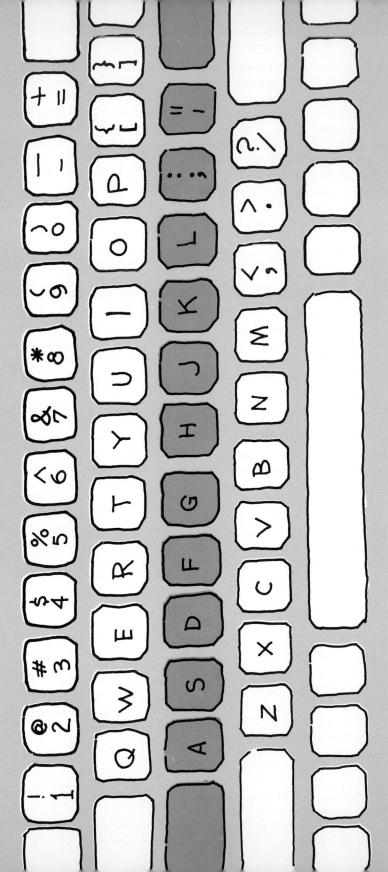

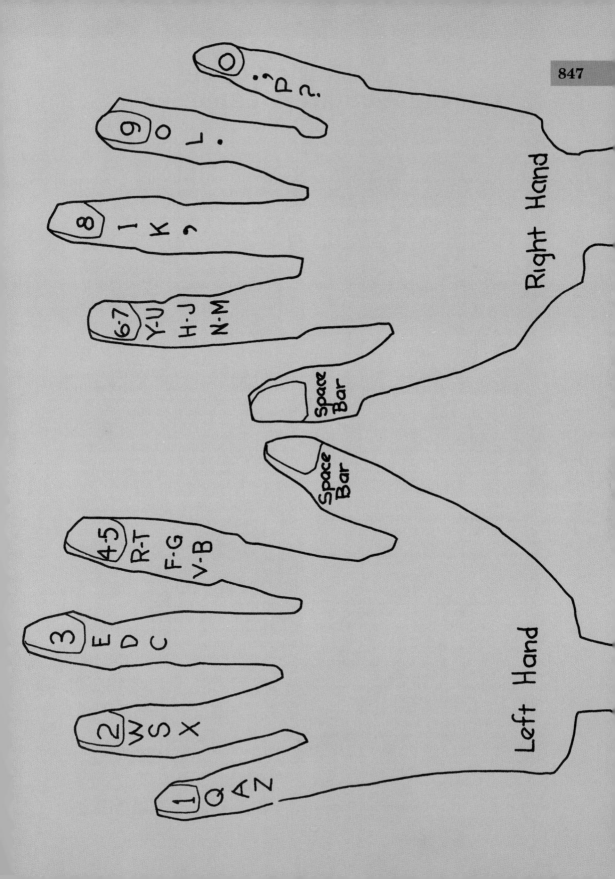

Right Hand

Left Hand

Space Bar

Space Bar

0 .?P?.

9 O L.

8 I K?

6-7 Y-U H-J N-M

4-5 R-T F-G V-B

3 E D C

2 W S X

1 Q A Z

Constitution of the United States of America

Note: The original text of the Constitution has been edited to conform to contemporary American usage. The bracketed words have been added to help you locate information more quickly; they are not part of the Constitution.

The oldest federal constitution in existence was framed by a convention of delegates from twelve of the thirteen original states in Philadelphia in May, 1787, Rhode Island failing to send a delegate. George Washington presided over the session, which lasted until September 17, 1787. The draft (originally a preamble and seven Articles) was submitted to all thirteen states and was to become effective when ratified by nine states. It went into effect on the first Wednesday in March, 1789, having been ratified by New Hampshire, the ninth state to approve, on June 21, 1788. The states ratified the Constitution in the following order:

Delaware	December 7, 1787	South Carolina	May 23,1788
Pennsylvania	December 12, 1787	New Hampshire	June 21,1788
New Jersey	December 18, 1787	Virginia	June 25,1788
Georgia	January 2, 1788	New York	July 26,1788
Connecticut	January 9, 1788	North Carolina	November 21,1789
Massachusetts	February 6, 1788	Rhode Island	May 29,1790
Maryland	April 28, 1788		

[Preamble]

We the people of the United States, in order to form a more perfect Union, establish justice, insure domestic tranquility, provide for the common defense, promote the general welfare, and secure the blessings of liberty to ourselves and our posterity, do ordain and establish this Constitution for the United States of America.

Article I

Section 1

[Legislative powers vested in Congress] All legislative powers herein granted shall be vested in a Congress of the United States, which shall consist of a Senate and House of Representatives.

Section 2

1. **[Make-up of the House of Representatives]** The House of Representatives shall be composed of members chosen every second year by the people of the several States, and the electors in each State shall have the qualifications requisite for electors of the most numerous branch of the State Legislature.

2. **[Qualifications of Representatives]** No person shall be a Representative who shall not have attained to the age of twenty-five years, and been seven years a citizen of the United States, and who shall not, when elected, be an inhabitant of that State in which he shall be chosen.

3. **[Apportionment of Representatives and direct taxes—census]** (Representatives and direct taxes shall be apportioned among the several States which may be included within this Union, according to their respective numbers, which shall be determined by adding to the whole number of free persons, including those bound to service for a term of years, and excluding Indians not taxed, three-fifths of all other persons.—*Amended by the 14th Amendment, section 2.*) The actual enumeration shall be made within three years after the first meeting of the Congress of the United States, and within every subsequent term of ten years, in such manner as they shall by law direct. The number of Representatives shall not exceed one for every thirty thousand, but each State shall have at least one Representative; and until such enumeration shall be made, the State of New Hampshire shall be entitled to choose three; Massachusetts, eight; Rhode Island and Provi-dence Plantations, one; Connecticut, five; New York, six; New Jersey, four; Pennsylvania, eight; Delaware, one; Maryland, six; Virginia, ten; North Carolina, five; South Carolina, five; and Georgia, three.

4. **[Filling of vacancies in representation]** When vacancies happen in the representation from any State, the Executive Authority thereof shall issue writs of election to fill such vacancies.

5. **[Selection of officers; power of impeachment]** The House of Representatives shall choose their Speaker and other officers; and shall have the sole power of impeachment.

Section 3

1. **[The Senate]** (The Senate of the United States shall be composed of two Senators from each State, chosen by the Legislature thereof, for six years; and each Senator shall have one vote.—*Amended by the 17th Amendment, section 1.*)

2. **[Classification of Senators; filling of**

vacancies] Immediately after they shall be assembled in consequence of the first election, they shall be divided as equally as may be into three classes. The seats of the Senators of the first class shall be vacated at the expiration of the second year, of the second class at the expiration of the fourth year, and of the third class at the expiration of the sixth year, so that one-third may be chosen every second year; and if vacancies happen by resignation, or otherwise, (during the recess of the Legislature of any State,) the Executive thereof may make temporary appointments (until the next meeting of the Legislature, which shall then fill such vacancies.— *Amended by the 17th Amendment.)*

3. **[Qualification of Senators]** No person shall be a Senator who shall not have attained to the age of thirty years, and been nine years a citizen of the United States, and who shall not, when elected, be an inhabitant of that State for which he shall be chosen.

4. **[Vice President to be President of Senate]** The Vice President of the United States shall be President of the Senate, but shall have no vote, unless they be equally divided.

5. **[Selection of Senate officers; President pro tempore]** The Senate shall choose their other officers, and also a President pro tempore, in the absence of the Vice President, or when he shall exercise the office of President of the United States.

6. **[Senate to try impeachments]** The Senate shall have the sole power to try all impeachments. When sitting for that purpose, they shall be on oath or affirmation. When the President of the United States is tried, the Chief Justice shall preside: and no person shall be convicted without the concurrence of two-thirds of the members present.

7. **[Judgment in cases of impeachment]** Judgment in cases of impeachment shall not extend further than to removal from office, and disqualification to hold and enjoy any office of honor, trust, or profit under the United States; but the party convicted shall nevertheless be liable and subject to indictment, trial, judgment, and punishment, according to Law.

Section 4

1. **[Control of congressional elections]** The times, places, and manner of holding elections for Senators and Representatives shall be prescribed in each State by the Legislature thereof; but the Congress may at any time by law make or alter such regulations, except as to the places of choosing Senators.

2. **[Time for assembling of Congress]** The Congress shall assemble at least once in every year, (and such meeting shall be on the first Monday in December, unless they shall by law appoint a different day.—*Amended by the 20th Amendment, section 2.)*

Section 5

1. **[Each House to be the judge of the election and qualifications of its members; regulations as to quorum]** Each House shall be the judge of the elections, returns, and qualifications of its own members, and a majority of each shall constitute a quorum to do business; but a smaller number may adjourn from day to day, and may be authorized to compel the attendance of absent members, in such manner, and under such penalties as each House may provide.

2. **[Each House to determine its own rules]** Each House may determine the rules of its proceedings, punish its members for disorderly behavior, and, with the concurrence of two-thirds, expel a member.

3. **[Journals and yeas and nays]** Each House shall keep a journal of its proceedings, and from time to time publish the same, excepting such parts as may in their judgment require secrecy; and the yeas and nays of the members of either House on any question shall, at the desire of one-fifth of those present, be entered on the journal.

4. **[Adjournment]** Neither House, during the session of Congress, shall, without the consent of the other, adjourn for more than three days, nor to any other place than that in which the two Houses shall be sitting.

Section 6

1. **[Compensation and privileges of members of Congress]** The Senators and Representatives shall receive a compensation for their services, to be ascertained by law, and paid out of the Treasury of the United States. They shall in all cases, except treason, felony, and breach of the peace, be privileged from arrest during their attendance at the session of their respective Houses, and in going to and returning from the same; and for any speech or debate in either House, they shall not be questioned in any other place.

2. **[Incompatible offices; exclusions]** No Senator or Representative shall, during the time for which he was elected, be appointed to any civil office under the authority of the United States, which shall have been created, or the emoluments whereof shall have been increased during such time; and no person holding any office under the United States shall be a member of either House during his continuance in office.

Section 7

1. **[Revenue bills to originate in House]** All bills for raising revenue shall originate in the House of Representatives; but the Senate may propose or concur with amendments as on other bills.

2. **[Manner of passing bills; veto power of President]** Every bill which shall have passed the House of Representatives and the Senate,

shall, before it becomes a law, be presented to the President of the United States; if he approve, he shall sign it, but if not he shall return it, with his objections to that House in which it shall have originated, who shall enter the objections at large on their journal, and proceed to reconsider it. If after such reconsideration two-thirds of that House shall agree to pass the bill, it shall be sent, together with the objections, to the other House, by which it shall likewise be reconsidered, and if approved by two-thirds of that House, it shall become a law. But in all such cases the votes of both Houses shall be determined by yeas and nays, and the names of the persons voting for and against the bill shall be entered on the journal of each House, respectively. If any bill shall not be returned by the President within ten days (Sundays excepted) after it shall have been presented to him, the same shall be a law, in like manner as if he had signed it, unless the Congress by their adjournment prevent its return, in which case it shall not be a law.

3. **[Concurrent orders or resolutions to be passed by President]** Every order, resolution, or vote to which the concurrence of the Senate and House of Representatives may be necessary (except on a question of adjournment) shall be presented to the President of the United States; and before the same shall take effect, shall be approved by him, or being disapproved by him, shall be repassed by two-thirds of the Senate and House of Representatives, according to the rules and limitations prescribed in the case of a bill.

Section 8
[General powers of Congress] The Congress shall have the power:

1. **[Taxes, duties, imposts, and excises]** To lay and collect taxes, duties, imposts, and excises, to pay the debts and provide for the common defense and general welfare of the United States; but all duties, imposts, and excises shall be uniform throughout the United States; (*See the 16th Amendment.*)

2. **[Borrowing of money]** To borrow money on the credit of the United States;

3. **[Regulation of commerce]** To regulate commerce with foreign nations, and among the several States, and with the Indian tribes;

4. **[Naturalization and bankruptcy]** To establish a uniform rule of naturalization, and uniform laws on the subject of bankruptcies throughout the United States;

5. **[Money, weights, and measures]** To coin money, regulate the value thereof, and of foreign coin, and fix the standard of weights and measures;

6. **[Counterfeiting]** To provide for the punishment of counterfeiting the securities and current coin of the United States;

7. **[Post offices]** To establish post offices and post roads;

8. **[Patents and copyrights]** To promote the progress of science and useful arts, by securing for limited times to authors and inventors the exclusive right to their respective writings and discoveries;

9. **[Inferior courts]** To constitute tribunals inferior to the Supreme Court;

10. **[Piracies and felonies]** To define and punish piracies and felonies committed on the high seas, and offenses against the law of nations.

11. **[War; marque and reprisal]** To declare war, grant letters of marque and reprisal, and make rules concerning captures on land and water;

12. **[Armies]** To raise and support armies, but no appropriation of money to that use shall be for a longer term than two years;

13. **[Navy]** To provide and maintain a navy;

14. **[Land and naval forces]** To make rules for the government and regulation of the land and naval forces;

15. **[Calling out militia]** To provide for calling forth the militia to execute the laws of the Union, suppress insurrections, and repel invasions.

16. **[Organizing, arming, and disciplining militia]** To provide for organizing, arming, and disciplining the militia, and for governing such part of them as may be employed in the service of the United States, reserving to the States, respectively, the appointment of the officers, and the authority of training the militia according to the discipline prescribed by Congress;

17. **[Exclusive legislation over District of Columbia]** To exercise exclusive legislation in all cases whatsoever, over such district (not exceeding ten miles square) as may, by cession of particular States, and the acceptance of Congress, become the seat of the Government of the United States, and to exercise like authority over all places purchased by the consent of the Legislature of the State in which the same shall be, for the erection of forts, magazines, arsenals, dock-yards, and other needful buildings;—And

18. **[To enact laws necessary to enforce Constitution]** To make all laws which shall be necessary and proper for carrying into execution the foregoing powers, and all other powers vested by this Constitution in the Government of the United States, or in any department or officer thereof.

Section 9
1. **[Migration or importation of certain persons not to be prohibited before 1808]** The migration or importation of such persons as any of the States now existing shall think proper to admit, shall not be prohibited by the Congress prior to the year one thousand eight hundred and eight, but a tax or duty may be imposed on such importation, not exceeding ten dollars for each person.

2. **[Writ of habeas corpus not to be suspended; exception]** The privilege of the writ of habeas corpus shall not be suspended, unless when in cases of rebellion or invasion the public safety may require it.

3. **[Bills of attainder and ex post facto laws prohibited]** No bill of attainder or ex post facto law shall be passed.

4. **[Capitation and other direct taxes]** No capitation, or other direct, tax shall be laid, unless in proportion to the census or enumeration herein before directed to be taken. (*See the 16th Amendment.*)

5. **[Exports not to be taxed]** No tax or duty shall be laid on articles exported from any State.

6. **[No preference to be given to ports of any State; interstate shipping]** No preference shall be given by any regulation of commerce or revenue to the ports of one State over those of another: nor shall vessels bound to, or from, one State, be obliged to enter, clear, or pay duties in another.

7. **[Money, how drawn from treasury; financial statements to be published]** No money shall be drawn from the Treasury, but in consequence of appropriations made by law; and a regular statement and account of the receipts and expenditures of all public money shall be published from time to time.

8. **[Titles of nobility not to be granted; acceptance by government officers of favors from foreign powers]** No title of nobility shall be granted by the United States; and no person holding any office of profit or trust under them, shall, without the consent of the Congress, accept of any present, emolument, office, or title, of any kind whatever, from any king, prince, or foreign state.

Section 10

1. **[Limitations of the powers of the several States]** No state shall enter into any treaty, alliance, or confederation; grant letters of marque and reprisal; coin money; emit bills of credit; make anything but gold and silver coin a tender in payment of debts; pass any bill of attainder, ex post facto law, or law impairing the obligation of contracts, or grant any title of nobility.

2. **[State imposts and duties]** No State shall, without the consent of the Congress, lay any imposts or duties on imports or exports, except what may be absolutely necessary for executing its inspection laws: and the net produce of all duties and imposts, laid by any State on imports or exports, shall be for the use of the Treasury of the United States; and all such laws shall be subject to the revision and control of the Congress.

3. **[Further restrictions on powers of States]** No State shall, without the consent of Congress, lay any duty of tonnage, keep troops, or ships of war in time of peace, enter into any agreement or compact with another state, or

with a foreign power, or engage in war, unless actually invaded, or in such imminent danger as will not admit of delay.

Article II

Section 1

1. **[The President; the executive power]** The executive power shall be vested in a President of the United States of America. He shall hold his office during the term of four years, and together with the Vice President, chosen for the same term, be elected, as follows:

2. **[Appointment and qualifications of presidential electors]** Each State shall appoint, in such manner as the Legislature thereof may direct, a number of electors, equal to the whole number of Senators and Representatives to which the State may be entitled in the Congress: but no Senator or Representative, or person holding an office of trust or profit under the United States, shall be appointed an elector.

3. **[Original method of electing the President and Vice President]** (The electors shall meet in their respective States, and vote by ballot for two persons, of whom one at least shall not be an inhabitant of the same State with themselves. And they shall make a list of all the persons voted for, and of the number of votes for each; which list they shall sign and certify, and transmit sealed to the seat of the Government of the United States, directed to the President of the Senate. The President of the Senate shall, in the presence of the Senate and House of Representatives, open all the certificates, and the votes shall then be counted. The person having the greatest number of votes shall be the President, if such number be a majority of the whole number of electors appointed; and if there be more than one who have such majority, and have an equal number of votes, then the House of Representatives shall immediately choose by ballot one of them for President; and if no person have a majority, then from the five highest on the list the said House shall in like manner choose the President. But in choosing the President, the votes shall be taken by States, the representation from each State having one vote; a quorum for this purpose shall consist of a member or members from two-thirds of the States, and a majority of all the states shall be necessary to a choice. In every case, after the choice of the President, the person having the greatest number of votes of the electors shall be the Vice President. But if there should remain two or more who have equal votes, the Senate should choose from them by ballot the Vice President.—*Replaced by the 12th Amendment.*)

4. **[Congress may determine time of choosing electors and day for casting their votes]** The Congress may determine the time of choosing the electors, and the day on which they shall give their votes; which day shall be the same throughout the United States.

5. **[Qualifications for the office of President]** No person except a natural born citizen, or a citizen of the United States, at the time of the adoption of this Constitution, shall be eligible to the office of President; neither shall any person be eligible to that office who shall not have attained to the age of thirty-five years, and been fourteen years a resident within the United States. (*For qualifications of the Vice President, see the 12th Amendment.*)

6. **[Filling vacancy in the office of President]** (In case of the removal of the President from office, or of his death, resignation, or inability to discharge the powers and duties of the said office, the same shall devolve on the Vice President, and the Congress may by law provide for the case of removal, death, resignation or inability, both of the President and Vice President, declaring what officer shall then act as President, and such officer shall act accordingly, until the disability be removed, or a President shall be elected.—*Amended by the 20th and 25th Amendments.*)

7. **[Compensation of the President]** The President shall, at stated times, receive for his services, a compensation, which shall neither be increased nor diminished during the period for which he shall have been elected, and he shall not receive within that period any other emolument from the United States, or any of them.

8. **[Oath to be taken by the President]** Before he enter on the execution of his office, he shall take the following oath or affirmation:—"I do solemnly swear (or affirm) that I will faithfully execute the office of President of the United States, and will to the best of my ability, preserve, protect, and defend the Constitution of the United States."

Section 2

1. **[The President to be Commander-in-Chief of army and navy and head of executive departments; may grant reprieves and pardons]** The President shall be Commander-in-Chief of the Army and Navy of the United States, and of the militia of the several States, when called into the actual service of the United States; he may require the opinion, in writing, of the principal officer in each of the executive departments, upon any subject relating to the duties of their respective offices, and he shall have power to grant reprieves and pardons for offenses against the United States, except in cases of impeachment.

2. **[President may, with concurrence of Senate, make treaties, appoint ambassadors, etc.; appointment of inferior officers, authority of Congress over]** He shall have power, by and with the advice and consent of the Senate, to make treaties, provided two-thirds of the Senators present concur; and he shall nominate, and by and with the advice and consent of the Senate, shall appoint ambassadors, other

public ministers and consuls, judges of the Supreme Court, and all other officers of the United States, whose appointments are not herein otherwise provided for, and which shall be established by law: but the Congress may by law vest the appointment of such inferior officers, as they think proper, in the President alone, in the courts of law, or in the heads of departments.

3. **[President may fill vacancies in office during recess of Senate]** The President shall have power to fill up all vacancies that may happen during the recess of the Senate, by granting commissions which shall expire at the end of their session.

Section 3
[President to give advice to Congress; may convene or adjourn it on certain occasions; to receive ambassadors, etc.; have laws executed and commission all officers] He shall from time to time give to the Congress information of the state of the Union, and recommend to their consideration such measures as he shall judge necessary and expedient; he may, on extraordinary occasions, convene both Houses, or either of them, and in case of disagreement between them, with respect to the time of adjournment, he may adjourn them to such time as he shall think proper; he shall receive ambassadors and other public ministers: he shall take care that the laws be faithfully executed, and shall commission all the officers of the United States.

Section 4
[All civil officers removable by impeachment] The President, Vice President, and all civil officers of the United States shall be removed from office on impeachment for, and conviction of, treason, bribery, or other high crimes and misdemeanors.

Article III

Section 1
[Judicial powers; how vested; term of office and compensation of judges] The judicial power of the United States, shall be vested in one Supreme Court, and in such inferior courts as the Congress may from time to time ordain and establish. The judges, both of the supreme and inferior courts, shall hold their offices during good behavior, and shall, at stated times, receive for their services, a compensation, which shall not be diminished during their continuance in office.

Section 2
1. **[Jurisdiction of Federal courts]** (The judicial power shall extend to all cases, in law and equity, arising under this Constitution, the laws of the United States, and treaties made, or which shall be made, under their authority; to all cases affecting ambassadors, other public min-

isters and consuls; to all cases of admiralty and maritime jurisdiction; to controversies to which the United States, shall be a party; to controversies between two or more States; between a State and citizens of another State; between citizens of different States, between citizens of the same State claiming lands under grants of different states, and between a State, or the citizens thereof, and foreign states, citizens, or subjects.— Amended by the 11th Amendment.)

2. **[Original and appellate jurisdiction of Supreme Court]** In all cases affecting ambassadors, other public ministers and consuls, and those in which a State shall be party, the Supreme Court shall have original jurisdiction. In all the other cases before mentioned, the Supreme Court shall have appellate jurisdiction, both as to law and fact, with such exceptions, and under such regulations, as the Congress shall make.

3. **[Trial of all crimes, except impeachment, to be by jury]** The trial of all crimes, except in cases of impeachment, shall be by jury; and such trial shall be held in the State where the said crimes shall have been committed; but when not committed within any State, the trial shall be at such place or places as the Congress may by law have directed.

Section 3

1. **[Treason defined; conviction of]** Treason against the United States, shall consist only in levying war against them, or, in adhering to their enemies, giving them aid and comfort. No person shall be convicted of treason unless on the testimony of two witnesses to the same overt act, or on confession in open court.

2. **[Congress to declare punishment for treason; proviso]** The Congress shall have power to declare the punishment of treason, but no attainder of treason shall work corruption of blood, or forfeiture except during the life of the person attainted.

Article IV

Section 1

[Each State to give full faith and credit to the public acts and records of other States] Full faith and credit shall be given in each State to the public acts, records, and judicial proceedings of every other State. And the Congress may by general laws prescribe the manner in which such acts, records, and proceedings shall be proved, and the effect thereof.

Section 2

1. **[Privileges of citizens]** The citizens of each State shall be entitled to all privileges and immunities of citizens in the several States.

2. **[Extradition between the several States]** A person charged in any State with treason, felony, or other crime, who shall flee from justice, and be found in another State, shall on demand of the Executive authority of the State from which he fled, be delivered up, to be removed to the State having jurisdiction of the crime.

3. **[Persons held to labor or service in one State, fleeing to another, to be returned]** (No person held to service or labor in one State, under the laws thereof, escaping into another, shall, in consequence of any law or regulation therein, be discharged from such service or labor, but shall be delivered up on claim of the party to whom such service or labor may be due.— *Eliminated by the 13th Amendment.*)

Section 3

1. **[New States]** New States may be admitted by the Congress into this Union; but no new State shall be formed or erected within the jurisdiction of any other State; nor any State be formed by the junction of two or more States, or parts of States, without the consent of the Legislatures of the States concerned as well as of the Congress.

2. **[Regulations concerning territory]** The Congress shall have power to dispose of and make all needful rules and regulations respecting the territory or other property belonging to the United States; and nothing in this Constitution shall be so construed as to prejudice any claims of the United States, or of any particular State.

Section 4

[Republican form of government and protection guaranteed the several States] The United States shall guarantee to every State in this Union a Republican form of government, and shall protect each of them against invasion; and on application of the Legislature, or of the Executive (when the Legislature cannot be convened) against domestic violence.

Article V

[Ways in which the Constitution can be amended] The Congress, whenever two-thirds of both Houses shall deem it necessary, shall propose amendments to this Constitution, or, on the application of the Legislatures of two-thirds of the several States shall call a convention for proposing amendments, which, in either case, shall be valid to all intents and purposes, as part of this Constitution, when ratified by the Legislatures of three-fourths of the several States, or by conventions in three-fourths thereof, as the one or the other mode of ratificatian may be proposed by the Congress; provided that no amendment which may be made prior to the year one thousand eight hundred and eight shall in any manner affect the first and fourth clauses in the ninth Section of the first Article; and that no State, without its consent, shall be deprived of its equal suffrage in the Senate.

Article VI

1. **[Debts contracted under the confederation secured]** All debts contracted and engagements entered into, before the adoption of this Constitution, shall be as valid against the United States under this Constitution, as under the Confederation.

2. **[Constitution, laws, and treaties of the United States to be supreme]** This Constitution, and the laws of the United States which shall be made in pursuance thereof; and all treaties made, or which shall be made, under the authority of the United States, shall be the supreme law of the land; and the judges in every State shall be bound thereby, anything in the Constitution or laws of any State to the contrary notwithstanding.

3. **[Who shall take constitutional oath; no religious test as to official qualification]** The Senators and Representatives before mentioned, and the members of the several State Legislatures, and all executive and judicial officers, both of the United States and of the several States, shall be bound by oath or affirmation, to support this Constitution; but no religious test shall ever be required as a qualification to any office or public trust under the United States.

Article VII

[Constitution to be considered adopted when ratified by nine States] The ratification of the conventions of nine States shall be sufficient for the establishment of this Constitution between the States so ratifying the same.

How a Bill Becomes a Law

When a senator or a representative introduces a bill, he sends it to the clerk of his house, who gives it a number and title. This is the *first reading,* and the bill is referred to the proper committee.

The committee may decide the bill is unwise or unnecessary and *table* it, thus killing it at once. Or it may decide the bill is worthwhile and hold hearings to listen to facts and opinions presented by experts and other interested persons. After members of the committee have debated the bill and perhaps offered amendments, a vote is taken; and if the vote is favorable, the bill is sent back to the floor of the house.

The clerk reads the bill sentence by sentence to the house; this is known as the *second reading*. Members may then debate the bill and offer amendments. In the House of Representatives, the time for debate is limited by a *cloture rule*, but there is no such restriction in the Senate for cloture. Instead, 60 votes are required to limit debate. This makes possible a *filibuster*, in which one or more opponents hold the floor in an attempt to defeat the bill.

The *third reading* is by title only, and the bill is put to a vote, which may be by voice or roll call, depending on the circumstances and parliamentary rules. Members who must be absent at the time but who wish to record their vote may be paired if each negative vote has a balancing affirmative one.

The bill then goes to the other house of Congress, where it may be defeated or passed with or without amendments. If the bill is defeated, it dies. If it is passed with amendments, a joint Congressional committee must be appointed by both houses to iron out the differences.

After its final passage by both houses, the bill is sent to the president. If he approves, he signs it, and the bill becomes a law. However, if he disapproves, he *vetoes* the bill by refusing to sign it. He then sends the bill back to the house of origin with his reasons for the veto. The objections are read and debated, and a roll-call vote is taken. If the bill receives less than a two-thirds vote, it is defeated and goes no farther. But if it receives a two-thirds vote or greater, it is sent to the other house for a vote. If that house also passes it by a two-thirds vote, the president's veto is *overridden*, and the bill becomes a law.

Should the president desire neither to sign nor to veto the bill, he may retain it for ten days, Sundays excepted, after which time it automatically becomes a law without signature. However, if Congress has adjourned within those ten days, the bill is automatically killed, that process of indirect rejection being known as a *pocket veto*.

Amendments to the Constitution
of the United States

Note: Amendments I to X popularly known as the Bill of Rights, were proposed and sent to the states by the first session of the First Congress. They were ratified Dec. 15, 1791.

AMENDMENT 1

[Freedom of religion, speech, of the press, and right of petition] Congress shall make no law respecting an establishment of religion, or prohibiting the free exercise thereof; or abridging the freedom of speech, or of the press; or the right of the people peaceably to assemble, and to petition the Government for a redress of grievances.

AMENDMENT 2

[Right of people to bear arms not to be infringed] A well-regulated militia, being necessary to the security of a free State, the right of the people to keep and bear arms, shall not be infringed.

AMENDMENT 3

[Quartering of troops] No soldier shall, in time of peace be quartered in any house, without the consent of the owner, nor in time of war, but in a manner to be prescribed by law.

AMENDMENT 4

[Persons and houses to be secure from unreasonable searches and seizures] The right of the people to be secure in their persons, houses, papers, and effects, against unreasonable searches and seizures, shall not be violated, and no warrants shall issue, but upon probable cause, supported by oath or affirmation, and particularly describing the place to be searched, and the persons or things to be seized.

AMENDMENT 5

[Trials for crimes; just compensation for private property taken for public use] No person shall be held to answer for a capital, or otherwise infamous crime, unless on a presentment or indictment of a Grand Jury, except in cases arising in the land or naval forces, or in the militia, when in actual service in time of war or public danger; nor shall any person be subject for the same offense to be twice put in jeopardy of life or limb; nor shall be compelled in any criminal case to be a witness, against himself, nor be deprived of life, liberty, or property, without due process of law; nor shall private property be taken for public use, without just compensation.

AMENDMENT 6

[Right to speedy trial, witnesses, counsel] In all criminal prosecutions, the accused shall enjoy the right to a speedy and public trial, by an impartial jury of the State and district wherein the crime shall have been committed, which district shall have been previously ascer-

tained by law, and to be informed of the nature and cause of the accusation; to be confronted with the witnesses against him; to have compulsory process for obtaining witnesses in his favor, and to have the assistance of counsel for his defense.

AMENDMENT 7

[Right of trial by jury] In suits at common law, where the value in controversy shall exceed twenty dollars, the right of trial by jury shall be preserved, and no fact tried by a jury, shall be otherwise re-examined in any court of the United States, than according to the rules of the common law.

AMENDMENT 8

[Excessive bail, fines, and punishments prohibited] Excessive bail shall not be required, nor excessive fines imposed, nor cruel and unusual punishments inflicted.

AMENDMENT 9

[Reserved rights of people] The enumeration in the Constitution, of certain rights, shall not be construed to deny or disparage others retained by the people.

AMENDMENT 10

[Rights of States under Constitution] The powers not delegated to the United States by the Constitution, nor prohibited by it to the States, are reserved to the States, respectively, or to the people.

AMENDMENT 11

(The proposed amendment was sent to the states March 5, 1794 by the Third Congress. It was ratified Feb. 7, 1795. It changes Article III Sect. 2, Para. 1.)
[Judicial power of United States not to extend to suits against a State] The judicial power of the United States shall not be construed to extend to any suit in law or equity, commenced or prosecuted against one of the United States by citizens of another State, or by citizens or subjects of any foreign state.

AMENDMENT 12

(The proposed amendment was sent to the states Dec. 12, 1803, by the Eighth Congress. It was ratified July 27, 1804. It replaces Article II, Sect. 1, Para. 3.)
[Manner of electing President and Vice President by electors] (The electors shall meet in their respective states, and vote by ballot for President and Vice President, one of whom, at

least, shall not be an inhabitant of the same state with themselves; they shall name in their ballots the person voted for as President, and in distinct ballots the person voted for as Vice President, and they shall make distinct lists of all persons voted for as President, and of all persons voted for as Vice President, and of the number of votes for each, which lists they shall sign and certify, and transmit sealed to the seat of the government of the United States, directed to the President of the Senate; the President of the Senate shall, in the presence of the Senate and House of Representatives, open all the certificates and the votes shall then be counted; the person having the greatest number of votes for President, shall be the President, if such number be a majority of the whole number of electors appointed; and if no person have such majority, then from the persons having the highest numbers not exceeding three on the list of those voted for as President, the House of Representatives shall choose immediately, by ballot, the President. But in choosing the President, the votes shall be taken by states, the representation from each State having one vote; a quorum for this purpose shall consist of a member or members from two-thirds of the states, and a majority of all the states shall be necessary to a choice. And if the House of Representatives shall not choose a President whenever the right of choice shall devolve upon them, before the fourth day of March next following, then the Vice President shall act as President, as in the case of the death or other constitutional disability of the President. The person having the greatest number of votes as Vice President, shall be the Vice President, if such number be a majority of the whole number of electors appointed, and if no person have a majority, then from the two highest numbers on the list, the Senate shall choose the Vice President; a quorum for the purpose shall consist of two-thirds of the whole number of Senators, and a majority of the whole number shall be necessary to a choice. But no person constitutionally ineligible to the office of President shall be eligible to that of Vice President of the United States.— Amended by the 20th Amendment, sections 3 and 4.)

AMENDMENT 13

(The proposed amendment was sent to the states Feb. 1, 1865, by the Thirty-eighth Congress. It was ratified Dec. 6, 1865. It eliminates Article IV, Sect. 2, Para. 3.)

Section 1

[Slavery prohibited] Neither slavery nor involuntary servitude, except as a punishment for crime whereof the party shall have been duly convicted, shall exist within the United States, or any place subject to their Jurisdiction.

Section 2

[Congress given power to enforce this article] Congress shall have power to enforce this article by appropriate legislation.

AMENDMENT 14

(The proposed amendment was sent to the states June 16, 1866, by the Thirty-ninth Congress. It was ratified July 9, 1868. It changes Article 1, Sec. 2, Para. 3.)

Section 1

[Citizenship defined; privileges of citizens] All persons born or naturalized in the United States, and subject to the jurisdiction thereof, are citizens of the United States and of the State wherein they reside. No State shall make or enforce any law which shall abridge the privileges or immunities of citizens of the United States; nor shall any State deprive any person of life, liberty, or property, without due process of law; nor deny to any person within its jurisdiction the equal protection of the laws.

Section 2

[Apportionment of Representatives] Representatives shall be apportioned among the several States according to their respective numbers, counting the whole number of persons in each State, excluding Indians not taxed. But when the right to vote at any election for the choice of electors for President and Vice President of the United States, Representatives in Congress, the executive and judicial officers of a State, or the members of the Legislature thereof, is denied to any of the male inhabitants of such State, being twenty-one years of age, and citizens of the United States, or in any way abridged, except for participation in rebellion, or other crime, the basis of representation therein shall be reduced in the proportion which the number of such male citizens shall bear to the whole number of male citizens twenty-one years of age in such State.

Section 3

[Disqualification for office; removal of disability] No person shall be a Senator or Representative in Congress, or elector of President and Vice President, or hold any office, civil or military, under the United States, or under any State, who, having previously taken an oath, as a member of Congress, or as an officer of the United States, or as a member of any State Legislature, or as an executive or judicial officer of any State, to support the Constitution of the United States, shall have engaged in insurrection or rebellion against the same, or given aid or comfort to the enemies thereof. But Congress may by a vote of two-thirds of each House, remove such disability.

Section 4

[Public debt not to be questioned; payment of debts and claims incurred in aid of rebellion forbidden] The validity of the public debt of the United States, authorized by law, including debts incurred for payment of pensions and bounties for services in suppressing insurrection or rebellion, shall not be questioned. But neither the United States nor any State shall assume or pay any debt or obligation incurred in aid of insurrection or rebellion against the United States, or any claim for the loss or emancipation of any slave; but all such debts, obligations, and claims shall be held illegal and void.

Section 5
[Congress given power to enforce this article] The Congress shall have power to enforce, by appropriate legislation, the provisions of this article.

AMENDMENT 15
(The proposed amendment was sent to the states Feb. 27, 1869, by the Fortieth Congress. It was ratified Feb. 3, 1870.)

Section 1
[Right of certain citizens to vote established] The right of citizens of the United States to vote shall not be denied or abridged by the United States or by any State on account of race, color, or previous condition of servitude.

Section 2
[Congress given power to enforce this article] The Congress shall have power to enforce this article by appropriate legislation.

AMENDMENT 16
(The proposed amendment was sent to the states July 12, 1909, by the Sixty-first Congress. It was ratified Feb. 3, 1913.)

[Income taxes authorized] The Congress shall have power to lay and collect taxes on incomes, from whatever source derived, without apportionment among the several States, and without regard to any census or enumeration.

AMENDMENT 17
(The proposed amendment was sent to the states May 16, 1912, by the Sixty-second Congress. It was ratified April 8, 1913. It changes Article 1, Sect. 3, Para. 1 and 2.)

[Election of United States Senators; filling of vacancies; qualifications of electors] The Senate of the United States shall be composed of two Senators from each State, elected by the people thereof, for six years; and each Senator shall have one vote. The electors in each State shall have the qualifications requisite for electors of the most numerous branch of the State Legislatures.

When vacancies happen in the representation of any State in the Senate, the executive authority of such State shall issue writs of election to fill such vacancies: Provided, that the legislature of any State may empower the executive thereof to make temporary appointment until the people fill the vacancies by election as the legislature may direct.

This amendment shall not be so construed as to affect the election or term of any Senator chosen before it becomes valid as part of the Constitution.

AMENDMENT 18
(The proposed amendment was sent to the states Dec. 18, 1917, by the Sixty-fifth Congress. It was ratified by three-quarters of the states by Jan. 16, 1919, and became effective Jan. 16, 1920. It was repealed by the 21st Amendment.)

Section 1
[Manufacture, sale, or transportation of intoxicating liquors, for beverage purposes, prohibited] After one year from the ratification of this article the manufacture, sale, or transportation of intoxicating liquors within, the importation thereof into, or the exportation thereof from the United States and all territory subject to the jurisdiction thereof for beverage purposes is hereby prohibited.

Section 2
[Congress and the several States given concurrent power to pass appropriate legislation to enforce this article] The Congress and the several States shall have concurrent power to enforce this article by appropriate legislation.

Section 3
[Provisions of article to become operative, when adopted by three-fourths of the States] This article shall be inoperative unless it shall have been ratified as an amendment to the Constitution by the legislatures of the several States, as provided in the Constitution, within seven years from the date of the submission hereof to the States by Congress.

AMENDMENT 19
(The proposed amendment was sent to the states June 4, 1919, by the Sixty-sixth Congress. It was ratified Aug 18, 1920.)

[The right of citizens to vote shall not be denied because of sex] The right of citizens of the United States to vote shall not be denied or abridged by the United States or by any State on account of sex.

[Congress given power to enforce this article] Congress shall have power to enforce this article by appropriate legislation.

AMENDMENT 20
(The proposed amendment, sometimes called the "Lame Duck Amendment," was sent to the states March 3, 1932, by the Seventy-second Congress. It was ratified Jan. 23, 1933; but, in

accordance with Section 5, Sections 1 and 2 did not go into effect until Oct. 15, 1933. It changes Article 1, Sect. 4, Para. 2 and the 12th Amendment.)

Section 1
[Terms of President, Vice President, Senators, and Representatives] The terms of the President and Vice President shall end at noon on the twentieth day of January, and the terms of Senators and Representatives at noon on the third day of January, of the years in which such terms would have ended if this article had not been ratified; and the terms of their successors shall then begin.

Section 2
[Time of assembling Congress] The Congress shall assemble at least once in every year, and such meeting shall begin at noon on the third day of January, unless they shall by law appoint a different day.

Section 3
[Filling vacancy in office of President] If, at the time fixed for the beginning of the term of the President, the President-elect shall have died, the Vice President-elect shall become President. If a President shall not have been chosen before the time fixed for the beginning of his term, or if the President-elect shall have failed to qualify, then the Vice President shall have qualified; and the Congress may by law provide for the case wherein neither a President-elect nor a Vice President-elect shall have qualified, declaring who shall then act as President, or the manner in which one who is to act shall be selected, and such person shall act accordingly until a President or Vice President shall have qualified.

Section 4
[Power of Congress in Presidential succession] The Congress may by law provide for the case of the death of any of the persons from whom the House of Representatives may choose a President whenever the right of choice shall have devolved upon them, and for the case of the death of any of the persons from whom the Senate may choose a Vice President whenever the right of choice shall have devolved upon them.

Section 5
[Time of taking effect] Sections 1 and 2 shall take effect on the 15th day of October following the ratification of this article.

Section 6
[Ratification] This article shall be inoperative unless it shall have been ratified as an amendment to the Constitution by the legislatures of three-fourths of the several States within seven years from the date of its submission.

AMENDMENT 21
(The proposed amendment was sent to the states Feb. 20, 1933, by the Seventy-second Congress. It was ratified Dec. 5, 1933. It repeals the 18th Amendment.)

Section 1
[Repeal of Prohibition Amendment] The eighteenth article of amendment to the Constitution of the United States is hereby repealed.

Section 2
[Transportation of intoxicating liquors] The transportation or importation into any State, territory, or possession of the United States for delivery or use therein of intoxicating liquors, in violation of the laws thereof, is hereby prohibited.

Section 3
[Ratification] This article shall be inoperative unless it shall have been ratified as an amendment to the Constitution by convention in the several States, as provided in the Constitution, within seven years from the date of the submission thereof to the States by the Congress.

AMENDMENT 22
(The proposed amendment was sent to the states March 21, 1947, by the Eightieth Congress. It was ratified Feb. 27, 1951.)

Section 1
[Limit to number of terms a President may serve] No person shall be elected to the office of the President more than twice, and no person who has held the office of President, or acted as President for more than two years of a term to which some other person was elected President shall be elected to the office of the President more than once. But this article shall not apply to any person holding the office of President when this article was proposed by the Congress, and shall not prevent any person who may be holding the office of President, or acting as President, during the term within which this article becomes operative from holding the office of President or acting as President during the remainder of such term.

Section 2
[Ratification] This article shall be inoperative unless it shall have been ratified as an amendment to the Constitution by the legislatures of three-fourths of the several States within seven years from the date of its submission to the States by the Congress.

AMENDMENT 23
(The proposed amendment was sent to the states June 16, 1960, by the Eighty-sixth Congress. It was ratified March 29, 1961.)

Section 1
[Electors for the District of Columbia]

The District constituting the seat of Government of the United States shall appoint in such manner as the Congress may direct:

A number of electors of President and Vice President equal to the whole number of Senators and Representatives in Congress to which the District would be entitled if it were a State, but in no event more than the least populous State; they shall be in addition to those appointed by the States, but they shall be considered, for the purposes of the election of President and Vice President, to be electors appointed by a State; and they shall meet in the District and perform such duties as provided by the twelfth article of amendment.

Section 2
[Congress given power to enforce this article] The Congress shall have the power to enforce this article by appropriate legislation.

AMENDMENT 24

(The proposed amendment was sent to the states Aug. 27, 1962, by the Eighty-seventh Congress. It was ratified Jan. 23, 1964.)

Section 1
[Payment of poll tax or other taxes barred in federal elections] The right of citizens of the United States to vote in any primary or other election for President or Vice President, for electors for President or Vice President, or for Senator or Representative in Congress, shall not be denied or abridged by the United States or any State by reasons of failure to pay any poll tax or other tax.

Section 2
[Congress given power to enforce this article] The Congress shall have the power to enforce this article by appropriate legislation.

AMENDMENT 25

(The proposed amendment was sent to the states July 6, 1965, by the Eighty-ninth Congress. It was ratified Feb. 10, 1967.)

Section 1
[Succession of Vice President to Presidency] In case of the removal of the President from office or of his death or resignation, the Vice President shall become President.

Section 2
[Vacancy in office of Vice President] Whenever there is a vacancy in the office of the Vice President, the President shall nominate a Vice President who shall take office upon confirmation by a majority vote of both Houses of Congress.

Section 3
[Vice President as Acting President] Whenever the President transmits to the Presi-

dent pro tempore of the Senate and the Speaker of the House of Representatives his written declaration that he is unable to discharge the powers and duties of his office, and until he transmits to them a written declaration to the contrary, such powers and duties shall be discharged by the Vice President as Acting President.

Section 4
[Vice President as Acting President] Whenever the Vice President and a majority of either the principal officers of the executive departments or of such other body as Congress may by law provide, transmit to the President pro tempore of the Senate and the Speaker of the House of Representatives their written declaration that the President is unable to discharge the powers and duties of his office, the Vice President shall immediately assume the powers and duties of the office as Acting President.

Thereafter, when the President transmits to the President pro tempore of the Senate and the Speaker of the House of Representatives his written declaration that no inability exists, he shall resume the powers and duties of his office unless the Vice President and a majority of either the principal officers of the executive department or of such other body as Congress may by law provide, transmit within four days to the President pro tempore of the Senate and the Speaker of the House of Representatives their written declaration that the President is unable to discharge the powers and duties of his office. Thereupon Congress shall decide the issue, assembling within forty-eight hours for that purpose if not in session. If the Congress, within twenty-one days after receipt of the latter written declaration, or, if Congress is not in session, within twenty-one days after Congress is required to assemble, determines by two-thirds vote of both Houses that the President is unable to discharge the powers and duties of his office, the Vice President shall continue to discharge the same as Acting President; otherwise, the President shall resume the powers and duties of his office.

AMENDMENT 26

(The proposed amendment was sent to the states March 23, 1971, by the Ninety-second Congress. It was ratified July 1, 1971.)

Section 1
[Voting for 18 year-olds] The right of citizens of the United States, who are 18 years of age or older, to vote shall not be denied or abridged by the United States or by any state on account of age.

Section 2
[Congress given power to enforce this article] The Congress shall have power to enforce this article by appropriate legislation.

861 Emancipation Proclamation

January 1, 1863

By the President of the United States of America:

A Proclamation

Whereas on the 22d day of September, A.D. 1862, a proclamation was issued by the President of the United States, containing, among other things, the following, to wit:

"That on the 1st day of January, A.D. 1863, all persons held as slaves within any State or designated part of a State the people whereof shall then be in rebellion against the Union States shall be then, thenceforward, and forever free; and the executive government of the United States, including the military and naval authority thereof, will recognize and maintain the freedom of such persons and will do no act or acts to repress such persons, or any of them, in any efforts they may make for their actual freedom.

"That the executive will on the 1st day of January aforesaid, by proclamation, designate the States and parts of States, if any, in which the people thereof, respectively, shall then be in rebellion against the United States; and the fact that any State of the people thereof shall on that day be in good faith represented in the Congress of the United States by members chosen thereto at elections wherein a majority of the qualified voters of such States shall have participated shall, in the absence of strong countervailing testimony, be deemed conclusive evidence that such State and the people thereof are not then in rebellion against the United States."

Now therefore, I, Abraham Lincoln, President of the United States, by virtue of the power in me vested as Commander-in-Chief of the Army and Navy of the United States in time of actual armed rebellion against the authority and government of the United States, and as a fit and necessary war measure for suppressing said rebellion, do, on this 1st day of January, A.D. 1863, and in accordance with my purpose so to do, publicly proclaimed for the full period of one hundred days from the first day above mentioned, order and designate as the States and parts of States wherein the people thereof, respectively, are this day in rebellion against the United States the following, to wit:

Arkansas, Texas, Louisiana (except the parishes of St. Bernard, Plaquemines, Jefferson, St. John, St. Charles, St. James, Ascension, Assumption, Terrebonne, Lafourche, St. Mary, St. Martin, and Orleans, including the city of New Orleans), Mississippi, Alabama, Florida, Georgia, South Carolina, North Carolina, and Virginia (except the forty-eight counties designated as West Virginia, and also the counties of Berkeley, Accomac, Northhampton, Elizabeth City, York, Princess Anne, and Norfolk, including the cities of Norfolk and Portsmouth), and which excepted parts are for the present left precisely as if this proclamation were not issued.

And by virtue of the power and for the purpose aforesaid, I do order and declare that all persons held as slaves within said designated States and parts of States are, and henceforward shall be, free; and that the Executive Government of the United States, including the military and naval authorities thereof, will recognize and maintain the freedom of said persons.

And I hereby enjoin upon the people so declared to be free to abstain from all violence, unless in necessary self-defense; and I recommend to them that, in all cases when allowed, they labor faithfully for reasonable wages.

And I further declare and make known that such persons of suitable condition will be received into the armed service of the United States to garrison forts, positions, stations, and other places, and to man vessels of all sorts in said service.

And upon this act, sincerely believed to be an act of justice, warranted by the Constitution upon military necessity, I invoke the considerate judgment of mankind and the gracious favor of Almighty God.

U.S. Presidents

(*Did not finish term)   **862**

1	George Washington .... April 30, 1789 - March 3, 1797 .... John Adams	1
2	John Adams .... March 4, 1797 - March 3, 1801 .... Thomas Jefferson	2
3	Thomas Jefferson .... March 4, 1801 - March 3, 1805 .... Aaron Burr	3
	Thomas Jefferson .... March 4, 1805 - March 3, 1809 .... George Clinton	4
4	James Madison .... March 4, 1809 - March 3, 1813 .... George Clinton	
	James Madison .... March 4, 1813 - March 3, 1817 .... Elbridge Gerry	5
5	James Monroe .... March 4, 1817 - March 3, 1825 .... Daniel D. Tompkins	6
6	John Quincy Adams .... March 4, 1825 - March 3, 1829 .... John C. Calhoun	7
7	Andrew Jackson .... March 4, 1829 - March 3, 1833 .... John C. Calhoun	
	Andrew Jackson .... March 4, 1833 - March 3, 1837 .... Martin Van Buren	8
8	Martin Van Buren .... March 4, 1837 - March 3, 1841 .... Richard M. Johnson	9
9	William Henry Harrison* .... March 4, 1841 - April 4, 1841 .... John Tyler	10
10	John Tyler .... April 6, 1841 - March 3, 1845	
11	James K. Polk .... March 4, 1845 - March 3, 1849 .... George M. Dallas	11
12	Zachary Taylor* .... March 5, 1849 - July 9, 1850 .... Millard Fillmore	12
13	Millard Fillmore .... July 10, 1850 - March 3, 1853	
14	Franklin Pierce .... March 4, 1853 - March 3, 1857 .... William R. King	13
15	James Buchanan .... March 4, 1857 - March 3, 1861 .... John C. Breckinridge	14
16	Abraham Lincoln .... March 4, 1861 - March 3, 1865 .... Hannibal Hamlin	15
	Abraham Lincoln* .... March 4, 1865 - April 15, 1865 .... Andrew Johnson	16
17	Andrew Johnson .... April 15, 1865 - March 3, 1869	
18	Ulysses S. Grant .... March 4, 1869 - March 3, 1873 .... Schuyler Colfax	17
	Ulysses S. Grant .... March 4, 1873 - March 3, 1877 .... Henry Wilson	18
19	Rutherford B. Hayes .... March 4, 1877 - March 3, 1881 .... William A. Wheeler	19
20	James A. Garfield* .... March 4, 1881 - Sept. 19, 1881 .... Chester A. Arthur	20
21	Chester A. Arthur .... Sept. 20, 1881 - March 3, 1885	
22	Grover Cleveland .... March 4, 1885 - March 3, 1889 .... Thomas A. Hendricks	21
23	Benjamin Harrison .... March 4, 1889 - March 3, 1893 .... Levi P. Morton	22
24	Grover Cleveland .... March 4, 1893 - March 3, 1897 .... Adlai E. Stevenson	23
25	William McKinley .... March 4, 1897 - March 3, 1901 .... Garret A. Hobart	24
	William McKinley* .... March 4, 1901 - Sept. 14, 1901 .... Theodore Roosevelt	25
26	Theodore Roosevelt .... Sept. 14, 1901 - March 3, 1905	
	Theodore Roosevelt .... March 4, 1905 - March 3, 1909 .... Charles W. Fairbanks	26
27	William H. Taft .... March 4, 1909 - March 3, 1913 .... James S. Sherman	27
28	Woodrow Wilson .... March 4, 1913 - March 3, 1921 .... Thomas R. Marshall	28
29	Warren G. Harding* .... March 4, 1921 - Aug. 2, 1923 .... Calvin Coolidge	29
30	Calvin Coolidge .... Aug. 3, 1923 - March 3, 1925	
	Calvin Coolidge .... March 4, 1925 - March 3, 1929 .... Charles G. Dawes	30
31	Herbert C. Hoover .... March 4, 1929 - March 3, 1933 .... Charles Curtis	31
32	Franklin D. Roosevelt .... March 4, 1933 - Jan. 20, 1941 .... John N. Garner	32
	Franklin D. Roosevelt .... Jan. 20, 1941 - Jan. 20, 1945 .... Henry A. Wallace	33
	Franklin Roosevelt* .... Jan. 20, 1945 - April 12, 1945 .... Harry S. Truman	34
33	Harry S. Truman .... April 12, 1945 - Jan. 20, 1949	
	Harry S. Truman .... Jan. 20, 1949 - Jan. 20, 1953 .... Alben W. Barkley	35
34	Dwight D. Eisenhower .... Jan. 20, 1953 - Jan. 20, 1961 .... Richard M. Nixon	36
35	John F. Kennedy* .... Jan. 20, 1961 - Nov. 22, 1963 .... Lyndon B. Johnson	37
36	Lyndon B. Johnson .... Nov. 22, 1963 - Jan. 20, 1965	
	Lyndon B. Johnson .... Jan. 20, 1965 - Jan. 20, 1969 .... Hubert H. Humphrey	38
37	Richard M. Nixon .... Jan. 20, 1969 - Jan. 20, 1973 .... Spiro T. Agnew	39
	Richard M. Nixon* .... Jan. 20, 1973 - Aug. 9, 1974 .... Gerald R. Ford	40
38	Gerald R. Ford .... Aug. 9, 1974 - Jan. 20, 1977 .... Nelson A. Rockefeller	41
39	James E. Carter .... Jan. 20, 1977 - Jan. 20, 1981 .... Walter Mondale	42
40	Ronald Reagan .... Jan. 20, 1981 - Jan. 20, 1985 .... George Bush	43
	Ronald Reagan .... Jan. 20, 1985 - Jan. 20, 1989 .... George Bush	
41	George Bush .... Jan. 20, 1989 - .... J. Danford Quayle	44

Order of Presidential Succession

863

1. The Vice President
2. Speaker of the House
3. President pro tempore of the Senate
4. Secretary of State
5. Secretary of the Treasury
6. Secretary of Defense
7. Attorney General
8. Secretary of the Interior
9. Secretary of Agriculture
10. Secretary of Commerce
11. Secretary of Labor
12. Secretary of Health, Education, & Welfare
13. Secretary of Housing and Urban Development
14. Secretary of Transportation

Index

Your *Write Source 2000* index contains **topic** numbers, not page numbers. You will find topic numbers at the top of each page and next to each new piece of information in the handbook. Those entries in *italics* are words from the "Using the Right Word" section. For a more detailed explanation of how to find information in your handbook, see "Using the Handbook" at the front of the book.

G

H

I

876 Handwriting Models

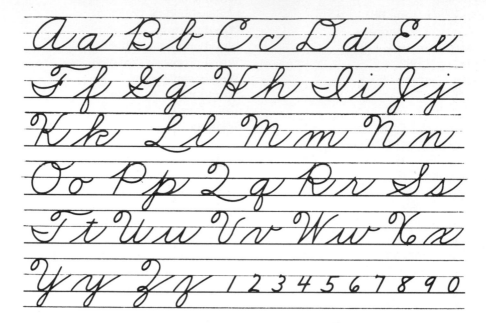

877 Symbols of Correction

ab.	do not abbreviate	¶	paragraph
agr.	agreement	‖	not parallel
ambig.	ambiguous	pro. ref.	pronoun reference
avoid	this should be avoided	p.	punctuation
awk.	awkward expression	?	questionable statement
cap.	capitalization	red.	redundant
c.f.	comma fault	RO	run-on sentence
d.	faulty diction	s.s.	sentence structure
d.m.	dangling modifier	shift	shift in agreement
d. neg.	double negative	sp.	spelling
fl.	flowery	sub.	subordinate
frag.	sentence fragment	t.	verb tense
gen.	be more specific	◯	this is wrong
gram.	grammar	trans.	weak transition
inc.	incomplete	TS	topic sentence
inf.	too informal	u.	usage
logic	not logical	w.c.	word choice
mis. mod.	misplaced modifier	w.f.	word form
mix	mixed pair	w.o.	word order
n.c.	not clear	wordy	more words than needed
∧	omission (word/s left out)	X	find and correct error

12-Year Calendar

1989

January	February	March	April	May	June
S M T W T F S	S M T W T F S	S M T W T F S	S M T W T F S	S M T W T F S	S M T W T F S

July	August	September	October	November	December
S M T W T F S	S M T W T F S	S M T W T F S	S M T W T F S	S M T W T F S	S M T W T F S

1990

January	February	March	April	May	June
S M T W T F S	S M T W T F S	S M T W T F S	S M T W T F S	S M T W T F S	S M T W T F S

July	August	September	October	November	December
S M T W T F S	S M T W T F S	S M T W T F S	S M T W T F S	S M T W T F S	S M T W T F S

1991

January	February	March	April	May	June
S M T W T F S	S M T W T F S	S M T W T F S	S M T W T F S	S M T W T F S	S M T W T F S

July	August	September	October	November	December
S M T W T F S	S M T W T F S	S M T W T F S	S M T W T F S	S M T W T F S	S M T W T F S

1992

January	February	March	April	May	June
S M T W T F S	S M T W T F S	S M T W T F S	S M T W T F S	S M T W T F S	S M T W T F S

July	August	September	October	November	December
S M T W T F S	S M T W T F S	S M T W T F S	S M T W T F S	S M T W T F S	S M T W T F S

1993

January	February	March	April	May	June
S M T W T F S	S M T W T F S	S M T W T F S	S M T W T F S	S M T W T F S	S M T W T F S

July	August	September	October	November	December
S M T W T F S	S M T W T F S	S M T W T F S	S M T W T F S	S M T W T F S	S M T W T F S

1994

January	February	March	April	May	June
S M T W T F S	S M T W T F S	S M T W T F S	S M T W T F S	S M T W T F S	S M T W T F S

July	August	September	October	November	December
S M T W T F S	S M T W T F S	S M T W T F S	S M T W T F S	S M T W T F S	S M T W T F S